BAHAMA SAGA

The Epic Story of The Bahama Islands

By

Peter Barratt

ISBN: 1-4107-9830-5 (e-book)
ISBN: 1-4107-9829-1 (Paperback)

This book is printed on acid free paper.

Also by Peter Barratt:
'Grand Bahama' published in two editions by Macmillan, and by David and Charles Publishers, Stackpole Books and IM Publishing, Freeport

Front cover photograph: Family Island beach scene.
Back cover photograph: A collage of photographs of the Bahamas.
Photographs courtesy of the Bahamas Ministry of Tourism

Text set in 10 point Book Antiqua

Copies of this book are obtainable on-line at
AuthorHouse 1-800 839-8640 and Amazon.com
In the Bahamas contact: *Media Enterprises 242 325-8210* in Nassau and in Freeport *RAM (Records, Archiving and Management)* at 242 351-7250

1stBooks - rev. 09/13/04

For Isabelle, Phaedra and CM

Contents

MAPS

Credits for Illustrations

Book cover photographs and **Rawson Square, Nassau** (courtesy of the Bahamas Ministry of Tourism).

PART ONE (frontispiece) and Chapter 2 - **Lucayan Indians** *(Dance the first dance and Lucayan Traders)* original paintings by courtesy of Abaconian painter Alton Lowe.

Sound out of Hearing, (Chapter 1) original woodcut by Robert Rosewarne.

Natives in Canoe, Native House, Suicides and Native Hammock from Girolamo Benzoni's, *La Historia del Mondo Nuovo*, 1565.

New World 'Indians', Vespucci, The British Library, London.

Indians Panning for Gold, Fernandez de Orviedo, *History of the Indies 1535.*

Cannibals from Thevet's *Sinulitez...*, 1558.

Columbus Vessel, woodcut by Carlo Veradi.

Engraving of **Columbus** from Caoriolo's, ***Ritratti***, 1596.

The *Santa Maria* at San Salvador, from the original illustration by Richard Schlecht from *The Log of Christopher Columbus* by Richard Fuson.

Ponce de León, Mansell Collection, London.

The Horrors of Syphilis, 15th century woodcut.

PART TWO (frontispiece) - **The Eleutherian Adventurers** illustration by P. Barratt.

'Abbaco' advertisement, from Riley, Sandra, *Homeward Bound*, Miami, Florida, 1983.

Woodcuts of **Fort Charlotte** and **Fort Montagu** from Bacon, *Notes on Nassau,* 1926.

Illustration of **S.S. Corsica,** from *Nassau Guardian,* 1944.

The prints of **Colonel Andrew Deveaux, William Bowles, Sunday Morning after Chapel, Sponging** and the **Blockade and Bootlegging** scenes have been reproduced from *Sources of Bahamian History,* Cash, Gordon, Saunders, Macmillan, 1992.

The map of the **Route According To Becher 1856** (the suggested route taken by Columbus through the Bahamas in 1492) has been taken from *In the Wake of Columbus,* edited by Louis de Vorsey and John Parker published by Wayne State University, 1985.

The abstract of a page from the **Log of Columbus** edited by Carlos Sanz, 1962. (the original is in the Biblioteca Nacional, Madrid).

Photograph of the **Duke and Duchess of Windsor with Adolph Hitler** from Marigny, Alfred, *Conspiracy of Crowns,* New York, 1990

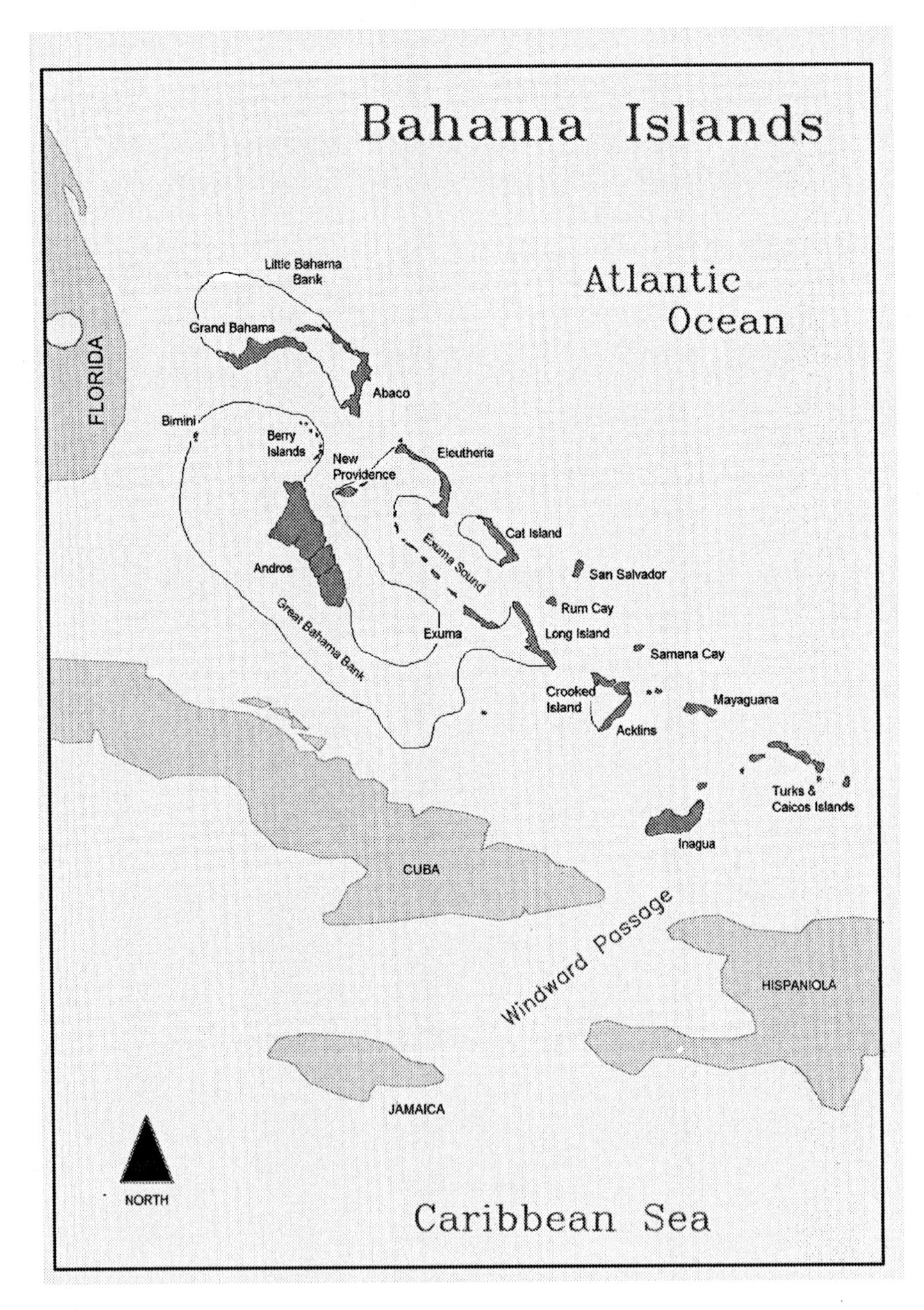

Map 1 -The Islands of The Bahamas

Foreword

The beauty of these islands surpasses that of any other and as much as day surpasses the night in splendour.

Christopher Columbus

The story related in this book sketches the course of human history in the Bahama Islands from its distant beginnings to the present day. As will be immediately apparent, fictional 'colouration' has been added to the account to give a more human dimension to the story. Indeed, since there were no written records of the era before Columbus and but scant records thereafter (right up until the nineteenth century in fact), the narrative has utilised the sometimes hazardous literary device of combining both fact and fiction. The fictional portions of the book cover much of the pre-Columbian phase but hopefully also serve to add a human dimension to the story in historic times. They also present another viewpoint on certain historical events that would be inadmissible in a strictly factual work. To paraphrase the old truism: 'it might be foolish to expect the absolute truth to fall open on pages of ink'.

So to anticipate the question: 'what then is fact and what is fiction?' The answer in most cases is left for the reader to decide (though a brief elucidation of some of the more important nuances in the text is included in the Epilogue). Additionally, to clarify the source of some of the text, recorded quotations (in 'single' quotation marks or *italic* print) have been included in an attempt to give appropriate tenor to the story, while words put into the mouths of the cast of characters (in "double" quotation marks) are solely from the author's imagination. In similar vein, many references to the Christian religion in early historic times have been included which, more so than today, pervaded most aspects of daily life.

Doubtless someone like Edward W. Said, the perennial critic of imperialism, would argue the story has more to do with a few people—often foreigners—who were in positions of authority rather than the general mass of the population. And he would be right. However human history, both that which is inspirational and that which is lamentable, is often disproportionately shaped by those few persons (generally of masculine gender) who had jurisdiction and authority and these are also the same people who keep the records that eventually find their way into historical texts.

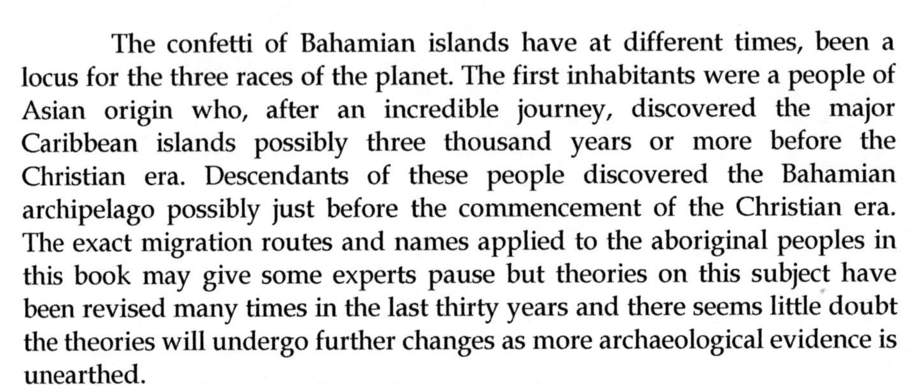

The confetti of Bahamian islands have at different times, been a locus for the three races of the planet. The first inhabitants were a people of Asian origin who, after an incredible journey, discovered the major Caribbean islands possibly three thousand years or more before the Christian era. Descendants of these people discovered the Bahamian archipelago possibly just before the commencement of the Christian era. The exact migration routes and names applied to the aboriginal peoples in this book may give some experts pause but theories on this subject have been revised many times in the last thirty years and there seems little doubt the theories will undergo further changes as more archaeological evidence is unearthed.

The (Caucasian) Europeans, a mere five centuries ago, stumbled upon the Bahama Islands and a so-called 'new world', a 'world' already inhabited for eons by people of Asian ancestry. (As a sad footnote to this event, as we shall later see, almost the entire native population of the Bahamas perished shortly thereafter).

The Bahamas then remained uninhabited for nearly 150 years until people from Bermuda - largely of English stock though there were some Africans among them - re-settled the islands commencing in 1648. Not long afterwards many more Africans were brought to the Bahamas in bondage. Their descendants today hold the destiny of the islands in their hands.

The geographical location of the Bahamas allowed the islands to play a brief, but important part in the history of the modern world. The eastern islands protrude out into the Atlantic Ocean so as to make them one of the nearest parts of the Americas to Europe and it was here that an explorer from Europe made a historic landfall at what, for him at least, was a 'New World'. It was just over five hundred years ago in the year 1492 that Christopher Columbus *'sailed the ocean blue'*.

The islands on the western side of the Bahamas abut the narrow margin of the Florida Channel that is the narrowest and fastest flowing section of Gulf Stream. The Channel separates the Bahamas from the United States of America which, at its nearest point, is a mere fifty miles away. Throughout time, events on the North American continent have had a major affect upon the human history of the Bahama Islands as the story relates.

In historic time it should be readily admitted that actual events are perhaps more compelling, bizarre even, than any that could be invented. Such is the nature of the recent human history of the Bahamas.

BAHAMA SAGA is a chronicle of the human presence on a unique archipelago in the Americas from the earliest times to the present day. The story takes its title from a few invented characters and the romantic and beautiful country of seven hundred sub-tropical islands.

I have borrowed extensively source material of scholarly authors of historical texts written about the Bahamas; the late Dr. Paul Albury who wrote the **Story of the Bahamas**; Michael Craton, an old friend from happy days in Nassau in the 1960's, whose book, **A History of the Bahamas** is a standard text about the Bahamas and who, together with Gail Saunders, wrote the two volume work, **Islanders in the Stream,** the most thorough social history of the Bahamas yet written. I also consulted Sandra Riley who has done such excellent research on the often overlooked Loyalists of the Bahamas in her book, **Homeward Bound**. Also another most useful book has been **Sources of Bahamian History** edited by Cash, Gordon and Saunders. For the pre-historic phase I consulted the new work by Irving Rouse, **The Taínos,** the publication entitled **Taíno** by the Monacelli Press and **Bahamian Archaeology** by William Keegan. The story of Columbus has been gleaned from the informative work with a new English translation of the log by Robert Fuson in his, **The Log of Christopher Columbus,** and **In the Wake of Columbus**, edited by Lousis de Vorsey and John Parker and several other popular works. For general information about the other attempts at English colonisation of the 'new world' I consulted **Saints and Strangers** by George F. Willison and **American Genesis** by Alden T. Vaughan.

Chapter 3 contains a short extract from a poem taken from Sandra Riley's **The Lucayans.** From the same work I would like to thank Abaconian painter Alton Lowe for allowing me to reproduce his evocative paintings of the Lucayan Indians: ***'Dance the first dance...'*** and ***'Lucayan Traders'.*** The episode involving Louis Powles has been gleaned from the book he authored: **Land of the Pink Pearl** and material for the Oakes murder was taken largely from **Conspiracy of Crowns,** by Count Alfred Marigny the main suspect at the murder trial. The charming poem about the 'chick charney' is by Telcine Turner. The verse quoted at the end of the chapter is part of a curiously apt work called **In the Strange Isle** by poet Michael Roberts and in Chapter 12 is an excerpt from a poem **Marchin' On** by Grand Bahamian, Susan Wallace. The words from the *Goombay* song about the Duke of Windsor were written by Blind Blake one of the best loved of the Bahamas' balladeers.

I should like to thank archaeologist Dr. Julian Granberry who provided expert advice concerning the pre-Columbian inhabitants of the islands (but, since this work has a strong fictional element, I should apologise for not following his advice too closely). And Gerald Groves, who was brought up in West End, Grand Bahama in the bootlegging era by a Missouri mother and returned thirty years later after spending many years in a Trappist monastery. For a few years he lived on Petersons Cay Beach in Grand Bahama as a hermit. Later he became a Professor of English and Latin was kind enough to offer exacting advice on syntax (that I admit was also not followed with painstaking exactitude I am sure he would have preferred). I should also like to acknowledge Dr. Gail Saunders OBE of the Bahamas Department of Archives for her help. In addition my thanks go to Keva Bethel (née Eldon) and Sally Lightyborn for reading the manuscript and offering helpful suggestions also Jerry Coleborn for the use of his extensive library on Bahamiana. Finally my thanks go to my wife Isabelle who was uncomplaining as I spent long hours at the word processor writing this highly personalised and, indeed cathartic, history about the beautiful 'islands of the shallow sea'.

Peter Barratt
Grand Bahama
(Columbus Day,)
10th October 1996

PART ONE

The Lucayans of the Bahama Islands

Chapter 1 - A Land Revealed (c.50,000 BC - 600 AD)

An age will come after many years when the ocean will lose the chains of things and a huge land lie revealed.

Seneca, Medea

THE GOBI DESERT, *one of the most desolate places on the planet, might seem an unlikely starting point for a story about the Bahamian islands. Yet, there is compelling reason to believe that it was from this remote region of central Asia - the most inland place on earth - that one of the greatest migrations in human history commenced. It was a migration that would bring the first human visitors to the continents of the Americas and eventually to the necklace of islands known as The Bahamas.*

The great migration started when a small tribe set out on a hurried eastward trek to escape hostile invaders who were entering the steppes from western Asia. After trekking for many centuries, the fleeing migrants crossed a narrow strait and arrived on a new continent. Eventually they were to create new 'nations' on the vast uninhabited lands of the Americas. During this incredible hegira, the migrants crossed deserts, mountains, plains and, when confronted with water, learned how to make watertight craft to allow them to navigate streams, rivers, lakes, and later, even oceans. On their journey they explored and eventually colonised the continents of North and South America. And, just before the end of the great migration, a spearhead of explorers visited, and colonised, the Bahama Islands which were some 15,000 miles from their original starting point near the centre of the Asian continent.

PART ONE

It might be difficult to find two places on the surface of the now-inhabited globe that are physically and climatically as different as central Asia and the islands of the Bahamas. But, strange as it may seem, the human history of the islands of the Caribbean Basin, and indeed of the great continents of North and South America, begins with some tribes of primeval Stone Age nomads who subsisted on the margins of the frigid Asian desert somewhere between 20,000 to 50,000 years ago.

BARELY DISCERNIBLE in the midst of the vast undulating steppes a straggling caravan of man and beast trekked slowly eastwards.

Watercourses and thinly iced lakes forced the tribe and its animal herds to meander wildly across the barren and snowy terrain like some wounded creature seeking its last resting place. In the distance, far to the northeast, some low foothills could be just vaguely discerned but otherwise the treeless landscape offered the weary travellers little in the way of landmarks and nothing in the way of shelter.

As the sun's pallid orb edged toward the horizon the frail old leader raised his staff as he had done every day during the long trek to bring the ragged caravan to a halt. It was a daily ritual that signaled the end to yet another day in a historic odyssey. After he had slowly lowered his staff the diminutive figure then shielded his eyes with his hand and peered through failing eyes straining to see what lay far beyond the eastern horizon. A small gesture from the old leader indicated that this would be their resting place for the night. Now, before nightfall, the tribe would make camp on a traverse of deeply scarred greyish bedrock surrounded by the luminous whiteness of the cheerless desert.

The small nomadic tribe was of Mongolian stock, short in stature, but all having powerful muscular physiques. Apart from their apple ripe faces, with mere slits for eyes, their bodies were completely covered by roughly cut sheepskin hides with the fur turned inward for warmth and all sewn together with the sinews of animals. Their captive animals were a diverse mixture of two humped Bactrian camel, yaks, goats, bighorn sheep and a small equine species whose biological forebears, like the camel, had travelled an evolutionary route in the opposite direction eons before.

To help them on their forced journey, and away from the aggressive fair-skinned foreigners who were advancing from the west, they had herded together some of the more docile animals of the Siberian steppes. This was accomplished by maiming some of the beasts so they could not easily escape, others they kept tethered. In this way the tribe had a ready supply of both milk and meat while they could also use the animals to carry their supplies of animal furs, hides, fodder, wooden poles, kindling and, when the need arose, for human transport. The furs were used for clothing and to act as blankets to cover the frozen ground, while the animal hides were dressed over a skeleton of wooden poles to create one of the earliest seminal inventions of mankind: the tent. This architectural artifact would later develop into the tent-like *yurt* and *ger* of the Asian steppes today.

As the tribesmen set about erecting the tents, the old leader produced a small leather pouch in which he kept a supply of knapped flints and a few other implements with which to create fire. Also secreted in the pouch was a smooth semi-translucent green stone that, over the years, had become a sacred talisman of the tribe.

Withdrawing away from the others, the shaman huddled over some kindling and within a few minutes had produced the magic of fire. Camel meat cooked over an open fire was the only food they would consume that day. The tribe ate hungrily and the meal was over long before the prolonged twilight of central Asia dissolved into blackest night. Sentries were now posted at the perimeter of the encampment while the exhausted tribe prepared themselves for sleep. Finally the flaming orange red sun descended below the horizon in the darkling sky, shadows slowly lengthened and congealed into a huge eclipse that gradually covered the whole plain then, in the heavens above, like piercing points of light, the stars came out of hiding.

AT FIRST LIGHT the camp came to life and, as on every day since their journey started, the tents were quickly taken down, the animals were marshalled back into herds, and the eastward trek recommenced.

On this day the hills to the east became a little more distinct.

With the arrival of spring, the northern fringe of the inscrutable Gobi Desert became more difficult to traverse as there was a continuing increase in the number of streams and rivulets feeding the brackish *talas*. By now many boulders had emerged from the mantle of snow and, on exposed knolls, the gnarled bedrock emerged, protruding upwards and taking on the appearance of fortress-like bastions. To the north and east the steppes undulated like giant oceanic swells disappearing towards the distant hills.

After trekking for several days towards the higher ground, the cold bright sun that had been a constant beacon for the tribe for the past many weeks, disappeared behind a greyish haze. And, as the caravan pressed deeper into the foothills, the weather grew much colder and control of the animal herds became increasingly difficult. The forbidding terrain of the rock-strewn scrubland now emboldened the furtive Siberian snow leopards, who followed the caravan ever more closely, to seize upon any of their animals that strayed too far from the herd.

The twisting passage through the foothills now led the nomadic migrants into a confrontation with the difficult terrain of the Sayan Mountains.

From bushy scrubland the vegetation gradually changed to towering evergreens whose snow covered leafy vaults shut out the sky. As they slowly started to ascend the mountain valleys, for the first time in many months, they completely lost sight of the day and nighttime sky that until this time had been their unerring compass. The tribe had not encountered terrain like this before, indeed they found the confining wooded mountain landscape a completely new and bewildering experience.

Their old leader realised they must set a different course.

As the woods turned to dense forest he directed the tribe to follow a small stream that started to flow eastwards though, after some time, it turned towards the north. Even so, following the bank of the stream was easier than trekking directly through the primordial forest and it had the added advantage of providing fish as a source of food.

Weeks became months as their forward progress was slowed by both weather and terrain. But worst of all, their animals were constantly attacked by day and by night. Most of the small horses had bolted and the greater part of their goats and sheep had escaped only to be brutally killed by predators. The colder weather turned foul and driving sleet slowed their forward movement even more. The rivulet they had been following became a raging torrent and could no longer be forded to allow access to the eastern bank, yet the water still flowed north taking them further and further away from their intended eastward course.

Unbeknown to them they had joined the headwaters of the Orchon River.

For weeks the depleted caravan slowly picked its way through the forest. Every night man and beast encamped in a tight circle under the towering trees with guards posted every few yards to ward off the omnipresent predators. Now, by day and night, added to their other adversaries, wolves occasionally descended upon them and sometimes hungry bears blocked their way.

But, fearful for their lives they trekked ever onwards.

One afternoon as they were looking for a suitable campsite, a fierce wind suddenly blew up bringing forward movement to a premature halt. All hands were put to work to help corral what was left of their animals and to erect temporary shelter. But so fierce was the storm that the cold and frightened wanderers were unable to prepare food and were forced to go hungry, cowering under such cover as they could improvise during the raging blizzard.

The storm continued to worsen and, some time after midnight, a freak gust from the swirling cyclone uprooted two of the tents and tossed them, occupants and all, high in the air and into the raging river. Shrill cries were heard over the noise of the storm only to dissolve and meld with the tempest until only the furious sound of the wind remained. By the following morning the storm had subsided sufficiently for the battered tribe to re-assemble though it was amidst a muttered litany of grumbles and fearful angry accusations. Reluctantly the tribe pushed further northwards still following the western bank of the river.

The nomads were now near to complete despair.

But they pressed slowly onward knowing that to remain where they were, or to turn back, might only hasten their demise. And as they trekked painfully and slowly onwards they grieved for their lost kinfolk acutely aware that they too, might soon suffer a dire fate. Then, only a few hours into their trek, the tribe was startled by shouting coming from an advance party of young men. Far ahead, the small vanguard had heard cries which they realised were from the other bank of the river. To their great surprise they could see in the distance that their kinsmen were alive.

When the young men drew level with their comrades they screamed questions across the river to find out how they got there - and were astounded at the reply - for what had saved them seemed miraculous. A shout carried across the swollen river:

"The tents became…floating things!"

"What?" The advance party shouted back.

"…on the tents…" and they pointed to a pile of hides and poles on the river bank, "…we floated here!"

It seems that the tents, when they became airborne, had turned upside down and landed in the river whence they carried their astonished and drenched occupants careening down the raging torrent.

Strange events often provide the spark to fire invention. They quickly reasoned that with the skills the tribe had acquired over the years to create a tent, those same skills could now be employed to fashion floating craft to carry people. Thus the idea for the canoe was born.

That day under the direction of their old leader, the people worked with new purpose, cutting wood and preparing hides and leathern thread to make a primitive craft that would float. The older men delighted in putting their skills to work fashioning a new floating vessel and, from their labours, a crude and nearly waterproof coracle resulted.

At dawn on the following day, two courageous young men launched the vessel and managed to maneuver it across the rapidly flowing river to the opposite bank. After the kinfolk were re-united with their brethren other coracles were constructed and soon there were enough crudely-built craft to hold the entire tribe. The few remaining animals were slaughtered and skinned, and their meat was placed in leather panniers to be carried aboard the craft. Then, with many spills, patching and rebuilding as they went, the small flotilla of people allowed the spring-flooded river to carry them racing downstream.

The waterborne tribe now reverted to becoming hunters and gatherers of food. It would be many centuries before the migrants would again revert to herding animals as a customary mode of husbandry.

After a month and more of travel, the pace of the Orchon River slowed, widened and veered to a more easterly direction. Finally the river terminated by flowing into a vast lake which then, as now, is a repository for nearly one fifth of all the fresh water of the planet earth.

The migrants had arrived at the great Lake Baikal.

Chiefs and shamans came and went in the course of the pilgrimage but always the tribe pushed on steadily eastwards. From Lake Baikal they joined the mighty Lena River and, using their floating craft and crude paddles, they followed its eastward course for over eight hundred miles.

News of the new land they had discovered filtered back to their former homeland and in time, other people slowly followed in the wake of the great pilgrimage that the solitary tribe had started.

As the years passed, the Megalithic wanderers became quite skilled in the art of building craft that by this time were narrow of girth and pointed at both ends thus resembling canoes. Sensibly they kept the size small and the weight low, so that the craft could be portaged at impassable rapids and shallows or where the water was frozen.

The expanded tribe followed the broad Lena River until it turned abruptly northwards. Remembering the directives of their ancestors that had by now passed into folklore of the tribe, they struck out directly eastwards. They crossed the extensive mountain range, called in the modern Russian language of today Chrebet Sette Daban and in course of time arrived at the Sea of Okhotsk near the Kamcatka peninsula in eastern Siberia.

It was the first time the central Asian nomads had ever looked upon the open sea.

From here the ever-expanding tribe followed the shore of the vast Pacific Ocean eastwards for many years until they arrived at a temperate savanna-like region that would later be called Beringia (named in historic times for the Danish explorer Vitus Jonassen Bering). The sea level at this time was considerably lower than today and the sub-continent of Beringia was virtually free of permanent ice sheets. Indeed paleo-botanists suggest that at this time the region may have been open prairies with grasslands on the lower terrain and with thick forests on the higher elevations where today there is only tundra. Surprisingly too, there may not have been deep coverage of either snow or ice in this sub-continental region.

Though exactly on a line with the Arctic Circle, the time of their arrival in Beringia coincided with a mild Arctic winter. The tribe trekked across the narrow 'land bridge' and, with their flimsy canoes, navigated some of the finger-lakes that would later expand to become the Bering Strait.

Finally, after many years of travel through some of the most difficult terrain and one of the harshest climates in the world, the migrants made the first human landfall on a new continent.

The Asian nomads had arrived at the threshold of a veritable 'new world'.

THE FIRST CROSSING was accomplished by less than three hundred souls. But these Stone Age people had succeeded in accomplishing more than half of their bold mission; they had made the longest sustained trek in the history of mankind from the western edge of the Gobi Desert to the western-most point of the mainland of the northern American continent.

It is doubtful however, the migrants realised they had reached a new continent. The terrain and much of the wildlife they found on setting foot in America would have been very familiar to them and the visitors could see this 'new world' was uninhabited by humankind. Indeed, for most of the period between 100,000 and 10,000 before the Christian Era there was little open water between Asia and northern half of the continent of America as the sea level was considerably lower because of the ice retained in the polar ice caps. This land bridge permitted animals, and later humans, to migrate with comparative ease between the two landmasses.

Once established on the new continent, the new immigrants followed the Alaskan coastline southwards in their canoes for a few hundred miles then headed inland when confronted by the giant mountainous arm of the Alaska Peninsula. They passed Nunivak Island, travelled up the Kuskokwim River and finally made camp at a site which would be called 'Bethel' by Moravian missionaries about twenty millennia later (interestingly in that same age the same name would also be applied to a small Christian chapel 4000 miles away in the Bahamian islands).

From 'Bethel' their travels took them further inland past the highest point in North America known by the first visitors as *Traleyka,* but today called Mount McKinley. The migrants trekked to the north then east of the great range of towering rock-strewn mountains following the great Yukon River.

They were pleased to find many familiar animals in this new land and were particularly awed at the vastness of the herds that flourished on the northern continent. One animal, which was very familiar to them and greatly prized for its meat was the woolly mammoth that they found grazing in large numbers on the lower slopes of the formidable Rocky Mountain range. The explorers set about hunting these giant beasts and finally, with perseverance and skill, they managed to wound one juvenile in the leg. It limped away with the hunters following at a safe distance. After some time it rested for a moment and the hunters pelted it with a barrage of rocks and, when it was sufficiently weakened, they battered the ill-fated beast to death. They then took huge chunks of meat to Bluefish Caves in what is today called the Yukon and there made a great feast. The bones were later broken to create spearheads and simple tools - evidence of which were discovered nearly twenty millennia later.

By this time more people had caught up with the vanguard tribe as they slowly pursued their journey both east and south. The expanded tribes followed the mighty Yukon River upstream trekking past sleeping goldfields, oil deposits and tar sands while all the time pushing south until they reached the great plains.

During their migration southwards they found the climate was becoming more temperate and the land more fertile. They doubtless noted too, that the length of the days had changed. At different times of the year there were no longer excessively long days and nights. The summers became uncomfortably hot. Their dress changed to clothes that could be carried and used only when needed and these found expression in wearing apparel like the *serape,* the blanket and the shawl. Their fur-lined footwear evolved into moccasins.

The canoes they used changed too. They were no longer sturdy craft suitable for navigating icy waters, instead they developed a lighter kayak made of bark or skins sewn over a wooden framework. For transporting their womenfolk and possessions they developed a larger boat, the *umiak*. And, with these craft, they completed the task of migrating from the Arctic cold of one hemisphere to the Antarctic cold of the other.

By the time they had finished their migration, they had travelled the entire range of north, central and south America. They colonised mountains, valleys, plains, swamps, pampas and even desert. And that was not all. There is even a suggestion that their descendants later travelled by craft, not so very different from those conceived by the original tribe, to settle in the distant islands of the great South Pacific Ocean. Though the theory remains in doubt, one recent expedition at least proved it was possible to travel great distances in locally made craft across a immense ocean.

The Stone Age people who came to the 'new world', by some accounts arrived between twenty and fifty thousand years ago. They were incredibly ill-equipped to conquer a new continent. They did not possess metals and had a technology limited to what could be cut and shaped by a bone or a piece of rock. They were technically so unsophisticated that some early ethnologists even suggested that the Asian peoples of this time did not have a sufficiently cohesive social structure to permit the tribal cooperation necessary to organise so great a migration. But, against fierce odds, they did indeed succeed in reaching, exploring and colonising the American continents. The vanguard migration was an important model for other peoples in Asia and, as the years passed, many others followed in their tracks.

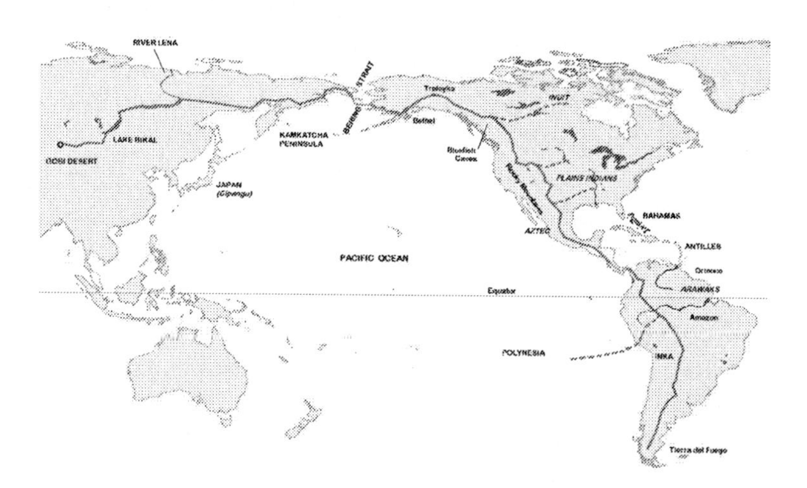

Route taken by the Asian peoples to the Americas

Much later some of the migrants would cross the Bering Strait but instead of following the time-honoured route south, they continued to head east and...north! These were the Eskimo, or Inuit people, and they created a very special place for themselves in the science of human adaptation by surviving in incredibly adverse environmental conditions. But that is another story.

As the main migration spread slowly southwards, tribes and nations were formed. The mound builders, the nations of the plains, the hill tribes, the pueblo dwellers and later the great sedentary empires of the Maya, Aztecs and Inca were established on the new continents. Indeed the migration took place over such a long period of time that their origins were long forgotten. The new people were spread over the entire land area and each community developed a specialised niche to guarantee its survival.

Some tribes hunted the great herds of bison on the plains, others lived in small cities cut into rock cliffs, some were experts at fishing, and yet others lived off agriculture and created great sedentary empires. Some tribes even inhabited the inhospitable region at the far extremity of the southern continent over 9000 years ago and, not unreasonably, found it necessary to make fires so frequently to keep warm that their country became known as *Tierra del Fuego* (the Land of Fires).

Many remarkable peoples lived in the great forests of the southern continent in a very special relationship with the luxuriant vegetation and abundant wildlife of the jungle. Their descendants and lifestyle have endured to the present day. The homeland of some major tribes was just north of one of the world's greatest rivers near the middle of the largest and ecologically most important woodland on the face of the planet earth: the vast Amazonian rain forest. Later, several branches of these peoples would migrate northwards to the coast of the southern continent to re-discover a sea surrounded on three sides by land and on the fourth by a chain of islands. Using canoes, the newcomers colonised most of the islands of this small inland sea.

Several tribes gave their names to geographical landmarks in the inland sea but almost all of these 'native' Americans perished within a few years of the discovery of this 'new world' by European explorers. The sea would be named 'Caribbean' for the warlike Caribs who were one of the last peoples to colonise the islands. A handful of their descendants still live on the West Indian island of Dominica.

The first people to actually migrate to the islands of the inland sea were a jungle tribe that lived near the Honduras coast. These were the Casimiroid people, speakers of a Tol language, whose existence in the jungle had taught them much about how to survive in such an environment but little about the outside world. In their early period they carved in stone but, as far as is known, made no pottery and knew but little about science except perhaps possessing a keen knowledge of the properties of herbs and plants. The jungle nurtured people who learned its ways. Their population grew.

The Casimiroid people did not need to till the land as they were gatherers of the bounty of the Central American rain forest but they needed to expand their territory continually in order to survive. After they had claimed all the available land in the region they were forced to add seafood in their diet. Then, when the need arose to further expand their range, the Casimiroid people followed the mode of their distant ancestors. From a headland that would later be known as *Cabo Gracias a Dios* they paddled their canoes towards the east, sometime around 5000 years before the Christian era.

Canoes by this time had changed from the light kayaks of the earlier migrants to commodious, stout, hollowed-out trunks of giant trees. These new canoes were created by burning out part of the heartwood of the trees and then completing the work of hollowing out the trunk with stone adzes. The result was sturdy sea-worthy craft capable of carrying up to two dozen people.

The inland sea, later called the Caribbean Sea in the south and the Gulf of Mexico in the north, nestled between the north and south portions of the new continents and was different in its morphology in the early years of man's arrival on the new continent. A large shallows existed in the west of the basin which almost formed a land bridge between the Yucatan peninsula and Cuba. This ancient land bridge, once identified as the Central Caribbean Island Chain, is evidenced by some shallow banks that divide the Caribbean Sea from the Gulf of Mexico. These banks today line the route followed by the Casimiroid people.

In the fifth millenium before the century before the Christian Era the Casimiroids were able to land at many low-lying islands which have long since disappeared below the sea. In time they reached the magnificent chain of mountainous and sometimes volcanic islands that make up the Greater Antilles that, besides Cuba, includes the islands that today go by the names of Hispaniola, Jamaica and Puerto Rico.

Cuba was almost certainly the first land to be colonised by the Casimiroids. Later they were to push on further eastwards to settle the island of Hispaniola (modern Haiti and the Dominican Republic). To reach these islands of the Greater Antilles the Meso-Americans and their forebears had travelled an incredible circuitous route of nearly 15,000 miles. For them it was nearly the end of an incredible journey which led them to a primitive island paradise, a veritable Stone Age *Utopia* set in the sparkling Caribbean Sea.

These first visitors to the Antilles, were a Lithic or Stone Age people who left only for posterity a distinctive decoration applied to stone artifacts and shell ornaments. The earliest radiocarbon date from a Cuban rock shelter suggests it was inhabited by the visitors as early as 4190 BC. These new 'Antilleans' settled on two major islands and, in time as their population increased, they made temporary visits to some low-lying limestone islands to the north.

The new arrivals can best be identified by the few workshop sites that have been found which contained flaked stone workings and also food remains in the form of piles of shells and the bones of hutias (a kind of large rodent), lizards and snakes. Their burial practices were not distinctive and evidence of their occupation has been exceptionally difficult to find. Though a few fine stone carvings have been found, they left not a trace of their dwellings. Indeed there is a regrettable paucity of any physical evidence for a remarkable people who had travelled so far and had surmounted incredible obstacles to arrive at these distant islands. Nevertheless the vanguard of the great migration had arrived near to its final destination and was almost within sight of the Bahama Islands. By now the Meso-Indians had inhabited the Antilles for nearly four thousand years which was an incredible stretch in terms of time and territory. The fact that they survived so long in the Antilles suggests that the resources of the islands were sufficient for their needs and they clearly must have effected a happy balance with nature.

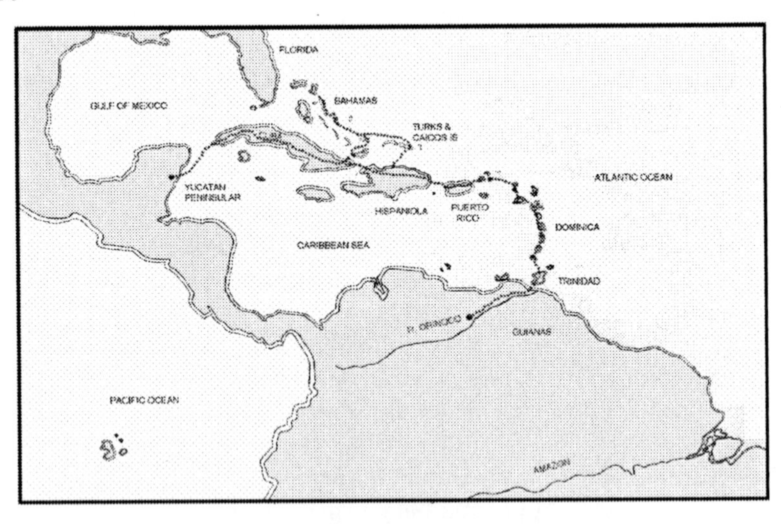

Meso-Indian migrations to the Caribbean

After this juncture the picture of immigration to the Caribbean and the cultures that they produced is a little more complex. No more people came to the Antilles from Central America but instead several waves of immigrants originating from South America made their way up the chain of islands. Commencing about 2000 BCE the first were a people originating in the Orinoco Basin archaeologists refer to as the Ortoiroid peoples. They migrated to the southern islands of the West Indies (the Lesser Antilles) and, in time, melded with the Casimiroids. This new intermixture of peoples may be referred to as 'Antilleans'.

Then, some time just before the Christian era, people of Arawak stock from the Orinoco River basin began to move north into the Lesser Antilles. On their migration they would have encountered and assimilated several of the tribes of the original Antilleans. These 'Island' Arawaks island-hopped as far as the Greater Antilles but avoided conflict with the Antilleans by stopping their advance at the Mona Passage, the channel that divides Hispaniola from Puerto Rico. This frontier existed between the two peoples until about 400 BC.

After a few hundred years into the Christian era the Island Arawaks, who, by this date, had developed a culture that we know as 'Taíno', had hopped across the Mona Passage and almost totally absorbed the native Antillean peoples. But not all. A few people were completely unaffected by the Taíno incursion. In the northeastern corner of Hispaniola and in far western Cuba, the original inhabitants of Central American provenance, were left undisturbed right up to historic times. While in northeastern Cuba the Antilleans who came into contact with the Island Arawaks, adopted the Taíno language but practiced a different lifestyle. These were the Ciboney, a people of a Sub-Taíno culture who, by this time, were creolised to the extent that they spoke a Taíno dialect but were ethnically distinct, being originally from Central America. It was the Ciboney who were possibly the first aboriginal people to completely colonise the Bahama islands.

But it is possible the first people to actually set foot in the Bahamian archipelago were the original Antilleans. They may have visited Great Inagua by canoe from nearby Cuba sometime before the beginning of the Christian era and settled some of the Bahamian islands to the north. Inagua, the first island they visited, was hardly beckoning. The land barely broke above the surface of the water and cursory inspection showed that fresh water was almost non-existent and the land produced little that was edible. The islands did, however, produce salt and abundant shellfish that were a staple of the Antillean diet.

The Antilleans made temporary encampments in Inagua late in the first century before Christian era though their occupation was probably of short duration. Then, in about 600 AD, the Ciboney from Cuba began the process of colonising the Bahamian archipelago and some years later they were followed by the Taíno from *Aiti* (the former name of the island of Hispaniola) who also migrated to the islands first to the Caicos Islands and then later to the Bahamas proper.

But long before either Ciboney or Taíno permanently settled the flotilla of 'white islands', an Antillean trader-turned-discoverer had already made a voyage deep into the Bahamas. He was to discover for the first time in human history some of the wonders of the physical world of the Bahamian archipelago that, despite a dearth of natural resources, was truly an earthly paradise.

His name, as nearly as it may be written, was Tsgot.

THE SOUTHERN END of the Bahamian archipelago (the Bahamian island of Inagua together with the small island nation of the Turks and Caicos) starts about a hundred miles north of the island of Hispaniola and extends for about 550 miles in a northwesterly direction to about 60 miles east of the Florida peninsula. Including banks and islands the Bahamas have an average width of about 200 miles and occupy about 110,000 square miles or roughly the area of Italy. Of this total area, the islands and cays collectively account for about 5,382 square miles, about the same land area as Jamaica. There are estimated to be 700 islands in the Bahamas of which 30 or so are today inhabited, though depending on the definition of an island, others would have it that there are 29 islands, 661 cays and 2387 rocks (the word 'cay' in the Bahamas is pronounced 'key' and is derived from *'ka'* or *'ke'* which means small island in the Taíno language).

The geographical form of the Bahamas exhibits a striking incidence of narrow islands oriented northwest/southeast and what is also remarkable is the consistent presence of islands adjacent to deeper water generally on the eastern side of the banks. This is true of the Abaco's which are located east of the Little Bahama Bank, while Eleuthera, Cat Island, Great and Little Exuma and the cays, Long Island, the Ragged Islands and Andros are on the eastern side of the Great Bahama Bank (although Andros is actually positioned adjacent to the Tongue of the Ocean the strange deepwater channel which intrudes into the centre of the archipelago). Even Cat Island and the paired islands of Crooked and Acklins are both located on two smaller banks and demonstrate the same phenomenon. The only major exceptions are the two southern islands of Mayaguana and Inagua which are not associated with shallow water.

Geologists surmise that some 115,000 years ago in the Pleistocene Epoch, gigantean waves brought debris from the floor of the Atlantic Ocean and deposited it on land sometimes as high as 60 feet above sea level. Some of the debris remained as a natural levée to supplement the terrain of the islands. In Eleuthera there are 2000 ton boulders near the ridge of the island that are sitting on bedrock which is around 220,000 years younger than the boulders. Since these mega boulders did not drop from the sky and could hardly be moved by the wind one can only conclude the sea must have transported them there. Scientists hypothesise there must have been cataclysmic waves at least 100 feet high moving at speeds of 60 miles per hour - or more - to move the giant boulders to this location.

Seen from the air, small shallow lakes formed of near-perfect circles and segments of circles can be seen generally on the leeward side of many of the larger islands. These were formed by the slow concentric chemical dilution of the limestone. Another matter of geological interest is the perimeter of the shallow water banks of the Bahamas that are almost everywhere formed of segments of geometric arcs - in contradistinction to irregular or straight lines. Especially noteworthy in this regard, is the lower portion of the Tongue of the Ocean that approximates three quarters of a near perfect circle.

The morphology of the Bahama and Caicos islands is a minor wonder of the world. The explorer Tsgot saw only small islands in a kaleidoscopic sea. But, if the sea could have been drained, Tsgot and his colleagues would have discovered that the present banks were the tops of incredibly high plateaus protruding nearly four kilometres above the ocean floor! They would also have understood that the islands they found were little more than very small ripples on tops of the giant plateaus. The sides of these mountains were precipitous, yet, all of this great bulk was comprised of limestone, the by-product of chemical reaction in the sea with sunlight to which had been added the detritus of coral and other marine organisms. Around most islands this marine debris has resulted in the formation of beaches of the purest white sand and, without rivers, the result is sediment-free inshore waters which are crystal clear.

But, like the land, the banks also have great stretches of virtual desert resulting in the luminescent turquoise colour so characterstic of the archipelago. The sandy bottom of the shallow banks sometimes extends for many miles without obvious features or marine life. The reefs, which often identify the outer extremity of the banks, are perhaps the most interesting natural phenomenon of the Bahamian archipelago. One such reef is composed of a stromatolite limestone on the eastern shore of Exuma that some believe is the oldest evidence of life on earth! Formed mainly of living coral the reefs are the habitat for a myriad variety of fish and other marine life and through the ages they have acted as a larder for the inhabitants of the islands. The yawning depths of the sea between the plateaus are a vast Neptunian domain inhabited by the larger pelagic fish.

The vegetation of the islands is a product of its proximity to other land, fertility of the soil, latitude and most importantly, climate. The larger islands which are generally in the north, receive fairly substantial rainfall of about 50 inches a year. This helps support considerable pine forests on the islands of Abaco, Andros, Grand Bahama and, to a lesser extent, New Providence. The rainfall diminishes in travelling south and so it is on the southern islands, especially Inagua and the Turks and Caicos group, that solar-evaporated salt is to be found. The climate is sub-tropical with a temperature in the 80 degree Fahrenheit range for most of the year. Although it is fairly humid in summer, Tsgot and later visitors would have found little variation in temperature throughout the islands. In fact so pleasantly mild is the climate that a Privy counselor of Charles V of Spain wrote: *'these islands were called fortunate for the temperate ayre which is in them'*, and a hundred years ago a visitor from a temperate island in the North Sea christened them the 'Isles of Perpetual June'.

In summer it is common for cloud banks to form especially over any land however small the land mass. Sometimes the cumulus clouds are so diminutive that it is not unusual to have a downpour a few yards away from bright sunlight while on other occasions enormous cumulous nimbus clouds build up rapidly bringing several inches of rainfall in one hour. Between May and October tropical disturbances which often form off the coast of Africa sometimes develop into hurricanes to cause much damage in the islands. In winter the islands are more affected by 'fronts' coming from the North American landmass and can bring a temporary sharp drop in temperatures though frost is virtually unknown.

The vegetation of the central and southern islands consists mainly of dense shrubs and low trees. There is however, a considerable difference of flora on these islands between the lee and windward sides. To leeward the water's edge is often occupied by three types of mangroves. Red mangroves are the pioneer genus often surviving with their tangled roots in several feet of water. The mangroves are able to filter out much of the salt water but some salt rises to the leaves which then yellow and drop off. These leaves soon break down and become the first building block of the marine food chain. Over time the red mangroves, supported further inland by the black and white mangroves, are able to stabilize the land to create small islets or cays. The black mangrove is found in periodically flooded areas while the white mangrove tends to thrive in salty marsh land.

To windward are sea oats, bay geranium, creeping vines and low shrubs which are sometimes overtaken by the sea but in time generally manage to re-establish themselves. On the larger islands, coarse grasses abound together with shrubs like pigeon plum and coco plum (the latter sometimes used to stem dyspepsia and diarrhea). Small trees include cinnecord, the dyewood brasiletto, seagrape, yellow elder (the national flower of the Bahamas) and the purple flowered 'five fingers' *(Tabebuia bahamensis)* with shrub palmetto and the cactus-like agave filling out the centre of the landmass in which scattered hardwood 'coppices' may be found.

The coppices are diverse eco-systems where sometimes non-native species of flora may appear having been introduced to the islands by migratory birds. The coppices often include the sabal palm, sapodilla (the chewing gum tree), wild tamarind, poison wood, gumbo limbo (sometimes known as gum-elemi but better known as the 'tourist tree' since it tends to peel!), mahogany and the prized West Indian red cedar tree. On some islands the calabash tree provided the aboriginal settlers with gourds for carrying precious water. Occasionally present is wild cane, wild grape and the wild coffee plant *(Psychotria nervosa)* and often a mantle of orange love vine can be found in the coppice slowing smothering its host. In damp conditions the limbs of mangroves and other trees are sometimes laiden with delicate and colourful epiphytes and orchids like *Epidendrun nocturnum, Cattleyopsis* and *Oncidium lucayanum,* the latter named for the first inhabitants of the islands.

But here it is perhaps important to add a sad postscript. Towards the end of the second millennium of the Christian era much of the original beach vegetation would succumb to an invasion of 'exotics' (that is to say vegetation not native to the islands). The Australian pine in particular, by the late twentieth century, had probably claimed more land in the islands—and destroyed more native vegetation—than all that occupied by human development in buildings and roads.

The land animals of the Bahamas are few. The indigenous hutia, a rodent related to the agouti, was a food source for the early inhabitants though today it is nearly extinct in the islands. The iguana was once widely distributed throughout the islands and was also eaten as a delicacy. It too, is rarely found today. Many varieties of frogs, lizards and a few non-poisonous snakes round out the reptile population.

Most other wild land animals like hogs and cattle, have been imported in recent times and reverted to a feral state. Of the other mammals, bats are probably the most noteworthy. For millennia the caves of the islands have been home to vast colonies of nocturnal bats. The Bahamas is home to twelve species of bats that are derived from Hispaniolan and Cuban forebears. Most bats live off wild fruit though some play a useful role in keeping down the flying insect population.

The birds of the Bahamas are many and varied due the islands being located on an important north/south migration route. Perhaps the most interesting bird, now greatly restricted in its range, is the flamingo. Wading birds like the flamingo, heron and spoonbill were was almost certainly an important food source of the early inhabitants and were almost certainly captured and eaten by the first explorer Tsgot. The Bahama islands also supported numerous herons, hummingbirds, spoonbills and parrots. The latter of which is also much diminished in number from when the first European visitor noted great flocks in the islands 'darkening the sky'.

Of the sea birds, the frigate bird (with a seven foot wing span and the greatest ratio of surface area to weight of any bird), and the osprey (sometimes called a sea or fish hawk) are not uncommon. The brown pelican is unevenly distributed in the Bahamas being found only in the northern islands and the southern island of Inagua. When Columbus, on his first visit to the 'new world' neared the Bahamas, he noted in his log that he saw petrels convincing him that land was near. In all, there are approximately 300 species of birds in the Bahamas but only three are endemic, the Bahama woodstar, the Bahama swallow and the Bahama yellowthroat.

It is the sea however that most captures the interest, for although the islands are generally undistinguished, below the surface of the lambent turquoise and blue water is a veritable wonderland. Many interesting corals are to be found like the beautiful plant-like purple or yellow sea fan which grows to two or three feet in height and adds its almost unreal colours to the inshore waters. Others are formed of innumerable polyps in calcareous cups like the aptly-named ochre-coloured brain coral and the bright orange 'stag horn' coral. At shallow depths below the inshore waters are often great beds of turtle grass *(Thalassia)* which is a habitat and a primary source of food for many marine creatures. Turtle grass also helps stabalise the shallow sea bed.

Coral is important to the very terrestrial existence of the ephemeral Bahama islands since colonies of numerous species over the centuries have built up underwater calcareous ridges or mounds commonly known as coral reefs. Most Bahamian islands have a fringing reef lying offshore on the windward side. It is this reef which is often credited with protecting the island by breaking up the ocean swell. Even dead coral which becomes detached has its uses for it supplements the marine debris and aids in silting inshore waters or building up beaches. It is interesting to consider that because of the detritus from the reefs, the beaches of the Bahamas are probably larger today than they have ever been.

Of the gastropods, the conch, especially the Queen Conch, *(Strombus gigas),* is found in great numbers on the banks. From the earliest times this lowly mollusc has been an important food source for the inhabitants of the islands. The Bahamian varieties of conch are among the largest univalve shellfish in the oceans. Most conchs feed on algae although some related varieties of Helmet Conchs are carnivorous and inedible. The variable colours of pink and white inside the shells make them especially suitable for making into cameos or simply preserving as curios. Conch would have been the staple food of Tsgot and the first inhabitants, a status it has held ever since. In addition to the Queen Conch, the waters of the Bahamas are a habitat for considerable numbers of species of beautiful shellfish like Apple Murex, Measled Cowrie, Decussate Bittersweet as well as Bleeding Tooth and Codakia the latter of which proved to be a special delicacy with the earliest inhabitants.

A crustacean of economic importance is the crawfish or spiny lobster *(Panlirus argus)* which, until recently, was a principal export of the Bahamas. Crawfish are easily spotted by their large antennae that they leave projecting from their habitat under rocky ledges and crevices. An interesting event in the life cycle of the crawfish happens around October every year when the crawfish 'march' in teeming thousands to deeper water obeying some now archaic instinct learned in the final Ice Age.

The banks provide an ideal habitat for sponges that were once the basis of an important industry in the Bahamas. These lowly animals, yes animals(!), spend their lives anchored to the sea-bottom and for a brief period also formed the basis of an important industry in the Bahamas. One marine biologist has identified eighty-two species of sponge in the western Bahamas alone. The early inhabitants of the islands would certainly have been aware of their utilitarian properties for retaining liquid.

Tsgot and his colleagues would have seen fish of myriad hues and shapes swimming below the surface in the crystal clear water around the islands from microscopic small fry to giant 500lb Jewfish. The principal food fish then as now are grunts, porgies, yellow tails, grouper and snapper to name but a few. Other fish include some with spectacular markings like the foureye butterfly fish, squirrelfish, parrotfish and several kinds of angelfish. Some fish retain a more silvery guise like the tarpon, needlefish, the shallow water bonefish and the predatory barracuda. The monk seal, now extinct in the Bahamas, was probably another food source for the early inhabitants and an even more important food source was the turtle as evidenced by the numerous turtle bones found at excavation sites. At sea, Tsgot and his comrades would have caught flying fish, shrimps and small crabs on the floating weed. And other early inhabitants would have used spears to catch fish though later nets were used.

Inhabiting the inshore waters are several species of the ray family, which include the sting ray, the leopard ray (so called on account of its brown spotted markings) and generally in deeper water the manta or devil ray. Mantas found in Bahamian waters sometimes attain an astounding width of twenty feet across and a weight of 2000 lbs.

Game fish are abundant in the deeper water. Many varieties of fish leave the deep water to feed or spawn on the banks and are often preyed upon by barracudas and other predators. Sharks too, are ubiquitous though they generally only visit the shallower water to feed at night. A few manatees or sea cows still inhabit secluded creeks and blue holes. Porpoises can often be seen in both deep and shallow water and that other large marine mammal, the whale, is also a frequent visitor especially to the southern Bahamas.

In short, the islands were a marvelous natural environment for a people acquainted with the sea. And, it was to this beautiful sea-oriented world, that the first people to visit the Bahamas were to settle and eventually make their home.

Chapter 2 - Mission of Discovery (c. 150 BC

But the Lord sent a great wind into the sea, and there was a mighty tempest in the sea, so that the ship was likely to be wrecked.

Book of Jonah 1 v. 4

*A**FTER THE DISCOVERY** of the Greater Antilles the great migrations in the Americas came to an end. Life now for the inhabitants of the islands remained virtually unchanged for the next four thousand years. The seasons ruled their lives and the bounty of both land and sea responded to their unvoiced requests for sustenance.*

It might be thought strange that anyone would wish to break out of such a tranquil self-sustaining environment yet, for reasons unknown, a small number of the Antillean people just before the dawn of the Christian era left the tranquility of the island of Cuba to make some temporary settlements in the islands about one hundred miles to the north of their homeland. To survive, the transplanted visitors lived off the meagre resources of the islands and traded with the nearby islands of Cuba and Hispaniola.

Traditionally most trade in the Antilles was carried on between the larger islands though very occasionally, a small convoy of canoes would head out for the low, swampy isles and cays north of Hispaniola today known as the Turks and Caicos Islands. One such trading voyage to the Caicos resulted not only in commerce but in the discovery of a distant shrine cave far to the north in a small flotilla of islands today known as the Bahama Islands.

Woodcut of a Taíno Canoe

SHORTLY BEFORE THE START OF THE CHRISTIAN ERA, a lone canoe appeared out of the morning mist headed for the distant fishing grounds far off the northeastern end of the island of Cuba. In the canoe was an Antillean youth named Tsgot and his four companions. The Casimiroid occupants of the canoe were bronzed, sinewy men of medium build...and all quite naked. Another common feature among them was their long torso, a mop of jet-black hair that stopped just short of their eyes, an absence of facial hair and narrow almond-shaped eyes, all of which clearly betrayed their Asian origin. In common with most Casimiroids, the young men tended to be fairly impassive and spoke sparingly in the fluid Tol language of their mainland ancestors.

On this day Tsgot and his friends were following a line of seaweed that they knew often concealed larger fish feeding near the surface. Very occasionally fish would break the surface near their canoe and they would swiftly strike at the fish with their spears. Invariably the fish would avoid their thrusts but, very occasionally, one of the men would spear a fish of such size that their whole village could feast off it. But on this day they were unsuccessful even though they had followed the line of seaweed out to sea for many miles.

They paddled further and further away from their village, striking unsuccessfully at fish, when they observed, below a cloudbank, the line of a dark object rising above the horizon to the north. Tsgot was aware that they had travelled out of sight of land and at first he thought they were disoriented and the indistinct line they saw above the horizon was their Cuba. But, on checking his bearings from the sun, he realized that the object was a distant land. Paddling a few miles nearer, they confirmed Tsgot's assumption that the image on the horizon was indeed land and, from what they could see, it seemed to be a largish island but, unlike their homeland it was without hills or mountains. Amazed at their discovery they returned swiftly to their Cuban village to carry news that they had discovered a new island only a day's journey by canoe from their coastal settlement in Cuba.

The discovery of this island had great historical significance since it was part of the last group of islands in the Americas that would one day become a sovereign nation. The indistinct line that Tsgot had seen turned out to be the second largest island of an archipelago that would later be known as the Commonwealth of the Bahamas. The humans that were soon to settle the island were the most dominant—and almost the last—of a long line of life forms to arrived in the islands from Cuba and the other islands of the Greater Antilles.

On their return to Cuba, long after midnight, the adventurers woke up the village and excitedly told them of their discovery. After a discourse that lasted long into the night, the Antillean tribal chiefs decided to call for a reconnaissance of the newfound island and appointed Tsgot to be in charge of an exploration party of four canoes. A new island, they reasoned, would open up new resources for them to draw upon and might even become a suitable place to settle. As hunter-gatherers the Antillean people needed to continually expand their territory to survive.

A few days later a small fleet of canoes headed by Tsgot circumnavigated the newfound island and reported back to the elders that it was generally flat but quite large and had an extensive lake near its centre and a long peninsula that extended to the northeast. They noted the extensive bird life that included enormous flocks of pink flamingos wading in the lake all striding together in unison, waving their slender necks and occasionally flashing their black flight feathers in a courtship ritual. They also saw parrots, flamingoes and herons and a plethora of iguanas and some strange fresh water turtles. Around the great lake they found piles of white crystalline salt. In the inshore water they observed numerous brightly coloured fish besides shellfish in abundance, codakia, mussels and conch. Though the vegetation of the island was not as lush as their homeland they recognized many plants and trees as being similar to those in Cuba. They drew the conclusion that the island would support humankind.

In course of time, the Antilleans established a small settlement on the 'Island of the Iguanas' (the island would later be called Great Inagua, the name a derivative from 'iguana' that were found in abundance on the island). The village the Casamiroid's established on Great Inagua served as a trading post at which the settlers at first collected salt to send back to their mother village in Cuba. Later they also made good trade exchanging iguana and flamingo meat for stone implements and vegetable produce of the mainland.

After only a few years Tsgot became the chief of his small tribe. At this time he inherited the sacred green stone that had been passed down by shamans through many generations and he commissioned a craftsman to carve onto the egg-shaped talisman a bat's head as homage to the souls of his ancestors. As chief of his tribe, Tsgot was to lead many trading parties in the voyages between eastern Cuba and the 'Island of the Iguanas' and, on such occasions, he proudly wore the *zemi* around his neck as a symbol of his authority.

One auspicious day several years later Tsgot, now a seasoned old man aged 38 years, headed out to sea from his village in Cuba on one of his customary trading voyages to Great Inagua. On this voyage Tsgot was in the lead of five dug-out canoes that were carrying a small cargo of knapped flints, shell implements, herbs (including a mild narcotic) and the root vegetable cassava all of which would be put up for barter.

Their destination was the small settlement near the southwest headland of the island that Tsgot had discovered more than twenty years before. The village was located just behind a beach on a peninsula surrounded on three sides by the incredibly deep indigo sea while, on the landward side from the settlement, there was the large lake that, after the autumn rains, partly evaporated leaving miles crystalline salt. The traders, as they had done countless times before, would exchange their cargo of goods for salt and for the salted flesh of flamingos and iguana.

The small Inaguan community saw the traders in the distance and came to greet them at the beach and, in the time-honoured way, the villagers crowded round the canoes and the bartering began. As soon as exchange had been concluded the visitors and settlers sat down to the customary feast of roast flamingo. The method of cooking over an open fire was called by the Antilleans *'barbecu'* from which we derive the word 'barbecue'. Around the hearth the conversation traversed the many obvious topics of recent births and deaths, storms and drought, news from the homeland, news from the island. But one unexpected item of news that Tsgot gleaned from the parley was that a few of the original villagers had broken away from the settlement on Great Inagua and had gone to live at one of a group of 'white' islands to the northeast that had been newly discovered.

The Inaguan villagers implored the traders to visit the islands claiming that the new settlers had need of many things and the traders would fare well from the barter. As Tsgot still had a few items still left to exchange he decided he would visit the 'Caicos' as these new isles would be called. So, all of the salt and most of the salted meat they had acquired by barter was unloaded from their canoes with a promise made that it would be kept for them to pick up on their return.

For Tsgot it was actually the promise of a new adventure and not trade that stirred him to visit the Caicos Islands. As time would tell he would experience a greater adventure than he could ever have predicted. The salt and salted meat the traders had acquired by barter was unloaded from their canoes with a promise that it would be kept for them to pick up on their return. Tsgot and his crew then made ready for a long journey to these intriguing new islands.

Tsgot was informed it would not be difficult to find the new settlement because the village was located on the lower slope of a small hill that was clearly the highest point of land on the most centrally located island of the Caicos. Near the top of the hill was an opening that led into a series of large caverns. All caverns possessed significance for the Antillean people but these caves were extraordinary, they were told, because they were the provenance of an oracle and had just recently become revered by the Casimiroid settlers as a 'shrine' cave. Thousands of sacred bats that were thought to be the souls of departed kin, inhabited the labyrinth of caves that contained the oracle. This was a place, the Inaguans insisted, the traders must not fail to visit.

After rounding the finger headland of Great Inagua, Tsgot and his crew passed the uninhabited island of Little Inagua and after two days of hard paddling, the indigo colour of the sea turned glass green and some faint shadows appeared deep in the water below them. Far to the northeast they saw the hazy outline of islands. They rounded the most westerly Caicos island keeping about half a mile off the northern shore of the main Caicos islands. They passed the wide sweep of Grace Bay on the island that would later be named for Divine Providence. Next they passed a string of pretty cays then rounded the headland of the island of North Caicos. Now, following the coast in a southeasterly direction they could see the lush vegetation of this island and, as they paralleled an offshore cay they encountered the mouth of a creek that later would be known by the strange name of Bottle Creek Mouth. As the small convoy got closer a man in the lead canoe stood up and hailed his comrades.

"This was the creek that we were told to look out for", Tsgot remarked, "some time soon we should see some high cliffs and a sentinel rock." The small convoy crossed the mouth of the creek and continued to follow the northern coast until a man in the lead canoe stood up and hailed his comrades, "look!" he said pointing straight ahead, "...see a rock poking out of the sea...and there is a hill...over there!"

Tsgot too had seen the hill and shouted his reply.

"Let us steer towards it...follow me, I can see a channel!" and Tsgot expertly negotiated a course through a break in the reef with the other canoes following closely behind. The canoes crossed the breakers that separated the dark blue water of the deep channel from the turquoise 'white' water of the inshore waters. Once safely across the reef, the canoes, aided by the breaking surf, skidded across the shallow inshore waters floating giddily above herringbone sand ridges on the sea bottom and finally came to rest in a small bay overshadowed by a high cliff. Not far inland they could see a small settlement of beehive-shaped huts near the hill that was the goal of their journey.

Their approach had been witnessed from the clifftop and the traders were joyfully met by the few people who now lived in a small settlement on the island in circumstances, as they would soon discover, of considerable deprivation. As hunter-gatherers their situation on the barren island had forced them to conserve their food resources and to rely on trade to supplement their meagre rations.

No sooner had the visitors disembarked from their canoes than they were immediately besieged with anxious questions:

"Have you brought cassava?"

"...and agouti?" (agouti was a small rodent much favoured by the Antilleans for its meat).

"I would like to taste the meat of Inaguan turtles again," another settler remarked, "...and what about corn, pigeon peas, akee, and...?"

It was clear to the villagers who had been eagerly searching the cargo in the canoes found a deficiency of things to eat. A young mother with a child at her breast mouthed an obvious fact: "...we are almost destitute of food except for conch!"

Tsgot was able to give the settlers some of the salted meat they were carrying.

Another voice from the crowd pleaded, "...also we need more knives." (The knives referred to were actually stone flints with a sharp cutting edge since hard metals and rocks were unknown in the limestone islands). A young man happily agreed to exchange some crudely made fish bone necklaces for the flints.

From the back of the crowd an old crone anxiously complained, "...and we have great need of the sacred herb so we can commune with the spirits of the cave..."

At his remark some of the villagers hid their faces in amusement. Already anticipating a negative response to his question, yet oblivious to the reaction of the other settlers, the old man slowly limped away. Tsgot was about to reply that he had indeed brought a small quantity of *cohaba* leaves when an elder interjected:

"Oh, pay him no heed! I want to see what trade goods you bring...I need another hard hammer stone and knives...I can exchange for salt." He was to be disappointed. Tsgot did not have the items desired and he certainly did not need more salt.

A tearful young woman asked, "...have you any news from my family on the great island?—my natal mother is kin to the chief named Moua..."

Tsgot had heard of the Casamiroid chief of a village neighbouring his own and was able to assure her that her family was in good health though he expressed sorrow that he had little other news to impart. By way of explanation he stated that it had not been his original intention to visit the Caicos Islands. All the while he was reassuring the tearful woman the villagers kept up a veritable litany of questions, complaints and entreaties. Even the customary hospitality of islanders to offer food and drink to visitors had temporarily been forgotten. Meanwhile the trade goods Tsgot had brought were soon bartered for almost worthless exchange.

It was soon apparent that some of the settlers were distant kin to Tsgot's companions and were disillusioned about the attempt to settle in the Caicos. Their sojourn on the island had clearly been difficult and many of them stated openly they wished to return to Inagua or even the 'great' island from where their ancestors originated. Finally, to put an end to the persistent complaints, demands, questions and banter, Tsgot promised to faithfully relay their requests back to their kin in Inagua and Cuba and, with this spoken, he asked to be shown the way to the miraculous shrine cave.

"We must not delay our visit to the oracle", Tsgot quietly reminded his colleagues, then turning to the people of the settlement he raised his voice and continued, "...we have heard that the secret voice of the oracle tells of things from another world...we wish to hear from this wonder for ourselves..."

The settlers happily acceded to Tsgot's request and accompanied the visitors to the hilltop situated just south of the village. Walking past small patches of cultivated land the visitors could see for themselves the wizened state of the vegetation.

Soon they approached the entrance to the cavern that opened into the side of the hill. The settlers stopped some distance from the cave entrance while Tsgot and his men approached the mysterious cleft in the hillside.

At the mouth of the cave all conversation ceased. The villagers lit flaming torches for the visitors and reverently Tsgot and his comrades entered the cavern in single file when suddenly, at the moment of their entry, aerial waves of shrieking bats made a noisy escape to the open air. The visitors were awestruck. It was believed that cave openings like this were the entrance to the underworld where the souls of the dead were thought to reside. The bats, they thought, were the metamorphosised souls of the dead who would occasionally depart their shadowy abode to re-visit the world of the living.

Quietly they proceeded into the dim interior of the cavern treading carefully around large holes that punctuated the floor of the caves. They held onto each other to avoid falling on slippery cavern floor. As they proceeded their whispered voices echoed eerily off the walls of the caverns.

Suddenly, a voice from the dim interior of the cave, speaking in a strange but intelligible dialect of *Aiti*, startled them;

Proceed no further!

You are to leave this place to seek on a far-away isle in a sea of islands, another sacred cavern, a cavern which is lit by the sun at daybreak. There you must leave a sacred token displaying an image of the blessed soul of the dead. You will find the cavern in the contrary direction to the mid-day sun. Do not return until you have counted as many moons as there are fingers on your two hands.

Do as the oracle commands...!

As the oracle was speaking Tsgot instinctively touched the green jade amulet depicting the face of a bat that he was wearing round his neck. Mesmerised for a moment by the command of the unseen oracle, the visitors were rooted to the spot. Then, when they realised the pronouncement had ended, they hurriedly retreated from the cave and, once outside, heatedly discussed among themselves the meaning of this strange decree.

"No one has ever explored the unknown sea to the north!" exclaimed one of the younger men in a voice tinged with apprehension, "how can anyone be certain that there are more islands?"

"...and how can we survive - possibly for months at sea - if there is no land to the north of here?" questioned another.

"...and what if we encounter sea monsters that are reputed to live in that region...?"

The oraclular conundrum generated questions but no answers. Tsgot held up his hand to silence the controversy.

Pondering for several minutes he said thoughtfully:

"I do not doubt we shall find land and, let us not forget this is a sacred command!...It is true that no-one has ever travelled to the region of the northern sea...but the oracle has wisdom and knowledge known only to the sacred *zemi.*" Then, peering towards the distant sea he continued quietly but with stern authority, "...it is not for us to decide, the *zemi* has spoken...we must prepare to leave without delay!"

His colleagues found the gently spoken command difficult to accept with equanimity. But Tsgot gradually managed to persuade the young seamen by asking them to consider that a great adventure might lie ahead of them. He asked them to recall the oral sagas long recited by the elders of their people recalling the heroic crossing of a vast inland sea to the island of Cuba from the great western continent and even of the long voyages made to islands within the inland sea. Though competition between the Antilieans was almost unknown, they all understood an epic adventure would enhance the reputation of any seaman and might even be recorded in the oral history of his tribe. This promise of a chance of recognition, fame even, eventually convinced them. So, after much discussion, the men were gradually won over and they left the cave entrance to return to the village and prepare for a voyage into the unknown.

The prospect of a major expedition with its starting point in the insignificant Caicos islands stimulated the villagers to action. Hunting parties were sent out to trap *biaya* (flamingos) from the salt flats, the conch corrals were emptied and fishermen donated some of their catch. A paltry supply of beer made from cassava was made available and even the precious store of tubers and corn was raided to furnish the expedition. Flints and fireboards were also stowed aboard the canoes.

With the help of the settlers the provisioning of the canoes was soon complete, but once the stored food had been eaten, Tsgot and his men would have to live off both sea and land in time-honoured fashion. Their most important provision would be drinking water and this they collected in gourds that they secured in the bottom of their canoes. They knew from long experience that they could survive on half a gourd of water per man per day. To this they added leaves from various shrubs. Once under way they would dilute the fresh water with about a quarter of seawater. The Antilieans had long found that adding seawater helped quench their thirst and the leaves would impart flavour and nutrients while at the same time replenishing the salt their bodies would loose through perspiration.

Because of Tsgot's calm but persuasive reasoning the men became reconciled, and later even eager, to embark on an adventure to the forbidding northern ocean. They were not unduly dismayed that it might entail a journey of up to five months and the only directions they had received was that the distinguishing feature of this mysterious cave they were to seek was that its entrance would be illuminated by the rising sun. There was little thought for the kin they would be leaving behind. The seamen now clearly understood that the oracle was a messenger of the sacred *zemi* and the command must be obeyed.

This was to be a sacred mission!

At dawn the following day Tsgot and his men bade farewell to the people of the settlement and launched their canoes. They paddled through the shallow creek between the islands and for two hours followed the northeast coast of the main Caicos islands. Then, once abeam the northern cape, the adventurers turned towards the open ocean and set a course due north.

The canoes were at one with the sea. They floated above the surface of the water with a draft and freeboard of only a few inches. The measured drop of the paddles created only a ripple on the surface water. By day a great variety of life was visible all around them. Terns skimmed across the waters never far from landfall while pelicans stayed with them longer at sea alighting gracefully on the water when they needed rest. Boobies would skim the surface of the ocean near them hoping for an easy meal, and cormorants and gannets would scream at them from overhead. Sometimes majestic frigate birds soared high in the sky in giant circles searching for floating weed that often concealed a shoal of fish. Occasionally the surface water around the weed would churn as predatory fish homed in on the concealed shoals in a frenzy of feeding and then the seabirds would swoop down to catch a mouthful of fish in their beaks. In the ocean, sharks, turtle, jellyfish, shrimp and pelagic fish of many species made their appearance from time to time then moved on. Often they would catch shrimp and small crabs from the weed which floated by and, sometimes in deeper water, flying fish would stun themselves by flying into their canoes and would be quickly gathered on board.

At night the marine life would change to a different genus of marine animals with luminous eyes which seemed to flicker on and off. At times the phosphorescence of the surface water flashed around them like a reflected image of the stars. Occasionally the grunt of a turtle - or it might have been a porpoise or whale - hauntingly punctuated the nocturnal silence. Sometimes they could hear the eerie sounds of whales calling to each other in the depths below. Generally the seamen found travelling at night easier since on cloudless nights the north star was visible so they could be sure of their direction and it was cooler and the sea was often calmer. The paddling was exhausting but far over the horizon they were sustained by the belief that distant islands, like beautiful virgins, awaited the arrival of mariners ready to reward the brave men who dared to find them.

After travelling for two days across the yawning blue-black water of the Caicos Passage, they were overjoyed to catch sight of land far to the west in the morning light of the third day. Their faith in the oracle now confirmed, the canoeists altered course and, with a following wind, made landfall later that day. Apart from the isolated island of Great Inagua - that is even further south than the Caicos chain - Tsgot and his colleagues had now discovered yet another island in the Bahamian archipelago. The isle Tsgot had found, like Inagua, was populated with numerous iguana that scuttled about its rocky surface so the island became known as *Yaguna.*

Mayaguana, as *Yaguna* would later be known, seemed to be flatter than the islands they had left with only shrub and cactus protruding from its parched landscape but apart from that, and the dearth of pine trees, they concluded its vegetation looked very similar to the Caicos Islands. After stretching their legs Tsgot and his tired companions hauled the canoes above the tell-tale line of seaweed at high water after landing on a white sand beach. They walked through the narrow margin of sea oats and spider lilies and found some gnarled seagrape bushes to rest under and, lulled by the melodious thunder of the surf, soon fell into a deep sleep.

Tsgot and his men were the first of humankind to ever to set foot in the Bahama Islands.

Some hours later the visitors stirred. Once awake they were able to reflect on the fact that they had indeed found a new island. Tsgot was quick to remind the canoeists that the pronouncement of the oracle appeared to be coming true.

First, they gathered some of the acrid sweet berries from the canopy of saucer-sized seagrape leaves over their heads and chewed upon some of the succulent herbs which grew near the beach strand. They also smoothed the sap of the aloe plant on their skin that served to keep insects away and also helped as a balm against the fierce rays of the sun. After this the adventurers trekked inland in search of water. The Antilleans, like many people who live close to nature, had an instinctive sense of knowing where to find life-sustaining drinking water.

In less than half an hour Tsgot found a deep slit in the ground revealing a water hole which was partly covered by ferns and other overhanging vegetation. He tasted the water from his cupped hands and announced that it was drinkable. Then he and his companions drank deeply and replenished the gourds. That done Tsgot then led his men on an iguana hunt. The giant, dragon-like creatures had never known a natural enemy and were soon caught and roasted. Meat not eaten was readied for the next stage of their journey.

It was twilight when they returned to the beach to sleep. Some of the men laughingly separated from the others to pursue an intimacy that later ages of mankind would declare abhorrent but the taboos of the Antilleans extended only to incestuous relationships, it would take several centuries before other ideas of morality would invade their culture. The waves washed laconically upon the anvil of the beach and a warm breeze fanned the low bushes around them. A beautiful starlit heaven was above in which shooting stars left fluorescent markers in the sky but the contented Antillean adventurers soon drifted off to sleep oblivious of the awesome nocturnal spectacle.

Morning brought the golden gift of sunshine. A chorus of seabirds awoke them just before dawn and the seafarers helped themselves to a last meal of seagrapes and smoked iguana meat. With every man knowing his duties, they were soon ready to re-commence their odyssey. With hardly a word spoken they quickly re-launched their canoes into the breaking foam and were at sea once again.

Once more the seafarers headed north but the drift of current and wind fortuitously caused their track to be more northwesterly which, within a day, carried them to some small idyllic isles that would later be called Plana Cays. After landing on the cays they soon discovered they were almost barren of edible vegetation and without fresh water so they decided to leave the isles and continue onward the following day. Before leaving however, they made a meal of eggs taken from seabirds' nests, gathered conch and caught reef fish in the shallows that they stowed in their canoes as provision for the voyage ahead.

Far out at sea late the following day they were delighted to sight more land on the western horizon and, as they headed in closer, they were able to discern the customary long white line of surf breaking against a fringing reef. As they approached closer still they could hear the menacing hiss of the swells breaking up on the underwater coral.

Confident now that the oracle had been correct about the presence of land in the forbidding northern ocean Tsgot and his colleagues finished what was left of their sun-dried meal of raw fish then unhurriedly rode the surf into a wide bay. As before, they landed on a pristine white sand beach and found that this island seemed to be blessed with more vegetation than Mayaguana.

Pulling their canoes above high watermark on a sandy beach, they obeyed the call of nature and climbing to the top of a sandy ridge, they rested. Twilight was rapidly approaching and, as the sun rapidly disappeared into the placid sea, it emitted a momentary silent green flash, but it went unnoticed. The exhausted seamen were already asleep.

At dawn the adventurers started a reconnaissance of this new island from locations that in the present age have acquired picturesque Bahamian place names. They first walked from what is today known as Hard Hill and crossed the narrow island to Snug Corner which faces a shallow turquoise-coloured bay known as the Bight of Acklins. There they gathered more of the edible succulent beach vegetation and berries before continuing on to the broad sweep of white sand now known as Delectable Bay. From here they left the mangroves at the south end of the bay and climbed to the ridge that was covered with low flowering shrubs among them the beautiful dwarf yellow elder tree destined one day to be declared the national tree of the islands.

Atop the ridge they had a commanding view of the cerulean blue ocean on one side of the island and the shallow milky coloured turquoise water of the bank on the other. At the highest point of the island they could see to the east a small cay just off a promontory. The islet in a later age would be named Jamaica Cay. Pressing further south they climbed another knoll which in historic times would be named Binnacle Hill as it was reminiscent of the stand upon which ship's compasses are mounted. And, at the southernmost point of the island they found an extensive natural salina where they gathered salt and observed a fortress-like cay that would later be fittingly named Castle Island.

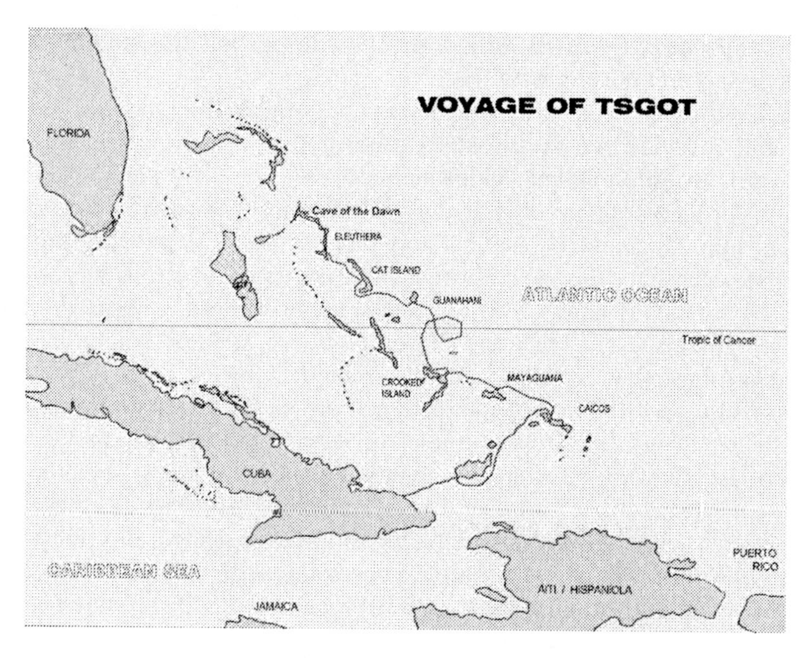

Figure 4 - The voyages of Tsgot to the Bahama Islands

On their return to Hard Hill they followed the east coast of the island passing charming sheltered coves defined by low ironstone promontories. Their ramble brought them finally to a brackish inland lake populated by flocks of snowy egret, herons and other waterfowl. Crossing the island they retraced their steps to Spring Point where they were found fresh water left after a rain storm which allowed them to replenish their gourds. Later they trapped a hapless visiting flamingo in the tidal flats which they roasted over an open fire. But in their thorough reconnaissance of the beautiful island they found no significant caves.

Back at Hard Hill the seamen spent the remainder of the day at ease anticipating a lifestyle that future visitors would imitate. The day following was spent in similar fashion though they found time to catch reef fish in the shallows by submerging branches of the native dogwood tree into the water. The poison in the dogwood momentarily stunned the fish that they then deftly scooped into their canoes. Some fish they cooked on shore but most were gutted, salted and stowed on board to be eaten raw later. They then harvested the plentiful conch in the shallows. Since the seamen did not need the extra weight of the conch shells in their canoes the conch was separated from its shell by breaking the shell at the exact point the mollusc is attached to the hard shell. This was achieved by expertly hitting one conch with the point of another and 'juking' the animal from its shell by the bony 'heel', more properly called an operculum, that the animal uses to move or to secret itself into its shell.

With the canoes fully provisioned once again they re-launched their craft and rounded the northeastern cape of this newfound isle that long afterwards would be called Acklins Island.

After passing Lovely Bay they paddled across a narrow channel that opened into the Bight of Acklins and then another island came into full view. As Tsgot and his men approached they noted that this new isle had many bays and headlands and, from what they could see, appeared to be of very irregular shape. For good reason it would later be named Crooked Island but these first explorers called the island: *Samoet*.

So up to this time, though they were slightly less than one moon into their voyage, the adventurers had discovered for the first time in human history, some cays and three new Bahamian islands. The enigmatic command of the oracle had been to 'seek out the Cave of the Dawn' and it was soon clear that *Samoet*, like the others they had visited, did not possess any significant caverns, and certainly none facing east.

As was customary, Tsgot and his men searched for food and found berries in profusion on the island. They sampled the fruit of the Bahamian cocoa plum bush but wisely avoided the tempting-looking but poisonous berries of the poison wood tree. Afterwards they caught and roasted the nimble land crabs that raced about the scarred surface of the island. Later that day the visitors replenished their water containers, repaired some of their paddles and re-stowed what was left of the tradeware in the canoes. A storm was approaching so Tsgot decided they should stay longer to enjoy the tranquility of *Samoet* for one more night especially now that the wind had made the flying insects less of a nuisance. That night was inky black but was surrealistically illuminated with distant flashes of lightning. If the adventurers had only been conscious, the pyrotechnic explosions of light might have intimated to them impending disaster.

At daybreak the canoeists left *Samoet* just as the orange orb of the sun appeared above the eastern horizon. By now the canoes were floating a little lower in the water since the tree trunks had absorbed seawater so that, even in moderate seas, the holds were now often awash. Occasionally it would rain and when this happened the canoeists would quickly bail out their canoes to let their holds fill with rainwater. The fresh water would then be collected by the canoeists sucking the bilge water into their mouths and regurgitating it into the gourds. However, undeterred by the weather, Tsgot and his men paddled northwards all day and all night in a choppy sea.

The following day dawn arrived almost unnoticed. The world at first light was murky and eerily quiet. Later the wind picked up and soon varied only between storm and gale. Sea birds shrieked loudly on their way to make land. The wind and surface current turned a full circle so they were able to make little headway in any direction. As the day wore on, scuds of low clouds passed quickly overhead and the wind became shifty. Later thunder and lightning surrounded them and the driving rain bit into their naked skin. The wind now whipped up the sea like a boiling cauldron and there were breaking white crests on the wave swells all around them. These hardened seamen knew only too well what by now would be obvious to anyone: this was a prelude to a deadly cyclone.

It was clear they could make no distance in any direction and since they had lost all sense of direction they could not paddle back to *Samoet* even if it had been an option. By noon the wind was blowing even more fiercely with a noise that was deafening. The canoes bobbed about like corks on the turbulent ocean.

The storm raged on for hours.

At times, walls of water threatened to submerge them but just as they were about to be overwhelmed, the natural buoyancy of their wooden craft floated them to the crest of the swell. Moments later though they found themselves at the bottom of a trough again fighting fiercely to paddle their canoes into the face of the giant swell to avoid being swamped. But often waves broke right over them and then the natural buoyancy of the solid wooden craft was of no avail.

In time one by one all of the canoes were over-turned. The men hung onto the hulks of wood with all their might for, to become separated from their canoes at this time they well understood would mean certain death. The canoeists, some of whom had been in a similar predicament before, shouted instructions and encouragement to each other. But their voices hardly carried above the roar of the ocean and soon some of the canoes drifted well out of earshot.

The hurricane raged for a full night and throughout the following morning. Gradually the breaking waves gave way to precipitous swells and only then were the men able to sit astride the upturned craft. Tsgot could see only three canoes, two others were completely lost to sight. Though fearfully exhausted the men in the remaining canoes paddled with a following wind towards the north hoping to catch sight of their comrades and the welcome sight of land.

They tried shouting again but only the wind replied.

By daybreak they found themselves close to foundering onto a reef. Beyond lay a large shallows that a future visitor would claim could hold all the ships of Christendom. For now it was enough that three rough hewn wooden canoes would find shelter. The Antilleans had arrived at an island they called *Guanahani* (in their language it meant the Place of the Iguana) the island would later be re-named for the Holy Saviour, then for a cold-blooded pirate, and then once again for the Holy Saviour.

Tsgot and his men glided their canoes through the surf onto a silver beach and staggered out onto the warm sand. For seamen who prided themselves on being able to stay at sea for many days at a time, the ordeal of the hurricane had made them appreciate the unyielding solid and dry land.

After a deep long sleep born of exhaustion, the survivors of the hurricane beat a path inland to explore the small hills and pretty irregular-shaped lakes of the island. They were surprised to find many lakes were of different colours (due in fact to the lake depth and bloom of different types of algae) and were quick to discover that the largest lake was brackish, while some of the smaller lakes contained sweet water. They also found iguana and turtles in abundance. But their explorations revealed no important caves. They found too that *Guanahani* was more extensive north to south than it was east to west and was like a bent oval in shape not unlike a peanut.

Tsgot sensibly decided they should stay some time on this island to recuperate, repair and re-provision the canoes. To create shelter they built small huts looking much like the tents of their ancient Asian ancestors, but instead of animal hide, they covered them with interlaced palmetto fronds.

The loss of their colleagues greatly disturbed them, but little was said of the matter. Several times each day they would climb the low hills to scan the horizon for a distant sign of their friends but saw only a deceptively tranquil sea. The inshore waters were a kaleidoscope of turquoise, jade, and several shades of blue with even a magic intrusion of purple and gold. While about a mile from shore was an ever-changing white margin of breaking waves with the ominous dark Prussian blue of the expansive Atlantic Ocean beyond.

After three days of scanning the beautiful sea from a hilltop, they were alarmed to catch sight of several sharks at the distant reef circling something in the water. The seamen rushed down to the beach and paddled their canoes towards the thrashing beasts. On arriving at the reef their worst fears were confirmed: the frenzied sharks were tearing one of their lost comrades to pieces. For one brief moment, in a gruesome mocking irony, a dismembered arm appeared above the surface of the water as if to hail them then quickly disappeared below the waves. The men beat their paddles on the seawater turned red with blood and screamed helplessly at the sharks but to no avail. Minutes later the thrashing animals disappeared and suddenly the terrible scene was but a grisly memory. But the full horror of the sea devils started to haunt their minds and the seamen began to think with longing of returning to their mountainous homeland.

But the decree of the oracle was ever-present in their minds. Tsgot understood well the feelings of all his men and decreed tactfully:

"We shall do as we were commanded but we shall take no great risks on our journey. I promise we shall start our return to the Caicos by the fifth moon and not a day later!"

His colleagues reluctantly concurred. Thus, after five or so months into the voyage they would start their long journey home.

They stayed twenty days at *Guanahani*. During this time some necessary repairs were made to one of the canoes and several new paddles were fashioned. They also formed some long poles that were sometimes used at sea to act as temporary outriggers and on land to create ephemeral shelter. Though most of the tradeware was lost, the fireboard and some of the gourds and basketwork remained and Tsgot still had possession of the small crudely carved figurine representing the bat spirit of the dead on a string around his neck.

The gourds, as always, were re-filled with water, basketwork was fashioned into crude fishing nets, and berries, iguana, turtle eggs and crabmeat were stowed aboard the canoes. Despite the painful memories of their shipmates, their discovery of the island of San Salvador had both sustained and enchanted them. Of all the islands they had seen up to this time Tsgot mused this was the island that might be the most suitable site for future settlement. It was information he would be sure to carry back to the Great Island.

Then, with greater trepidation than before, the Antilleans recommenced their voyage. This time they hugged the leeward shore of *Guanahani* and followed the turquoise water of Exuma Sound northwards thus avoiding the open ocean. The cooler days of winter were now approaching and nights on the open sea were unpleasantly cold but the canoeists paddled valiantly onwards.

As before terns skimmed across the waters never far from landfall while now squawking seagulls stayed with them longer at sea, alighting on the water when they needed rest and eying them constantly in hopes of obtaining an easy meal. Towards evening, flocks of birds flew overhead with more purpose. No longer were the birds interested in making precipitous dives into sea to secure a meal but flew intently instead to the nearest island. By following the birds an experienced seaman knew where he would find land though of course the land-based birds would be home long before a navigator would see the gossamer thin line of land on a distant horizon. Sometimes islands would be capped by the tell-tale sign of a cloud. An isolated cumulus cloud will often form over a tropical island as the sun heats the earth and a stream of warm air is created which rises up and causes its vapour to condense in the upper colder strata of air. Experienced navigators at sea like Tsgot can sometimes tell the size as well as the direction of an unseen island just by observing the clouds in the sky.

After three days paddling northwards the adventurers saw a typical tell-tale cloudbank and shortly thereafter spied an island to westwards where they happily made a landfall.

This long narrow island, was called *Guanima* and later Cat Island (and mistakenly later still, San Salvador) but for the Antilleans their folkloric memory of a cat had been the jaguar of a now long-forgotten mainland existence. On landing on this island they found it rendered the usual provisions, similar scenery and another chance to recoup from the rigors of travel. They climbed to the top of a hill, which at just over two hundred feet was in fact the highest point of land for over two hundred miles. This gave them a good view of the island and the surrounding waters. From the summit of the hill they determined that more land lay northwest of them.

Seaborne once more, they hugged the lee of *Guanima* and, when they were not far from the northern cape, the adventurers could indeed discern more land almost due west. In a matter of hours they discovered some cays that to windward were protected by an extensive reef. The cays later were confusingly called Little San Salvador in the mistaken belief that the island they had just left was the landfall of Columbus. They did not land on the cays because once abreast of them they could see a larger island further west. Paddling with the full benefit of tide and current they made landfall at *Ziguateo* an isle which centuries later would be re-named by people from a faraway island across the great ocean. Its Greek name *Eleutheria* would commemorate freedom.

This new island they found was very narrow and extended on a north/south axis, as they would later discover, for about sixty miles. With the high bluffs to windward Tsgot was convinced that it was here that they would find the long sought-for cave. So they beached their canoes and set about their exploration on foot.

By day they marched northward along the windswept beaches on the Atlantic side of the island of *Ziguateo* occasionally taking time out to force their way through the hardwood coppices and thick shrubbery to view the leeward coast of the narrow island. Here the largely sandy shore was occasionally punctuated with gnarled 'ironstone' rocks containing solution-eroded rock pools. As they passed, the rocky foreshore emitted strange random clicking sounds as the tide rose and fell. In the shallows beyond the beach strand black shadowy stingrays moved stealthily across the sandy bottom and from time to time silvery shoals of bonefish would dart along the shore being chased, no doubt, by some unseen predator.

After three days the island narrowed and they crossed a natural bridge. On one side was the cauldron of the open Atlantic Ocean, on the other the placid saucer calm of Exuma Sound. They marvelled at the strange 'window' and continued on.

A day later, one of Tsgot's men made a great discovery. Carved out of the cliff, a little inland from the sea and near the northern cape of Eleuthera, was an entrance to a great cave that faced toward the northeast and would therefore just catch the first rays of the morning sun. This they reasoned must be what the oracle had predicted the long sought-after: cave of the dawn!

With the contradictory emotions of joy and foreboding they approached the cave. Tsgot summoned his men to remain outside while he slowly proceeded to enter the cavern alone.

"Stay here but make no sound!" Tsgot whispered, "I will enter and listen for a message."

The 'Glass Window', Eleuthera

Inside it was not so wide as the Caicos cave and it seemed too, not to be so deep. Twelve paces forward Tsgot stopped, motioning to the others to join him.

They all listened intently for a voice.

The distant sea pounded the shore, sea birds shrieked overhead, lizards scurried for cover but they could discern no other sound, no sign. Tsgot beckoned to the men to stay silent and, for many, many, minutes they waited intently.

But nothing happened.

Tsgot at last broke the silence:

"The spirits have nothing to impart to us, we have done as we were asked, the *zemi* are satisfied with our visit. It is now time to return..."

His tactful assertion satisfied his men, for they had indeed done their duty, and more. His words reassured the men that their mission had not been a failure and now, uppermost in all their minds, they could return to their distant home.

As the Antilleans were slowly leaving the cave Tsgot stopped for a moment, then returned. He took the jade amulet from around his neck and placed it high on a ledge in the cave. Tsgot took three steps back, stared in silence at the object for a moment, then hurried out into the bright sunlight to rejoin his comrades.

Up to this time, Tsgot and his colleagues, had been travelling four moons and twenty days.

THE RETURN JOURNEY was more carefree than the outward expedition. They encountered storms, but none so fierce as the hurricane, they endured hardships, cold, lack of food, water, and incredible physical exhaustion, but they were consoled by the knowledge that they would soon be home again. The adventurers followed the island chain southwards, retracing very nearly, the same course as they had followed on the outward journey.

At an island they called *Amaguayo* but later known as Samana Cay, over seventy miles southeast of *Guanahani*, Tsgot and his companions were amazed to see smoke rising. On landing on the cay they were overjoyed to meet up with comrades from one of the canoes they thought had been lost forever. The men from the lone canoe had hung together after the terrible hurricane and had been washed ashore. On Samana they had barely survived off the meagre resources of the island. Without lumber, or the skills to make a canoe, the seamen knew that they would surely perish unless Tsgot returned for them. So on seeing Tsgot in the distance approaching the cay they were overjoyed and knew for a certainty that the good *zemi* had interceded on their behalf.

The re-united seamen spent a few days on the Samana Cays celebrating, recuperating and preparing for the last leg of their heroic journey. Then, increasing the crew proportionately in each canoe, the Antilleans set course for home.

In just over four moons they arrived again at the 'middle' island of the Caicos group and were disheartened to find not a trace was left of the former settlement. Tsgot revisited the cave of the oracle on the middle Caicos island but there was no voice to either commend or rebuke his efforts in finding the distant cave. Tsgot reasoned the spirits did not need always to convey their thoughts into words. He knew that he, and his men, had done all that was asked of them. He would let that suffice. So, with some foreboding they set a course for Inagua and were relieved and happy to find that the people from the Caicos settlement had returned there safely. Once ashore the people of the expanded village greeted them joyously. Tsgot and his companions were made to recount the tale of their adventures over and over again. Their exploits soon became recorded into the oral folklore of the tribe and the fame of Tsgot and his comrades was spread to the Antilles for hundreds of miles around.

At the settlement in Inagua there was great feasting and ribaldry, for everyone was cognizant of what an epic journey had just been completed. Though other members of the tribe had been at sea for many days, weeks even, nothing could compare to the endevours of the incredible expedition led by the Antillean trader named Tsgot. As a tribute to his accomplishments, when he decided to leave for Cuba, the paultry trading items that the adventurers had left months before were now increased tenfold by the admiring villagers.

It is noteworthy to recall that this fantastic voyage of discovery, almost to the northern end of the Bahamian chain of islands, had been undertaken by a naked seaman who travelled with his companions over one thousand miles over a perilous ocean. Tsgot and his colleagues had lived off the land and sea as they travelled using only the sun and the stars for navigation, they survived numerous storms and a full-fledged hurricane, yet to accomplish their mission they employed nothing more than the hollowed-out trunks of a tree!

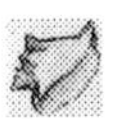 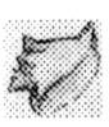 

***IN THE MIDDLE** of the seventh century before the Christian era, a crisis due to over-population arose in the small Aegean island of Santorini (modern Thera). This was exacerbated by a seven year drought which caused so much distress that it seemed to suggest that forced emigration would be the only solution. But before they decided on such a drastic step, the leaders of the community consulted the famed Oracle of Apollo at Delphi and were advised to establish a new community at Cyrene in Libya. The community obeyed.*

The role played by the priest in the oracle of the Caicos was a similar ruse. Had Tsgot and his colleagues not heeded the voice of the oracle and proceeded further into the caverns they might have discovered that the oracular voice emanated from an old shaman (who doubtless was under the influence of hallucinants). His reason for ordering the voyage was the desire on the part of the elders to have the Antilleans explore and colonise other islands. Shamans often resorted to trickery to gain compliance to their wishes. Experience had long taught them that people are never so motivated as when they think they are serving their gods!

Both oracles played on the religious piety of their followers and both were effective, in a small way, of changing the course of history.

Once the Greeks embarked on colonisation, they spread their culture throughout the world of the Mediterranean and beyond. Tsgot, because of his heroic voyage, was the first man to set foot in the Bahama Islands which were shortly thereafter to become a stepping stone for the colonisation of a whole new world.

Chapter 3 - The Lucayans (600 - 1513 AD)

> ***I...think their life most happye of all men, if they might therewith enjoie their anciente libertie. A fewe things content them, having no delite in such superfluities, for which in other places men take infinite paynes and commit many unlawful acts.***
>
> ***Peter Martyr***

THE ORIGINAL INHABITANTS of the Antilles enjoyed nearly four thousand years of undisturbed tranquility. Then, just before the dawning of the Christian era, Arawak tribes living in the northern part of the Amazon rain forest started to migrate downstream from the mid-reaches of the Orinoco River into what is today the country of Venezuela. When they reached the open sea they turned north. Soon their migration was to touch the lives of almost all the Stone Age people living in the necklace of islands that stretch between South and North America on the eastern rim of the Caribbean Basin.

The Arawaks were a gentle industrious people. They introduced a new progressive culture to the islands of the Caribbean that was continually being adapted to the environment as they progressed northwards towards the Bahamas. Outsiders who later met the Island Arawaks and the indigenous island peoples they influenced were full of praise for the Utopia like communities they developed. But as the human history of the world has shown all too often, in time weaker nations succumb to stronger forces irrespective of morality, religion or race.

With the coming of the Europeans, the Lucayans of the Bahama Islands were not chased away or absorbed but conquered, brutalized and exterminated. In a brief moment of time they disappeared as a race from the earth. Thus the original inhabitants of the Bahamas, a unique branch of the human family became, with conclusive finality...extinct.

The following account recalls the story of the migrants who visited the Caribbean islands from the South American mainland and later went on to colonise the Bahama Islands.

Woodcut of Hammock

ONCE OUTSIDE the Orinoco River delta, the Arawaks, entered the silt-laden and turbulent stretch of water known as the Serpent's Mouth. From there they headed their canoes towards a detached portion of the southern continent of the Americas. The island they discovered around 200 BC that would later be named by Christian Europeans for their triune concept of a Supreme Being. The time of the Arawak's arrival can be estimated with some degree of accuracy because of the boon of Carbon-14 dating which has placed a fairly accurate date on carbon samples found at a place called Cedros near the southern tip of Trinidad.

Some time before 100 AD the 'Island' Arawaks recommenced their migration and started to travel by canoe northwards up the island chain of the Lesser Antilles towards Hispaniola. One theory has it that after finding a new island they would climb to its highest point to look for another island to explore. But whether they followed this practice or not, in course of time they were to arrive at the island of Cuba.

The Island Arawaks spoke a language which became the ancestor of the later Taíno language. They were a sedentary, agricultural people who were good at many crafts including weaving and the making extremely fine ceramics, which were named for convenience, after archaeological sites at which it was later found. It is of particular significance to archaeologists and historians that the Island Arawaks made much pottery since this was later to render much information about their culture. Pottery shards have even been found that captured the fingerprints of its maker. Arawak ceramics were made by coiling the clay instead of the more familiar method of using a potter's wheel. Some of their pottery carried intricate incised patterns while other ceramic objects they made displayed decorative motifs inspired by animals. Fortunately their movements and the various cultural changes they experienced can be traced fairly accurately from the pottery that the Island Arawaks made and sometimes discarded but was later found and analysed.

By 400 AD the Island Arawaks were well established as far north as Hispaniola. At this stage the Island Arawaks had become 'creolized' to the point that they became a new cultural entity that ethnologists identify as the 'Taíno'. In eastern Hispaniola it is possible the Taíno encountered large numbers of the original Antilleans who slowed the progress of their migration. But, in time, most of the original Antilleans were assimilated and adopted the language and the cultural traits of the Taíno. Interestingly the first Europeans noticed that wives often spoke a different tongue from their spouses and deduced that this was a societal norm. In fact it was much simpler than that. The womenfolk were original Antilleans who sensibly preferred to use their own language among themselves.

After Hispaniola the Taíno then pushed on to colonise Cuba. Again they were confronted by large numbers of the original inhabitants. This new wave of Taíno physically occupied most of Cuba but here too they did not totally assimilate all the inhabitants. Some small enclaves of the ancient Antillean people resisted complete absorption. One such were a people living in the northeastern portion of Cuba. But in time these earlier settlers adopted a form of Taíno speech and a few Taíno traits including the strange practice of flattening the foreheads of their children shortly after birth. It was through this encounter that the earlier settlers became a new cultural entity identified by ethnologists as 'Ciboney'. The Ciboney were so-named because they used caves for habitation or as religious shrines (the Taíno word 'ciba' meaning rocky land and 'eyeri' translating as man).

The Ciboney, probably due to increasing population pressure and their confrontation with the advancing Taíno, made some exploratory visits to the small limestone islands to the north. They first visited the Bahama islands from the Cuba in about 600 AD. Some time later, many of them were to migrate to the Bahamian archipelago and became, in course of time, the rootstock of the Lucayan Indians.

Like the other Antilleans, the Ciboney used canoes to travel great distances by sea. At first they were only occasional visitors to the low-lying 'white' islands where they would gather salt and catch fish. Later however, small communities were established, first in the Caicos islands, then later throughout the whole Bahamian archipelago where in time, they became another distinct cultural entity who were called by European visitors the '*Lucayos*' or Lucayan Indians.

Indeed by 800 AD, probably due to increasing population pressure, there was a major migration of the Ciboney originating from northeastern region of Cuba to both the western Caicos and the Bahama islands. This was followed, a little later by a similar migration of other creolised people originating in northern Hispaniola whose destination was primarily the eastern Caicos Islands.

The Ciboney could be described as fisherfolk and food gatherers and only in their late phase did they master the art of pottery-making which exhibited a strong Taíno influence. Their preferred medium was stone and their carvings of purely decorative items were exquisite in both form and decoration and were widely distributed throughout the islands. The Ciboney in common with many early cultures made celts that looked like stone axe heads though their function might in some cases, have been non-utilitarian. The shaping and polishing of these celts involved the tedious but exacting task of grinding basaltic rocks to pure shapes and then polishing them with extensive rubbing. The resulting artifacts represent an important cultural art form and indeed axe head celts have been found in most of the islands of the Caribbean Basin. Until very recently the celts, known locally in the Bahamas as 'thunderstones', were thought to be have been formed when a thunderbolt struck the ground. They were often placed beneath the masts of sailing ships to bring good luck.

Several sites where flint tools were made in the Antilles have been identified. The flints were almost certainly 'tradeware', that is to say, they were bartered with tribes on other islands. People living on islands consisting solely of soft limestone (like the Bahamas and the Turks and Caicos Islands) would have been obvious customers for the sharp-edged flints. Experts have confirmed that some flints they used were quite as sharp as the Spanish knives.

Another artifact all the Indians shared and which had immense utility value, was the canoe. All the Indians of the Caribbean region came from a culture that had used canoes in one form or another for thousands of years. The Lucayan canoe was not so different from those made by the Antillean people before them, though contemporary observers suggested the Lucayans favoured using the trunk of the large silk cotton tree. These trees were felled in the time-honoured way of chopping at the base of the trunk with stone axes and then causing fires to burn until the tree could be toppled. Fires were also used to hollow out the trunk. The shaping and finishing of the canoe was then done with stone axes and chisels.

The Genoese eyewitness who was the first European to meet with the Lucayans remarked, *'every chief has a great canoe for himself in which he takes great pride as a Castilian gentleman is proud of possessing a fine, big ship'*, and, continued Columbus, *'they have their canoes painted and carved both bow and stern with ornaments so that their beauty is marvelous.'*

All the peoples of the Antilles were incredibly good seamen and early writers suggest that they treated the sea as if it was their natural element.

'Their...dugouts which are fashioned like a long boat from the bole of a tree, and all in one piece, and wonderfully made (considering the country), and so big that in some came 40 or 45 men, and others smaller, down to a size that held a single man. They row with a thing like a baker's peel and go wonderfully (fast), and if they capsize all begin to swim and right it and bail it out with calabashes that they carry.'

Many of the Antilleans were traders and occasionally canoes would fan out from Cuba and Hispaniola, the main centres of the Antillean world, to barter tradeware and agricultural and marine produce with other islands.

As to the appearance of the Lucayans we have an excellent description from Columbus:

'...their forms are well-proportioned, their bodies graceful and their features handsome, though they are marred somewhat by very broad heads and foreheads...Their hair is as coarse as the hair of a horse's tail and short. They wear their hair over their eyebrows, except a little hank behind, which they wear long and never cut. Some of them paint themselves black (they are the colour of Canary islanders neither black nor white), some paint themselves white; some red, and some with whatever they can find; some paint their faces, some their whole body, some their eyes only; and some their noses only...'

The Lucayans, like the aboriginal peoples before them, were distinctly oriental in appearance. Their 'neither black nor white' skin colour is an accurate observation by Columbus, for they were indeed of neither the white Caucasian nor black African race; they belonged rather to the Asian so-called 'yellow' race.

The reference by Columbus to the applied paint is also interesting. They were vain certainly, for they deformed the heads of their infants in an attempt to achieve some idealized facial type. Science has yet to study what psychological effects the cranial deformation produced. Could the increase in the brain cavity that sometimes resulted have increased their intelligence or have had some other psychic effect? The body painting referred to was also cosmetic though it has been suggested that the dyes used would also have had the effect of repelling insects. Another suggestion is that the colouration was used as a sign of rank. Possibly all three explanations are correct.

But it was the womenfolk that the male visitors found most captivating. Even allowing for the fact that sailors visiting these shores had sometimes been at sea for three months their descriptions waxed lyrical, *'they go about as naked as the day their mothers bore them...they are so beautiful that inhabitants of other countries, charmed with their beauty, abandon their homes...for love of them...'* (and surprisingly perhaps) *'...they have more civilized morals than others who live farther away.'* In fairness it should be admitted that these writers were the same people who confused the manatee with a mermaid! But a consensus agree, the women were very attractive and not reticent in sharing their feminine charms.

The Lucayans survived on a meagre but healthy diet. They had built up immunities to most diseases prevalent in the hemisphere. They were athletic, fond of life and captivated by sex which they believed should be a constant and collective pleasure; it is doubtful that they were even remotely monogamous. Because most of them were completely naked, sexuality developed earlier and was entirely without taboo. Onanism was practiced as was coupling in twos and more. The Indians also understood in part the female cycle and also used bush medicine to control unwanted births.

Visitors found the character of the Lucayans admirable. They seemed to have no idea of private property. All things were shared. Peter Martyr, the Spanish chronicler who never visited the Antilles but avidly collected a great deal of information about the native peoples of the 'new world' wrote, *'they seem to live in that golden world of which the old writers speak so much, wherein men lived simply and innocently without enforcement of laws, without quarrelling, judges and libels, content only to satisfy nature.'* An idyllic prospect and probably not so very far from the truth.

Bartolome Las Casas, a Spanish bishop who was both advocate and apologist gives us a further insight about the Indians by quoting the *palabras formales* (exact words) of Columbus:

'In order that we might win good friendship, because I knew they were a people who could better be freed and converted to our Holy Faith by love than force, I gave them red caps...' (a bizarre gesture to say the least!) *'...later they came swimming to the ship's boats in which we were, and brought us parrots and cotton thread in skeins and darts and many other things, and we swapped them for other things that we gave them, such as little glass beads and hawks bells. Finally they swapped and gave everything that they had, with good will; but it appeared to us that these people were poor in everything...they bear no arms, nor know thereof; for I showed them swords and they grasped them by the blade and cut themselves through ignorance; they have no iron...'*

Neither the Lucayans nor indeed any of the Caribbean Indians had a written language. Their folklore was said to have been transmitted down in songs from time immemorial, memorized (it is believed) exclusively by the sons of the *caciques.* The sagas were sung at festivals and sacred solemnities. They had a single instrument made of wood, concave and resonant, which was beaten like a drum. They were good sculptors and created designs on fabrics, basketwork and pottery and scratched other illustrations in the form of petroglyphs on rock surfaces, especially on cave walls. Petroglyphs depicting fish, semi-human and purely abstract decorative designs have been found in a cave on East Caicos island and in the Bahamas in Hartford Cave, Rum Cay.

The Lucayans spoke the Ciboney dialect of the Taíno language. This assumption is made from the only piece of speech that was recorded phonetically and has been passed down to us. Las Casas informs us that the Arawaks of the Greater Antilles and Lucayans were unable to understand one another, *'here'* (in Hispaniola), he wrote *'they do not call gold* caona *as in the main part of the island, nor* nozay *as on the islet of Guanahani* (San Salvador) *but tuob.'* It is interesting to note again in this lexical example how important it was to the Spanish to talk about gold! This brief hint of language tends to reinforce the theory that the Bahama Islands were first settled by people coming from eastern Cuba of the Sub-Taíno culture. Language experts have suggested that a dozen or so other words have come down to us from the original Arawakan language, these include: tobacco, potato, maize, cay, hurricane, hammock, cannibal, canoe, barbecue and iguana. Interestingly the islands of Inagua and Mayaguana both derive their names from 'iguana'.

The Lucayans enjoyed sports and played a game with a rubbery ball so similar to that played by the Maya of Mexico that it staggers credulity to believe that the two peoples did not know of each other's existence. If further evidence is needed, the Meso-Indians of Mexico also flattened the heads of their infants in similar fashion to the Island Arawaks and their relatives.

The Lucayans enjoyed dancing and feasting and brewed an alcoholic beer fermented from cassava. They smoked cigars and inhaled snuff and besides subjecting themselves to tobacco they also used herbal hallucinants from the *cohoba* plant. The smoke from these mild narcotics was inhaled through a two branched pipe called a *tobaco* which was drawn directly up the nostrils (the Spanish mistakenly called the plant 'tobacco'). To maximize the potency of the drug a 'vomit stick' was sometimes used to purge the stomach of food thus permitting the smoke to have a greater effect on the nervous system. The ceremony of absorbing the smoke of the plant was confusingly also called *cohoba*. Shamans or *tequinas* under the influence of *cohoba* would speak to *zemis* to request answers to important questions. The Lucayans told the Spaniards that in their trances they had a 'hundred hundred visions'.

The mind holds many worlds.
Breathe out one world.
Breathe in another.

Perhaps not all the traits of the early inhabitants were admirable. As a society they hardly improved upon their lot during centuries of existence. Though not brutish, they nevertheless removed sick and dying relatives from their villages to perish alone in the bush. A sick chief, perhaps as a mark of respect, was ritually strangled. The dead, it was hoped, would go to paradise after death. There is some evidence to suggest that in Hispaniola at least, the Taíno practiced *sati,* the ghastly practice of burying a wife alive with her dead husband. Habitual criminals were impaled alive upon trees.

The Lucayans lived in small communities in generally circular houses framed with specially cut and shaped tree branches. Onto this skeleton they applied canes, vines and withies to create a wall. The roof would be thatched with palm. Inside their houses furniture was sparse but almost every house had one or more hammocks. These hammocks were made of either cotton net or dyed cotton cloth and were strung from the centre pole of the house to the framing of the outside walls. Hammocks were an invention of such importance that after they had been demonstrated in Europe, they were adopted and used for over four hundred years by most navies of the world.

Lucayan villages were often 'paired'. That is to say there might be two villages within a mile of each other but other villages would be several miles away. The mile radius has been suggested as the area necessary to obtain resources and may also have something to do with the matrilineal system of marriage where a bridegroom moved to the village of his wife's mother. Clearly the close proximity would mean that not all social ties would be curtailed. Another reason given for the incidence of paired settlements may be that new villages remained close to abandoned villages in order to avail themselves of any fruit trees and other useful plants in the vicinity.

The needs of the newcomers to the Bahamian islands were small and they would have found adequate supplies of their favourite shellfish from the sea but their land-supplemented diet was seasonal and thus at times quite meagre. The principal source of food was the sea though it is thought on some islands nearly half of their diet came from plants. While the land was not very fertile it supported their transplanted cassava tubers and provided some natural fruits and berries. The Antilleans and their descendants seemed to understand intuitively how the contrasting segments of life fitted together in their wonderful symbiotic natural world and they altered their life style and diet accordingly.

The islanders fished with nets bows and arrows, and sometimes built check dams to trap fish and, if they were fortunate, used fish hooks to catch larger fish — some of which were made of gold. Broken branches of coral were used from the earliest times as an implement for scaling fish. The Lucayans consumed great quantities of shellfish especially conch, codakia (a kind of scallop) and a small shellfish known in the Bahamas as 'bleeding tooth' so called because the lip of the shell looks very similar to a bloody incisor tooth. If they were even more fortunate they supplemented their diet with agouti (a small rodent), seals and birds.

The Arawaks and their island cousins also cultivated maize, yams, yucca, sweet potatoes and cassava. The latter was probably their most important food source and from it they made a pancake-like bread called *casabe.* They grew both sweet and poisonous varieties of cassava, though the Indians seem to have much preferred the poisonous variety and developed a way to draw off the poison before preparing the bread. A common dish was the stew pot in which seafood and vegetables were mixed with *axi,* a hot pepper.

The chief of a village was a *cacique.* Often a shaman, the cacique settled disputes and was responsible for the allocation of the communal food. The *cacique* wore robes on special occasions and the length of his robe, it is theorized, was a sign of rank. Several villages in the larger islands would make up a 'kingdom'. Chiefs would hold audience sitting on a small carved wooden seat called a *duho.* These seats were often exquisitely carved with zoomorphic motifs, a favourite subject being the head of a bat.

Priests and shamans presided over a religion that had several gods. The Catholic Spaniards at first suggested that there was a three-headed deity but were later to find out that the Arawaks believed in two supreme gods, one male, the lord of cassava and the sea, and the other female, the goddess of fresh water and fertility. There was also a dog-headed *zemi* named *Opiyelguobiran* and other *zemis* depicting the sun, bats, tortoises, conch and other zoomorphic beings. Even some trees and mountains were considered sacred. The religion and history of the tribe were recorded in sagas committed to memory by the sons of the *caciques*. Friar Pane, a Spanish priest who studied the religion of the Taíno noted:

When our people asked the islanders from where they had got those vain and harmful rites, they answer that they have inherited them from their ancestors; they say those things have been transmitted in that way in songs from time immemorial, and it is not licit to teach them to anyone other than the sons of the lords. They learn them by heart, since they have never had writing, and singing them to the people on holidays, they recite them as sacred solemnities.

From the scant records we have of their lifeways, the Arawaks advanced no great detailed explanation for their conception of the world. They knew however that the 'Great South Land' (South America) was their ancestral home. This land was traversed by Shingu the 'Great River' (the Amazon) and to the north was the 'Gentle Flowing River' (the Orinoco) which flowed into a 'North Sea' (the Caribbean Sea). To the west was the 'Land of the Sun' (Mu) and to the east was the unexplored 'Great Ocean' so vast and forbidding that if anyone should ever appeared from that direction then, the Arawaks believed, they surely must be gods.

The Arawaks thought the genesis of humankind commenced with the appearance in the Great South Land of the Jujo or snake-like men with entwined arms and legs. One day the men decided to make women by tying woodpeckers to the some of their stick-like comrades and the birds, thinking they were sticks of wood, bore a hole in them that became the female part.

It has been suggested that deep in the race memory of the Amerindians there was a still connection with eastern Asia, like the use of jade in death rites, the symbolism connected with the tortoise and the bat, divination and ritual burning to effect prayer. They believed in a heavenly afterlife, *coyaba*, where they would go after they died. Besides the principal spirits the Lucayans had many other sacred talismans or *zemis*. These were the personification of spirits or divas and they would portray them in their sculpture often as the head of a bat, a monkey or even as the stylized head of the Supreme Being, *Yocca Hu*, the Giver of Food. A female *Atabeyra* was the diva of fertility while *Guabancex* was the mistress of the hurricane.

They believed that good luck or misfortune was the work of the *zemis* and so they sought to propriate the spirits by keeping many of their images in their homes and, on occasion, by throwing a great festival in their honour. But they did not believe in supplication, that is to say they did not earnestly beg their gods for favours, it was enough that the gods had given them life and for that they were supremely thankful.

Las Casas quotes Friar Pane on the subject of *zemis* in a letter he wrote to the Cardinal of Aragon: *It is well known that nocturnal spirits appear to the islanders so as to lure them into vain errors, and this is known from the idols they worship in public. For they make seated images of stuffed woven cloth that look like the nocturnal spectres our painters paint on the walls. Since you yourself have seen four of those images, which I ordered sent to you, you can personally show his Highness the King, your uncle, better than I can describe them, how they are like the painted spectres'.*

The islanders had an innocent trusting nature and although they believed in an animate and possibly female devil, they also believed it could be overwhelmed by the intercession of benevolent *zemis*. As a precaution, before the act of making love, a man would first feel to make sure his partner had a navel to make certain he was not having intercourse with the devil!

Las Casas wrote of the Amerindian religion making special reference to the Lucayans:

I always gathered and understood that the peoples of the neighbouring islands had the same kind of religion as that of this island of Hispaniola, but they did not have very consequential idols (we found none on the island of Cuba), nor did they offer them sacrifices excepting those fasts and a certain part of their harvest, nor any other ceremonies excepting those cohobas with which they nearly intoxicated themselves. And I have always understood, the purest of all in this matter were the very simple people of the Bahamas...we believe they lived simply with the universal and confused knowledge of a first cause, which is God, and that he dwelt in the heavens...

At death the Lucayans would intern the deceased with great solemnity. The skulls of chiefs would sometimes be kept as sacred objects, some were even fashioned as vessels. A report from a Cat Island planter in 1784 notes that he had found evidence of many cave burials on that island; *'Great quantities of their Bones are to this Day found in different Cavities of the Rocks...'* And numerous sites have been discovered all over the archipelago where the deceased were actually interned under water in caves and this represents the strangest custom of all. It seems to have been a practice peculiar to the Lucayans of the Bahamas and Turks and Caicos Islands.

Like the Antilleans and the Island Arawaks, the Lucayans were superb seamen. They had canoes that could hold up to fifty people in which they regularly traversed the islands. If a canoe overturned, and they probably did quite often, the Lucayans were good swimmers and would right the craft and continue on their way. Contemporary observers were amazed at the proficiency of the Lucayans in the water and reported having seen them swimming several miles from shore. They seemed to have been good navigators too and there is even a theory that they built aids for navigation in the Caicos Islands. Certainly they used the stars for navigation. They had names, long since forgotten, for the heavenly bodies and they knew those which were fixed in position (the stars) and those which moved (the planets).

The Lucayans inhabited most of the larger islands of the Bahamas with their settlement sites being near to good fishing reefs and, if also possible, to fertile land. In so locating they were able to cultivate the best land and live off the bounty of the sea. In the southern islands of the Bahamian archipelago they may have met with their distant relatives, the Antillean people. The younger women they almost certainly claimed as wives, the others were probably chased away. Thus, within a short space of time the ancient Antillean people of the Bahamas disappeared leaving hardly a trace.

In the Antilles for eight hundred years the Island Arawaks had settled into living in peace and harmony with themselves and their environment. They were quite unprepared to adapt to different ways. But, it was different in the southern islands of the Lesser Antilles where the Island Arawaks had started to fight a losing battle against their distant but warlike relatives the Island Caribs who were advancing northwards. By some accounts one whole Arawak nation, the Igneri, had been decimated by the Caribs in the first millennium of the Christian calendar. And the Caribs were continually moving north, pillaging villages, ravaging their womenfolk but worse still the Caribs were cannibals who sometimes ate the flesh of their victims!

'I saw some with scars on their bodies,' reported Columbus, *'and to my signs asking what these meant, they answered in the same manner, that the people from the neighbouring islands wanted to capture them and they defended themselves; and I did believe, and I do believe, that they came there from the mainland to take them prisoners.'* Thus the Island Arawaks and their cousins, the Lucayans, may have already been doomed before three sailing ships appeared in the east.

The awful finality of the Spanish Conquest was recorded by Friar Pane who recounted what the son of a *cacique* told him and what the *zemis* had prophesied:

Listen, finally, illustrious prince, to another thing worthy of memory…they recounted that the zemis *had answered them that not many years would go by before a people covered with clothes would reach that island, and they would end all those rites and ceremonies of the island and would kill all their children or deprive them of freedom. Conjecturing that this referred to the cannibals, the youths had resolved to save themselves by flight when they saw them approaching, and never again did they enter into combat with them.*

But when truly they saw the Spaniards who had invaded their island, consulting among themselves about this matter, they resolved that they were that people of the prophesy. And they were not mistaken; they are all now subject to the Christians, and all those who resisted are dead: not even a memory is now left of the zemis, *who have been transported to Spain so that we might be acquainted with their mockery and the devil's deceptions: you have seen many of them, illustrious prince, through my diligence.*

A gruesome engraving of 'cannibals' preparing a feast

THE BAHAMA ISLANDS, unlike most of the islands of the Greater and Lesser Antilles, are not visible from the high point of one island to the next. Instead, the Ciboney heard of the existence of the Caicos Islands from an Antillean concubine named Iya.

Iya was a slight girl with features that clearly suggested her Oriental heritage. Her hair was long and black with raven blue highlights, her small nose flat and her eyes mere slits in an oval face. She had a well-proportioned body with small firm breasts, narrow hips and a short torso atypical of her race. Like many of her kin, Iya affected the fashion adopted by some of the Taíno women by wearing a small apron about her loins and on special occasions, she would apply a variety of colours and patterns to her face and body. Her head was often surmounted with a fabric headband and a shell necklace always adorned her neck. But, unlike others in the settlement, Iya did not display any cranial deformation which custom was starting to be copied from the Taíno and was now being applied to most Ciboney infants.

One day in her small village, Iya was in the village plaza explaining to a group of inquisitive young men how she came to be on the great island of Cuba:

"...my father's grandfather's grandfather was a chief and he canoe across the great channel...", (indicating with her arm the direction of the island of Inagua that all the Ciboney in the village would have heard about though it was uninhabited at this time) "...then from the Island of the Iguanas he made journey to a great sea of flat white islands...that way," Iya said now pointing generally in a northeasterly direction. "Great spirits and the souls of the dead abide in a temple of rock on an island there and in a great cave is a voice which tells the thoughts of the gods from the other world..."

A tall young man in the shadows had overheard her and stepped forward. He was Caonca the eldest and most favoured son of one of the *caciques* (his name meant 'golden one' in the Sub-Taíno dialect). He had long admired Iya not only because of her important family associations but also because of her very obvious feminine charms. As the daughter of a chief and a one-time intimate of an important *caicique* she merited some prestige in the small settlement.

Caonca asked of her: "How far is this island?"

"...about a day to the Island of the Iguanas then two days and nights if the sea is favourable to make landfall in the Caicos and then perhaps another day to the island of the cave," Iya replied and added, "the cave is just inland from a small rocky outcrop which is separated from the island at high tide. It should not be difficult to find."

"...could we gather fruits and plant manioc on this island?" asked one of the young men.

"...and is there sweet water?" questioned another who, though of tender years, had been well taught to first ascertain the basics.

Iya said that she thought the island had a few plants which bore fruit and but little fresh water though she recalled the sea was teeming with fish, and added, "...there is also much dried sea salt which can be scooped up in great handfuls!"

The bystanders knew well that salt was an important preservative and could serve as a product for barter and trade. More young men showed their interest by gathering around Iya and asking further questions.

"...and when did your ancestors leave the white islands?" Caonca enquired.

Iya answered that she did not know exactly since she was very young when she had been brought to Cuba from Inagua and she added: 'Once my father took a pilgrimage of people to the great cave and I went with him. That is how I know about the great caverns.' Then she reminded them that she lost her parents in infancy had been adopted by the family of a *cacique*. As everyone knew, before he died she had been one of his concubines.

The young men were greatly interested to hear of a new cluster of islands not so far distant but, when they pressed the young girl for more information Iya admitted the 'white' islands had a dearth of vegetation and the clouds of insects and the barren flatness of the place were discouraging features. But she also reflected on her happy childhood memories in Inagua. And she explained more about the wonderful cave of the oracle:

"...it is bigger than anything I have seen in my life...and has many chambers and is, without doubt, the abode of the spirits of the dead."

The reference to the caves convinced Caonca and a few of the young adventurous Ciboney menfolk that they should explore this matter further. As the son of an important *cacique* he was charged with committing to memory the history of the tribe and also leading the tribe on trading missions and expeditions of exploration.

"Let us go to see this island cave for ourselves!" Caonca exclaimed, "who will come with me?"

About two dozen young men quickly agreed to go with him. It was understood that the voyage they were about to make would be for menfolk only. Iya tactfully started to move away but not before Caonca made eye contact with her, the portent of which the two young people understood instantly.

The men withdrew to a shade tree between two circular huts and immediately set about planning the expedition. Fishing nets were to be procured, fish and meats were to be salted, fire boards and flints readied, pots for food obtained, and containers for water filled. Next the canoes and paddles would need to be checked to make sure they were seaworthy. Caonca announced he would tell his father Coliquin about their plans. The *caicique* had reasons of his own to encourage the proposed adventure and so consented readily enough.

PART ONE

In just two days when all was ready the young men arranged their exquisitely fitted and adorned canoes to near the water's edge to await a benediction from the village shaman. Then, on a signal from Caonca, the young Ciboney adventurers launched their craft into the surf and leapt expertly aboard after each canoe was pushed up and over the face of the breaking wave.

They paddled out to sea in a convoy of six with each canoe taking the lead for a time, then, like migrating birds, the lead canoe would fall back to the rear. Terns accompanied them skimming across the water until they were nearly out of sight of land and then they flew back to the shoreline, gulls and boobies ever hopeful for a free meal then took their place. High in the sky a pair of ospreys floated on invisible thermal currents of air in an aerial ballet. Then, without warning they would dive down at great speed to catch a fish and ascend again with a fish still wriggling in its talons. The Ciboney considered the presence of the giant fish hawks a good omen.

Overhead sugarloaf mountains of pure white cloud appeared and vanished below a luminous azure blue sky. Sometimes a brief downpour would bring welcome relief from the burning tropical sun but for most of the daylight hours the sun's burning rays were unremitting. The golden twilight turned rapidly to night and their exhausted bodies would ache with the cold and exposure in their vigil on the high seas. The divine gift of dawn provided a spectacular collage of ethereal colours but with the advent of morning the same arduous physical conditions were repeated.

Their course took them over the dangerous turbulent shark-infested water of the Old Bahama Channel. After being out of sight of land for more than a day they finally made landfall at Inagua and found the old settlement that had been only intermittently occupied in the last half century. They stayed two days on the island principally hunting for iguanas and flamingo. Anxious to resume their journey they re-launched their canoes and rounded the island. At the northeast cape they were in clear view of the smaller sister island later appropriately called 'Little Inagua'. From here they changed direction and after paddling out of sight of land for more than a day they sighted a small, and most westerly island of the Caicos Chain: West Caicos. They landed on the isle and, in the distance to the northeast, they saw the larger island that later would be named by the Spaniards: Providenciales.

Anxious to be on their way the adventurers followed the fringing reef that led them to a great arc of a beach on the island of Providenciales. Conscious always of the need for water they searched for a natural spring or well but could not find a fresh water source. But, from long experience the men knew how to obtain sufficient life-sustaining moisture from the succulent native plants of the beach strand and in the lymph glands of the fish they had caught. With the fireboards and flints they made a fire and cooked a meal of the crabs and iguana they found in abundance on the island. The visitors stayed only one night on the island sleeping under the stars.

These new islands they had found were different from the Inaguan isles. The first thing they noticed as they approached the islands was the 'wall' at the edge of the bank. In the crystal clear water they could see an underwater precipice the top of which was just 30 or so feet below the surface. On its almost sheer sides they could discern exotic corals and shoals of small silver fish being stalked by predatory barracudas. Above the yawning deep a few tiger sharks patrolled the submarine 'wall'. Once inside the inshore waters the sea became an incredible medley of turquoise mixed with green, jade and blue. While below them, the sea was so clear they could see small forests of orange and white coral dancing just below the surface of the water. Their quick eyes soon observed great quantities and numerous varieties of colourful fish, many of which were quite new to them.

The morning following they resumed their journey and, as instructed by Iya, followed the northern coast of the island chain.

Exactly as Iya had told them, within less than two days they followed the intermittently rocky and sandy coastline of the North Caicos Island until they came to another island separated only by a narrow creek. There they found a large rock outcrop projecting into the sea. It was the landmark Iya had told them to look out for.

Caonca shouted orders and his men worked feverishly steering a tortuous course between the coral heads that were awash since they had arrived at low tide. Soon they were safely over the reef and, as they approached the shoreline, each canoe slid down the front of a breaking wave, shot through the shallow surf and with a crunch came to rest on the sandy margin of a small cove encircled by an unusually high cliff.

The Caicos beach on which they had landed was of the purest white sand. There were many pleasant coves in their mountainous island homeland but none, they agreed, that was as beautiful as this. The breaking waves ricocheted along the shoreline while tepid warm surf pulsed forward and backward. Occasionally a more powerful surge seemed as though it might overwhelm the grey and white sandpipers but they were so adept at avoiding the incursions of the surf the proudly strutting birds seldom seemed to get their feet wet. As the men approached the sandpipers stopped pecking at the seaweed and, at a single chirp from their leader, they would fly away in a shallow semi-circle to pursue their search for a meal a few yards further up the beach. Giant turtles higher up the beach using the same swimming action on land that they used in the sea stumbled towards the shallows and laconically swam out to sea at the approach of the human visitors. While at the margin of the beach strand, blue crabs danced zig-zag down the beach menacingly holding up their claws. The seamen laughed at their antics. And, on the rocks at the far end on the rocky outcrop, monk seals could be seen lying lazily in the sun. The island promised a varied diet.

A command from Caonca pulled the men out of their daydream.

"Let's stow the paddles! Pull the canoes beyond the line of seaweed, oh, and don't forget to bring the gourds there must be water on this island somewhere..."

After they had secured their canoes high up the beach and gathered their water vessels they headed in single file over the sand dune. It was then they realised that the beauty of the Caicos has mainly to do with the sea. The land was covered with coarse grasses and shrub-like bushes, few as tall as a man and offering no shade. Rock everywhere broke through to the surface suggesting the island would not be very suitable for cultivation. As they walked huge iguanas skittered noisily through the sparse undergrowth. They saw a few giant agave plants and an occasional spherical cactus with a bizarre red headdress that later explorers would say resembled a Turkish fez. The similarity of the cactus to the Turkish headgear was later to be recorded in the name of the island country. The Ciboney on seeing the cactus made the raunchy observation that it reminded them of the posterior of the giant sloth of their homeland.

As they trekked inland the insects attacked them unceasingly. About half a mile from the beach was a steep rise.

"That is the hill Iya told us about", Caonca announced, "on the south side we should find the entrance to the sacred cave."

Any visit to a cave was, for all native Antilleans, a mystical experience but for the Ciboney, who were a people whose culture was intimately associated with caves, to enter a cave was nothing less than an act of communion with the supernatural. Like Tsgot centuries before they approached the great opening of the cave with trepidation. Cautiously they peered inside.

It was everything Iya had described.

As the visitors waited momentarily outside the cave, flocks of bats swirled above their heads as they had done for thousands of years when disturbed. The flying 'souls of the dead' soared in all directions. Once inside, the Ciboney were too awed to notice the guano on the cave floor that attested to the bats' lengthy residence in the caverns.

After a few paces inside they were captivated by arched chambers of rock on three and more levels, pendulous stalactites, reciprocating stalagmites, and plays of shimmering light and shade. Their other senses perceived the eerie echoes of their voices, dripping water, and musky aromas.

On exploring deeper into the caverns they found a veritable labyrinth of passages that compounded the mystery and drama of their experience. The caves continued to play upon all their senses. They looked for the oracle Iya had described and then found, in the far recesses of the caverns a small, almost spherical chamber. But the former Antillean settlers had disappeared from the Caicos Islands many years before so there was no priestly shaman in residence to proffer self-serving demands. As the sun began to set, the sun's rays played with surreal colours and shapes on the walls of the caves.

"Surely", they whispered, "this is a sacred place!"

Caonca spoke the thoughts of all of them:

"Iya spoke truly! The gods have created this temple of rock as a sanctuary for the sacred flying souls. We shall carry the news of our great discovery to our king!"

The men enthusiastically voiced their agreement. An older seaman offered another thought, "...and now we have seen for ourselves that the spirits of the dead inhabit this place, the next time we visit we should bring the sacred *zemis* to pay them homage!"

Caonca agreed and suggested that a shaman too should also be brought to the island to see and pay homage to the incredible caverns of the Caicos.

The seamen left the cave in awe. And, after making a cursory exploration of the island they returned to the beach to make preparations for the return journey to their Cuban homeland with the news of their great discovery.

ON THE ADVICE of the explorers, the king of the loose confederation of Ciboney chiefdoms in Cuba ordered the *caciques* to aid Caonca to mount an expedition of colonisation to the Caicos Islands. The king had many good reasons to think about expanding his realm. For years his domain had been growing and the shortage of good land and resources from the sea were being felt especially now that the Taíno shared with them the bounty of their island. The new-found islands promised supplies of rare ambergris, salt, iguana and monk seal meat. Colonisation would further act as a diversion from the irritant of internecine squabbling. And, was it not propitious too to visit a sacred cave for who knew what beneficence might ensue? But, most important of all, the chief had just received ominous news: Carib warriors had raided the sister island of *Aiti* once again!

The king issued a solemn decree:

"All but the first and second born children of the same mother who have reached adulthood must take part in an expedition to settle these new islands. They will go together with such spouses and children as they have. The expedition will be led by Caonca, son of Cacique Coliquin. The expedition shall leave at dawn immediately after the next full moon..."

The king requested the shamans to donate fire boards and to select suitable *zemis* which would be offered to the spirits of the cave and an especially wise old shaman was nominated to accompany the expedition. The nobles gave canoes and provisions for the journey and the womenfolk provided manioc tubers to be replanted in the new land. They also took care to carry with them their specially carved dibbing sticks, plant cuttings and water-soaked grain. A mating pair of a small mammal called an agouti was also included in canoeists' cargo.

It was a solemn assembly of young people that appeared on the beach at dawn two weeks later. A large fleet of canoes was assembled, last minute preparations were made, farewells were bidden, and then, at a signal from the king, Caonca and his small flotilla paddled out to sea.

The king imparted a blessing as the small convoy headed for deep water:

"May the good spirits travel with you! Find for yourselves and your children and your children's children a bounteous new haven of peace...!"

The crossing was uneventful but the more timid among the emigrants feared that the monstrous whales, which cavorted perilously close to their canoes, would devour them. The voyagers were unaware they had disturbed a pod of humpbacked whales during the breeding season near their annual gathering site at the extensive shallow later known as Silver Bank. As the canoes cut through the surf the noisy air-breathing leviathans would swim right up to them sometimes spraying great torrents of water from their blowholes and then, at the last moment, would dive under the canoes disappearing as blue-black hulks into the ponderous depths below. Other times they would suddenly breach the surface and create such a splash that they feared the canoes would be swamped. It was not unknown for whales to submerge themselves just beneath floating vessels to try to scrape the barnacles off their backs. Sometimes it had deadly results, but this day the good *zemi* saw to it that the Ciboney adventurers came to no harm.

Occasionally porpoises would play follow-my-leader with the small convoy then, as if they got bored of their game, they would disappear as quickly as they came. But the most constant feature of this and other voyages was the rhythmic strokes of the paddles striking the water and the intermittent commands shouted over the noise of the sea as the lead canoe slipped to the rear to be replaced by another leader.

Upon arrival at Grand Caicos, the middle island of the small archipelago, the women and children were completely distressed when they saw the barren landscape of the island. Crying some of them sorrowfully expressed their desire to be transported back to the lush tropical country of their birth. Caonca tried to explain again the reason for the migration while Iya tried to ease their anguish by teaching them the ways of her ancestors that she had learned at her mother's knee.

"See! You can eat the roots of this plant and…that one will make a needle and thread!" and she demonstrated how the sharp point of a spiky agave plant could be peeled off with some fibre attached and used for sewing, "…this plant when rubbed on the skin will keep the insects away…and this is a medicine for the stomach…" Then she went on to explain how to make a herbal brew from selected shrubs.

Another important activity she taught them was how to harvest the shallows for bonefish, conch and other shellfish. Iya demonstrated how to trap the reef fish and open one conch with the sharp point of another and, she pointed out the plants that could delay a pregnancy and, most intriguing to the men, plants which were an aphrodisiac. Later in the day, she promised the men they could test its potency with her in the seclusion of the sand dunes if they wished…

As the moon rose high in the night sky a few dark shadows appeared in the dunes to hold the seductress to her promise. As the skulking human shadows moved into the moonlight, Iya said,

"Alright then who is first?" and the youngest, a boy of only ten, shyly moved forward. The men remained in the shadows intent on watching the lovemaking.

"No! it is his first time…the rest of you must go away or I will not keep my word!"

The men ambled away laughing. It was over an hour later that a flushed young lad re-appeared.

"He was so young," Iya clarified, "I had to explain everything to him…but he was eager and quick to learn!…now who is next?" Two men stepped forward but another shape appeared from out of the darkness.

The newcomer quickly moved forward. Iya immediately recognized him as Caonca. "Ai! A man of experience, this will take time…now you can all leave!"

Reluctantly they started to go, "...and I mean leave!" she called out after them. The men laughed but did as she said. They had many other options for a sexual encounter in the village and this experience with a new herb was starting to pleasantly cloud their minds with a numbing ecstasy. In their soporific state they were anxious to find a partner in the new Caicos village...

Iya spent the whole night with her last lover. After her coquettishly erotic dance of seduction Caonca gently pulled her towards him and with his arm about her waist, swept Iya into the air and carried her deeper into the dunes. Wriggling slightly she mussed her hair in his face and pressed her lips...to his. When he had placed her among a bed of soft sea oats he pulled away her short fabric loin cloth. Canonca ran his fingers all over her body; her hair... her lips...her nipples ... her navel. The latter yielding proof positive that Iya was indeed flesh and blood. They then became entwined and settled gently to the ground. Caonça slipped his hand between her legs and she drew them up. Pushing them gently apart he exposed a moist petal in her underbody. As he penetrated her she groaned and murmured, "...slowly...there is much time..."

After a while Iya took control of the tryst. Caonca was amazed by Iya's inventive sexual ingenuity and for the remainder of the night their pursuit of love undulated like the distant tide.

All the Ciboney menfolk who felt their passions soar that night could only agree with the aphorism of the contemporary Romans a lost world away: *ubi bene, ibi patria,* a rough translation of which might be: *'where I am content, there will be my country!'*

The new colonists visited the cave and, as bidden by the king, the old shaman lit small fires to burn sweet-smelling incense. They built a bower of sticks and wattle over some sacred manioc which they had brought with them as homage to *Yocca Hu* the supreme deity of their pantheon of gods. The visitors placed the *zemis* on natural rock shelves and decorated them with garlands of leaves and wild flowers. After which they formed a circle and intoned prayers for many hours in a low monotone. Floating on the evening air was a dulcet plain chant overlaid the universal:

'ommmmm...ommmmm...ommmmm...'

When at last the shaman had finished the long ceremony of consecration the Ciboney visitors felt spiritually enriched and retreated from the cave to return to the site of their new settlement.

They started immediately to create shelter for themselves and their families. At the same time the womenfolk set about planting the cuttings and the manioc tubers. The framework of the houses was completed in few days and, by the end of the first week, all the circular houses of the small village were virtually weather-tight. But, even though they had shelter, in just a few weeks it was clear to the new settlers that little would grow in the infertile ground and arid climate of the Caicos.

The little community spent a few years near the cave, living principally off the sea then, as the population slowly multiplied, they spread out into other little settlements all over the Caicos islands. Caonca reasoned to his people, "…if we are to survive, we will need to occupy much land and harvest the bounty of both land and sea." The small community agreed with his reasoning.

In time, they headed northwards again and in time settled on the major islands of the entire Bahamian archipelago. And by so doing they developed a culture quite distinct from the Ciboney of the Greater Antilles. In their own language they became *'Lukkunu Kairi'* or Lucayans - the people of the islands.

After slowly island-hopping northwards, the Lucayans revisited and then colonised, the islands Tsgot had first discovered several hundred years before. And they discovered many new Bahamian islands. They made the first human landfall on the isolated island of Rum Cay that they named *Manegua*. In time this became the fabled 'island of women' and was sought by men from all over the Caribbean region. The island, like the mythical Greek island of the Amazons, was visited briefly by men just once a year to couple with the women and then leave. Female children remained on the island while all the male children, when they were two years old, were sent away with the men folk. At *Manegua* the solitary Lucayan womenfolk scratched sacred petroglyphic designs on the walls of a large cave that allude to the act of coupling with symbolic representations of male and female genitalia. The purpose of the *graffiti* was to transmit to the *zemi* their desire to have a fruitful liaison with their erstwhile partners…

Everywhere the Lucayans went they followed the nighttime flight of the revered bats and, by so doing, were able to find almost every major cave in the archipelago many of which they utilised and embellished. After Rum Cay they settled the verdant island of *Yuma*, only late in the nineteenth century was the name they gave the island dropped in favour of 'Long Island', and they made many settlements all along the coastline. Indeed, because of the great number of settlements on Long Island it developed into a major ritual and ceremonial centre of the Lucayans as later evidenced by the number of ceremonial stools known as *duhos* found there. He may have had a special case to argue but the first European visitor to the Bahamas suggested that Long Island was the most beautiful island he had ever seen!

After rounding the northern cape of Long Island the jeweled pendant at the base of the necklace of the Exuma chain of islands was discovered. This was the island of Great Exuma (named *Koreto* by the Lucayans). Several permanent settlements were also established on Great Exuma and, since Long Island was less than a day's journey by canoe away, the two islands had close social and economic links which was not so true of the other islands of the archipelago. Great Exuma, like Long Island, supported thick shrub-like vegetation that the Lucayans cleared with a kind of hardwood cutlass called a *macana*. Once cleared the land was planted with various kinds of squashes, arrowroot and cassava. The root vegetables were destined for a kind of pepper-spiced stew that consisted of the vegetables mixed with fish, turtle, shellfish, bird flesh and, on rare occasions hutia meat. Once a year some of the men folk of Great Exuma and Long Island joined together in a festive convoy of canoes bearing food and gifts to visit *Manegua,* the 'island of women', where they indulged their sexual fantasies. Sometimes however, jealous rivalries over the women erupted into fighting. The first visitors to the islands were surprised to find these hitherto peaceful people in conflict and noted the fact in the ship's log. The Europeans noted at *Guanahani* that, '*many of the men have scars on their bodies, and when I made signs to them to find out how this happened they indicated that people from nearby islands come to the island to fight with them.*' This may possibly be the earliest account of a lover's quarrel in the Bahamas!

From Great Exuma the Lucayans followed the line of pretty cays to the north of the island for ninety miles which led them to the future nucleus of the Bahamas: the small but strategically located island of *Nema* (later to be known as New Providence). They sighted first the eastern point of the island and noted an extensive pine forest - the first they had encountered since leaving the Caicos. Following the northern coast of *Nema* they came across a cay a few hundred yards north and parallel with the main island. The cay was later named for the hogs that were kept on the isle that served as a 'paddock without fences' but in recent times it would be more poetically renamed: Paradise Island.

In the channel between the island and cay their canoes passed over dancing sea gardens and shoals of brightly coloured fish in the exceptionally clear water below. They landed on the rocky foreshore of the main island just below a small ridge. This site, they agreed would make an excellent site for a settlement. It was a good choice for the place they chose has been continually inhabited since the Lucayans first landed there. Today it is the site of the capital city of the Bahamas.

From their new settlement site the Lucayans travelled along the coast visiting some sea caves on the northern shore of the island then set off in a westerly direction which carried them into a strange deep water 'tongue' of the ocean. In the distance they saw an enormous bank of cumulous clouds the highest of which had anvil-shaped heads from which intermittent lightning flashes were orchestrated as if by some pyrotechnic genie. The clouds suggested there might be a land mass hidden somewhere below. Fierce rainstorms heralded their approach to what turned out to be a huge island indeed, in fact the largest in the entire archipelago. Below the blackened sky they could see an extensive pine forest and, as they approached the islands in their canoes, they had to negotiate their way through two parallel fringing reefs before landing on a rock strewn shore.

So in less than one day from *Nema,* they set foot on the largest island of the Bahamas that until now had lain undiscovered by humankind: the island of Andros. From their explorations they deduced that Andros was not one island but three or four islands separated by wide creeks. The northern portion of Andros they called *Kanimisi* the southern part *Habakowa.* In the extensive and forbidding pine forest they encountered a strange flightless bird almost the size of a man. The bird was quite docile and soon became the favoured meat for the stew pots of the Lucayans. Later myths implied that the 'chick charney', as the gigantic bird came to be named, was malevolent but in fact it was a poor trusting creature that was soon driven to extinction. The creature was later remembered in a children's rhyme:

He had a queer and mixed up form
Like none I'd ever seen.
His arms were bird, his ears were mouse
His legs were in between.

The Lucayans explored only the east side of Andros where they made a few settlements near to the shoreline. They explored the few caves that were on the island and were captivated by the strange deep blue holes they found inland which they used as burial sites for their dead. But despite the large landmass of this great western island they preferred the more central and easterly islands of the Bahamas as settlement sites.

Returning to *Nema* the Lucayans fanned out in an easterly direction and, in course of time, arrived at the northern tip of *Ziguateo* (Eleuthera) and there they discovered the cave that Tsgot had found several centuries before. On finding the necklace that Tsgot had left in the cave, they added a three-cornered stone *zemi* as a talisman of their own reverence for the spirits of the cave. The Lucayans pondered who could have left the necklace but then remembered stories about a woman called Mother Iya who, generations before, had first told their ancestors about the 'white islands'. They immediately reasoned that their ancestors must have been the first people to visit this sacred place.

The Lucayan explorers continued on northwards, crossing the straits between the low Aeolian cliffs of Eleuthera and the strange rock formation known as the 'Hole in the Wall' and explored for the first time in human history, the island of *Lucayoneque* (Abaco). Travelling east of Great Abaco the visitors canoed past yet another extensive pine forest and then joined a necklace of pretty cays parallel to the main island. But, apart from some small cays at the far end of Little Abaco, for the first time in their island-hopping migration, they found no more islands to the north.

So the vanguard of Lucayans then turned south, crossed a shallow bank (from which the country would derive its name) and passed through a shallow creek at the lobster tail end of a new island. This took them to the southern shore of *Bahama,* an island that because of its size would later be called 'Grand' Bahama.

The Lucayans now followed the coastline of this island paddling through the white water inside the fringing reef. Occasionally they passed close to deep and mysterious blue holes in the sea which were teeming with marine life. Near one of them they encountered head on a black and grey speckled manta ray that was wider than their twenty-man canoe. The monster creature with two strange horns projecting on its leading edge was quite harmless and slowly moved out of their way as they approached. They took the appearance of the harmless sea monster as a favourable omen. Looking towards the shore of Grand Bahama they could discern behind the beach dunes another large pine forest and the rare spectacle of a forest fire. The phenomenon of a natural fire excited their curiosity.

After they had travelled westwards for almost half the length of this newly discovered island when towards evening a man in the lead canoe, standing and holding his paddle aloft, shouted.

"Look, a golden isle!"

And they followed his eyes to see a small gold-coloured cay in the foreground of a surreal multi-coloured sunset projecting out of the reef lying no more than half a mile from the shore. They paddled up to the rock as light was failing. The myriad colours of the sea disappeared but were quickly transmuted upwards into the furiously luminescent sunset. The leader inched up to the cay in his canoe and circled it. He tried to land but cautioned, "...take care!...it is not easy to get ashore...the rock is as prickly as a sea urchin...! It would be better if we headed for the beach!"

So the Lucayans pointed their canoes towards a wide sand bight and in a short while beached their canoes on an expansive white sand beach. That night they spent at an encampment amid tall sea grass and flowering white lilies on the seaward side of the high secondary sand dunes opposite the golden cay.

The day following they discovered that the 'gold' rock served as a sentinel for a creek which flowed out into the sea from a thick onshore mangrove coppice. The pretty creek invited them to explore further so they headed their canoes inland and followed the serpentine route of the watercourse inland.

The narrow fast-flowing creek was arched over by vegetation and beneath them, the crystal clear water revealed a great variety of fish: large and small, yellow and blue, turquoise and green, silver and grey all darting in different directions below their canoes. Solitary barracudas waited motionless in the current awaiting their prey, needlefish swam almost invisibly near the water's surface while stingrays glided stealthily like phantoms on their way upstream. The branches of the trees above their heads were alive with birds and, when they encountered a clearing, they discovered herons, flamingos and other majestic wading birds while the sky above their heads was darkened by great flocks of colourful screaming parrots.

For the Lucayans this was a magical journey.

The visitors were in great anticipation to discover where the creek might lead. They continued paddling their canoes for nearly three miles up the fast-flowing creek and found at its end a large 'boiling' hole that was miraculously welling up sweet water into the brackish water of the creek. Near to the boiling hole the Lucayans pulled their canoes ashore, then beat a path inland through mangroves weighed down with multi-coloured flowering orchids and air plants. Butterflies fluttered around their heads, crabs scurried about their feet. Walking became easier as the tangled black and red mangroves gradually thinned out to give way to white mangrove, buttonwood and prickly, oriental-looking Ming trees. Finally they reached the vast pine barren which seemed to cover most of the island. From here onwards they found walking was considerably easier.

After just a few hundred yards into their tramp through the pinelands they espied a small rise and clambered up the slope to discover the yawning opening of a cave in the ground beneath their feet. About fifteen feet below the surface opening was a bell-shaped chamber in which a tiny island was located surrounded by iridescent clear water.

The Lucayans were spell-bound.

"*Ee ee!*" they exclaimed in their native tongue, "*we-ne-cay-na*" (Look!...an island in a deep cave!) Everyone present understood that this was without doubt a sacred opening to the underworld. Their leader slid down the aerial roots of a tree and sampled the water.

This is fresh water too! And there are many sacred bats in the cave...and just look at the fish!" And fish there were in great numbers in a giant natural fish tank that were attracted by the light and sustenance that filtered down through the cave opening to the water below.

The visitors explored further inland and discovered an even larger cavern cut into the side of the high bluff of a rocky outcrop that in their tongue they called a '*hammock*'. This cave had a semi-circular water channel at the base which the Lucayans later found, was connected by underground passages to yet another underground bell-shaped cave. This smaller cave was lit by a small hidden aperture that served as a skylight.

The discovery of the caves in the island of *Bahama* would seem to agree with reports of the creationist folklore of the Taíno that was dismissively reported by Peter Martyr: *'...note what they childishly say about the origin of man in their land: there is a region on (an) island...where it is said human kind emerged from two caves...the larger cave, Cazibaxagua; the smaller Amaiauna'.*

The caves they had found were in fact only isolated openings to an underground labyrinth of caves and caverns which, when they were explored in a later age, were found to be among the longest such systems in the world. The Lucayans quickly decided to create a settlement near the enchanting caverns to benefit from the fresh water source for cultivation and for the nearby fishing in the caves, the creek and the sea. The site they had stumbled upon enjoyed the greatest resources and ecological diversity to be found anywhere on the entire island.

When news of the discovery of the great cave complex on the island of *'Bahama'* was announced, people from other islands came to visit a place where they believed their Lucayan ancestors had gone to an afterlife. In time, a mystical cult of shamans served as custodians of the caverns that, in a few years, would become the principal place of pilgrimage for the Lucayan people of the Bahama Islands. The incredibly clear fresh water of the caverns was used for drinking and ritual bathing, bestowing on all participants the gift of peace of the soul and the promise of a long and healthful life.

But, when death occurred, in one of the strangest practices anywhere on earth, chiefs and their families were solemnly interred after death underwater in the dimly lit bell-shaped hypogeum. Since the Lucayans believed the caves were the entrance to the underworld, people of importance were interred underwater at the mouth of the cave to ensure them an easy passage to the afterlife. Indeed it was believed the attributes of the deceased beings could be attained by drinking the water of the caverns.

Strange phenomena in the heavens and the earth made of the cavern of the Lucayans an otherworldly place.

Voices cry out in trees, and fingers beckon
The wings of a million butterflies are sunlight eyes
There is no sword
In the enchanted wood
Branches bend over like a terror,
The sun has darkened,
The white wind and the sun and curling wave
Cradle the coral shore and the tall forest.
Trees crash at midnight unpredicted,
Voices cry out
Naked they walk, and yet with no fear,
In the strange isle, the wise and gentle.

Assuredly the caverns were soon to demonstrate miraculous curative properties. Young and old joined in the *arieto* dances. Cripples threw away their sticks. The infirm left their hammocks. Great feasts and séances were held outside the large apsidal cave, which eons before, had been gouged out by a tempestuous sea into the side of the large hammock outcrop. Most ceremonies were held after nightfall at which time fish oil lamps and incense candles illuminated the cavernous apse where considerable quantities of hallucinants where ingested by the priestly guardians whose rites, prayers, divinations and soothsayings were eagerly followed by the faithful. Free love was promoted by bronzed athletic young men and half-naked maidens clad in diaphanous white sarongs. Infant children were cared for in communal nurseries where their heads were gently bound to cause the cranium deformation favoured by Lucayans as a sign of beauty. A large plaza was created surrounded by beehive shaped huts for visiting acolytes and from the plaza, pathways were cut through the forest to connect to the creek. Cultivated areas were laid out near to the fresh water sources and fishing became an important occupation for the expanding population. The cavern site of *Bahama* became an important place of pilgrimage and a major trading centre.

The fame of the amazing Caverns of the Lucayans was spread by Indian traders as far as the mountainous islands six hundred and more miles to the south. Indeed it was in Puerto Rico in the early sixteenth century that 'round-eyed' visitors from Europe who had recently made a brutal epiphany to the region first heard of the Lucayans Caverns as being 'in the vicinity of Bimini'.

The words spoken excitedly by the native Indians were, "*baxaweka I bimini bahama*", which translates roughly as, "there is a great rock cave with a natural fount in *Bahama* near *Bi mi ni.*" But, with the difficulty of translating the Lucayan Ciboney dialect of Taíno into Classic Taíno, and then into Castillian Spanish, the exact geographical location of the fountain was translated as being 'at' the island of *Bimini* instead of 'near' the island of *Bimini*.

However, the locational error notwithstanding, this marked the beginning of the romance of the fabled:

Fountain of Youth

Chapter 4 - Admiral of the Ocean Sea (1492)

nudo nocchier, promettitor di regni
(a pauper pilot, promising kingdoms)

Without the persistence of Columbus, permission and support for a voyage into the unknown would never have been granted. The fact that he obtained ships at a time when all available vessels were being utilized to carry the former citizens of Spain to North Africa who had been declared heretics is even more remarkable.

But it should be noted that Columbus was not the first person from the 'old world' to have visited America. The strongest contenders for that honour are probably the Vikings, who around 1000AD discovered Greenland and Labrador, snow-covered lands in the throes of almost perpetual winter. The existence of Labrador, like Greenland, was certainly long known to European travellers but it may not have seemed of much consequence and thus accounts for why so little was made of the discovery. But it is doubtful in any case the Lucayans would have heard of these wild adventurers of the north. It was commonly believed that St. Brendan visited some islands in the Western Ocean in the sixth century and, in 1436, a German cartographer had actually shown an island on a chart in roughly the position of Newfoundland. And just recently another interesting theory hypothesizes that the famous Chinese Admiral Zheng He, who is known to have had a fleet of 100 ships, beat Columbus to the Americas by 72 years!

Then there is the very real possibility that mariners from Northern Europe or the Mediterranean may have made a one-way journey across the ocean only to perish on reaching the shores of the new continent. There is even an intriguing theory that Columbus was in possession of a secret map and so he knew exactly where he was going. In the 1480's the Spanish ambassador in England reported that some seamen from Bristol had, for seven years, sought an island in the Western Ocean prophetically named Hy Brasil (!) without success.

But what is perhaps most surprising is that the new continent had not already been discovered by the Portuguese. For, in the latter half of the fifteenth century, the Portuguese, who were the most experienced navigators in the world, had travelled with ease distances greater than the width of the Atlantic Ocean on their way to the Horn of Africa and beyond.

But fate decreed that the man to find the new world for the Europeans would be from a city state in northern Italy sailing under the colours of the king and queen of a newly unified country: Spain. Christopher Columbus made many informed notes about the new lands and people he found on his four voyages. In his lifetime he was convinced that he had found islands off the coast of Asia. He was quite unaware that his islands were but stepping stones to two vast, hitherto unknown, continents. In fact when he finally sighted the continent of South America he was unsure whether it was a simple land mass or another large island.

A fanciful engraving of Columbus taking his leave of King Ferdinand and Queen Isabela at Palos

CRISTOFORO COLOMBO, to give Columbus his Italian name, was born in the port city of Genoa in 1451. The Europe into which Columbus was born was beset by the expansion of the Ottoman Empire. Constantinople had been captured in 1453, and the Ottomans had advanced into the Balkans, occupied the whole of Asia Minor and the lands bordering the south and eastern shores of the Mediterranean. Thus access to the East by land was now impossible, the only route to the East involved a difficult voyage around the entire African continent. Most important of all, the brutual Christian Crusades had failed and the Holy Land was inaccessible to Christian pilgrims. Christendom seemed powerless to liberate Jerusalem from the infidels. Christopher Columbus like many people, hoped that one day somebody would mount a successful crusade against the Turks and rebuild the Jews' Holy Temple and herald in a new 'Age of the Holy Spirit'.

Columbus was the son of a middle class weaver and, from his childhood, he dreamed of going to sea. His ambitious father encouraged his son into a business career. This tall red-faced man first made his way on a trading mission to Portugal and from there made several long sea voyages to the Mediterranean, to West Africa and one which, remarkably, carried to him to near Iceland. He could have been under no delusions that the earth was flat, few blue water mariners of his day believed such nonsense.

While in Lisbon in 1479 he married into an aristocratic seafaring family and his Portuguese wife bore him a son. For a time the young couple moved to Madeira where their son, Diego was born. When he was not away sailing, Columbus worked with his younger brother Bartholomew in Lisbon as a map-maker. The gap in their knowledge of what exactly lay both east and west of the Mediterranean must have taunted the enquiring mind of Columbus. During this period he developed the great desire to one day complete the charts they were drawing. In fact while residing in Lisbon, Columbus conceived a bold plan. He would discover for himself what lay beyond the Western Ocean! The problem now became: who would offer him financial support for his 'enterprise of the Indies', a quest to find a short route to India by travelling west?

King John II of Portugal showed interest in the idea but refused Columbus financial support since the Portuguese knew by this time that the Orient could be reached by rounding the Horn of Africa. Not surprisingly, the English and French monarchs may have found this foreign dreamer difficult to understand and even more difficult to take seriously. The Spanish had the greatest preoccupation of all the European monarchs at this time as they were locked in deadly conflict with the powerful Moors that would decide the very existence of Catholic Spain. Thus help from Spain at this time was all but inconceivable.

But Columbus tried anyway.

A contemporary chronicler penned the following report: (Christopher Columbus),...*came to the Court of King Ferdinand and Queen Isabela and he told them of his dream to which they did not give much credit...And he talked to them, assuring them that what he said was true, and he showed them a map of the world. The result was that he instilled in them the desire to know about those lands*...or, much more probably, the monarchs were politely dismissing him with a courtly "...we will consider this matter at a future time..."

To be fair they did appoint a commission to study the matter and though one member of the commission, a Franciscan friar, was on the side of Columbus, the majority was unswayed by his arguments. Their reasoning was stated very succinctly as follows:

First, we know the Western Ocean is infinite.

Second, since the voyage he proposes would require at least three years, it would be impossible for him to get there and back.

Third, if he did reach the Antipodes on the other side of the globe, how would he sail back up against the slope?

Fourth, St Augustine has clearly said: There can be no Antipodes because there is no land down there.

Fifth, of the five zones into which the earth is divided, the ancients have assured us that only three can be inhabited.

Sixth, and most important, if so many centuries have passed since Creation, is it reasonable that any lands still await to be discovered?

Only a fool would argue against Saint Augustine and the ancients...

Columbus spent a large part of his time following the Court as it moved from city to city. In so doing, if he failed to convince the monarchs, Columbus caught the eye of Luis de Santangel, the Keeper of the Privy Purse. Columbus knew well that the man who controlled the purse strings could be critically important to his enterprise.

In 1485 his wife died and Columbus left Lisbon to reside in Palos in Andalusia, Spain. By now impoverished and frustrated, he lodged with the monks at the Monastery of La Rabida. At Palos he confided his grand design to the abbot, Fray Juan Perez who had once been the confessor of Queen Isabela and who encouraged him to continue to pursue his dream. The friar even went so far as to write to the monarchs to plead with them to grant another interview to Columbus.

"Your Majesties, Señor Colon has made me privy to his plan to find a shorter route to Cathay...'*bustar el levante por el pontiente...*'" (to reach the east by travelling west)...I beseech your Highnesses to reconsider..." And, referring to letters of the Italian scholar Toscanelli, he explained that China lay only 5000 nautical miles west of the Canary Islands due west.

The replies to this and other requests must have been brief and discouraging as Ferdinand and Isabela hurriedly travelled from place to place in the pursuit of the holy war. But Columbus persisted and history suggests that it was Queen Isabela who saw something special in this zealous Italian.

In January 1492, Granada, the last stronghold of the Moors fell and Queen Isabela was able to turn her mind to other matters of state. The Queen again put the proposed enterprise in the hands of a committee, which again turned the idea down. Besides refuting Columbus' estimates as to the distance to China they were concerned that he was now demanding titles, to rule the lands that he discovered and be able to pass the privileges on to his sons. During this time Columbus lived with another woman who gave birth to his second son, Ferdinand in 1488, who was illegitimate.

In April 1492 it must have appeared like the answer to a prayer when Queen Isabela, then in the little town of Santa Fé some six miles from Granada, informed Columbus that she would provide the aid he sought. Columbus was again ushered into the presence of the Queen and her Court. Now thinking he was in better position to bargain, he was emboldened to make some astonishing demands:

"First", he announced, "I wish to be created to the position of admiral", there was a gasp from some of the courtiers but undeterred he continued on, "also I would like to given governership over any lands I might find, and I think it only fair that I should receive one tenth of all gold and an eighth part of the profits of all trading ventures carried on in the new possessions." The Queen and her Court were incredulous at the demands of the presumptuous foreign mariner and he was dismissed from Court.

Columbus was crushed and set his mind to leave Spain and try his fortune elsewhere but history records that, on the day Columbus left the Court, Luis de Santangel the state comptroller, *'went to find the Queen…and with words…to persuade her suggested…that, if any other prince should undertake what the admiral offered to her, it would be a great damage to her Crown, and a grave reproach to her…'* Not four miles from Santa Fé Columbus heard the hoofbeats of the Queen's messenger. He was informed that his extravagant demands would be met. This was indeed the miracle he had long prayed for.

Matters now started to move quickly. He was informed that the town of Palos in the southwest corner of Spain at some unspecified time had committed an 'offence' against the Crown. Accordingly it had been 'condemned and ordered' by the State to provide, should it ever be required, two caravels fully equipped and prepared for a whole year's service. That judgement was now invoked by the Crown.

Columbus returned to Palos and outfitted a fleet of three ships taking on sufficient supplies for a voyage of one year. He was fortunate indeed to find any ships at all, for at this very moment in history almost all of the available ships were being pressed into service to carry 'heretic' Sephardic Jews, (calculated to number about 100,000) and even more Muslims, away from Spain to North Africa. Of this agonizing exodus Columbus has little to say except to make a small note that the monarchs had decreed to expel all the 'heretics' by January 1492. He was wrong by four months.

The flagship of the small fleet was a Galician *naõ* of 100 tons or thereabouts, renamed for the Holy Virgin and chartered by Columbus. It was owned by a man named Juan de la Cosa who sensibly decided to travel with his property on the intended voyage. The two smaller caravels provided by the town of Palos were the *Niña* and the *Pinta* ('*pinta*' translates as 'painted one' or '*puta*' while *Niña* or 'little girl' may have similar implications). As time would tell, the two smaller ships were more suited to exploration and sailing the high seas. The captains of these two ships were two brothers, Martin and Vincent Pinzon, whom history has largely overlooked, for in terms of seamanship they were the equal or perhaps even better sailors than Columbus though the admiral was unquestionably the better navigator.

The 90-man crew was drawn principally from Palos and the surrounding towns of Andalusia. Indeed there were only a few non-Spaniards besides Columbus; some would include a Portuguese, a Calabrian, an Italian and possibly two crewmembers from the British Isles. Contrary to some reports most of the crew were good, hardy and competent seamen. Many of them had sailed before with the popular Pinzons and, as time would tell, they owed the Pinzons' a strong loyalty.

Despite myths, local folklore and fanciful engravings the monarchs were not at Palos to bid the small fleet farewell. Instead the event was witnessed only by the fearful relatives of the sailors who were traveling into a voyage into the unknown. '*Sale para alta mar!*' ("cast off for the high seas!") was shouted at dawn on the second day of August 1492 and the small flotilla weighed anchor. The ships were maneuvered down the river and Columbus recorded in his log that he could hear the monks at the La Rabida monastery chanting their morning office as they gently slid by:

Deo Patris sit Gloria
eiusque soli Filio
cum Spiritu Paraclito
et nunc et in Perpetuum

'...and now and Forever!' were the final words of the chant and, with those words ringing in their ears, they joined the sea and set sail for the Canary Islands with following northeast trade winds. Columbus opened his log:

We sailed on this (second) day of August, 1492 at 8 o'clock in the morning, from the bar of Saltes, the wind is strong and variable, and we had gone 45 miles to the south by sunset. After dark I entered the course for the Canary Islands, to the SW and south by west.

In the Canaries they paused at the small port of Gomera and used the time to change the lanteen sail of the *Niña* to a square rig. Columbus noted in his log: *'some say the Spaniards, through treachery and cruelty, enslaved the Canary Islanders and forced them to convert the Catholic Faith. I am sure these are but rumours...'* In fact it was very much a harbinger of events to come.

On the 6th September they finally set out on a westerly course of the most celebrated sea voyage of all time. Columbus kept a log of the voyage which has become one of the most researched documents in history, in the preamble to the log he wrote: *Your highnesses, as Catholic Christians and Princes devoted to the Holy Christian Faith and to the spreading of it, and as enemies of the Muslim sect and of all idolaters and heresies, ordered that I should go to the East but not by land as is customary, I was to go by way of the West whence, until today, we do not know with certainty that anyone has gone...*and then Columbus promised: *to write down everything I might do and see and experience, from day to day, and very carefully...*He recorded the false alarms given when crew members thought they saw land, he noted that they took a celestial 'fix' which put them in the region of Labrador (an obvious error) but most worrisome to Columbus was the morale of the crew. Some of the entries in the log he kept on the 'outward' passage from the Canary Islands are an eloquent testimony of the famous voyage:

Thursday 6 September 1492

Shortly before noon I sailed from the harbour of Gomera and set my course due west...

Saturday 8 September 1492

The Santa Maria *took in so much water forward progress was impeded...*

Sunday 9 September 1492

This day we completely lost sight of land...

Monday 10 September 1492

Today I made 180 miles at a speed of 7½ knots. I recorded only 144 in order not to alarm the sailors if the voyage is lengthy.

Many of the men were proud Andalusians and, having sailed with the Pinzon's many times before, they had difficulty understanding why they were travelling on a perilous journey into the unknown and why an upstart Italian was in command of Spanish ships - and by now they had time to doubt his honesty (because it was immediately rumoured Columbus was lying about the distance travelled each day).

Tuesday 11 September 1492

I held my westward course and made 60 miles or more…

Wednesday 12 September 1492

…99 miles again reckoning less…

Thursday 13 September 1492

…our compasses declined to the NW and in the morning declined to the NE.

Friday 14 September 1492

I sailed day and night to the west for 60 miles…

Life aboard the three ships was arduous. There was endless work handling the sails, pumping bilge water out of the hull and continually cleaning and repairing the relatively frail wooden vessels that were built for coastal waters not traversing oceans. The sailors slept on deck in good weather and below decks when it was foul. Only Columbus and the other ship's captains had bunks that they shared with other important members of their crews. Juan de la Cosa as owner of the *Santa Maria* 'hot bunked' with Columbus.

Saturday 15 September 1492

…I sailed day and night to the west for 81 miles…

For a time they enjoyed goat cheese they had acquired in Gomera. The cook used a wooden stove to make a stew of fish and, on rare occasions meat, all eaten with hard biscuits. But the further they travelled, the more monotonous the menu became. All food was washed down with watered-down wine, if the wooden barrels it was stored in held up, they had enough food, water and wine, for about a year.

Saturday 15 September 1492

…I sailed day and night to the west for 81 miles…

Sunday 16 September 1492

…gone about 117 miles, but logged only 108.

Monday 17 September 1492

I saw a great deal of weed today…I take this to mean we are near land.

Ten days into their trans-Atlantic voyage and they encountered the rust-green Sargasso Sea, a floating morass of weed that they feared any moment would entrap them, *'vieron muchas yerbas'*, Columbus entered in the log for many days. All the while the winds were favourable, blowing constantly from the east. But this also raised a problem in the minds of the sailors: could they beat back against such a steady wind? The seed of dissention was starting to germinate.

Tuesday 18 September 1492

Martin Pinzon…is a fine captain but his independence disturbs me somewhat…

The Pinzons' had more experience and, in their faster vessels, they irritated Columbus by continually forging ahead. Columbus had written in his log that the ocean between the Canary Islands and *Cipangu* (Japan) was a mere 750 leagues, *'but if we miss that island we shall surely reach the mainland of China'*, and he continued with a sailor's universal prayer, *'Lord spare us from storms and calms'*. The Pinzons were now starting to doubt Columbus' navigational ability.

Wednesday 19 September 1492

...almost becalmed.

Thursday 20 September 1492

...changed course for first time since leaving Gomera.

A momentous moment on the voyage, almost lost in a short phrase, was this momentary shift in the position of the rudder that put them on a more southerly course.

Friday 21 September 1492

...saw a whale, which is another sign of land.

A lot of the sailors aboard the *Santa Maria* doubted Columbus' reasoning when he explained this to them. Surely the further they travelled from civilization the more numerous and fearsome the monsters and became...? They thought Columbus was feeding them untruths again...

Saturday 22 September 1492

The crew is still grumbling...

Monday 24 September 1492

I am having serious trouble with my crew...said it was insanity and suicidal on their part to risk their lives following the madness of a foreigner...the Pinzons have sided with them.

Tuesday 25 September 1492

...some of the men went swimming.

And this was an opportunity for some of the men to supplement their monotonous diet by fishing. The men were getting anxious and this led some men to imagine they saw land in the distance.

Wednesday 26 September 1492

...what we thought was land last evening was nothing more than squall clouds.

Thursday 27 September 1492

...72 miles by day.

Friday 28 September 1492

...west for 42 miles.

Saturday 29 September 1492

This morning I saw a frigate bird, which makes terns vomit what they have eaten and then catches it in mid air...never is found more than 60 miles from land.

Sunday 30 September 1492

...making only 42 miles.

Each day the zealous Columbus, as the acting chaplain of the fleet, called the men to Mass and the chanting of *Salve Regina* was heard for the first time upon the deep waters of the mid-Atlantic Ocean. *'We sing'*, Columbus wrote, *'"Holy Queen, Mother of Mercy, hail!" each of us chanting after our own fashion, for mariners are fond of music.'*

Monday 1 October 1492

...calculated that we were 1734 miles west of the Canaries.

Tuesday 2 October 1492

...west night and day for 117 miles.

Wednesday 2 October 1492

I calculate we have come at least 2,379 miles.

Thursday 4 October 1492

So many birds are a sure sign of land.

Friday 5 October 1492

...many flying fish flew aboard the ship.

Saturday 6 October 1492

Despite their grumblings I have held fast to the west.

This entry in his log suggests that Columbus was following a line of 'latitude'. On the 6th October Columbus was urged to change course. It was almost two weeks since they mistook the sky for land. Two nights later, flocks of migratory were seen against the background of the moon flying west-south-west. Martin Pinzon remarked perceptively to his men, *'those birds know their business'*, meaning they knew where they would find land. Columbus then followed Pinzon's advice and changed course to follow them. In so doing, fate decreed that he would open a door to the southern half of the great continent instead of the north. The change of a few degrees in the position of the tiller that night literally changed the course of world history. Vicente Yanez Pinzon, captain of the *Niña* admitted to the *'grumblings'* noting: *'The men on board said in a shameless and public way that they had been betrayed and were lost, and that the King and Queen had used them badly and cruelly by trusting a foreigner who did not do what he was doing...'*

Sunday 7 October 1492

I went about 69 miles to until an hour before sunset, but told the crew 54...This morning we saw what appeared to be land to the west, but it was not very distinct...Joy turned to dismay as the day progressed.

Everyone aboard would have been quite aware that Queen Isabela had promised a reward of 10,000 *maravedis* a year for the first man to sight land and that doubtless spurred them to claim sight of land (even when none existed).

Monday 8 October 1492

...continued on my new course to the SW and made 15 miles...

Tuesday 9 October 1492

...we must be very close to landfall.

Wednesday 10 October 1492

...I reproached the crew for lack of spirit...for I had started to out to find the Indies and would continue until I had accomplished that mission.

On the 10th of October tempers flared on the *Santa Maria* and there was a near mutiny. The explanation from the log was that the men were restless at having been out of sight of land for so long and they doubted there was enough food on board, even if rationed, for the journey back to Spain. This was certainly part of the problem but it is interesting to note that the trouble was mainly aboard the *Santa Maria,* the Pinzon brothers were able to keep their crews in the *Niña* and the *Pinta* under control and indeed it was the Pinzons who eventually quashed the insurrection on the flagship. Their intervention was just in time. The chronicler Peter Martyr, who later heard the story from Columbus himself in Europe, recalled:

His Spanish crew first began to grumble in low voices, then speaking insults to his face; finally [Columbus] thought he was going to be killed or thrown into the sea, they said they had been deceived...and they were heading for an abyss from which they would never return...blind with anger, they beseeched him to go no further but to go back...but, with gentle persuasion and big promises [Columbus] saw their anger giving way and he pointed out that the Sovereigns would punish them for treason if they tried to do something against him or did not obey him...

Columbus had used his great eloquence to good effect once again. As part of the settlement Columbus promised to turn back if they did not make landfall within the next three days. Then they all pledged to sail those three days 'with determination and in harmony' - but for not one hour more! At Vespers Columbus invoked the Blessed Virgin to protect them and promised the seamen he would not abandon them to a cruel fate and, certain of the ultimate success of his mission, he reminded himself in his log: *'I know we have passed the island the Portuguese call – the seven cities. But I must not miss China where the roofs are made of gold...!'*

The next day, providence sent a sign that land was near. Forty petrels flew by the vessels, a boy hit one with a stone, a branch with flowers was seen floating in the water, then they saw a stem of something looking like cane and a fragment of carved wood. All talk of returning was forgotten. Everybody now realised they were near the goal of their voyage.

Thursday 11 October 1492

I now believe that the light I saw earlier was a sign from God…then, at two hours after midnight, the ***Pinta*** *fired a cannon, my pre-arranged signal for the sighting of land…*

Under the moonlight on the distant island the natives in their huts were enjoying their last sleep of innocence. Like the Spaniards, the Lucayans would wake up the next morning into a new world.

Chapter 5 - Worlds Collide (1492)

"Come and see the men who have come from heaven; bring them food and drink."
Reputed to have been spoken by the Lucayans - extract from the log of Columbus

AFTER ABOUT TEN WEEKS AT SEA, having weathered calms, storms and a near mutiny in three vessels unsuited to crossing a great ocean, Columbus was near to his goal. As he lay out to sea he thought he must be near Japan but, after he landed, he revised that assumption to an offshore island of India. The morale of his crew improved somewhat but soon they were all disappointed at the poverty of the inhabitants they found in the islands.

The islands they found were the site of the most publicized, though certainly not the first, European landfall in the 'new world' of the Americas. It was an event that took place a little over 500 years ago. A recent controversy has put in doubt which island was the actual landfall of Columbus. But, within living memory of the historic landing, Spaniards visiting the landfall island called it by the same name as Columbus. And, from the historical evidence to hand, there are other compelling reasons to believe that the Spanish explorer first landed at modern-day San Salvador and nowhere else (for more discussion on this matter the reader is invited to refer to Appendix A).

The arrival of Columbus, the 'Admiral of the Ocean Sea', was accepted by the natives of the islands to have been preordained. The Lucayans had long believed that a race of demi-gods would one day arrive from across the eastern ocean. They may have heard tell of other visitors who came from the east for indeed, before Columbus, several adventurers had ventured across the western ocean to the 'new world'. Some may possibly have arrived in the region of the Indies, never to return.

Columbus had great difficulty administering the new island territories he found, but his greatest disappointment was not being able to find tangible exploitable wealth (especially gold) in the new world. He first discovered an easterly island of the Bahamas chain but left after a relatively short stay and, though he saw the islands on a subsequent voyage, he was never to set foot in the islands again.

As a footnote to the historic find of Columbus, it is interesting, almost ironic, to recall that Columbus in being the first European to find the 'new world' by his landfall in the Bahamas, actually found the last land to be discovered by the original Asian 'explorers'.

Christopher Columbus

At 10 pm, before the moon had risen, Columbus wrote a dramatic phrase in archaic Spanish in his log that he saw, *'vna candeli lla de cera q se alcava y levatava'* (a light ahead like a candle rising and falling). There is some speculation that this was to place on the record that he, Christopher Columbus, had first seen land and therefore was entitled to the reward of 10,000 *marevedis*. He further noted in the log that two other crewmembers verified his claim. The lookout in the rigging of the lead vessel would surely have been the best able to see the supposed lights but recorded no such claim.

Historians disagree, in any case, as to his position. If he was thirty-five miles out, as many contend, land would have been well over the horizon. Could sparks from a fire have been carried high up in the air? Possible but unlikely. Could the Lucayans have been fishing with flares at night in the open ocean? Again possible but unlikely.

But, four hours later when the ships were further west and the moon was glowing, there was no question about the sight of land. Rodrigo de Triana, at the masthead lookout of the *Pinta* screamed:

Tierra! Tierra!

De Triana had discerned the same dark line of an island on the horizon that Tsgot had seen over a millennium before.

The fleet hove to and awaited daybreak. Columbus wrote in his log:

The moon, in its third quarter, rose shortly before midnight. I estimate that we were making about 9 knots and had gone 67½ miles between the beginning of the night and 2.00 o'clock in the morning.

Two hours after midnight, the *Pinta* fired its cannon that was the signal for a sighting of land. Columbus continued writing in his log:

...we caught up with the Pinta, which was always running ahead because she was a swift sailer, I learned that the first man to sight land was Rodrigo de Triana, a seaman of Lepe...The land is about six miles to the west.

The crew then swarmed around the forecastle lookout on the *Pinta*. One crew member shouted to de Triana:

"*Felicidades primo Rodrigo*! You have won the reward...remember we are of the same lineage...pray do not forget me when you receive all those *maravedis*!"

"*Rodrigo! que buena fortuna!* I trust you will recall before God that this was to be my watch before we swapped!" The ship's carpenter reminded him.

"With 10,000 *maravedis* a year you can buy a ship...or perhaps a farm!"

"Ay! Perhaps you could learn to plough!" Francisco, another of the Pinzon brothers joked.

The *Santa Maria* then caught up with the *Pinta* and Columbus hailed them.

'Señor Martin Pinzon, you have found land!'

Pinzon replied enigmatically, 'Sir, my reward is not lost.'

Columbus called back, 'I give you five thousand *maravedis* as a present!' Which gesture seems to suggest that Columbus had already decided to lay claim to the prize of 10,000 *maravedis*.

Pinzon did not hail back but under his breath he muttered, "I wonder if I will ever see it! Anyway this should at least convince the Genoese upstart who are the better seaman!"

The yearly prize of 10,000 *maravedis* would allow a seaman to live comfortably for the rest of his life and the Pinzons and de Triano would certainly have shared the prize money with their comrades. The crew very much doubted the Italian would prove so generous.

The dislike of the crew for Columbus later turned to something nearer hatred when Columbus later boldly claimed that it was he who had first sited land and was thus solely entitled to the entire reward. But for the moment the anticipation of landing in the realm of the Great Khan occupied their thoughts.

It had been an exceptionally long voyage for those times but now there was the hope that shore leave would provide them with a chance to procure some of the fabled wealth of the Orient: gold, silver, perfumes…and what about the sultry Oriental maidens? At the local taverns in Andalusia it was reputed their private parts were erotically different from European women by being slit from side to side…

Finally a landfall, territory to claim, treasure, perhaps an exotic sexual liaison…it is doubtful anyone slept aboard the ships that night in anticipation of the next day. Least of all Columbus.

Columbus was acutely conscious that he represented the Spanish sovereigns and so when he met with the envoys of the Great Khan he was anxious his bearing should create a favourable impression. In characteristic fashion he first gave private thanks to God. Afterwards he ordered his courtiers clothes to be laid out. Then he summoned Luis de Torres, his translator to his side, and together with Rodrigo de Escobedo the royal notary and Rodrigo Sanchez the comptroller, they discussed the manner of their deportment as befitted emissaries of the Spanish Crown. It would be the duty of Escobedo, secretary of the fleet, to draft diplomatic correspondence with any dignitaries they should encounter.

As dawn broke they could clearly see there were no harbours or inlets, indeed strong waves were beating against the shore along the entire eastern side of the island. Several of the men clambered up the rigging to get a better view of verdant sub-tropical island in the distance. Besides getting a better view of the magical isle they could see in the turquoise depths below them brilliantly coloured fish and strange antler-like corals which, though beautiful, promised imminent danger to their fragile vessels. Staying clear of the coral they sailed parallel to the island and towards the end of the island came to a gap in the reef through which Martin Pinzon, without instructions from Columbus, boldly sailed the *Pinta.* She was followed shortly afterwards by the *Niña.* The impulsive Pinzons waited impatiently for the *Santa Maria* to negotiate the channel and catch up with them, then all three ships anchored in calmer water on the western side of the island.

Columbus and his senior officers, now fully dressed in their regalia, were rowed in a dinghy across the turquoise blue water and landed on an idyllic white sand beach. The Pinzon brothers followed at a respectful distance. The first words Columbus recorded in his log on Friday the 12th day of October 1492 read:

At dawn we saw naked people, and I went ashore in the ship's boat, armed...

The standards of Ferdinand and Isabela were planted in the sand, Columbus fell to his knees, shed tears of joy and offered a prayer to Almighty God.

...and all this is set forth at large in the testimonies there set down in writing. Forthwith the Christians hailed him as Admiral and Viceroy and swore to obey him as one who represented Their Highnesses with as much joy and pleasure as if the victory had been all theirs, all begging his pardon for the injuries that through fear and inconstancy they had done to him.

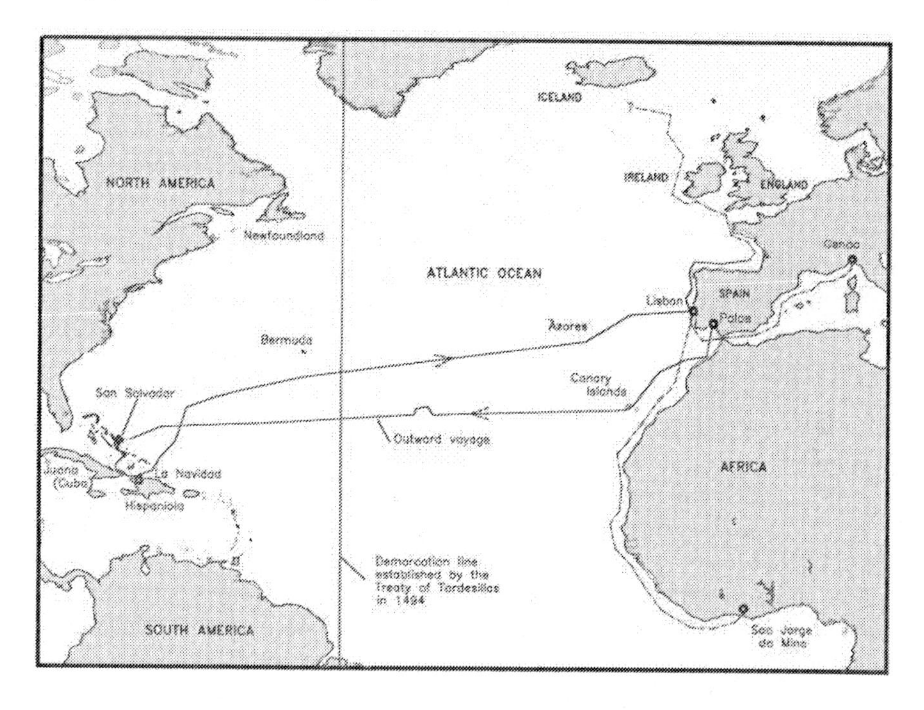

Voyages of Columbus up to the end of his first Trans-Atlantic Voyage

It is highly doubtful that this piece of mummery recorded in the log was the whole truth. And what the natives thought of this performance is not recorded but they had long believed that gods from the east would visit them so they pondered, could this strangely-dressed man with blue eyes and giant ships be a god?

A small party of naked wide-eyed Lucayan natives now left the safety of the bushes and came on the beach to meet the visitors.

The first words spoken to the Lucayans were in Arabic believed at this time to be the mother of all languages. The Lucayans were in awe but made no response. De Torres then reverted to Spanish, to Hebrew, to Aramaic. The natives were still speechless. Columbus grasped the problem and told de Torres to cease his efforts. It was clear to Columbus that if the natives did not respond to Arabic, the most widely-spoken language of the known world, or to Hebrew - and thus they could be discounted as one of the Lost Tribes - then they must indeed be in India where it was known they spoke a quite different tongue. After that there was their appearance to consider. Escobedo whispered to Columbus that it suggested an Oriental origin since, to repeat a myth popular at the time he whispered, "their narrow slit-like eyes came from sun worship which is caused by looking directly at the sun..."

So that was it! They were on an off-shore island of the great continental landmass of India (so from this day forward the indigenous people he met were known confusingly as 'Indians'). They were at least in or near the domains of the great Khan, "God be praised..." or were they? for now Columbus did something very strange. He gave the island the name 'San Salvador' and,

...in the presence of many natives of that land assembled together, took possession of that island in the name of the Catholic Sovereigns with appropriate words and ceremony...

Some historians have suggested that Columbus knew that this was not India and that is why he knew he could, with impunity, claim it for his masters, or he might even have written this embellishment in the log for the benefit of the Spanish authorities. We may never know the exact truth.

When the Lucayan Indians realized that the visitors meant no harm, more of them came out of the woods. They were given hawk's bells, glass beads and red caps that were exchanged for darts, skeins of cotton and green parrots. The more daring of the natives swam out to the boats to exchange their wares. The natives were astonished at the Spaniards' *'beards and fairness of their skin'* they were also captivated by the clothes the visitors wore, especially the red doublet of Columbus that marked him as a person of authority. The Spanish had brought items of paltry worth with them but it seems they followed the pattern set by the Portuguese who traded similar items with the Sub-Saharan Africans. Later Columbus noted that the sailors were exchanging pieces of broken glass and other rubbish with the Indians and he tried to forbid the practice.

After landing on *Guanahani* and making a cursory inspection of the island on the 12th October 1492 Columbus noted in his log:

The people here call this island Guanahani in their language, and their speech is very fluent, although I do not understand any of it. They are friendly and well dispositioned people who bare no arms except for small spears, and they have no iron…I showed one my sword, and through ignorance he grabbed it by the blade and cut himself. Their spears are made of wood, to which they attach a fish tooth at one end, or some other sharp thing.

The collision of the two cultures was peaceable enough though it must have been clear that the wealth the Spanish hoped to find must be elsewhere (on the mainland perhaps?) Trading and social intercourse, such as it was, lasted two days and then Columbus ordered his men to explore the island in two small boats.

From the site of their landfall the log describes how they headed off in a nor-north easterly direction and rounded the northern tip of the island to explore the eastern coast that had been their first view of land in the 'new world'. They found the island was surrounded by a reef which encircled a small bank to the north of the island which had a narrow entrance. Columbus noted the bank was sheltered but, there were visible rocks (probably coral heads), just below the surface. The log explains what he saw,

…the water was as smooth as a pond…and deep enough to shelter all the vessels in Christendom…there is a large lagoon in the middle of the island and there are no mountains…also I saw what looks like an abandoned quarry, but it is natural. I have been very attentive and have tried very hard to find out if there is any gold here. I have seen a few natives who wear a little piece of gold hanging from a hole made in their nose…the island is fairly large and very flat…

He even found a promontory which he noted would be suitable as the site for a fort. As defence against whom he does not say. He also stated in his log that they could see many other islands—which is impossible—but suggests that they either travelled far out to sea in the small boats or, more likely, Columbus completed his log later when they had, in fact, discovered more islands. On the east coast of the island of *Guanahani* they found more people, and Columbus noted in his log:

…and I soon saw two or three (people)…calling and giving thanks to God. Some brought us water, others various foodstuffs; others, seeing I was not inclined to land, threw themselves into the water and swam up to us…(and asked)*…if we had come from heaven. One old man…shouted to the rest…" Come and see the men who have come from heaven; bring them food and drinks"…calling to us that we should land. But I was afraid to do so, for I saw a great reef of rocks which circled the whole of the island.*

It is highly doubtful those were the exact words of the old man but his gesticulations must have indicated a similar intention. So, at least discerning all the natives were friendly, Columbus sailed to rejoin the ships on the calmer western side of the island where they readied the ships to continue their voyage. So, after only two days Columbus left San Salvador, never to return.

And it was here the whole enterprise started to go amiss.

As they were leaving the island in the small boats to reach the ships that were anchored in deeper water, Columbus took six Lucayan Indians with him, ostensibly as guides but really as hostages and exhibits for the Sovereigns. His sinister intentions can be discerned from the log:

'They ought to be good servants of good skill, for I see that they repeat very quickly all that is said to them; and I believe they would easily be made Christians...'

The entry in his log for October 14th further develops his thinking:

'...these people are very unskilled in arms. Your Highnesses will see this for yourselves when I bring to you the seven (the log elsewhere suggests the number six) that I have taken. After they learn our language I shall return them, unless your Highnesses order that the entire population be taken to Castile, or held captive here. With fifty men they could all be subjected and made to do all that one wished.'

History is silent about what the Pinzons' thought about the encounter but they were surely starting to become disillusioned. Though doubtless religious, they did not share the same strong faith as Columbus and knew they could expect no great honours on their return to Spain. That, they could see only too well, would be reserved for the upstart Italian. So what could they hope to get from the voyage? The answer would probably be accurate for any epoch of the western world but was especially true for the mediaeval era: they craved...gold!

Juan Reynal, a deck hand, disgusted with the savage and impoverished islanders, spoke for all of them: "...and have seen their goods? - worthless!"

One of the more pious members of the crew, who just happened to be within earshot looked skyward and offered, "I fear these people are god-less pagans!"

To which the cabin boy added giggling, "...and shamelessly naked!"

"Well now we know for a fact the wenches are not split from side to side!"

The sailors laughed.

The self-appointed cook, one of the least-regarded men aboard ship, pronounced a self-serving observation: "*Ellos son barbaro!*" (they are such savages!) "do you not see, they eat the meat of the sea snail!"

The seamen were starting to get into a rebellious mood again. They had come so far, taken so many risks and yet found so little of tangible value. For that was how it now seemed. But, they reminded themselves, there was a chance that to the west - or perhaps it was the south - there must be gold! So they declared with the Pinzons' that they would continue onwards to find a reward for their pains in voyaging to this god-forsaken place!

"I want at the very least a golden locket for my wife..." Cristobal Quintero the owner of the *Pinta* stated.

"...for your mistress you mean!" Rodrigo de Escobedo countered.

The crew sniggered.

Somebody whispered quickly. "The Italian 'admiral' is coming!" and the crew rapidly resumed their duties.

Columbus had heard the laughter.

"Well", he mused, "I am glad the crew are happy, but just wait until we find *Cipangu* and the mainland...with courtiers dressed in silken robes, and...ahh...the jewels, the spices, the gold..." It was the gold that most obsessed Columbus: *It is true that, if I should find gold...in quantity, I shall wait and collect as much as I am able. Accordingly I am doing nothing but sailing on until I find it.* But Columbus is clearly anxious to move on. *I keep moving in order to see all of this so that I can give an account of everything to Your Highnesses.*

If Columbus had any doubt about what he had found to date in the Bahama Islands, he did not disclose it in his daily journal. His log is full of optimistic and informed observations. Now convinced that there was not much more to be gleaned from *Guanahani.* Columbus returned to the *Santa Maria.* He set a course southwest since the Lucayans, in response to their gesticulated questions about the source of their gold trinkets, pointed in that direction.

As the three ships disappeared into the distance the Indians gathered on the beach and discussed the cataclysmic events of the last two days.

"My daughter has seen only twelve years...one of the bearded men took her into the woods and raped her!" an older woman shrieked.

"One tried to rip the nose ring from me...look I am still bleeding!"

"...and they took six of our menfolk against their will," some of the women wailed, "will they ever come back to us?"

An older man who was wearing a Spanish buckle on a string round his neck - he could have had no idea of its proper use - remarked, "I fear it may be a punishment brought upon us by the *zemi,* perhaps we should have given the strangers more of our gold!"

The *caicique* of the island reasoned, "no, I believe they are but men with strange and different customs. I think we should follow them to warn others of their intentions, also we should try to rescue the men that have been taken. I will take the fastest canoe with my sons and go in the direction of *Manegua.*"

The *caique* launched his canoe as the small Spanish fleet started to disappear over the horizon. Columbus, on a southwesterly course, had only travelled about eight miles when he caught sight of an island in the distance. It was clearly smaller than *Guanahani,* was surrounded with a reef, and on drawing closer Columbus noted it had no visible physical features of interest. The Lucayans had called the island *Manegua* but Columbus christened it grandly, *'Santa Maria de la Concepcion',* later in the swashbuckling era, it would be called, Rum Cay.

It was still early in the day and Columbus could see other islands to the north and west. The Lucayans with him were excited and, *'made signs indicating there were so many islands that they could not be counted, and they named, in their language, more than a hundred',* so with this information in hand Columbus decided to continue on. The wind was freshening but the *Santa Maria* was making heavy weather against the current and the choppy sea so he ordered the *Pinta* and the *Niña* to go ahead. Columbus sighted an island to the north that would later be named Conception Island (in the erroneous belief that it was the second island to be discovered). Columbus got within sight of Great Exuma and then turned back. Later that night the *Pinta* and *Niña* returned with news that they had seen the 'many islands' extending in a long string to the north. They had seen a few of the 365 islands of the Exuma chain. Columbus, giving no credit to the Pinzons, recorded in his log: *all the islands...were level and most of them were inhabited...*But small islands did not interest Columbus. His log records...*finally I looked for the largest island and decided to go there. It is probably 15 miles from San Salvador, though some other islands are nearer.* Columbus was wrong to assume (modern) Conception Island was closer to San Salvador than Rum Cay in fact it is slightly further from *Guanahani* than *Manegua* (Rum Cay). Before nightfall Columbus back-tracked to within sight of *Manegua.*

*I had lain-to last night for fear of approaching the shore in the dark and because I did not know if the coast were clear of rocks...*He sailed round the island and anchored at sunset but Columbus did not land until noon on the 15th October. The Indians with him insisted that there was much gold on the island but Columbus thought this was a ruse to get him to land. This seemed to be confirmed when one of the Indians they had captured, escaped by swimming ashore during the night.

The following day Columbus disembarked on the island of *Manegua* and was convinced the people living there were as simple and gullible as those on *Guanahani*. He stayed only two hours on the island having decided the information about the gold was false. But just as he was preparing to leave a big native canoe pulled alongside the *Santa Maria* and he heard the men in the canoe shout something in the native language. Suddenly one of his Indian prisoners leapt overboard and was picked up by the canoe which then sped off. Columbus was furious and sent armed men to follow the canoe but *'they could not catch up…those boats go very swiftly…'* he reported. The *caicique,* his sons and the escaped prisoner returned immediately to their island home of *Guanahani.*

While this was happening the sailors seized another Indian who was trying to sell a skein of cotton alongside the *Niña* from his canoe. Columbus tactfully ordered them to let him go, *'…for this reason I used him thus, in order that they might hold us in such esteem that on another occasion when Your Highnesses send men back here the natives may not make bad company.'* Five other Indians, however were still left sweating and imprisoned in the hold. Columbus confided his motives to the log: *I wanted them to think that the men who had fled had done us some harm…*

On board Columbus wrote that the Lucayans told him that to the southwest they would find *'…a lot of gold, and they wear it in the form of bracelets on the arms, legs, ears and neck.'* So they set sail again and cruised along the coastline of a long narrow island that Columbus named *Fernandina* in honour of King Ferdinand. Here, in mid-channel they picked up a Lucayan in a canoe whom they presumed had just paddled from *Guanahani* because he had in his possession a string of beads and two small Spanish coins. He also carried *'a lump of bright red earth powdered and then kneaded,'* (some historians suggest that this was body paint but it was more likely clay for ceramics mixed with crushed conch shell tempering) *'…and some dry leaves which must be something valued by them.'* This latter was, in all probability, the first recorded sight of some leaves of the pernicious tobacco plant.

The native canoeist from *Guanahani* left them for the nearby island and must have given such a good account of the strangers that a flotilla of canoes came out to greet them. The Indians from the 'long island' were carrying gourds and pots of water which the native seaman understood they would need. Columbus was again incredulous at their generosity and naiveté. He wrote, *'nothing was lacking but to know the language and to give them orders, because every order given to them they would obey without opposition.'* The natives of *Fernandina* (Long Island) wore short cloaks of linen which covered their nakedness and this must have pleased his sense of propriety and Columbus was happy to note too, that they seemed to know how to drive a bargain.

As he sailed up and down the coast Columbus caught the scent of perfumed air on the off-shore breeze. It convinced him the vegetation of the island must contain valuable spices. Another observation Columbus made of Long Island had to do with the land. He lavished great praise on the verdant landscape that he claimed was, *'the best and most fertile and temperate and level and goodly land there is in the world'*. He observed that in this 'Garden of Eden', trees had *'branches of different kinds all on one* trunk' - which sounds remarkably like epiphytes or a 'strangler' ficus tree which so encompasses its host or hosts as to make it seem as if all the different branches are growing from a single bole. And he noted for the first time that he saw a patch of corn, regretted the lack of animal life but recorded that he was captivated by the birds, especially the parrots, and of course, the multi-coloured fish, *'...and all these days since I've been in the Indies it has rained more or less'*, Columbus added. In the Bahamas, autumn is the rainy season.

The southern tip of Long Island, near where the settlement of Roses is today, Columbus named *Cabo Verde* and from here they sailed in a generally southeast direction. *Before we had sailed three hours we saw an island to the east, for which we steered, and before midday all three ships reached a small island at the north point...the men on board from San Salvador called this large island Samoet, but I gave it the name Isabela.* The island they had found is today called Long Cay or Fortune Island. The Indians told Columbus the island was named for their chief, Samoet. Barely a stone's throw away to the north was the irregularly-shaped island first discovered by Tsgot known today as Crooked Island. The three ships found a mooring place just offshore and visited an Indian settlement where Columbus first records that *'their beds were like nets of cotton.'* On the 'crooked island' they had seen their first hammock. The hammocks were inside buildings Columbus described as looking like Moorish tents, *'...very high and with good chimneys'*, which were *'...very simple and clean inside.'* He also noted that married *'women...wore clouts of cotton, the wenches nothing.'*

On Long Cay Columbus met additional Indians who were a little more sophisticated than those of *Guanahani* and they confirmed the provenance of the small gold trinkets they possessed was *'colba'* which Columbus believed to be a reference to Kubla (Khan). On enquiring where the great Kubla Khan might be found the natives pointed him again towards the southwest. This land towards which the Indians were pointing, a hesitant Columbus entered into his Log, *'must then I think, be Cipangu'* (Japan). Significantly Columbus makes no mention of meeting with Samoet the chief of the loose confederation of Lucayans who lived on the island…and for good reason.

Samoet had been advised of the arrival of the 'gods from east' by messengers sent out from *Guanahani* shortly after the Spaniards arrived. He frankly was at a loss as to what to do.

"Go quickly to meet these gods!" advised one shaman.

"No", advised another, "they were to travel in this direction. Wait for them to come here!"

An old female *tequina* had another suggestion, "what I have heard does not make me think these men are gods - it would be better if we were to conceal ourselves and see how they disport themselves when they arrive here…" The other shamans mumbled that her advice could do no harm. "For if they are indeed gods your diffidence will be understood sire, but if they are not…" the point made her voice tailed off.

Samoet agreed that he would remain unseen when the Spanish arrived.

A few days later a mysterious vessel appeared on the horizon. Hours later two others appeared either side of the first. As the vessels got closer it could be seen that each of the floating craft were much larger than any building the Lucayans had ever constructed. The Indians surmised the hull must have been built of wood but the lack of paddles and the flapping fabric above deck filled the onlookers with wonder.

"These are wondrous canoes" Samoet said admiringly, "they must be great people who own such vessels."

"True sire, the vessels are indeed great but fine adornments do not necessarily make a fine person." It was the old woman again.

"And I am told they wear such fine clothes!"

The *tequina* persisted, "but recall sire that the *zemi* foretold that a people who wear clothing will come and rule over us, and kill us, and we shall die of hunger!"

The ships took a long time tacking up and down the island. Finally Columbus dropped anchor in shallow water and went ashore at a small island off the north coast of *Samoet.* Columbus noted in his log that somewhere on the island *'was a village and its king'* but later complained, *'there was no village but only a single house.'* Finally he found a small village, *'half a league from where I am anchored.'* Here he asked for water and the Lucayans ran to accommodate him and *'came presently to the beach with their gourds full.'*

Samoet and the shamans watched the activity from the verdant cover of the beach strand. The seamen tried to organise the Lucayans to pour the water into the casks. The Lucayans who had never seen a cask before were unsure what was required of them and were roughly handled by the sailors in an attempt to make them hurry. While they were doing this one sailor saw a black shape moving among the rocks. He quickly

Lucayan canoeists greet the arrival of three ships at *Samoet*

unsheathed a sword and chopped a long black snake in two. Columbus who was nearby and inspected the dead snake then stamped on its head.

"You see! You see!" the old woman whispered, "they may be gods, but they are evil gods!"

This 'crooked island' that Tsgot had once visited, Columbus renamed for Queen Isabela. Satisfied he had seen enough, dinghies carried Columbus, together with the precious water casks to the small fleet lying at anchor off island. As soon as he was aboard Columbus immediately opened his log and, with his superlatives ready again, wrote, *'it is the most beautiful thing that I have ever seen, nor can I tire my eyes looking at such handsome verdure, so very different from ours. And I believe that there are in it many plants and trees which are worth a lot in Spain for dyes, and for medicines of spicery; but I do not recognize them which gives me great grief.'* In suggesting the flora may have important utilitarian and medicinal uses he was exactly right.

Columbus then left the reported speech of his log and set out what he intended to do next: *'I here propose to leave to circumnavigate this island until I may have speech with this king and see if I can obtain from him the gold that I heard he has'*...if Samoet had heard these words he might have laughed. Columbus continues, *'...and afterwards to depart for another much larger island which I believe must be Japan according the descriptions of these Indians whom I carry, and which they call 'Colba' (Cuba), in which they say there are ships and sailors both many and great; and beyond this is another island which they call, which also they say is very big; and the others which are between we shall see as we pass, and according as I shall find a collection of gold or spicery, I shall decide what I have to do. But in any case I am determined to go to the mainland and the city of Quinsay, and to present your Highnesses' letters to the Great Khan, and to beg a reply and come home with it...'*

There are several matters from this curious entry in the log which provoke comment, the first of which is surely: why should the Great Khan, or anybody else, give him gold? The word *'Colba'* which he had heard before, he now understood referred to a large island, probably Japan (in fact it was 'Cuba'); and he believed *'Bohio'* referred to another country but it was in fact, a reference to *'bohio'* (house) in the native tongue. The city of Quinsay, the 'City of Heaven' actually referred to Hangchow, which had been described in glowing terms in a well-thumbed copy of Marco Polo's book which Columbus carried with him on the voyage. Columbus had no idea 'Hangchow' was actually over ten thousand miles further to the northwest!

To find this 'Japan' of his imagination he sailed in a southwestly direction but soon the lead ship found itself in shallow water near the centre of the channel. To warn the other ships from following onto the bank the lookout yelled 'Look out for yourselves!' The passage from that day onwards has been called in the archaic Spanish of the time 'Mira por Vos'. With disaster narrowly avoided the three ships continued onwards passing some islands with low sandy cliffs which Columbus called, Islas de Arena (the 'sandy' isles Columbus saw are today known as the Ragged Islands). The ships then crossed another shallow bank, that is today appropriately known as Columbus Bank and is the only geographical landmark to personally commemorate the Admiral's visit to the Bahamas (the Columbus Bank is actually a fairly insignificant southern extension of the Great Bahama Bank). Their course almost due south now took them to the great island of Cuba. Columbus had been but fifteen days in the Bahamas and though he came within sight of the Bahamas on the next of his three voyages to the new world, he would never go ashore in the Bahama Islands again.

On arriving at Cuba Columbus was ready with his superlatives again.

Sunday 28 October 1492

At sunrise I approached the coast and entered a very beautiful river. I have never seen anything so beautiful. The country around the river is full of trees, beautiful and green and different from ours...

Columbus explored the coast of Cuba with perceptive comments about the vegetation and the beauty of the land but noted that the inhabitants were about as uncivilized as those of the Bahama Islands. From one of his Indian prisoners the Pinzons' had gathered that there was gold to be found at an island called *Babeque* (Inagua). Columbus decided to look for the island and sailed nearly 45 miles northwards but *Babeque* lay to the east and, since Columbus could not beat against a contrary wind, he decided to return back to Cuba. But Martin Pinzon had other ideas.

Monday 19 November 1492

I saw the island of Babeque (Great Inagua) *due east about 45 miles distant.*

It is impossible to see a low island from 40 miles away but, as on many other occasions, Columbus presumably completed his log after he later verified his observations.

Wednesday 20 November 1492

This day Martin Pinzon sailed away with the caravel Pinta without my will or command. It was through perfidy. I think he believes an Indian I had placed on the Pinta could lead him to gold, so he left without waiting and without the excuse of bad weather, but because he wished to do so. He has done so many other things to me…

Martin Pinzon had informed his crew about his intention to break away and all had agreed with his intention to a man.

"After travelling this far, risking our lives, living like monks…" Bartolome Garcia grumbled.

"…more like rats!" Pedro de Arcos, another sailor, corrected.

Pinzon stepped forward and added, "…I speak frankly to you…our ships are leaking and need proper caulking not this sticky resin we using from the native trees. I am fearful that we may never return to Spain!" And, after a moment continued, "…yes, let us seek for the gold otherwise this dangerous voyage has been for naught!"

The seamen grunted their approval.

The tiny *Pinta* was better able to beat against the wind than the *Santa Maria* and in two days Martin Pinzon and his crew arrived at the island *Babeque*. After only an hour after going ashore on the west coast of the island Pinzon was near to despair. The large flat island of Inagua with its extensive swashland and a huge salt lake in its centre was clearly not a suitable venue to pan or mine for gold. But now, knowing that he and his crew might be accused of mutiny, his resolve was even greater to find the illusive gold. He reasoned to himself that only if they found gold would he receive a pardon for his treachery.

Pinzon ordered the Indian who had insisted there was gold on *Babeque* to be released from the hold. With hands tied together he was dragged into the middle of a circle of crew members to be interrogated. Pinzon demanded of him:

"Where is the gold...*coana...nozay?"* (to make clear his demand he used Indian words he had picked up to indicate gold)

He repeated, *"coana...nozay!!!"*

The poor Indian looked helplessly at the sky. Unseen by the Spaniards some Lucayans were watching the scene from the cover of the bush.

"We have to make him talk! Remember these barbarians have been misleading us all the time as to where gold is be found. Remember at San Salvador they told us there was gold at Santa Maria de la Conception, at Santa Maria they told us there was gold at Fernandina. We went to Colba and now they say it is back in the islands...!" This was spoken by Cristobal Quintero the owner of the caravel. He knew only too well that without finding gold on the expedition he would suffer a huge financial loss.

Pinzon agreed, "well if you all agree we can flog him until he tells us where it is to be found!"

There was a unanimous cry of agreement from the crew.

"Tie him to that tree", Pinzon ordered. "Now you all agree that these infidel barbarians have tried to mislead us...right?"

The crew again cried their agreement.

"Right bosun...deliver the punishment!" and with a knotted whip the bosun delivered five hard strokes on the poor Indian's naked body before he was stopped.

"Wait! Let us see if he can remember now..." Pinzon cried, and he went up to the unfortunate Lucayan and grabbing him by the hair and again demanded:

"Now are you going to tell us where we can find gold?...*coana?...nozay??!"*

The Lucayan uttered some unintelligible words in his native language and the boatswain re-commenced the punishment, stopping occasionally to bark,

"coana??...nozay??"

The Lucayan who had learned a few rudimentary Spanish words while in the hold of the ship gasped, *"no, nunca!"* (no, never!)

At this Pinzon was furious, "Pedro, make sure the damned savage never again makes more babies..."

And Pedro de Arcos, drew his knife and castrated the Lucayan. The air was pierced with horrific screams that only ceased when the Indian had lost so much blood that he fainted.

The onlookers in the bushes silently disappeared back to their villages.

"Well, we will have to search for gold ourselves", Pinzon declared angrily. "I will take ten men and Don Quintero you can take another ten and we will travel in opposite directions following the shore until we will meet up."

The reconnaissance, predictably, achieved nothing. They found deserted villages, a plethora of strange wading birds and nothing but the broken surface of the whitish limestone of the island that they knew could not possibly contain veins of the illusive gold. But when they had almost completed the circle of the island they stumbled across two naked young Lucayan girls who were searching for bird's eggs near the edge of the great lake. The first instinct of the seamen was to rape the girls but Martin Pinzon by this time was more desperate for gold than a sexual encounter.

"No!" he cried to some seamen who had already taken possession of the Lucayans, "there's time for that later! Let's get these girls to take us to their king and we will get him to give us his gold!"

The men made the terrified girls lead them to their village and with signs they made the girls call for the villagers to return. After more than an hour a wizened old *tequina* appeared and by signs to her they made it known that they wanted gold. Some words were exchanged between the frightened Lucayan girls and the *tequina* who then indicated by signs she would leave but return later with gold provided she was not followed.

Pinzon grudgingly agreed to the arrangement and less than hour later the old woman returned with nose rings, neck ornaments and pendants. The objects were quickly divided up by the crew and secreted away. The *tequina* also provided larger pieces that had been donated by the *caicique* and were later recorded by Columbus as: 'good pieces of gold the size of two fingers, and at times as large as a hand'. The arrangement concluded the *tequina* indicated that the girls should be released but she was curtly informed her usefulness was over and she was forced to leave immediately.

Once she disappeared the men took the girls to the woods.

While all this was happening Columbus was sailing across the Windward Passage. On the 6th December 1492 he stumbled across the great island of *Aiti*. Again he had his superlatives ready.

Thursday 6 December 1492

At the hour of vespers we entered the harbour...I marvelled at its beauty and excellence. Although I have praised the harbours of Cuba greatly, this one is even superior...

But Columbus was still understandably furious at Martin Pinzon's desertion and in the middle of the night on Christmas Day 1492 his anger was to increase even more at the disloyalty and cowardice of his crew.

Tuesday 25 December 1492

I jumped up immediately, no one else yet had felt we were aground. The master and many others jumped into the small boat, and I assumed they were going to follow my orders. Instead their only thoughts were to escape to the Niña.

Being Christmas night the crew had been celebrating and left the steering of the *Santa Maria* in charge of a cabin boy. The ship had strayed into the shallows and was firmly lodged against a submerged reef. Juan de la Cosa and most of the crew, caring only for themselves, launched the small boat and tried to escape to the *Niña* that was moored over a mile away. But they were turned away and it was the *Niña's* boat that actually came to take the crew off the sinking *Santa Maria.*

I ordered the mast cut and the ship lightened as much as possible, to see if it could be refloated. But the water became even more shallow, and the ship settled more and more on one side. Although there was little or no sea, I could not save her. Then the seams opened...

Fortunately, as they were close to shore, at daybreak the crew had time to remove the stores from the *Santa Maria* but that was about all. Of greater consequence was the fact that they could now not all travel back to Spain in the *Niña* and in any case, one small ship alone crossing the great Atlantic Ocean, they all understood, would be an exceptionally risky venture.

However in the days that followed there was one small satisfaction for Columbus. By his charm and diplomacy he gained the confidence of the local Taíno king who showed him where gold could be found on the interior of the island of *Aiti.*

But matters were still desperate. Columbus continued confiding to his log:

Tuesday 1st January 1493

The sailor who had been sent out with the Indian canoe to look for the Pinta returned without finding anything.

Thursday 3rd January 1493

If I had the Pinta with me, I would certainly have obtained a cask of gold. If I were certain that the Pinta would reach Spain in safety with Martin Pinzon, I would not hesitate to continue the exploration. But...since Pinzon would be liable to lie to the Sovereigns to avoid the punishment he deserves for leaving me...I feel confident that Our Lord will give me good weather and everything will be remedied.

Sunday 6 January 1403

I ordered a sailor to climb to the top of the mast to look for shoals. He saw the Pinta approaching from the east, and she came up to me. Martin Pinzon came aboard the Niña to apologise, saying that he had become separated against his will. He gave many reasons for his departure but they are all false. Even so I am going to ignore these actions in order to prevent Satan from hindering the voyage…

After a difficult meeting between the Admiral and the mutinous Captain the small convoy of two ships prepared to leave the Indies to return to Spain.

Unbeknown to Martin Pinzon, through his forced sexual liaisons with Lucayan women he had been infected with a new strain of syphilis. While in *Guanahani,* the young girl whom he had raped, suddenly developed a high fever and sores broke out all over her body. The Indian inhabitants of the islands were left pondering the visitors. Were they of heaven or of hell? Their miraculous arrival, their appearance and demeanor suggested one thing; their hauteur, avarice and malevolence suggested another.

They would soon find out.

Indians panning for gold in Hispaniola

BECAUSE OF INADEQUATE SPACE on his ships and because he wanted to pursue his quest for gold, Columbus hurriedly decided to establish a colony on *Aiti*. Accordingly he chose a site for the settlement not too far from the wreck of the *Santa Maria* on the north shore of the island. As the city was founded on Christmas day he named it, La Navidad. He left many of the crew of the *Santa Maria* at the settlement with instructions to continue building the city and to persist in seeking gold. Diego de Arana, Master of the Fleet, was appointed captain and Rodrigo de Escobedo, Secretary of the Fleet, was made lieutenant at La Navidad. The latter had kept a detailed secret diary of the voyage that differed in some important respects from the log written by Columbus—but fate decreed it would never be read.

Promising to return with a handsome recompense for the new settlers, Columbus then provisioned the two remaining ships and set sail for Europe.

The new residents of La Navidad had already vowed to obtain a reward for their labours without waiting for the beneficence of Columbus. As soon as the two ships disappeared over the horizon they confronted the friendly Taíno natives and demanded they show them where more gold was to be found. Then they enslaved them to work the mines. But worse was to come. With the men out of the way, the colonists ravished the Taíno maidens. The native peoples needed to ponder the character of their visitors no more.

The entire garrison was slaughtered.

Chapter 6 - Islands Of The Golden Road (1513 - 1648)

The first European colony in America was conceived as a means of converting infidels and acquiring gold; in practice the higher object became completely submerged by the lower.

Samuel E. Morison

THE SPANISH EXPLORERS *may have left the Bahamian islands to settle the larger Caribbean islands to the south but one terrible aspect of their visit remained: disease. The Lucayans had no immunity to diseases brought by the Europeans and soon they were swept by fierce epidemics. Over one half of the population perished.*

And, as if that was not enough, other Spaniards returned. This time not as explorers but as conquistadores (conquerors). The Spanish were now, with the sanction of Church and State, embarked on creating an empire in the new world. Such was the ascendancy of Spain at this time that many accepted the pronouncement of a Spanish mystic who had prophesied that soon there would be 'but one shepherd (meaning the Pope), one flock (meaning the universal Roman church), one monarch (meaning Philip II of Spain), one empire (meaning the Spanish empire), and one sword (meaning a triumphant world crusade).' Even Borja Pope Alexander VI (elected in a corrupt conclave in 1492) was Spanish. With his assent the Treaty of Tordesillas was signed in 1494 that granted Spain the exclusive right to colonise any new lands discovered 370 leagues west of the Cape Verde Islands while Portugal was permitted to colonise lands found east of the demarcation line. The inhabitants of the Lucayan islands were thus unwittingly, now part of a great new Spanish empire.

Las Casas records a deceitful ruse on the part of the new Spanish colonists: '...the islands of the Lucayos...were full of people who were idle...and would never become Christians in their own islands. They begged His Majesty to equip several ships in which they might transport the Lucayans...where they could become Christians...and would be of use in the mining of gold.'

And with this, the first episode in the story of the Bahamas ends. In the few years after the visit of Columbus all the known inhabited islands were completely de-populated. It was as if the clock had been turned back. Apart from a slight change in sea level the Bahamas were almost no different from how they had been some 1500 years before.

The Spanish now concentrated on the colonisation of the larger islands of the Antilles to the south and, in course of time, they found the treasure they had sought so earnestly in the great southern continent. Thereafter great convoys started to carry the plundered wealth to Spain.

Their course to Spain carried them through the waters of the Bahamas.

ALONSO DE HOJEDA, who commanded a caravel on the second voyage of Columbus, was probably the first to return to the Bahama Islands on a slaving mission. He was the first of many. De Hojeda was a ruthless man of the new mould. It was said of him, he *'...was always the first to get into a fight, whether it was a war or a private quarrel.'* De Hojeda had previously come to notice because he had cut off the ears of a Taíno in Hispaniola and was about to behead two others until a *cacique* interceded with Columbus for their lives. The two Indians had merely been guilty of taking some discarded Spanish clothes.

It was de Hojeda who, early in the sixteenth century sailed to the Caicos on a slaving mission. When his caravels arrived off the island the Spanish called *Providenciales* the Indians ran down to the shore to greet them. The giant canoes of the round-eyed people by now were quite familiar to the Lucayans, indeed one of them had actually landed a few months previously and traded fairly with the natives. At that time the Spanish had exchanged steel knives and glass beads for hammocks and basketware. Perhaps this time, the Lucayans hoped, they could acquire more of the wonderful goods from the bearded white men.

After landing, the Spaniards demanded through an interpreter that all the people of the villages nearby should be brought to the beach for what they believed would be a grand bazaar. It was many hours before nearly two hundred jubilant and expectant Lucayans were gathered together on the white sand arc of *Bahia de Gracia* (Grace Bay). Suddenly, at a sign from de Hojeda, soldiers with swords drawn appeared out of the bush and drove the Indians towards the ships. Most of the Lucayans, though bewildered, complied. The few that resisted were cut down. Terror gripped the Lucayans as they were sorted into lots. Some children screaming for their parents were killed, others were chased away, while the able-bodied among them, both women and men, were forced onto the ships. Mother Iya was one of the older people, rejected at spear point, by the Spaniards.

After the caravels sailed away with their human cargo Mother Iya collected together the few young and elderly Lucayans that were left, then she sent messengers to the other islands of the Caicos for help. Two days later, four canoes arrived with the sad news that their communities too had been decimated. But fortunately there were some young men among the new arrivals. Iya arranged for the remnant of the Lucayans to hide in the bush so they could care for the infants and elderly until they were able to travel. Then she directed a small flotilla of canoes to carry the largest part of the Lucayan survivors to the island of Little Inagua and there they settled far inland. In that island they were concealed from the Spaniards and lost to history for nearly two centuries.

Yet another of the new breed of *conquistadores* was Amerigo Vespucci (the Italian explorer who gave America its name) who paid a visit to the Bahamas. He explained with brutal simplicity to his patrons, the Medici of Florence, how in 1499, he captured 232 Lucayans in the Bahamas and carried them off to Europe:

'We agreed together to go in a northern direction, where we discovered more than a thousand islands and found many naked inhabitants. They were all timid people of small intellect; we did what we liked with them...Since the seamen were worn out from having been nearly a year at sea and were rationed down to six ounces of bread a day to eat and three small measures of water to drink, and the ships were becoming dangerously unseaworthy, the crew cried out that they wished to return to Castile to their homes and that they no longer desired to tempt fortune.

Therefore we agreed to seize shiploads of the inhabitants as slaves and to load the ships with them and turn towards Spain.'

Treating patients with measles

IN THE EARLY SIXTEENTH CENTURY a Spanish adventurer by the name of Juan Ponce de León, obtained a *'Capitulation'* from King Ferdinand of Spain, to seek the fabled ***Fountain of Youth*** on the island of Bimini in the northern Bahamas though some historians suggest that a secondary (and more cynical) purpose of the voyage was to search for slaves. It is probable that news of the 'miraculous fountain' had been brought to Puerto Rico by Indian traders visiting the island. The *'Capitulation'* allowed de León to be invested for life with the governorship and administration of justice of any new lands he might discover in the region.

Though the king required de León to pay the cost of outfitting the expedition, he allowed that any forts erected could be charged to the Royal Treasury (defence, it seems, was ever on the minds of the Spanish). The monarchy also claimed ninety percent of all profits from the venture for the first twelve years and one hundred percent thereafter. And it further stipulated that no foreigners would be allowed to participate in the venture.

On the 3rd March 1513 a fleet of three ships on a mission of discovery sailed north from Puerto Rico. They kept the islands of the Lucayans to their left, passing *Yaguna* (Mayaguana), *Amaguayo* (Samana Cay) and *Manegua* (Rum Cay) before arriving at *Guanahani* (San Salvador). Ponce de León had no hesitation in identifying *Guanahani* as San Salvador (Watlings Island) and calling Samana Cay (a recent contender as the landfall site of Columbus) by its Lucayan name of *Amaguayo.* It is interesting to recall this was a mere twenty one years after the fateful landfall of

Columbus and thus well within living memory. Ponce de León discontinued his northward journey at *Guanahani* to careen one of his ships. He found much evidence of recent habitation on the island but not a single person came out of the woods to greet him. He could have been in no doubt what happened to the former inhabitants.

Ponce de León and his fleet were by no means the first Spaniards to have travelled this route. The sad fact is that the islands were almost entirely depleted of population as many of the natives had expired of diseases brought by the Europeans and those that survived had been carried off by Spanish raiding parties and forced to become slaves on the larger islands of the Antilles. We know from Spanish sources that by 1513 just over four hundred Bahamian islands had been discovered, explored, and presumably, deprived of their inhabitants.

From *Guanahani* the small fleet of de León followed the same route as the earlier Lucayan explorers but instead of landing at Cat Island, Eleuthera and Abaco they continued northward. Off their port bow they took note of the pretty islands and the offshore cays but flat limestone isles were really of little interest to them. If they were to pick up slaves they would leave that for the return journey, for the time being this was to be a voyage of discovery. At the northern extremity of the Little Bahama Bank they stayed clear of the angry surf foaming over a dangerous shoal that they thought bore a resemblance to a woman's veil. They dubbed the shoal the 'Mantilla Reef' (today, possibly due to a chart makers' error, it is called the Matanilla Reef).

From the north of the Little Bahama Bank the small convoy headed northwest and arrived on the 2nd day of April at a verdant mainland peninsula de León christened 'Florida' (for *Pascua Florida*, the Easter Day of Flowers or Easter Sunday). The landfall in Florida represented the first visit of the Spanish to the North American continent. Ponce de León then turned south and followed the North American coastline until he arrived in Cuba in the vicinity of modern Havana. After this brief landfall he turned his small fleet round and, assisted by the Gulf Stream current, sailed up the Florida Channel to revisit the islands of the Lucayans.

On approaching the most northwesterly of the Lucayan islands the lookout in the lead ship noted that they were rapidly approaching shallow water. He shouted a momentous warning from the crow's nest:

"Cuidado!...baja mar!" (Look out!...Shallow water!)

The appellation stuck, for the shallows, and later the country, using English phonetic spelling, became known as 'Bahama'.

Ponce de León made landfall on the 18th July upon an 'island of the great shallows' (*gran baja mar*) and the ship's log recorded, '*...navigated up to some islands that were in the banks of the Lucayos...in the 28th* (latitude)'. If their calculation of the course was correct they would already have passed the small Bimini islands on the Great Bahama Bank. But, if this was the case, it is strange de León made no mention of discovering or even being aware he was near the goal of his voyage, the fabled: ***Fountain of Youth.***

On arriving near the 28th latitude the log further records that they took on water, presumably from the mainland of Grand Bahama, and then anchored at a small cay just off the western point of the 'island of the great shallows'. The explorers found a solitary old Indian woman (recorded in the log as *'la vieja'*) on the cay. The islet is to this day known as Indian Cay. The old woman had in all probability been left on the cay to die since she had no commercial value to the marauding Spaniards.

The old woman told de León where he could find Bimini. Interestingly she pointed east and so de León cautiously explored the shallows of the Little Bahama Bank looking for the island of Bimini. He noted in his log '(on)...*the 25th went out from the islets, in lookout for Bimini, navigated among some islands which are overflowed and found it to be* "baja mar"' (literally 'under the sea'). This statement was a perceptive description of a mangrove covered sand spit which is often awash at high tide. He may have been describing Mangrove Cay or any one of a number of small mangrove covered cays north of the island of 'Bahama'. But it is clear de León was actually sailing further away from the island we today call Bimini.

Ponce de León continued sailing east to the northern tip of Eleuthera, then he back-tracked, skirted the island of New Providence upon which Nassau is now located, and sailed into the Tongue of the Ocean and down the east coast of the island of Andros. Realising that there was no way out of this strange 'tongue' of deep water they turned round and returned to New Providence. His ships passed the western tip of the island near what is today Lyford Cay and from here they continued on until they came to Hog Island. Seeing that nearby there was a deep natural channel they sailed into what was later to become the harbour of Nassau. De León immediately recognised that this was the best natural harbour he had seen in all the Bahamas. They landed at a clearing where they observed the remains of an Indian village, they then climbed the small hill that overlooked the harbour. De León affirmed that this would make a magnificent site for a Spanish fortress from which the Spanish might one day control the island archipelago. Events were to overtake him, however, and he never had a chance to put his dreams for New Providence into effect.

Even though he was excited by his discovery of New Providence, Ponce de León did not however, loose sight of his quest for the ***'Fountain of Youth'***, and left two navigators, Ortubia and Alaminos (the latter a pilot who had been with Columbus on his second voyage), to search the northern islands further. Several months later the navigators returned to Puerto Rico with the news that they had found the legendary fount. However, their bland description of the flat, fishhook-shaped island of Bimini invoked little interest and sparked no further explorations for it must have been quite apparent from the Spanish explorers' gaunt emaciated appearance that they could not possibly have found the veritable ***'Fountain of Youth'***! Ironically the legendary 'fount' of the Indians which de León had over-looked was located on the 'Island of the Great Shallows' which de León had in fact briefly visited. The island today is known as Grand Bahama.

After returning to Puerto Rico the Spanish Crown was nevertheless impressed by de León's description of his voyage and the explorer was granted the provisional title of *'Don'* and *'Adelantado de la Florida e Bimini'* providing he established a colony in the newly discovered lands within three years. The Ordinance permitted him to settle *'Bimini'* (which meant presumably all the Bahama Islands) and Florida but required that *'no men condemned by the Inquisition were to be settlers, nor their sons nor grandsons'*. Jews were ineligible, even if converted, and all foreigners (and the document made specific reference to natives of Genoa!) were also to be excluded. The first 500 settlers were to enjoy the use of 80 Indians apiece as slaves. The Church further provided de León with a *'requerimiento'* allowing him to make war on the natives in the Catholic cause.

But, due to preoccupations in Puerto Rico, he did not set out to found colonies on the American mainland and the Bahamas until 1521.

When de León finally mounted his expedition of colonization the 61 year old explorer was severely wounded at Estero Bay on the west coast of the Florida peninsula by some of the natives he sought, unsuccessfully, to subdue. He was carried back to Cuba where he died.

Juan Ponce de León, like Tsgot long before him, had travelled a great distance to seek an illusive and largely mythical landmark in the islands of the Bahamas which was of insignificant importance compared to the other discoveries of their respective voyages.

THE SEARCH FOR WEALTH in the new Spanish dominions continued unabated. But, since the fabled 'riches of the Orient' were not as readily available as the Spanish had hoped, they started to mine for precious metals—especially gold—and since pearls could not be picked up by the handful as they had been led to believe, they set out to dive the oyster beds. And when the sources of gold and pearls dried up they strove to get rich from farming. But farming needed labour. So Spanish slaving expeditions travelled even greater distances to seek workers for the plantations. Many of the Lucayans were tricked by the Spaniards into captivity. A chronicler set the scene:

Several vessels were fitted out for the Lucayans, the commanders of which informed the natives, with whose language they were now well acquainted, that they came from a delicious country in which their departed ancestors resided (and) by whom they were sent thither, to partake of the bliss they enjoyed. The simpletons listened with wonder and credulity, and fond of visiting their relations and friends in that happy region, followed the Spaniards with eagerness. By this artifice 40,000 were decoyed into Hispaniola to share the sufferings which were the lot of the inhabitants of that island.

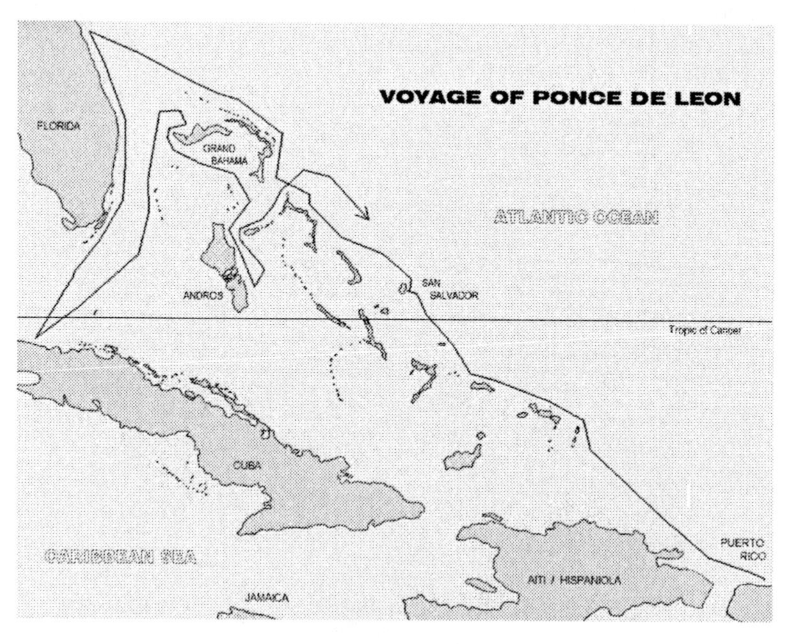

Voyage of Ponce de León in 1513

The Lucayans who passed into captivity were taken first to work on the land and at the gold mines of Hispaniola but because of their prowess in the sea, the Spaniards later put them to seek another source of treasure: diving for pearls at the island of Cubagua off the north coast of South America. Las Casa explains their plight:

The pearl fishers dive into the sea at a depth of five fathoms and do this from sunrise to sunset, and remain for many minutes without breathing, tearing oysters out of the rocky beds where pearls are formed. They come to the surface with a netted bag of these oysters where a Spanish torturer is waiting in a canoe or skiff and if the pearl diver shows signs of wanting to rest, he is showered with blows...The food given to the divers is codfish...at night the divers are chained so that they cannot escape. Often the pearl diver does not return to the surface for these waters are infested with man-eating sharks...

Even though by this time they had some immunity to European diseases the Lucayans soon died out through ill treatment and overwork. *'The tyranny which the Spaniards exercise against the Indians in the gathering or fishing for pearls is one of the most cruel and condemnable things which there would have been on earth'*, wrote Las Casas, one of the few Spaniards of his age who cared for the plight of the Indians.

Around 1515, Allyon sailing from Hispaniola with two ships confirmed that the Bahamas were by that time completely depleted of people. This fact was also confirmed by Bartolome de las Casas who continued to rail against the tyranny:

The conquistadors were responsible for terrible barbarity

'I have found many dead on the road, others gasping under trees, and others in the pangs of death faintly crying: "Hunger! Hunger!". Many others,' he recorded, *'killed themselves in despair, and even mothers overcame the powerful instinct of nature, and destroyed the infants at their breasts, to spare them a life of wretchedness.'* The Lucayans had been dragged, reported Las Casas, to join the Taíno Indians of Hispaniola where many were cut into pieces, buried alive, fed to the dogs, roasted over fires and even hanged in lots of thirteen (in memory, it was said, of the Saviour and the twelve apostles!) With all this, coupled with their failing health caused by white man's diseases, in

less than two decades perhaps as many as 40,000 Indians in the Bahamas in 1492 may have perished from the face of the earth.

THE RICHES OF THE NEW WORLD were being gradually amassed as fully laden convoys sailed regularly back to Spain carrying treasure from the new world. From the middle of the sixteenth century onwards there was a marked increase in the number of buccaneers and wreckers operating in the region who were drawn by the tempting prospect that the treasure fleets had to return to Spain by way of the Bahamas. If the Spanish were fortunate enough to evade the buccaneers they still had to contend with human error, dangerous shoals and the elements. Large numbers of ships, many laden with treasure, foundered on the reefs and sank. Captains of these days followed primitive sailing instructions called 'rutters'. One such rutter for ships leaving Havana for the Old World read as follows:

If from Havana thou wouldst set course for Spaine thou must go Northeast and so shalt have sight of the Martyrs (the Florida Keys), *which stand in 24 degrees and a half* (of latitude). *And the coast lieth East and West* (in other words ships would then be in the Florida Channel with the Florida peninsular to the left, the Bahama Islands to the right). *The marks be these, it sheweth like heads of trees, and in some places certain rocks with sandy beaches.* And the instructions continued: *shot out of the narrowest Channel of Bahama* (now called the Florida Channel), *goe Northeast until thou be in the 30th degree then goe East…*

In October 1655 the early morning sun was visible briefly above the horizon at Havana. But large threatening clouds were forming and soon the sky was completely overcast turning day into night. Later it would rain in torrents. The weather was a harbinger for the now immanent trans-Atlantic voyage of a fleet of proud galleons, caravels and transport ships. By noon the convoy was finally assembled and the final loading of the vessels was conducted in a flurry of activity. Under a darkening sky the fleet set sail from Havana harbour bound for Spain in command of a Spanish nobleman, the Marquis de Montealegre. His flag ship *Capitana*, and two other great ships of the line, *Nuestra Señora de Limpia Concepcion* and the *Nuestra Señora de la Maravilla* were carrying more than five million pesos in treasure: gold, silver, jewelry, precious stones and pearls besides cochineal, indigo, sugar and dyewoods. It was one of the largest treasure fleets ever to depart from the 'new world'.

But besides the importance that attached to commanding so a great treasure fleet, Montealagre had another reason to feel gratified. Among his passengers was the beautiful Condesa Ana-Maria, the second daughter of the Duke of Soria y Ridruejo with whom the Admiral was secretly infatuated. Her father, a noble Castilian Duke, had taken up temporary residence in the 'new world' to avail himself of the King's largesse towards Spanish grandees. Their arrival in the 'new world' allowed the King's conspicuously loyal and noble favourites minor administrative responsibilities coupled with the opportunity to amass enormous riches in the new Spanish dominions.

Certainly the family wealth and ancestry of the young Condesa attracted Montealegre, but even more important to him was the Condesa's dazzling charm and beauty. Though there was a gap of twenty and more years in their ages they had previously exchanged furtive glances at vice-regal receptions in Havana which hinted at a mutual attraction. A week before the intended voyage Monteleagre was formally invited to visit the family at their *estancia* near Havana so that the Admiral could meet the young ward who would shortly be a passenger aboard his ship. At the Duke's residence it was explained to Monteleagre that it was her parent's ardent desire for Ana-Maria to join her aunt at the Spanish Court where, it was hoped, a suitable marriage would be arranged for her. Once their daughter was properly settled in Spain her parents affirmed they would happily quit the barbarous 'new world' and return to their homeland to resume their place among the Castilian nobility.

At first the young Condesa had been reluctant to join the expedition but after secretly exchanging admiring glances with the Admiral at receptions and now having been formally introduced to Monteleagre she could hardly hide her impatience for the voyage to begin. She reasoned that since the Admiral was noble, married and considerably older than herself her parents could have no possible suspicion of the attraction that she felt for Monteleagre.

The Condesa wore her long jet-black hair in several spiral curls which cascaded either side of a pale complexioned face, a face dominated by startlingly dark and flashing eyes. She walked with a natural haughtiness, her head high, her glance imperious. Her small feminine frame was hidden beneath a tight bodice, hooped skirts and yards of crinoline. She had a wild spirit, which so much concerned her confessor that he suggested to her father that she should never be without a chaperon. Taking his advice, the

Duke of Soria y Ridruejo dispatched a saintly old Benedictine nun to be the constant companion of the young Condesa on the voyage.

Montealegre cut a fine figure in his military uniform. He was of slim, athletic build with an unmistakably aristocratic bearing. His face was angular with an aquiline nose and a precisely trimmed and pointed beard. A stern glance from the admiral could disarm an inferior, a command could terrify. And yet he had a vulnerable side known only to handful of people. When situation required he had great social charm and on rare occasions he could be passionate and even pliant. It was no secret that his arranged marriage to the eldest daughter of the dowager Duchesa de Marchena had been a failure. His wife had brought him wealth and lineage but little else.

Shipboard would not be a convenient place to arrange a furtive meeting with the young noblewoman the admiral mused, but it would certainly be easier to circumvent the social formalities found ashore due to the confined space aboard ship. Montealegre, as commander of the fleet, was in the opportune position of being able to establish the routines and accommodation of the ships. But even the interior of a proud Spanish galleon was at best like a cramped wooden trunk. Furniture was almost non-existent and beds resembling bunks were a luxury and were for important passengers only. The Condesa and nun were fortunate to have one bunk each separated by a flimsy curtain which swayed in concert with the creaking timbers of the vessel. A tiny porthole admitted little light and no air. The less fortunate crew slept on pallets in the cramped under decks though a few hammocks strung from the ship's framing were starting to be used.

Twice every day the Marquis, the Condesa, a Jesuit priest, and chaperone assembled aboard the *Capitana* for meals in the state room. Occasionally they were joined by the captains of the other ships. Montealegre arranged for the Condesa to have a cabin adjacent to his state room that served as his bedroom, office and refectory. On the open deck of the ship Montealegre and the Condesa, accompanied always by her diligent chaperone, saw each other frequently when polite bows and curtsies were mimed. Monteleagre could see that any chance of arranging a private meeting with Ana-Maria would be exceptionally difficult.

The convoy, now out of sight of land, headed north keeping the shallows and reefs of the Cay Sal Bank, the most westerly portion of the Bahamian archipelago, far to starboard. Two days out from Havana travelling through intermittent thunderstorms the Bendictine sister became violently seasick and was confined to her cabin. Then fortuitously, on the third day, while only three of them were present in the refectory in the evening, the priest was called away to investigate an incident in which a sailor was accused of heretical blasphemy. For the first time on the voyage, Montealegre and the Condesa were completely alone.

Both realised the rare opportunity presented to them.

The Marquis enquired stiffly of the Condesa, "I trust your accommodations are adequate Ana-Maria?" He used her Christian name without the customary title.

"Adequate sir, but hardly luxurious," she made eye contact with Montealegre and smiled coyly.

The Admiral's voice changed to a gentler tone. "That I know too well Ana-Maria, however, I promised your esteemed father, that I would ensure that you were inconvenienced on the voyage as little as possible...but life aboard ship..." his voice tailed off as the Condesa boldly interrupted,

"...that is kind of you sir and I perceive your concern for my well-being but my most devout wish is for my personal freedom and for congenial company...away from the rigours of my inquisitors!"

This remark all but confirmed to Montealegre that the attraction he felt for the Condesa was reciprocated. For a moment they looked knowingly into each others' eyes then, as a young steward re-appeared to serve them, the conversation moved to other subjects. Montealegre for the briefest moment rested his hand gently on top of Ana-Maria's below the tabletop.

A few minutes later the Jesuit priest returned in an angry mood. He crossed himself before he sat down.

"Excellency, the sailor we spoke about was apprehended by the officer of the watch. I shall not, of course, repeat what he said but it was grievous enough to deserve the lash - if not the ultimate penalty for heresy!" the priest announced. His two listeners understood very well what the 'ultimate penalty' would have to be delayed until they arrived in Spain when the Inquisition might arrange for an *auto de fe* - or a burning at the stake, the punishment reserved for a convicted and unrepentant heretic. The Condesa shivered slightly at the thought and cast a quick glance at the Marquis.

"Come Padre that is too severe a punishment surely! Anyway I will give orders for the matter to be resolved by the Commander of the *Capitana* on the morrow. And now...I believe it is time the young Condesa retired to her quarters..."

A long prayer was mumbled in Latin, Montealegre rose first from the table, looked for the briefest moment into the eyes of Ana-Maria, then he bowed formally to each of the assembled company as Ana-Maria left the refectory in a rustle of taffeta.

Later that evening a note from Montealegre was slipped under the door of the cabin the Condesa shared with her chaperon. Within minutes Ana-Maria slipped inside his stateroom.

It was the start of many such captured moments on a long and eventful voyage.

Meanwhile the convoy fell in with the fast-moving Gulf Stream and slipped past the Bahamian island of Andros on its northward course. Pretty white clouds billowed below an azure blue sky. A brisk easterly wind filled the sails. The nautical environment was an alien but intriguing world for somebody like Ana-Maria who was not familiar with sea travel under sail. There was the unrelenting crashing of the ship's bow as it sliced through the reluctant sea, the constant creaking of the ship's timbers and the unnerving circling of sea birds that accompanied the fleet squawking their defiance at the intruders to their private world. Occasionally a shouted command could be heard and sailors would run to their posts. The constant motion rolling and pitching of the ship was at times so severe that even hardy seamen sometimes had to steady themselves against the wooden structure of the ship.

A first seaboard conference of the senior captains of the convoy was called by Monteleagre to be held aboard the *Capitana.* Sails were furled and sea anchors dropped. Dinghies were then dispatched to the *Capitana* from the ships that made up the fleet. Once on board the flagship they were greeted aboard by rows of sailors standing at attention holding their forelock as a mark of respect. The stateroom was soon filled with men who were the pride of the Spanish navy. The agenda for the meeting mainly concerned the security of the fleet. The Admiral in his opening remarks noted that just fifty miles to the east was a nest of pirates and stressed the need for extreme vigilance.

"All ships must stay in a tight formation within the convoy. As you will be aware pirates may try to engage stragglers with their cowardly surprise attacks. For this reason I am requesting the *Maravilla* and *Limpia Conception* to sail slightly to eastward of the main fleet since the fire power they can bring to any naval engagement is far greater than those damnable brigands from the Bahamas. The flag ship *Capitana* will bring up the rear".

If there were to be an attack the most likely point of engagement the captains all agreed would be where the Northwest Providence Channel meets the Gulf Stream between Bimini and Grand Bahama Island.

"I have long believed it is time we re-claimed the Islands of the Lucayos for Spain", the Admiral continued, "those English pirates have for too long been like jackals barking at our heels..." All the captains present heartily agreed and there was general affirmation that it would be a matter that should be discussed jointly with the Admiralty on their return to Spain. "And gentlemen please let me remind you that all lights must remain doused on vessels at night while we are still near the banks and islands of the Lucayos," Monteleagre added.

Discussions continued on how to protect the convoy in case of attack, routines were amended, orders framed and administrative suggestions tabled. A few less important matters were discussed before the serious business of the conference was over and good humoured wit and gossip was exchanged. A fine dinner was laid out before the assembled company at which a loyal toast was drunk to the health of the Spanish monarch, King Philip IV. After the banquet the captains returned to their respective ships, checks were made to ensure the vessels were shipshape, then orders were given to unfurl sails, the ships were re-positioned and the convoy resumed its race northward.

Within hours the convoy passed the island of Bimini and the lead vessel searched the horizon for a sight of the Isaac and the Hen and Chickens rocks that identified the start of the Northwest Providence Channel. The crossing of the mouth of the Channel was uneventful and two days later in the morning light the lead vessels were in sight of the western tip of Grand Bahama. The fleet continued on northwards as land dropped from sight.

Just after midnight that same day the lookout on the *Maravilla* discovered that the convoy was straying dreadfully close to the shallow water of the Little Bahama Bank. From the rigging he screamed:

"Ojo! ojo! agua no profuda!" (Watch out! shallows!)

A cannon was fired to warn the other ships.

Confusion followed in the inky darkness and one of the ships collided with the *Nuestra Señora de la Maravilla* which sustained a large hole below her waterline. Hearing the sound of the cannon some of the other ships thought that a pirate ship had tried to attack them. But shortly afterwards the nearest ships were able to make out in the starless night that the *Maravilla* had turned half around in the water because of the collision and was foundering.

Grasping the problem, the captain of the *Nuestra Señora de la Maravilla* hailed the other ships to heave to.

Montealegre leapt from a gentle embrace in the privacy of his stateroom and ran to the bridge. It took the *Capitana* valuable time to arrive near the site of the collision. When he arrived, he shouted an order to the captain of the *Maravilla*:

"She's going to sink! Quickly, run her aground!"

The quick-thinking admiral hoped that running the vessel onto the bank would aid the salvage operations and, once on a sand bank, they would be able to repair the vessel and re-float her at high tide. But unfortunately as they were negotiating the shallow water in the darkness the *Maravilla* struck a submerged coral head that made an even larger hole in her hull. The ship immediately took on much water and started to list violently.

"Fools! you will answer for this when we arrive in Spain!" Montealegre screamed from the bridge of the *Capitana*, "...quick man the pumps!"

"*Madre de Deos!*"

"Help!...we are sinking..."

"...jump!"

For most it was too late. The ship drifted out from the reef, lurched sideways then, hastened by the weight of the treasure, sank rapidly in about fifty feet of water. For a few minutes the masts and the fore deck of the ship remained above water but then suddenly the vessel slipped sideways and disappeared below the waves.

The *Maravilla* began to break up almost immediately in the huge swells.

The vessel had settled on its side on the ocean bottom on the deepwater side of the reef. While this was happening the northeasterly wind intensified aggravating an already angry churning sea. Flotsam and men away floated away from the sunken vessel. Many of the sailors and people on board could not swim, while the few strong swimmers swam the hundred or so yards to the nearest vessel.

By sunrise only 45 survivors could be counted. Most of the 650 souls on board were lost in the darkness to the perilous sea.

Montealegre, comprehending their desperate situation, ordered the convoy to continue on to Spain but not before he left orders for the galleon *Nuestra Señora de Limpia Concepcion* to mark the location of the wreck of the *Maravilla.*

The convoy, now with the wind abeam, sailed rapidly northwards. Two days later they left the territorial waters of the Bahamas and the Admiral gave instructions that a few lights might be used after nightfall on the top deck. The fleet now sailed for a few hundred miles to where the Westerlies begin then, at a command from Monteleagre, the convoy changed direction to sail the familiar east-nor'-east course for a direct crossing of the Atlantic Ocean to Spain.

After the ominous sinking of the *Maravilla*, the Admiral and the Condesa stole every moment they could to be together. With a fatalistic passion and mature tenderness Monteleagre totally captured Ana-Maria's heart. Ana-Maria found herself in a state of almost constant ecstasy with her most extravagant and romantic daydreams becoming a daily reality. And for his part, for the first time in his life, Monteleagre was in the throes of irrational and hopeless love. The voyage for the lovers had become an erotic seaboard adventure.

Plying the priest, chaperon and crew with deceit and imaginative stratagems the couple made love with abandon.

AT DINNER a few days later the zealous priest announced that the charge against the blasphemer had prevailed. The sailor had been overheard, among other things, to proclaim a belief in the terrible Arian heresy which disavowed the Three Persons of the Holy Trinity a concept that both Jews and Muslims found difficult to comprehend. Under torture, it was also discovered he had a far better knowledge of the Old Testament than the New Testament and, to make matters worse, a shipmate further alleged his grandmother had been a Jewess. For heresy and 'attempting to pervert the Faith of his shipmates' the seaman was sentenced by the captain to thirty lashes.

On the morning the sentence was about to be carried out Monteleagre caught sight of Ana-Maria strolling on the afterdeck. He approached her formally and bowed stiffly,

"I regret Condesa this is no sight for a young lady. I should be grateful if you would retire below to your cabin directly..."

A few moments after these words were spoken the Admiral nodded to the man holding the cat o' nine tails then also left the afterdeck.

A drum roll announced the punishment was about to begin. The crew was called on deck to witness the flogging. When the crew was fully assembled the prisoner was dragged on deck, tied to the mainmast and stripped to the waist.

Meanwhile in the stateroom below deck Ana-Maria quickly untied her bodice and slipped her dress to the floor. Monteleagre swept Ana-Maria up into his arms and laid her gently on the bed. Moments later from the deck above, the lovers could hear the agonised screams of the sailor as the whip bit into his naked back, at the same time Monteleagre thrust deeply into the Condesa in a macabre and pulsating parody of torture and ecstasy.

The lovers remained in the stateroom until evening when Ana-Maria slipped out of the state room and into her own cabin only to re-appear half an hour later for dinner properly coiffed and powdered with the priest and the Marquis.

The seaboard quarters of Monteleagre on the *Capitana* far surpassed any other accommodation aboard ship. The spacious cabin occupied the entire width of the vessel with a large paned glass window in the stern of the vessel from which the lovers would sometimes gaze at the wake of the vessel. The churning white foam created two divergent furrows on the sea until they finally disappeared from sight, it was a poignant metaphor for the lovers—if one was indeed necessary—that soon their tryst would be over and they too would have to go their separate ways and these cherished moments would dissolve only into memory like the crested waves.

As the treasure fleet approached the 30th parallel it was suddenly becalmed. For the first time since the voyage began the sky was completely cloudless and there was hardly a breath of wind. The ships rode motionless in the millpond sea the sails luffing languorously. With the sudden calm, the Benedictine nun who, until this time had been confined to her cabin, immediately started to feel better. And, as she started to become active again, she became suspicious of her ward's long absences from her quarters. It did not take her long to discover that Ana-Maria was visiting the stateroom of the Admiral more often than was proper. She made an attempt to talk to the headstrong Condesa but was abruptly silenced. She did not dare to confront the noble Admiral with her suspicions nor did she wish to confide in the over-zealous priest so instead she kept a detailed journal of movements of the Condesa. If nothing else, she reasoned to herself, it would exonerate her if sinful mischief was alleged after their arrival in Spain.

After a few days of calm the southwesterly winds picked up and, now making good speed, the convoy steered a direct course to Spain. So urgent became the need to see each other that the lovers spent many hours every day in each other's company. Even the priest politely questioned the Admiral about the time Ana-Maria spent in the stateroom. He was given equally polite but contrived answers that he was "responding to the questions the Condesa had asked concerning geography and navigation" or that "it was important that she understand about protocol at the Spanish Court" or, yet another particularly devious response was that "she was daily growing more homesick and pining for New Spain and only the sternward view from the stateroom would stem her tears…"

The flotilla of ships meanwhile pitched, rolled and yawed in their headlong dash for Spain. As the convoy got closer to Europe below high herringbone cirrus clouds a continuous blanket of stratus clouds appeared already primed to carry precipitation in the form of rain, sleet and snow to a wintry Europe. With the change in cloud cover there was suddenly a pronounced change in the temperature, it now became much colder and the view of the horizon was so blurred as to disguise any demarcation between sea and sky. The convoy had suddenly entered a somber, misty and grey world. But for the lovers the change in climate was of no consequence. Sun, rain, storm or fair weather was of little significance, for them the stolen moments traversing the great ocean were all that mattered. The Admiral now even cancelled several conferences aboard the *Capitana* with his captains and the Marquis and the Condesa appeared at meals but only rarely on deck. Soon there was whispered gossip among the officers as to why the normally punctilious Admiral was so often indisposed.

As a military man the Marquis had spent most of his life away from home on voyages to Spain's far-flung empire that stretched far around the globe. However, on returning to Spain he knew he would have to answer serious criticism for the loss of the *Santa Maria de la Maravilla* off the Islands of the Bahamas. This realization made him only more reckless. Though in public he was courtly and dignified as he got older he became increasingly disconsolate that he had lost forever the joys of a happily married life. As time progressed he came to prefer his own company and resorted to the world of books. Then he even dabbled in poetry and secretly wrote love sonnets to the young girl of his dreams. But never did he imagine that he, a man old enough to be her father, might share not only his verse but also his bed with the subject of his phantasms. In their romantic sanctuary in the shipboard stateroom Ana-Maria listened adoringly to the recitation of the Admiral's intimate and passionate love poems and afterwards her total submission to Monteleagre gave actual substance to the lyrical imagery of his sonnets.

But, despite the blossoming love in the Admiral's stateroom, the voyage continued to be ill-fated. Just eight and a half weeks into crossing the Atlantic Ocean the lovemaking was disturbed yet again by a cry from the crow's nest of the leading ship.

A lookout screamed that a hostile fleet could be seen on the eastern horizon. The cry was echoed from ship to ship to ship.

As if the sinking of the *Maravilla* had not been misfortune enough, as the convoy neared Cadiz they found a large English fleet were lying in wait for them.

The tired Spanish convoy hastily prepared for a naval engagement. But due to the loss of the *Maravilla* and a lack of vigilance after leaving the Bahamas, the warships had neglected gunnery practice and were not battle-ready. Their lack of readiness would later be blamed on the Admiral. But in any case they were no match for the lighter, better armed and more agile English warships. After a bitter encounter with the exhausted convoy, the English sank the entire Spanish fleet except for two relatively unimportant transport vessels.

The Condesa, Benedictine nun, a few women passengers and infirm sailors were saved by a lifeboat put at their disposal by Montealegre. From their small boat they caught the distant sight of smoke and heard the eerily delayed booms of cannon fire. But worse, they saw the *Capitana* in the middle of the sea battle being pounded by English warships. As the smoke occasionally cleared they the saw sails on the vessel being ripped to shreds then, after one burst of accurate cannon fire, the main mast fell and finally the great ship caught fire and slowly heeled over and sank. Just a handful of men were seen to leap into the sea and swim for safety but, as the spectators to this grisly scene surmised correctly, the Marquis de Montealegre was not among them.

That night the occupants of the small boat spent a harrowing night adrift at sea.

At the terror of the event, and realising that in all probability her lover had perished, Ana-Maria entered into a mindless state of shock, staring blankly through unseeing eyes at the hellish world around her. The saintly nun, displayed great compassion for her headstrong ward and gently held the Condesa's head between her cupped hands reciting endlessly the comforting mantra of the Rosary. The good sister understood well the frailty of human flesh. As the shadow of darkness drew a veil across the awful scene, in a silent act of compassion, the nun felt under her habit for the journal she had been keeping and silently slipped it into the angry sea.

The following day the driving wind washed the dinghy into a small cove on the Spanish mainland.

The Condesa was carried to the Infirmary of the Hospitallier Brothers of St John of God in Cadiz where she received expert medical attention. But the doctors could cure only her physical ailments, she had lost the will to live and her life slipped away shortly afterwards. At her passing not one but two souls left her frail mortal body. The Condesa Ana-Maria de Soria y Ridruejo, it was rumoured, had died of a broken heart.

On a cold rain-swept day she was buried with little fanfare in the *Cementerio de Maria Imaculata* in Cadiz. Her interment was witnessed only by the local parish priest, the Benedictine nun and a few stalwart parishioners who felt it their duty to be present at the funeral of a Christian noblewoman. When her aunt received the message of her death she and her entourage made the arduous journey from Seville by horse drawn coach but were too late to attend the funeral.

The Duchesa arranged for a monument to be erected to record the passing of Ana-Maria's brief life. The simple epitaph read:

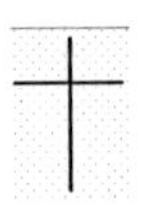

Condesa Ana-Maria de Soria y Ridruejo
De Nueva Espana
Pasandando este vida
20 Marzo, 1656
Requiem in Pace

The Marquis was severely criticized *in absentia* by the Spanish Council of State elite for having allowing the *Santa Maria de la Maravilla* to be wrecked in the Bahamas and also for being unprepared for the sea battle against the English foe. Though with hindsight it is doubtful if any preparations would have made a difference to the outcome of the naval engagement. The Spanish were understandably enraged at the surprise attack and the other depredations of the English seadogs and started to plan deliberate and violent revenge. The Great Armada launched against England some years before had failed so they vowed they would now turn their attention to the poorly defended English colonies in the new world...

A SALVAGING MISSION of six frigates with forty divers and a large number of soldiers was sent several months later from Cartagena to the wreck site near Memory Rock, north of Grand Bahama island. In thirteen days they managed to recover 480,000 pesos worth of treasure from the wreck until a storm forced them to abandon the search. But ill fortune continued to dog the Spaniards when four of the vessels carrying the treasure away were lost, though much of their bounty was later recovered. More salvage attempts were made on the submerged wreck of the *Maravilla* on the Little Bahama Bank and it is estimated that possibly a quarter of the treasure was recovered before the Spanish lost the wreck site location.

The main Florida Channel and other channels through the Bahamas were part of the 'Golden Road' back to Spain and yet the Spanish were delinquent in physically securing the islands. The forts that Columbus and de León had wanted to build as a defense against the harmless Indians were now necessary against more formidable foes. But, with rich lands being opened up in Peru, Mexico and the southern and western parts of North America, the Spanish ignored to their cost, the island country that had been their gateway to a new world.

THE NATIVE PEOPLES *of the Americas were devastated after the Spanish discovery of their hitherto unknown 'world'. However, as time went by, there was an exchange between the two 'worlds' which had some positive aspects. To understand some of the consequences of the resulting interaction between the 'New' and 'Old Worlds' the reader may wish to consult Appendix B.*

PART TWO

Adventurers at Preachers Cave, Eleuthera

Chapter 7 - From Bermuda to 'Freedom' (1500 - 1669)

> ***The Spaniards know this place well and have a yearly trade thither for the aforesaid commodities, and amongst the Islands are wracks of divers of their ships.***
>
> ***From an English report***

T **HE SPANISH** *were but the first of several European nations to exploit the 'new world'. John Cabot, a Venetian sailing in the English ship* ***'Matthew'****, sailed down the east coast of North America about the same time that Columbus was making his later epic voyages. Cabot is thought to have reached the south of the Florida peninsula before lack of supplies forced him to turn back. It was through his voyage that the English later laid claim to Canada and most of the coastal land on the eastern coastline of North America. Indeed only eight years after the celebrated landfall of Columbus there was an unsubstantiated Spanish claim that a ship, possibly English, ignored the Papal Bull against non-Spanish exploration of the 'new world' and was reported as 'roving the Indies'.*

The first English voyage to the West Indies of which there is positive evidence was in 1527 when John Rut sailed the ***Mary Guildford*** *to Santo Domingo on the southern coast of Hispaniola. On arrival at the town Rut weighed anchor outside the bar. The Spanish townspeople invited him to dock inside the harbour probably hoping to obtain much-needed supplies, but the cautious Rut sent spies into the town to determine the feelings of the authorities. It was well he did because his spies reported back that though the populace would indeed welcome any European, especially someone with whom they could trade, the Spanish governor was under orders to imprison all foreign visitors. Understandably Rut chose not to* *visit the town but instead sailed a few miles down the coast and, needing provisions, raided a hen house for its chickens. It was an inauspicious beginning to Anglo-Saxon expansion into the Indies for the first Englishman to set foot there to have been a chicken thief!*

In 1534 Henry VIII separated the English Church from the Roman communion. The English were henceforth no longer bound by the Papal Bull prohibiting trade and colonisation in the Caribbean. Sir John Hawkins, the first Englishman to transport African slaves to the Caribbean, made three illicit trading voyages to the West Indies between 1563 and 1568. In this latter year, Hawkins was attacked by the Spanish in the harbour of Vera Cruz, Mexico, and barely escaped with his life. The incident marked the beginning of a bitter struggle in the Indies for the right to trade and form colonies.

The Bahama Islands for more than a century after the arrival of the Spanish were de-populated. English settlers started to colonise Virginia in the late sixteenth century and arrived at Plymouth Rock in 1620 but it was not until the middle of the seventeenth century that the English considered colonisation in the West Indies. The stalwart colonists arrived from Bermuda in two small ships, one of which sank on arrival. The story related here follows the fortunes of a woman who had been caught in the then 'crime' of adultery and was exiled from Bermuda to the Bahamas. In this account she is destined to be the matriarch of a distinguished Bahamian dynasty. Appendix C traces (with sexist prejudice admittedly) the genealogy of the male line of which she was the progenitor and it takes up the story of her descendants to present times. Also included as Appendix D is a list of the governors of the Bahamas, both real and fictional which are referred to in the text.

AND THE ENGLISH were not the only intruders in the new Spanish 'new world'. At this same time French settlers were well established as *boucaniers* on some of the islands in the Spanish Main. These settlers, who gained their name by hunting cattle that had reverted to a wild state, soon gave a new meaning to the word by becoming 'buccaneers'. Their limited diet and the dispiriting situation of being virtual castaways soon led them to prey on an easy source of wealth: ships carrying treasure to Spain. As a result the waters around the Bahamas became so dangerous that a Spanish ordinance of the time forbade Spanish merchant ships from sailing through the Bahama Islands without an escort.

About this time there are records that Cardinal Richlieu, Prime Minister of France, granted the islands of Abaco and Inagua and presumably all islands in between to the protestant Baron Guillaume de Caen. But, though the Baron was permitted to build fortifications in the islands, the wily Cardinal was careful not to permit the Baron to colonise the islands with Protestants. So for the time being the Bahamas remained unsettled.

Eventually the English considered colonisation in the region. Sir Humphrey Gilbert was granted the right by Queen Elizabeth I to settle any land in North America not already colonised by the Spanish or the French. As a consequence of this new policy, in 1587 Sir Richard Grenville sailed through the Bahamas on his way to establish the first English colony in the new world. The Spanish, who saw the flotilla of seven ships off Portugal, thought that it was the advance party of an English expedition which possibly intended to settle the Bahama Islands. Don Alvaro de Bazan wrote to his superiors:

'Of their intentions nothing is known except that we expect more ships, they appear to intend to settle. It is presumed that they will go to Florida or to an island 30 leagues long which lies in the Bahama Channel,' and then, as if to underline his fears, he added, *'by which our fleets must sail'.*

The English ships however, continued on to the ill-fated colony at Roanoke in Virginia.

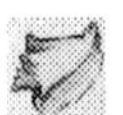  

THE MID-ATLANTIC ISLAND of Bermuda was settled by the English in 1609 and by mid-century was already becoming over-populated. The island was also becoming embroiled in the religious and political conflict that was affecting King and Parliament in the Mother Country.

When King Charles 1st ascended to the throne in England in 1625 he again tightened the grip on religious orthodoxy. Though the Six Articles (commonly berated as the 'Whip with the Six Strings') that was supposed to ensure conformity of belief promulgated in the reign of Henry VIII had been repealed, the English Church still rigourously enforced an orthodoxy not so very different from the Church of Rome. Though the Pope had been removed as head of the Church in England there were only two major changes from the Roman communion: the worship of 'idols' was forbidden and every church had to install a (chained) Bible in the common tongue for public use.

The hardest matter for religious reformers to accept was the Roman doctrine of transubstantiation—for some the awful and ineffable mystery which seemed to be a survival of a primitive blood rite. Yet, the established church maintained that no heresy was held to be more *'abhominable'* than not believing this doctrine - and many people paid with their lives for not espousing it. The reformers also took issue with many other tenets of the new English church; they would not kneel after the *'idolatrous Roman practice'*, nor would they have any truck with organs in churches calling them the *'divill's bagpipes'*. Yet surprisingly plain reading of the Bible was discouraged since many reformers felt the Sacred Text should always be followed by an explanation (which doubtless would be in conformity with their interpretation of Scripture). But most of all they felt they needed to restore the church to *'its primitive order, libertie & bewtie'*. English Archbishop Parker denounced these *'precise men'*. The phrase was graphic and so the exacting reformers were known for a time as 'Precisians' though not too long afterwards they came to be disdainfully called 'Puritans'.

The island of Bermuda was divided in matters of faith. On one hand were the royalist members of the established Church of England, on the other were the non-conformists, a varied group of dissident religious reformers—mainly Puritans - who emerged from within the Church of England during the mid-sixteenth century. Puritans in both England and Bermuda sought to extend the reforms by cleansing the culture of what they regarded as corrupt, sinful practices. They believed that the civil government should strictly enforce public morality by prohibiting vices like drunkenness, gambling, ostentatious dress, swearing, and Sabbath-breaking. They also wished to purge their churches of every vestige of Roman ritual and practice like the ruling hierarchy of bishops and the elaborate ceremonies in which the clergy wore ornate vestments and repeated prayers from a prescribed liturgy. Puritans further believed that only an elect of like-minded persons were pre-destined for salvation. But there were many reformist sects who were at great odds with each other on the most trivial of matters. With the restoration of the Stuart monarchy in 1660, Puritanism went into eclipse in England, but it persisted for much longer as a vital force in Bermuda and those parts of North America colonised by the English.

The Sheriff of Bermuda in 1647 wrote to the Governor of Massachusetts reporting that two ships had sailed for the Bahama Islands *'hoping there to enjoy Christ in the purity of his ordinances, without this Bermudian embitterment. But the lord has not answered us...and one of those vessels, with sundry precious souls in her, never returned'*. Indeed only last summer, he continued, the Bermudian non-conformists sent yet another vessel but *'without discovery of that island...and all through willful neglect of those employed...'* After this last disappointment the non-conformists looked to Captain William Sayle, an experienced sailor, of the protestant persuasion and sometime governor of Bermuda, to try again to allow them to emigrate to the Bahama Islands where they would not be subject to religious 'orthodoxy'.

This same year Captain Sayle and some of his friends published a pamphlet in England entitled, **'A Broadside Advertising Eleutheria and the Bahama Islands'** with a view to encouraging more of his like-minded countrymen to emigrate to a place where they could practice their religion without state control. The **'Broadside'** led to the formation of the curiously named ***Company of Eleutherian Adventurers*** that followed a similar format to the Bermuda and London companies which were responsible for the colonisation of Bermuda and Virginia respectively. Like the Pilgrim Fathers they looked for investors and potential colonists to finance a joint stock company. And, like the original Pilgrim Fathers who considered themselves *'saincts'*, they were nevertheless prepared to accept other people whom they dismissively called *'strangers'* as long as they were *'industrious and frugall...'*

Sayle's **'Broadside'** advocated a republican form of government, a single chamber parliament and religious toleration, but not the abolition of property or privilege (as such it represented the first proposal to establish a republic in the 'new world'). Investors in the venture, who were styled *'Adventurers'*, were required to pay £100 each to receive 300 acres of land in the main settlement plus another 35 acres for each additional person in the household. In addition, each investor was to receive a further 2000 acres outside the main settlement. Indentured servants were to be granted 25 acres when their term expired and all land was to be worked in common for the first three years.

Two remarkably commendable clauses in the Sayle's legal instrument **'Articles and Orders'** relate to the humanitarian treatment the Adventurers were to show to any natives they might encounter on Eleutheria, *'...no Inhabitant of these Plantations, shall in their converse with any of the Natives of those parts, offer them any wrong, violence, or incivility whatsoever; but shall deal with them with all justice and sweetness...'* and the other clause concerned those Indians already in captivity; '*...and whereas the Companie is informed that there are some Indians...(who)...have been taken and sold at some of the Caribe Islands; It is therefore agreed and ordered that the Indians shall be sought out and redeemed...*'

The reference to redeeming 'Indians' is interesting. Even though official Spanish reports suggested that by 1513 the Lucayan islands were uninhabited it is highly unlikely that an extensive archipelago of self-sustaining islands like the Bahamas could have been completely de-populated in so short space of time. Further, once the devastating effect of the foreign presence was known, the Lucayans would surely have concealed themselves from any Spanish marauding search parties looking to remove them.

Though there are no records suggesting the Adventurers met up with any Lucayans on Eleuthera and surrounding islands, it seems reasonable to assume that small pockets of survivors may have remained particularly on the more remote islands. These 'Indians' possibly survived for four or five generations and may later have been melded with the African population, free and slave, as happened in Florida. The numbers of Indians might also have been swelled by Taíno Indian slaves escaping from the Spanish colonies of Hispaniola and Cuba. (Interestingly as early as 1723, Bahamian legislation makes reference to 'Blacks' *and* 'Indians'. By this date it is known that a significant number of Amerindians were in the Bahamas, some of whom were from the American colonies but others conceivably, could have been indigenes or Amerindians from the Antilles.)

The Bill of Incorporation of the **Company of Eleutherian Adventurers** was debated in the English Parliament of 1648 but did not receive the Royal Assent because of the gathering storm between Crown and Parliament.

A year later King Charles I was to lose both his throne and his head.

As the political turmoil spilled over from England to Bermuda it pitted Royalist against Parliamentarian, Anglican against Non-conformist. Finding themselves in the weaker Parliamentarian/Non-conformist faction, William Sayle and seventy intending settlers (many of whom had recently arrived from England) and several Bermudans found it prudent to hurriedly leave Bermuda towards the middle of 1648. They embarked in the sailing ship *William* and a 'shallop', a small ship of six tons specially built for navigating shallow waters, and set sail for the Bahama Islands some eight hundred miles away.

Among the passengers was an octogenarian, the Reverend Patrick Copeland, who had just recently renounced membership in the established church. Copeland had had a most interesting career and was considered an especially valuable 'Adventurer'. In the early years of the seventeenth century he had been a minister, stockholder and spokesman of the London Company in the fledgling colony of Virginia where he lived for a time. In 1721 he raised money from the East India Company for the establishment of a school in Virginia for both colonists and Indians (in contemporary reports he referred to the native Americans as *'salvages'!*). A year later he was found preaching in Bow Church, London on *'the Happie Successe of the affayres in Virginia'* (though unhappily within weeks of his sermon the *'salvages'* massacred the colonists). Nevertheless it is quite possible Copeland's view that native Americans could be redeemed *'religiously and culturally'* as he put it, may have influenced the original humanitarian wording of the Eleutherian Adventurers **'Articles and Orders'.**

Another interesting but unlikely person aboard the *William* was William Latham who had been a servant boy at the first settlement at Plymouth in New England. He returned to the Mother Country after a few years in New England but then volunteered to return to the 'new world' as an indentured servant to one of the Eleutherian Adventurers. Also as a passenger on the ship was a sailor named Captain Butler who had once owned a fast lanteen rigged sailing boat in Cornwall. The Puritans aboard ship considered Butler a dissolute fellow and avoided his company. Hearsay had it that he had been both a wrecker and smuggler and was now running from the law. As time would tell, if he wished to pursue his profession of wrecker in the 'new world' he could not have chosen a better venue than the Bahamas.

On the voyage there was inevitably much discussion about religion. To add to their problems from the established church the Puritans were becoming disturbed by a sect of 'pietists'...*whose enthusiasm*...it was recorded...*as much exceeded their own as theirs had exceeded that of the orthodox clergy some twenty years earlier.* This new sect were called Quakers and already had created a furor among the Puritans of New England. As early as 1652 it was ordered in the New England Colony that...*none of that accursed sect shall be imported into the Colony...that Quakers convicted shall be banished, upon pain of Death.*

Even while William Sayle was in his first term as governor in Bermuda two people, George Rose and Richard Pinder, appeared before his Council for disturbing the peace. Sayle found it necessary to commit Rose to prison for preaching to the inhabitants, many of whom were, *'...convinced of the Truth they bore Testimony to, and began to separate from the usual Way of Worship, and form religious Assemblies among themselves.'* The fanatically devout leader of the Puritans, the Reverend Nathaniel White, was singled out for the Quaker's scorn and was even shouted down in church *'for the delivering of false doctrines...'* The Council further noted'...*it is difficult not to acknowledge that the clergy had some ground for the horror'* and the inhabitants

'...would tear the Quakers to peeces if they were not restrained...And to prevent murther and shedding of bloud wee were constrained to clap (the Quaker) in prison'. Despite the antagonism against him, the Reverend White would later carry his Puritan zeal to the Bahamas.

The heated discussion on the topic of religion drifted to news from the Puritans still in the 'old world'. One topic of great interest concerned the Puritan colony headed by Anne and Ebenezer Cartwright then living in the Netherlands who, it was reported, had urged Oliver Cromwell the Lord Protector of the Commonwealth to hasten the Second Coming of Christ. Since the Bible prophesied that Jews would be scattered *'to the ends of the earth'* (Deuteronomy Chapter 28 verse 64), the Cartwrights suggested to Cromwell: *'that this nation of England, with the inhabitants of the Netherlands, shall be the first and readiest to transport Israel's sons and daughters on their ships to the land promised to their forefathers Abraham, Isaac and Jacob for an ever-lasting inheritance'* (and thus presumably fulfill the prophesy to bring about the end of the world!). The Cartwights eventually left the Netherlands for the new world and settled in the Bahamas. The 'pilgrims' bound by sea for Eleutheria saw themselves as being on just such another spiritual journey as that suggested by the Cartwrights.

Sailing against the strong Gulf Stream current, the new 'pilgrims' followed a course sketched on the primitive chart Captain Sayle had procured in Bermuda of the Bahama Islands. The *William* took the lead while the shallop, manned only by sailors with a cargo of tubers, seedlings and a few chickens and goats, followed in its wake. Captain Sayle took a daily mid-day 'fix' on the sun which he then checked against his traverse tables to apply dead reckoning. He was forced to make the vessels tack often so they made slow progress but his calculations showed they were still on course.

The slow progress of the voyage got on everybody's nerves. The most fervent reformers argued *minutiae* of scripture amongst themselves and then combined their religious zeal to censure the less pious Adventurers. One pressing theological argument of the moment concerned Christian baptism. A New England minister had recently contended *'...baptism ought to be by dipping and putting ye whole body under water... sprinkling is unlawfull'*. The import of this statement meant that persons brought up in the established church who had not been immersed at baptism could not be considered Christians. Then there was another heated discussion about a youth from Duxbury who had slipped into *'strange and sinful ways'*. The main dilemma here involved three points: should death be inflicted on him for his unnatural sins, could the accused be subjected *'to bodily torments such as racks, hot-irons, &c.'* to effect a confession, and was one witness sufficient to convict a person on a capital offense? But history records there was no need to resort to *'racks, hot-irons &c.,'* since the youth confessed and was promptly executed, *'...according to ye law, Leviticus chapter 20 verse 15...'* The new pilgrims *en route* to the Bahamas could only concur with the rectitude of the judgement.

Finally the long awaited cry of 'Land-ho!' rang out from the lookout. Prayers were uttered, psalms were recited and hymns of praise floated on the early morning air. Slowly off the starboard side of the vessel the ether seemed to dissolve to reveal a long, low tree-covered island. However, on closer inspection they noted that intercepting a direct passage to the island were numerous small islands riding in a perilous froth of white foam.

Understanding the great anticipation on board Captain Sayle decided to call the ship's company together. Sayle revealed the island they could see in the distance was called on his chart *'Lucanoque'* or, an alternative name the chart offered was *'Habaco'*.

"The French once tried to settle there," he announced, "whether they moved on or perished...no one knows..."

Better they were gone was the unspoken un-Christian sentiment. The island was a tantalising sight and the captain brought the *William* round to give the passengers a better view.

"Aye...now I know ye are greatly anxious to make landfall but first we must make certain that Eleutheria—which is ye next island hard a' port - is uninhabited."

Captain Sayle now steered the ship to head south in the direction of Eleutheria and the passengers rushed to the other side of the vessel but their only view was of endless white crested waves forming and disappearing in a grey-green sea.

"There are reports that pirates abound in the islands and then there may be natives who may not welcome visitors to their shores...so, first I mean to follow the coastline closely. I should be much obliged if all of ye would keep a sharp lookout for signs of life..." Captain Sayle advised his shipload of pilgrims.

The passengers emitted a stifled groan.

Captain Sayle, well aware of the dangerous shoals around the Bahama Islands, inched slowly forward keeping about a half mile from the Abaco shoreline. Three hours later the passengers emitted a shout of joy as they saw Eleutheria, their destination island, gradually take form before their eyes. At first it was just a hazy line. But, as they approached closer, they could see that the land was generally flat but through the haze they could make out a central ridge which they guessed might be a hundred feet high. Closer still they could discern dazzling stretches of pink and white beach punctuated by grey coral headlands hedged by tangled mangrove while further inland they could see a few small coppices of trees but most of the island appeared to be covered with what looked like thick shrub.

But they saw no signs of life.

After travelling south for several hours they reversed course. On the return journey Captain Sayle's experienced eyes spotted what looked like a cave opening in a limestone bluff and he made a mental note of it. Just before nightfall the ships anchored in the lee of a small cay off the northern cape of the main island.

The following day they inched closer to the mainland and eventually landed at a small bay at the northern end of the island of *Zigateo* which they had already re-christened 'Eleutheria' (the name is Greek for 'freedom', later it would be spelled 'Eleuthera'). The landfall was adjacent to the cave Captain Sayle had seen the day previously. He sensibly reasoned that the cave would provide sanctuary from the elements until they were able to build more permanent shelter.

Upon arrival at the island (at what is today appropriately named Governor's Bay) an argument broke out between the immigrants almost immediately. No sooner had the 'Adventurers' set foot on the Bahamian Island than the shipboard disagreement followed them to shore and developed into a violent altercation. A contemporary report described like this:... *'in the way to Eleutheria, one Captain Butler, a young man who came in the ship from England, made use of his liberty to disturb all the company. He could not endure any ordinances or worship &c. and when they arrived...and were intended to settle, he made such a faction, as enforced Captain Sayle to remove to another island.'*

From these lines it perhaps may be inferred that the religious fervor of the Reverend Copeland and his colleagues had become too much for Captain Butler who baldly refused to take part in their Puritan services. For this he was declared to be a heretic. For his part Butler argued that a religious community that resorted to the use of *'bodily torments such as racks, hot-irons, &c.'* to maintain orthodoxy could itself hardly be considered Christian. Captain Sayle was unable to reconcile the parties and it was decided that they would separate into two settlements.

It would seem that many of the English 'pilgrims' had arguments aplenty before setting foot in the 'new world'. Some years before when a ship carrying immigrants to Virginia was wrecked in Bermuda there was also serious discord, some of the passengers not wishing to go further contending they *'would serve their whole life to serve the turnes of the* (Virginian) *Adventurers with their travailes and labours'* and when they landed finally in Virginia it was reported they were *'full of mutenie and Treasonable Intendments'*. Ten years later in 1609 there was a similar situation when the

Pilgrim Fathers arrived at Cape Cod at which time there were *'discontents & murmurings amongst some, and mutinous speeches and carriags in others...but fortunately ye better part...clave faithfully togeather in the maine.'* Clearly the nearer the English got to actual colonisation the greater was their disinclination to settle the forbidding 'new world'!

Faced with a near mutiny at his Bahamas landfall Captain Sayle parted company with the few troublemakers and decided to move from the first settlement site to St. George's Cay (where Spanish Wells settlement is located today) where he had anchored previously in the protected harbour. He took almost all the settlers with him but, as they were trying to navigate the shallows at Hawk Point near the northern tip of Eleuthera his ship, the *William,* struck a reef. One man was drowned and almost all their stores were lost. The sharp coral heads on which the ship had foundered were named for good reason, the Devil's Reef.

The resourceful Sayle ferried the colonists to shore then immediately took the shallop and with a few men sailed all the way to Virginia (a round trip of some 1600 miles!). A contemporary report expressed it thus: *'but finding their strength decaye and no hope of any relief Capt. Sayle took a shallop and eight men, with such provisions as they could get and set sail hoping to attain either the Somers Island* (Bermuda*) or Virginia: and so it pleased the Lord to favoure them that in nine days they arrived in Virginia, their provisions all spent.'* On arrival in Virginia the colonists generously offered supplies and the loan of a ship of 9 tons burthen. The generosity of the Virginians may well have reflected the high esteem in which they held their old friend, the Reverend Copeland.

Once in Virginia the indefatigable Sayle tried to recruit more colonists, "I beseech ye to harken to my advice! Give up this mainland Plantation and come with me to our Island of Freedom, we shall have no part with King or Commonwealth, we permit freedom of conscience, we offer indentures of land, the climate is fair..."

Sayle's energy and enthusiasm almost convinced the disheartened Virginians to join him until someone asked, "...and the soil, is it favourable for crops?...and what fresh water has this fair island?"

Sayle was obliged to admit that the presence of fresh water was not yet confirmed and the agricultural potential untried. They were perhaps better informed in London where it was reported: *'Letters from thence certifie that the Island they are upon, is a most barren Rock, shallow Earth, not hopeful to produce food for the Inhabitants...'* And when the Virginians later questioned Governor Winthrop of Massachusetts he also voiced his reservations. But the New England colonists were equally as generous as the Virginians to their spiritual brethren in the Bahamas and sent the Eleutherans abundant corn and other supplies. They arrived in the nick of time, for without them, the first Bahamian settlement would surely have perished.

Life for the Eleutheran 'pilgrims' was exceptionally harsh. Shortly after arriving in Eleuthera, the Reverend Copeland's name disappears from the records of the new settlers suggesting he may have been the first person from the 'old world' to have been interred in the Bahamas. His death left an opening for a Minister of the Gospel that would soon be filled by another of the many colourful characters to be washed up on Bahamian shores.

The early settlers had no doctors and in any case medicine at this time was a primitive science at best. Remarkably, 'bleeding' patients was the prescribed cure for many ailments. Sometimes bush medicine offered a cure, sometimes not. Teeth were an especial problem and rotting brown-stained teeth were removed with primitive pliers by a strong-armed man who often doubled as barber and butcher. If teeth were left to rot in the mouth the result was often fatal. Mothers watched in anguish as their children contracted a chain of diseases, many of them fatal, often caused by insect bites and exacerbated by poor nutrition. Happily those that did survive the tropical diseases developed an immunity they often passed on to their offspring. Nevertheless even settlers who survived childhood epidemics could still only look forward to something less than forty years more of arduous life and that was only if they avoided civil strife or accidents. Women died young, often in childbirth. It was not unusual for a man to bury two wives and then leave a third, much younger spouse to survive him, often with a brood of children to rear.

While Captain Sayle was away the colonists had the desperate task of fending for themselves by establishing plantations on the Eleutheran mainland. Having lost almost all their stores the need to be immediately self-supporting became critical for these first Bahamian 'pilgrims'. A first concern was to find a source of potable water for drinking and irrigation. William Latham who was of yeoman stock, brought experience with him from the first settlement at Plymouth in New England and came forward to claim he could use a dowsing-rod to find an underground water source. In his broad rural English accent William explained:

"Aye, it be like a gift from ye Almighty. Wi' a willow twig…though I 'spect any water-likin' tree will do…I walks around and ye twig just point out to whar water be…"

William's assertion that he could find water seemed to the Puritans to smack of witchcraft but, in their extremity they overlooked it and encouraged him to search for water with a divining rod he selected from a buttonwood tree. Whether the rod twitched or not was long open to argument but William selected a spot far inland on the narrow island and the men started to dig. Using old wooden barrels to line the well, just fourteen feet below the surface they found water. Even though it had a slight brackish taste it was drinkable and a vital resource for irrigating the planting on which, from then onwards, they would have to depend. Interestingly records show William complained much about the Eleutheran colony noting, *'...with some others, he was starved for want of food'* while they *'were forced (for diverse months) to lie in the open air, and feed upon such fruits and wild creatures as the island afforded'*. But William was also quick to remind his fellow colonists they were at least fortunate not to be facing the rigours of a New England winter!

Most of the farming was in potholes that were filled with a rich deposit of decayed vegetable matter to which was added guano excavated from the inland caves of the island. Because the bedrock was so near the surface they could readily understand it would be impossible to plough the fields in the European manner. And, since many of them had experienced life in Bermuda, they knew too that 'old world' cereals like rye, wheat and barley would not grow in the sub-tropics. Sensibly they found and adopted a strain of guinea corn that appeared to thrive in Eleuthera. Likewise they knew apples, pears and plums would also not survive so, over time, they planted mangoes, avocado and citrus that had been introduced to the nearby islands of the West Indies. Root vegetables too, like cassava, yams and pumpkins were planted and thrived.

In time they also cultivated a grove of the versatile coconut and in season collected the fruit of wild seagrape and cocoplum. Lumbering of dyewoods and structural and ornamental woods became an important cash crop for the new settlers. Indeed due to the increasing exploitation of forests in the new world by colonists Queen Anne would later try to reserve all the best lumber in her American dominions for exclusive use by the Royal Navy. But until the agricultural efforts of the Adventurers bore fruit the new colonists turned to the sea. Reef fish and spiny lobsters were caught but gradually their diet from the sea turned to the hitherto scorned Bahamian whelk known as the conch. From this time forward it has been a staple of the Bahamian diet.

To be near their plantations most of the Adventurers moved back to Governor's Bay on the Eleutheran mainland avoiding, as far as possible, any intercourse with Captain Butler and his associates. The communities survived principally by fishing and lumbering, supplemented by continuing aid from the English colonies of North America. In 1650 several churches in Boston raised £800 with which they purchased provisions for the destitute settlers. Mindful of their extreme generosity the Adventurers sent a cargo of ten tons of the dyewood Brasiletto to Harvard College, *'a moité of that grace bestowed on us, viz. ten tons of braziletto wood to be disposed of by them (with your approbation) as a stock for your college's use...and to avoid the foul sin of ingratitude so abhorred of God, so hateful to men.'* The note was signed by William Sayle and two others. The sale realized £124 and was one of the largest grants to Harvard in its formative years. But despite the help received from the mainland colonies many of the Eleutheran Adventurers returned to Bermuda within the first few years. Because of their political and religious persuasion they were hardly welcome and *'the ruder sort of people'* tried to turn them away and, as one of their letters attests, only *'by the blessing of the Lord'* were they allowed to remain in Bermuda.

Despite the victory of the Parliamentarians in England, the Bermudans remained staunchly Royalist. The same year that King Charles I was beheaded in London, another sixty Puritans found it prudent to leave Bermuda and sailed for Eleuthera under the spiritual guidance of their firebrand minister, the Reverend Nathaniel White. And, in the years that followed, still more Bermudans trickled down to the Bahamas seeking economic betterment and political and religious freedom.

As a matter of record during the early years of the migration to the Bahamas two colonists in Bermuda successfully petitioned for divorce because their wives, *'did lie with another man'* whilst they were away preparing a home in Eleuthera. And seven years later, after a civil disturbance in Bermuda, *'some troublesome slaves'* (and some) *'...native Bermudans and all the free Negroes'* were expelled. Most of the newcomers settled at Governor's Bay forcing Captain Butler to move a few miles south to a small cay which had a fine natural anchorage which was appropriately named: Harbour Island.

Just over a decade later, Neptuna Downham a beautiful young auburn haired woman, was 'transported' to Eleuthera for bearing a child, fathered by a young naval officer while her husband was away from the island. The winsome yet vulnerable Neptuna had given herself to the young naval surgeon before she had considered the calamitous consequences of her actions. Someone living alone and as attractive as Neptuna—even her name upset the older matrons—was a constant irritant to the chaste God-fearing townsfolk in the small island colony of Bermuda. So, when her indiscretion was made public the scandal caused a great furor in the island and she was shunned by her former friends and eventually 'bound over' to be brought to trial. English law at the time made little distinction between 'sin' and 'crime' and pursued both with cruel zeal to the full extent of the law. Meanwhile her disgraced erstwhile lover sailed away from Bermuda never to return except upon pain of death.

Neptuna spent a week in jail before she was brought before the authorities. At a Council Meeting held on the 21st June 1660, Captain William Sayle, who had been re-appointed governor of Bermuda shortly after his return from Eleuthera, was present when the case against Neptuna was brought:

...the case of Neptuna, the wife of Benjamin Downeham hath this day been taken into consideration, the which having been found guilty of Adultery, for that she hath (in her husband's absence) had a child begotten of her body by John Morgan chiurgian, whereby she hath made herself subject to the sentence of death by the present laws of England, nevertheless, an opportunity of sending her away to Eleutheria by Mr Thomas Sayle's ship now presented. The governor and Council in favour of her life, have thought fit, and ordered her banishment there hence, in lieu of the execution of the Law as aforesaid, in the said Mr Thomas Sayle's ship.

Neptuna stood in the dock as the sentence was read. She was dressed in a plain grey dress, her golden-brown hair covered with a mob-cap but the unflattering attire could not hide the fact that she was a beautiful young lady. A murmur rose in the court at the lightness of the sentence. But, though she had narrowly escaped death, her future seemed precarious indeed. Her parents were dead, her husband had spurned her, her lover had fled, she was alone, disgraced, penniless and was now about to be banished to the remote island of Eleuthera with a young child. Only the maternal bond to her young daughter gave Neptuna a reason to live.

Upon arrival Neptuna found life had been exceptionally difficult for everybody in the Eleutheran colony and many of the original settlers had drifted back to Bermuda or onward to the mainland colonies. Oliver Cromwell, hearing of the plight of the Adventurers in faraway London, ordered the Governor of Jamaica to send aid to the sixty or so residents of Eleuthera but, when help finally arrived, they found that the greater part had left the island. Those Adventurers that remained gratefully accepted the aid but indicated they would persevere with their small community where they were just managing to survive though they were enduring an austere existence. The small community was settled around Sayle's original wooden framed house using the cave for worship and council meetings.

The Rev. Nathaniel White the newly arrived Puritan minister was the first to use the cave at Governor's Bay, later appropriately called 'Preacher's Cave' for, what he termed, a 'Church of Christ'. Soon after his arrival on the island the black clad minister thoroughly inspected the cavern with a lantern and concluded its suitability as a temporary place for worship. He arranged to have the bat guano removed and ordered for a rock at the cave entrance to be carved to serve as a lectern. While making a visual reconnaissance of the cave his eye caught sight of a carved three-cornered stone and a knotted bundle of shells with an amulet high on a ledge. Minister White took careful note of the objects but left them undisturbed.

The first Sabbath after Neptuna arrived in Eleuthera every member of the small settlement was assembled in the cave while Minister White preached a sermon using texts from Psalms and the Book of Ezekiel:

"For it is written..." he intoned, "'*Confounded be all they that serve graven images, that boast themselves of idols...repent and turn yourselves away from idols, turn away your faces from all abominations...*'"

And with this spoken, the Minister left his stone pulpit, marched deep into the cave and thrust his hand up to the rock ledge. He grasped the jade *zemi* and the necklace of shells and then, holding the offending articles aloft for all to see, stormed from the cave and threw the objects far outside.

The congregation gasped.

Returning to the mouth of the cave he screamed an admonition to the people:

"Thus sayeth the Lord: 'For everyone which separateth himself from me, and setteth up idols in his heart...I will stretch out my hand upon him, and will destroy him from the midst of my people!'"

The astonished congregation voiced a discordant 'amen'. The wild-eyed preacher then returned to his lectern of natural rock to continue his preaching. His lengthy sermon gradually moved from the theme of idolatry to his favourite topics of fornication and adultery;

'"*...when thou sawest a thief, then thou consentest with him, and have been partaker with adulterers.*'" he raged. "And what did the Saint Paul in the Acts of the Apostles chapter 15 write about fornication?"

The congregation was in no doubt they would hear soon enough...

"'*Known unto God are all his works from the beginning of the world.* ***Known unto God!...***". He repeated the phrase for emphasis. '"*Wherefore my sentence is, that we trouble not them, which from among the Gentiles are turned to God: But that we write unto them, that they abstain from pollutions of idols, ...* ***pollutions of idols!*** *and from fornication,* ***... fornication! ...*** *and from things strangled, and from blood.*'"

Neptuna Downham, nursing her fretful infant, shuddered and blushed scarlet as he stormed into a further text the Minister identified as being from the Book of Ezekiel chapter 23 verse 37:

"'*...they have committed adultery...**adultery!**...and have caused their offspring, whom they bare unto me, to pass them through the fire, to devour them...*'"

When the lengthy sermon was finally over, small clusters of people huddled outside the cave thumbing their Bibles and debating the ambiguous portent of the sermon; "...could it be that God, in His wisdom, had meant that adulterers and their children should be put to the flames?" For, they reasoned, the text clearly referred to adulterers and their offspring *'passing through the flames...'* No one present needed to be reminded that their spiritual brethren in the Bay Colony of Massachusetts were severely censuring some of their backsliding members by burning them alive at the stake!

Neptuna guessed at the import of the whispered conversations and hurried towards her quarters, in an out-building on the Sayle property. Elizabeth, following closely behind her mother, spied a green stone lying on the ground and quickly picked it up and hid it under her clothes.

Pondering the dire horror of her situation Neptuna could hold back her fear no longer and started to sob convulsively while Elizabeth, seeing her mother so distraught, started to scream and wail.

Soon Neptuna's fears were heightened. There was a sharp knock at the door.

Quickly she dried her eyes, hid her auburn hair under a scarf then grasped the child in her arms and cautiously peeped outside. She gasped. It was Nathaniel White!

He called impatiently from outside.

"I would have a word with ye, Neptuna Downham!"

Reluctantly Neptuna opened the door.

"I suppose ye know why I am come hence?"

At the stern manner of the reverend minister, Elizabeth started to wail again and hid behind her mother's skirts.

"I...I fear it has something to do with your sermon Minister", Neptuna replied meekly.

"Aye Neptuna Downham, aye! Ye have committed a grievous sin I'll nay argue with that."

There was a dreadful moment of silence.

Then Minister White intoned, "...but, in His infinite mercy, Almighty God forgives a repentant soul". There was another dire moment of silence. Then he removed his black hat, made to dust off the wooden chair with it, but decided to remain standing.

"Ye surely know what holy upright people are saying - that ye deserve God's punishment for your heinous sin and...and I'll mince no words with ye - they are right! But...but if thou wouldst take a husband and were of contrite heart their vengeance for the cause of the Lord could be stayed..."

Neptuna looked desperately around her.

"How can I find a man...a husband, in this place? All the men folk are married," Neptuna replied.

"Except me..." the clergyman shot back, then added quickly; "...but of course, to marry a fallen woman would incur the wrath of God and the ridicule of the congregation...persons in such a union would have to remove themselves to where Almighty God only would know the shameful truth..."

Neptuna could hardly believe the turn the conversation had taken. "You mean...you are proposing to...you...you would marry me?"

The brittle clergyman replied stiffly, "We, hmm...in the sight of God...we could live chastely as man and woman."

Neptuna did not know what this meant and did not care to ask.

"Could I have a little time to think this matter over please Minister? I will give you my answer tomorr..." Neptuna stammered, Minister White's face appeared to stiffen,"...my answer...this very evening?"

"Very well, very well, at eventide then!" Minister Nathaniel White sniffed and, without so much as a further glance at Neptuna or her terrified daughter he picked up his hat and marched stiffly from the room.

Neptuna had narrowly escaped execution by hanging in Bermuda but now faced two further daunting prospects; to be burned at the stake by the Eleutheran Puritans or to become betrothed to this odious, sanctimonious man.

But were these her only choices?

Neptuna pondered the awful dilemma for some time. Then she made up her mind...she would flee!

Quickly she gathered her scant belongings together then, taking her daughter by the hand, crept silently out of the house. She was careful to avoid being seen by the people from the settlement. But she had no need of concern. It was the Sabbath, an obligatory day of rest. All the settlers were indoors peacefully asleep except for Will Latham who was tending his vegetable patch and did not notice as two figures stole into the woods.

The mother and child crept inland through the bush, skirted some planted fields, then joined up with the shoreline of the great bay in the lee of Harbour Island. Travelling in a giant arc in a generally southerly direction they fought their way through tangled mangroves and prickly underbrush. At times they clambered up the rocky spine of the island where they rested a little and Neptuna could check her bearings. Then they descended towards the shore to continue their escape. But they made slow progress. In places the foreshore was composed of razor sharp rocks and in other places the mangroves extended down to the water's edge. Elizabeth soon complained she was tired and hungry but Neptuna continued to scurry along, sometimes carrying, sometimes dragging her bewildered child, hoping all the time to catch sight of someone from the breakaway group of colonists on Harbour Island.

At nightfall Neptuna and Elizabeth huddled together in a natural clearing and slept fitfully until first light. Then they started walking along the foreshore again. Finally they reached a few crude planks that served as a mainland landing stage for Captain Butlers's island retreat. In the early morning light they could just barely see the cay some distance from the Eleutheran shore. About half way across the bay, half hidden in the morning mist, was a small fishing skiff.

Neptuna hailed the boat anxiously.

Her frantic waving was seen from the skiff and a lone powerfully built African slowly steered his boat to the shore. He did not seem in the least surprised to see two helpless souls on a deserted shore hundreds of miles from the nearest settlement of any consequence. With very few words the boatman helped them aboard and carried them the short distance to the island site of Captain Butler's settlement on Harbour Island.

On the small cay there were only two half-finished houses near the lee shore which were occupied by Captain Butler and a few blacks and people of mixed race who, Minister White had often proclaimed to his Puritan congregation, "...continually went a-wracking that was like sailing under ye black flag of piracy - may Almighty God forgive them!"

Neptuna had no time to hesitate, she quickly thanked the sturdy African then, grasping her child in her arms, she strode boldly up to the open door of the larger wooden dwelling.

"Come in! I have been expecting you." A voice announced from the interior of the dwelling before she could knock. "You must be tired and hungry!"

The voice belonged to a red-faced bearded man whose belly suspended over his belt. He was wearing calico breeches, a homespun shirt and a faded red bandana round his head. The inside of his one-room house was filled with a miscellany of objects: a blunderbuss, two empty rum barrels, some pieces of jewelry haphazardly strewn on the floor and several sea chests whose lids had clearly been forced open, all of which attested to Butler's nefarious occupation.

The captain screwed up the wrinkles around his blue eyes into an impish smile. "Well, you have missed your reverend friend! He has been here already by boat looking for you...aye, he guessed you would head this way!"

"What did he say, I…I mean what does he intend to do?" Neptuna enquired nervously.

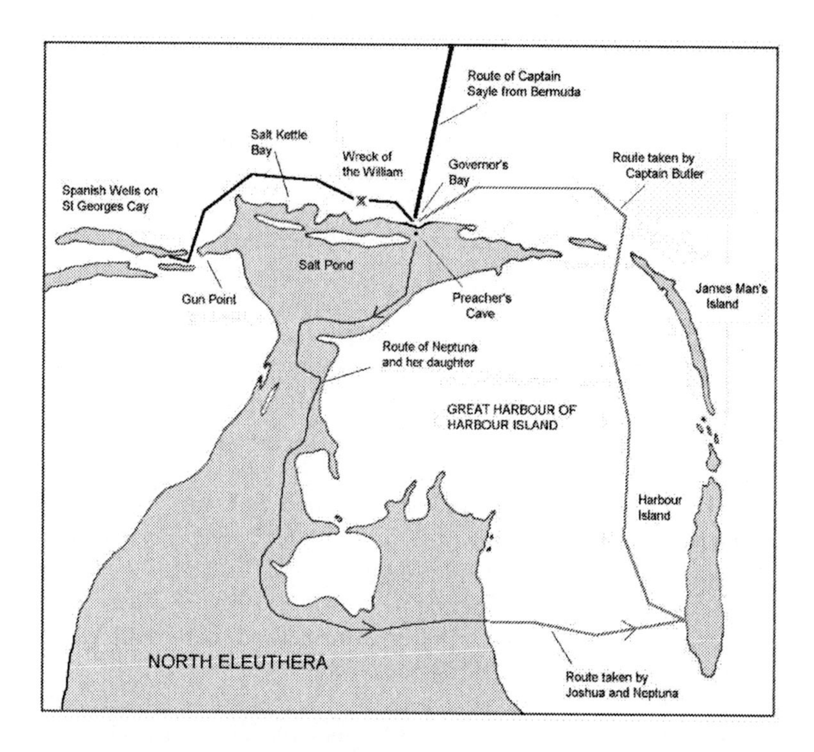

Chart showing early voyages of the Eleutheran Adventurers and Neptuna Downham's route to Harbour Island

"Well at first he hectored me with all that 'fire and brimstone' nonsense, then he was, well…rather pathetic. Wants me to return you back to the mainland settlement or at least to inform him if you came to these parts…"

"And will you?"

Captain Butler screwed up his face. "Nay, not if ye do not wish it."

"I want desperately to leave this place!" Neptuna sighed, continuing quickly, "did he tell you the people of the settlement want retribution for my child that was born out of wedlock?…and Minister White wants me…" her voice sank, "…for I know not what!"

Captain Butler nodded sympathetically and motioned for her to sit down on a sea chest that served as a chair.

"Thy reverend minister should study the 'Wicked Bible'", he chortled.

Neptuna looked shocked at what seemed to be a sacrilege.

"No it's not heresy—though that's not always a bad thing—no, you see a few years back they printed a Bible in England that had a printing error...in printing the Ten Commandments they mistakenly missed out the word 'not', so the passage read: 'Thou shalt commit adultery!'" Butler laughed uncontrollably for a minute until he saw that Neptuna did not find it so funny. His laughter subsided and he became serious again.

"Anyway, I believe I can help. Ye can stay here for the night - its rough and ready mind...! Then, if ye wish, ye can go with Joshua to Sayle's Island on the morrow. Joshua, is the name of the boatman who brought ye here - I have need of some supplies..." the captain added with a wink "...with a following wind ye could reach the isle in a matter of hours. There are quite a few houses already in the growing town and I know someone there who might offer ye shelter and vitals until ye both are settled."

At the happy thought of placing some distance between herself and the Puritan Minister and his flock, Neptuna broke down and sobbed her gratitude.

Sayles Island, had been colonised by people from Bermuda shortly after the first settlement on Eleuthera. Neptuna knew of its existence but since it was populated by Bermudans and pirates she had dismissed it as a possible place to live. *'There is about 300 people upon it myself having a plantation there with...8 Negroes and 5 English...'* a letter from a Bermudan settler in Sayles Island recorded in 1666. *'The people there have now no want of provisions, and...most inclinable to settle there, by reason the island is so healthful. It produces as good cotton as ever grew in America and gallant tobacco. They have made but little as yet. Their greatest want at present is small arms and ammunition, a goodly minister and smith...'* Neptuna could at least be pleased there was not minister of religion there yet to remind her of her sinful past...

Early next day Neptuna thanked the colourful sea captain profusely and bade him farewell as she and Elizabeth once more embarked on a boat manned by the African. On their journey she discovered the boatman was named Joshua Elding and was one of the free blacks that, like herself, had been expelled from Bermuda to the incongruously-named 'isle of freedom'. Their destination, Sayles Island, had just recently been re-discovered by Captain William Sayle, the kindly gentleman who had arranged for her to escape from a terrible fate in Bermuda. The island would later be known as New Providence since, as Sayle expressed it, only divine providence could have led him to this strategically important but hitherto uncharted island.

The route Joshua followed took them along the edge of the Great Bahama Bank that was dotted with small cays. Not long afterwards one of them would be purchased for six shillings—a name it still bears to this day. The water at the margin of the bank and the open sea was a veritable paint box. An azure sky above, the cobalt blue of the Providence Channel, the pink and green of the small islands and, where the bank began was every shade of blue intermixed with green that was imaginable. Neptuna was lost in her daydreams when suddenly Joshua cried:

"Pirates!"

And there, in the distance, she saw a square-rigged vessel bristling with guns bearing down on them.

"Lie down and keep out of sight', Joshua counseled, "I am going to sail closer to the reef so they will not be able to approach us, also if they see me only they will think that I am a native fisherman and will probably not draw near to us."

Neptuna and Elizabeth, both terrified, huddled together and did as they were advised. The galleon came close enough to observe the small craft but continued on its way. As it steered away it fired a shot in their general direction more as a taunt than in anger.

The incident gave Neptuna time to consider the hazards that fate seemed to constantly strew across her path. She realized that this short voyage was a like the throw of the dice, if all turned out well she would be able to embark on a new life with her young daughter and hopefully leave her unhappy past far behind, if not...but that prospect was too awful for her to contemplate.

On the remainder of their passage to New Providence, Neptuna and Joshua shared stories about their unhappy experiences. Joshua was to learn that white people too were sometimes also the victims of terrible injustice while Neptuna was able to discover much about Joshua and his fellow Africans. She learned that Joshua was possessed of uncommon good sense, a profound knowledge of the sea and an astute understanding, yet guileless compassion, for his fellow men of both races. She found out much too, about the dreams and aspirations of Africans transported to this alien 'new world'. She was surprised that Joshua expressed no wish to return to Africa but wanted only 'peaceful times' in what he called 'this country of islands'. For all the passengers on the small boat the short sea journey was to prove cathartic.

For little Elizabeth the journey became a turning point in her short life. As an infant she had narrowly escaped being orphaned in Bermuda only to be exiled with her mother in Eleuthera. There she remembered the hostility of the congregation when people were openly calling her 'bastard child' and, even though she was not exactly sure what the words meant, she knew they were not spoken kindly. Then there was the awful incident of the minister's visit to their house and the hatred he seemed to hold for her. She remembered vividly their recent escape and spending a night in the open under the stars. Then there was the visit to the strange sea captain on

Harbour Island. And now she had experienced what it was like to have been under fire from a pirate ship. Even in her four-year-old mind she had begun to realise that she would have to be strong if she was to survive in this cruel world.

When they finally reached Sayles Island and the few timber-framed buildings in the small waterfront community that went by the name of Charles Town (later it would be called 'Nassau'). Neptuna gave Joshua her heartfelt thanks and, carrying her few belongings and with little Elizabeth firmly clasping her hand, appeared on the doorstep of the house of Captain Butler's friend, Esekiel Tarp.

After knocking for some time at the small waterfront house the door finally creaked open and revealed Esekiel, a gaunt man prematurely old and stooped from having spent many years below deck on a ship of the line. Neptuna presented the letter she had brought from Captain Butler.

Esekiel read the letter slowly, painfully mouthing each word then, after a loud guffaw, she was offered the refuge she sought.

"Come in m'dear and the little darlint' too!...Martha! Martha!...Where are ye woman?...we have company!" And a double-chinned rosy-faced woman of enormous size wearing a bed cap and apron appeared from an inner room squinting at the visitors.

"Why bless us all! Now come with me m'dear...and the little 'un too...now let me hear your news...its not, I hope, a tale of woe..." and, fussing over the untidiness of her little house, she led them away to the back parlour of their waterfront abode.

Neptuna found the manner of the old salt and his busybody wife a trifle over-bearing but for the next few days their house provided welcome shelter indeed. While in Charles Town Neptuna used her time well to garner information about the mushrooming little town. Indeed in only three days after arriving in Charles Town, she was fortunate enough to find gainful employment. A newly opened tavern was in urgent need of help so she was most happy to accept the position of a serving wench. Neptuna was a welcome addition to the workforce in a town that was populated mainly by illiterate rough and ready seadogs. Though propositioned constantly at the inn Neptuna managed to retain her charm yet keep herself free from awkward entanglements. She soon proved herself an invaluable assistant to the innkeeper and within a short space of time was offered a room for herself and daughter in the attic of the small inn.

It was in the attic that Elizabeth showed her mother the pretty green stone she had picked up near the cave and had secreted in her clothing. Neptuna was at first bitterly reminded of the incident at Preacher's Cave but then was amused that her daughter had picked up the talisman. She pondered if Minister White had searched for the heathen *zemi* with a view to further exorcising it. The thought amused her and they both agreed that they would keep the green stone as a family keepsake.

At this time many people were moving into Charles Town on account of its fine natural harbour, its location near the geographical centre of the Bahama Islands and its free and easy lifestyle. It soon became the undisputed trading nucleus of the islands. The proximity of the island to Spanish shipping lanes was also an important factor in attracting residents. A contemporary report put it this way: '*The rovers* (pirates) *being now pretty strong…consulted together about getting some place of retreat, where they might lodge their wealth, clear and repair their ships and make themselves a kind of abode. They were not long in resolving, but fixed upon the island of New Providence, the most considerable of the Bahama Islands.*'

The hostelry business was brisk and, with perseverance, aided by her charm, tact and pleasant manner, within three years Neptuna had saved enough money to lease the tavern from its owner who found there was more money to be made with the 'rovers' at sea. Whereupon she renamed the inn, *The Wheel of Fortune*, a name she often asserted, capsulated her life in a single phrase.

The waterfront crowd was free with its money and the tavern continued to prosper. Indeed after just two years Neptuna was able to purchase the business from the estate of the owner who had mysteriously disappeared at sea. Neptuna and young Elizabeth, whom most people now called by her nickname 'Bahama', built a happy life for themselves in the bustling new settlement. Neptuna was beginning to enjoy her exile in the Bahamas and her daughter positively flourished in her new island home.

People from many places were drawn to Sayles Island. Besides former English sailors like Esekiel Tarp and his harridan of a wife, there were wreckers, pirates, fishermen, slaves, indentured servants and even a few Taíno Indians who had run away from Hispaniola. To round out the strange admixture of people there were also several scoundrels from London and the new American colonies who had escaped the law and found a new refuge from which to pursue their evil ways. In fact the town was growing so rapidly there was some idle talk that England might send out a governor to administer the unruly little island community.

Then one day, amidst the continuing influx of people, to Neptuna's pleasant surprise an acquaintance from Eleuthera moved to Charles Town.

Chapter 8 - Pirates and Commerce (1670 - 1733)

Expulsis piratis, restituta commercia
(Former motto of the Bahamas)

I **N 1670, EIGHT 'LORDS PROPRIETORS'** *obtained letters patent from the English Crown to add more territory to their already considerable possessions in the new world. The additional grants of land included the Bahama Islands that became the private property of a few absentee English noblemen. Sovereignty of the islands, however, remained firmly vested in the Crown. Thus for the original grant to William Sayle and twenty five other Adventurers who thought the term of their grant would be in perpetuity: '...the Said persons theire hiers and Assignes should have hold possesse and enjoye the Islandes* ***forever****...' (emphasis added) the 'forever' actually turned out to be a mere 20 years!*

Shortly thereafter the Lords Proprietors took physical possession of the Colony. The centre of government and commerce officially moved from Eleuthera to Sayles Island (now officially re-named New Providence) where it has been ever since.

The first census in the country taken in 1671 recorded a total of 913 inhabitants in New Providence of whom 413, or nearly half, were slaves. For a brief time there was honest commerce in salt, agricultural products, lumber and ambergris. But the lure of wrecking and piracy was too strong.

The first settlement on New Providence was named Charles Town in honour of the 'Merry Monarch,' King Charles II and was constructed along the waterfront which was an appropriate site for these new Bahamians who were first and foremost sailors who knew how to trade and live off the sea.

*The new **Charter** was drafted by John Locke the English philosopher who was secretary to Lord Ashley, one of the Lords Proprietors at the time. Despite the lengthy and strongly-worded **Charter** which established a bi-cameral parliament on the Westminster model, the change of administration ushered in a period of incredible lawlessness on both land and sea. Eventually it became obvious to the English government that it would have to take a more active role in administering the country if it was to remain an English possession. The virtual anarchy in the Colony was finally brought to heel by a remarkable English sea captain named Woodes Rogers who, in 1718, was appointed the first 'royal' governor of the Bahamas. Rogers was possibly the greatest governor the Bahamas has ever had.*

THE CHARTER OF THE LORDS PROPRIETORS was a very different document from William Sayle's **Articles and Orders**. Gone was any mention of treating the natives kindly or sharing of the workload. The tenor of this **Charter** was autocratic, militaristic, bellicose. It speaks of *'...whale, sturgeon and other "royal" fish'* and gives the Proprietors the right, *'...to make and execute laws upon the people...by penalty, imprisonment or death.'* And, unlike the republican status granted to the Adventurers, the **Charter** makes it clear that *'...all children born shall be denizens and Lieges to the King'* while the Proprietors are, *'...at pleasure to fortify, erect and pull down castles and...in case of rebellion...'* (after these bombastic clauses a likely event perhaps) *'...to proclaim martial law, either in the islands or on the sea.'* To its credit the **Charter** ends with a minor concession permitting the Proprietors or their representatives, *'...to grant indulgencies touching the liberty of conscience, etc.'*

With possibly only one or two exceptions the governors appointed by the Lords Proprietors were either a sorry bunch of incompetents or simply greedy and corrupt scoundrels. The first governor appointed to serve for the Lords Proprietors was to have been Hugh Wentworth but he died on his way to the Bahamas so his wayward brother John, a sea captain who, when a privateer, had captured Tortola from the Dutch, served in his stead. To the waterfront crowd John Wentworth was a kindred spirit.

By this time it was commonly reported that it was impossible to maintain law, order and morality in Charles Town since the ribald townsfolk were, quoting one account, used to living *'a lewd and licentious sort of life...'* Indeed a report reaching the lordly Proprietors in London suggested that Wentworth himself was their ringleader who, *'debauches himself and has corrupted the people to drink...and neglect their crops.'* No one has ever needed to be encouraged to drink in the Bahamas and farming was never a popular occupation but the Lords Proprietors allowed the charge to stand and John Wentworth, the first governor the Colony had ever known, was summarily dismissed.

A YEAR AFTER Neptuna and her daughter arrived in Charles Town news reached New Providence from Eleuthera that Captain Butler had died of the Spanish 'flux'. For the few people left at Harbour Island, this meant they had to find somewhere else to live since the isle and its 'immoveable' property had been forfeited to the Captain's many creditors. In fact the small island boasted little property, immoveable or movable. Captain Butler's house with a steep pitched roof and clap-boarding siding was still incomplete and the other smaller building of a similar type was as unfinished as when Neptuna had visited the cay. The remainder of dwellings were constructed of pine tree trunks with a raised platform for a floor and thatched with palmetto leaves that looked as if they would blow away in the first serious gale.

Joshua Elding who had faithfully served as Butler's boatman and sometime servant, inherited some of the irascible Captain's 'moveables' including the sailing skiff. But, even though Joshua could now claim to own, for the first time in his life, some capital in the form of possessions, for a black African finding somewhere to live in a strange country was a forbidding dilemma indeed. The worst of many problems for Africans in the 'new world' was the need to constantly prove that they were legally 'free'. Everywhere there would have been compelling physical evidence that most people of African descent were in bondage, a fact that could only have been both distressing and heart-rending.

So, because of circumstances over which he had no control, Joshua and his family were forced to move on. Joshua decided to go to Charles Town since he was quite familiar with the town and he remembered the sincere if brief friendship he had shared with Neptuna Downham who he had heard, was now a successful business woman in her own right. Also, of all the settlements in the Bahamas, it was Charles Town that had been considered important enough for the appointment of a resident governor. That meant that one day there might be law and order there and hopefully, justice too. Joshua sensed correctly that New Providence was about to eclipse Eleuthera to become the most important centre of commerce in the Colony.

With some trepidation Joshua Elding sailed with his African spouse, yet another 'exile' from Bermuda, and their young son Matthew to Charles

Town to begin a new life in a place where almost all the people sharing his African heritage were slaves.

Happily his worst fears were unfounded. Upon arrival in Charles Town, Neptuna and Esekiel Tarp helped Joshua find a shack near the harbour wharf and he soon commenced work. Relying on his woodworking skills, he offered his services to anyone needing a carpenter. Later he rented a larger lean-to structure and started a small business on the waterfront repairing boats. In course of time Joshua Elding earned the respected title of shipwright. His knowledge of woodwork and the ways of the sea soon meant that his services were much in demand. There were many orders for new vessels and a constant demand for the repair of old ones that had been damaged as a result of illegal commerce upon the high seas.

Joshua soon acquired a knowledge of the best woods to use for the various parts of a vessel. He soon knew where to find a heavy wood like horseflesh or dogwood with a natural crook for the keel, the frame ribs and knees. Local pine would be used for the masts and spars and the planking and deck would be finished in the highly prized Madeira (mahogany) wood. All the work would be cut with great precision with rudimentary two-handed saws. Seams would be caulked with local cotton or kapok from the silk cotton tree. Ropes could be made from local sisal and metal fittings would be supplied by a Charles Town blacksmith. Only the sails and tar for caulking would have to be imported. In efficiently providing an essential service to the maritime community Joshua's race and status as an 'African' never became an issue.

As soon as Matthew was old enough he too started work in the shipbuilding trade in Charles Town. Matthew Elding developed into a handsome youth. He had a finely sculpted face besides possessing an athletic physique inherited from his parents. His hair was jet black which he wore in long braids, inter-woven with a cotton fabric. And, like his father, he was widely acknowledged as an expert seaman. Over the years, with both perseverance and skill Joshua and Matthew built up a steady and profitable family business together.

In the small town Matthew was occasionally seen in the company of the fair young Elizabeth 'Bahama' Downham who often helped her mother at the tavern a few yards down the waterfront street from the small boat-builder's yard. Bahama could best be described as a pretty green-eyed tomboy even though her breasts were just asserting themselves. She had a strikingly beautiful face with golden hair which she wore in cascading curls but her demeanor belied her looks. She always stood pertly erect, often skipped and sometimes ran when it would have been more seemly to walk. And, most unladylike of all, she was fond of fixing things. Sometimes she found an outlet for her talents at the Eldings' boat repair yard and it was there she became acquainted with Matthew Elding. Unbeknown to the townsfolk, Bahama and Matthew spent almost all their free time in each other's company secretly going for long walks far away from public view.

Though they had much in common, the difference in their physical appearance and cultural background made them mutually inquisitive about each other. Added to this, the change brought about by adolescence awoke their latent sexuality.

When they were first alone they would shyly hold hands. Together they would explore the nearby pine barren then later they visited the deserted beaches to the west of the town and explored the old Indian caves that had first been discovered over 500 years before. It was on the western beach today known as Love Beach that they first coyly embraced.

Then one summer evening a few weeks later, they found themselves at the same beach shortly after the blazing sun had sunk below the horizon illuminating the sky in a collage of kaleidoscopic colours. Suddenly Bahama ran off to the next cove. Mystified as to why Bahama had disappeared so suddenly Matthew went to look for her and found her in the surf clad only in moonbeams. Splashing the water and beckoning with her arms she invited him to swim with her in the tepid surf.

Bahama teased, "...well Matthew, now let's see if you are brown all over!"

Matthew, peering through the moonlight countered shyly, "...well I can see you are certainly deliciously pink everywhere! Except...except for those buds on your err..." he stammered at the word, "...breasts...which, if my eyes deceive me not, are as brown as if they belonged to an African!"

In the lambent moonlight Matthew saw Bahama's nipples stiffen.

"Well perhaps they are trying to tell you something!" Bahama whispered.

It did not take long before their hands delicately explored the others' naked body in the pounding surf. After a while Matthew led Bahama by the hand to a small cove where they continued their tentative experiment with the novel and erotic functions of their bodies. Soon they experienced one simultaneous erotic explosion of passion followed by another.

Time raced by.

It was near 10 o'clock when they hurried back to town, each with an implausible excuse as to why they had been out so late.

It was not long before they were deeply in love.

Bahama had barely turned fifteen when, to the surprise of everyone, it was announced she was to be married. The surprise in the town was not so much her age as her choice of husband. The strong-willed Elizabeth Downham let it be known she wished to wed Matthew Elding. Neptuna, who was reminded of her own unhappy romantic experiences, soon acquiesced to the idea of the marriage of her young daughter fearing, needlessly as it turned out, that she might be 'with child'.

Even though in the 'new world' people of different races were for the first time starting to live in close proximity to each other, a marriage between a white female and a black African was entirely without precedent. Anywhere else the announcement might have created a dilemma but, in the devil-may-care atmosphere of Charles Town it was soon accepted as a unique but happy event. And, with the prospect of free ale and rum for all at *The Wheel of Fortune* to celebrate the marriage, not a soul in Charles Town demurred. Ever since Neptuna's first encounter with Joshua, the parents of the children had developed a friendship born of mutual trust and respect so the proximity of the two families in Charles Town brought perhaps, a predictable result.

After the banns had been declared, a solemn and simple marriage ceremony was performed by an itinerant Quaker elder who happened to be in Charles Town at the time. Just months before, the Quaker had been sentenced to death in Boston for his religious beliefs but then, after first being publicly whipped, his sentence was commuted and he was ordered to be transported to West Indies. He was more fortunate than some of his co-religionists. The Puritans in Massachusetts dubbed the Society of Friends '*notorious heretiques*' and several Quakers had been publicly whipped and *then* hanged.

The ship bound for the West Indies on which the Quaker was placed stopped at Nassau for a few days to take on supplies. While seeking any Quakers that might be in the town he was informed that there was '*no Godly minister*' to perform the rite of marriage between Matthew Elding and Elizabeth Downham. On hearing about the intended marriage the Quaker offered his services explaining that, "...we members of ye Society of Friends...believe in a personal God that speaketh directly to thee...there is therefore no need for priests or ministers to provide ye holy sacraments..." That was all Neptuna needed to hear for, from her experience, she had found Ministers of the Gospel to be little to her liking.

So, in his brief stay in Nassau, the Quaker performed the important task of pronouncing Matthew and Elizabeth, '*man and wife in the sight of God*' aided by Esekiel Tarp who served as guardian offering the bride's hand in marriage while the serving wenches from *The Wheel of Fortune* served as bridesmaids. Martha Tarp lent an impressive presence as the matron of honour.

As a memento of the marriage the visiting Quaker gave the bride and groom a hand-printed copy of the new English Bible acquired in Boston which version had been authorised by 'The Most High and Mighty Prince James, by the Grace of God, King of Great Britain, France and Ireland, Defender of the Faith, Etc.' - the venerable publication today better known as the King James Bible. The Bible would remain a prized possession of the Elding family for another eleven generations.

It may not have been necessary, but the Quaker elder slipped Biblical references into his homily at the marriage ceremony to illustrate that the idea of inter-racial marriages was hardly new: "...and in the Old Testament in ye Book of Numbers at chapter twelve verse one is not mention made of the great Israelitish leader Moses who took unto his bed a dark-skinned Ethiopian woman?...and remember how Miriam and Aaron spake against Moses and then Almighty God caused them to become as white as snow with leprosy...!" The congregation shuddered at the thought. Here was a ruling against racial prejudice from an unimpeachable source. The point made the Quaker continued, "...and now harken ye to the story of the Queen of Sheba as recounted in ye Old Testament..." and he reminded, at considerable length, his largely inebriated and growingly inattentive congregation about the dark-skinned queen from southern Arabia who visited the ancient land of Israel to test the wisdom of King Solomon.

After the service was over, the wedding party, which included almost everyone in Charles Town (though not the Quaker who considered strong spirits abhorrent), partied well into the night long after the newly wedded couple had slipped away on a sailing boat chasing the moonlight...

There was a further bond between the two families when, shortly after the marriage, Joshua and Neptuna entered into a business partnership and acquired two sloops to provide transport to the scattered Bahamian out island settlements. On one occasion their new business venture took them back to Eleuthera to work for a man named Richardson who had had a 'falling out' with his companions and had gone 'to live in the cave where they (the Adventurers) did formerly go to service'. Richardson had had the good fortune to discover a fully laden Spanish wreck on James Man's Island near to Preacher's Cave and urgently needed the services of a salvage sloop. Richardson, together with Joshua and Matthew, recovered £2,500 from the wreck that they divided up at Governor's Bay with *'a great deal of wrangling'*. But, with the dowry Bahama brought to the marriage and now the bounty from the wreck, the younger Eldings were now rich beyond their wildest expectations.

In 1672 the first entry in the new family Bible recorded that a son, Read Morgan Elding, had been born to Elizabeth and Matthew. The middle name was suggested by Neptuna and was, people privately but correctly speculated, the name of her former lover. Young Read displayed the best attributes of both parents. He carried himself well, was of athletic build and was exceptionally handsome with hazel-coloured eyes inherited from his mother. Charming and intelligent he also had that indecipherable charismatic attribute that suggested leadership qualities. Throughout his childhood Read Elding was never far from the sea. He could always be found on the waterfront and by age seven could handle a sailing skiff like an old salt. At age twelve, Read went to sea with the family business.

Bahama too, found time to learn her sea craft on the small sloops owned by the family enterprise which plied between the islands. The families grew in wealth and prestige. In fact when only in his early twenties, as the son of well-to-do and respected ship-owner parents, Read Elding was appointed to the Government Council which sat in Charles Town. The Council was headed by Nicholas Webb who was but one of many self-serving administrators appointed by the Lords Proprietors to enjoy absolute and tyrannical power in the Colony.

By now a major preoccupation of the Bahamas was wrecking. Often the wrecker was the cause of a shipwreck and the wrecker was invariably nearby and prepared for action as the vessel broke up against the rocks. Under the loose interpretation of maritime law a ship in distress which foundered, belonged (together with the ship's contents of course) to the finder. In fairness it might be noted that sometimes the wreckers made heroic rescues of the passengers of a sinking vessel though a handsome reward for their 'services' was expected. A naïve visitor to the Bahamas recorded for posterity a first hand conversation he had with a wrecker who was part of a fleet of forty boats that patrolled the Florida shore. The visitor questioned:

'Forty sail? Then certainly you must have had many opportunities of being essentially serviceable to vessels passing the Gulf Stream, by directing them to keep off places of danger, with which you made your business to be acquainted?'

The wrecker replied laconically, 'Not much of that - they went generally by night.'

'But then you might have afforded them timely notice, by making beacons on shore, or showing your lights?'

The wrecker laughingly replied, 'no, we always put them out for better chance by night.'

The shocked visitor responded, 'but would there not have been more humanity in showing them their danger?'

To which the wrecker retorted, 'we did not go there for humanity: we went for racking!'

Most of the wrecks in the Bahamas up to this time were Spanish and, if the position of the wreck were known, the Spanish would send their own crews to salvage the vessels. When this happened the Bahamian wreckers generally drove the Spaniards away and, on occasion, even made them give up what they had already salvaged. It was contributory factor to a grave and looming crisis involving two powerful rival maritime nations.

During this period Charles Town and smaller settlements were expanding all over the Bahamas, while at the same time, the islands were also becoming a haven for a different sort of inhabitant, the pirate or, when he was engaged in fighting the enemies of the Crown, he would claim the term 'privateer'. There were rich rewards for these fearless and unscrupulous seamen who sailed under the 'Banner of King Death'. The Spanish treasure fleets continued to sail through or near the Bahama Islands on the return trip to Spain and it was not too difficult to 'surprise' an over laden straggler in a convoy. From many a crow's nest a cry would alert the expectant pirate crew below:

"Avast! Lookee! Off the port bow, flying Spanish colours...a caravel...prepare to attack!"

After this cry the skull and crossbones would be hoisted and the pirate ship would close in. Generally the attacker would try to approach its prey from astern, or at least from where the Spanish ship could not use its long-range guns to advantage. Often the pirate ship, by expert seamanship and a burst of speed, would draw near its quarry and, with gunwales open, would open fire. Then, once the withering cannon fusillade from the pirate ship had found its mark, it would draw close enough so that grappling hooks could be thrown onto its victim's deck. Finally the cut-throat boarding party would leap aboard and commence their grisly work. Few people were spared for if they ever reached shore they would be sure to give damning evidence against the pirates.

If the disabled ship was not severely damaged it might be towed away as a 'prize'. The treasure would then be shared among the crew at a remote anchorage where the men would go on an extended binge. Port Royal, Jamaica was a favourite haunt of the pirates where rum was drunk, women were bedded and skulls were cracked. It came as no real surprise when an earthquake totally destroyed Port Royal in 1692. It was as if the Almighty had discovered in the new world yet another Sodom and Gomorrah.

The English government around this time was alternately at peace and at war with Spain and its policy vacillated between encouraging the privateers to harry Spanish shipping, followed by instructions to governors and the Royal Navy to suppress piracy. Acting on the latter instruction during a quiet interlude around 1682, Thomas Paine in the *Pearle*, a ship of eight guns and sixty men, received a commission from the governor of Jamaica to take pirates *'at the island of Bahama which is desert and uninhabited'.*

At the western end of Grand Bahama, Paine met with a few spirited ship's captains who were planning to dive for silver 'out of a Spanish wreck which lies about fourteen leagues from the island'. It was very likely the wreck of the sunken Spanish treasure ship *Santa Maria de la Maravilla.* At all events Paine was lured by the prospect of treasure and joined with the 'pirates' into what a contemporary report darkly called a 'confederacy.'

Paine had evidently chosen to ignore the instructions of the Royal Governor to apprehend pirates, and the following year it was reported that he was in Barbados seeking pilots to work the wreck 'without the limits of the Bahama islands'. But the sea did not readily yield its treasure. Paine and his men worked with six boats at the wreck site *'with thirty of the best divers available and six good drudges (dredges?) but had shared but seven and one half pounds of plate (silver) a man…'* They were reluctant to give up however, and reported that they *'…left six sails there* (north of Grand Bahama) *but considered their prospects poor'.*

Presumably, because the salvage operations were going so badly, Paine and the other ships' captains decided to sail under false colours to sack some Spanish settlements around St Augustine on the eastern Florida coast. For the Spanish this was the final straw and the Bahamas was shortly to receive a sharp rebuke. In January 1684 a small Spanish fleet from Havana sailed to the Bahamas to appear one morning off the north side of Charles Town on New Providence Island.

The inhabitants of the town were greatly alarmed by the hostile force about to invade their city. A few inaccurately aimed cannon balls arched overhead and landed harmlessly in the hillside cemetery instilling fear into the populace. But then as the first Spanish galleon crossed the bar outright panic erupted in the city. Men and women, black and white, slave and free, started to run inland. Some grabbed at their few belongings, their money, and more indiscriminately for other objects at hand: a silver tankard, a prayer book, a musket, a blanket or a memento or two. A few tried to utilize carts to carry more of their worldly goods but in the urgency of the moment soon discarded them. Some men carried invalided family members on their backs. Some loyal blacks helped their masters carry more of their valuables though after some time they jettisoned most of their load and joined the others disappearing southwards in a cloud of dust.

Robert Lilburne the governor of the day, was among the first rank of people running for their lives. He had been totally unprepared for the

Spanish attack and had been carousing at *The Wheel of Fortune* when the first cannon balls whistled overhead. Without a thought for his duty as the leader of the community he was the first to leave the inn. Neptuna and the Eldings on the other hand reluctantly left their properties' at the last moment and, trying to catch up with the other townsfolk, also raced toward the Blue Hills to seek sanctuary in the pine forest. Among the last to leave they were lucky to escape with their lives. Some were not so fortunate, a visitor to the Bahamas thirty years later reported that the Spanish *'carried off...half of the Blacks...*(and) *in October they came again and picked up most of the remainder of the Negroes'*. By this time most of the white inhabitants had already deserted the colony.

Robert Clark, the hapless former governor of the Colony and a few other foolhardy men put up a token defence near the harbour. The defenders were soon put to the sword but Clark's attire marked him as a gentleman of rank. He was quickly surrounded and captured by Spanish soldiers and, when his station in life was revealed, was turned over to a captain who had some bitter memories of English buccaneers. Clark refused to beg for his life and instead poured out his contempt for his captors. In a rage the Spanish captain declared that he would show him no mercy. He shouted for kindling to be brought and he had an iron rod that served as a spit set up in the town square. Then with Clark chained to an iron rod he ordered him to be roasted alive over the fire. As the flames rose, his piercing screams caused some of the younger Spanish soldiers to reel away in horror. The captain however, with arms folded seemed to relish the spectacle. In less than hour most of Clark's body had been consumed by the flames. The pyre was then left to smolder as witness to the unspeakably ghastly act. The appalling barbarity of the deed perhaps demonstrates some small measure of the hatred the Spanish held for Bahamian pirates and those who supported them.

The Spanish captain now gave orders to his men to totally destroy Charles Town that had been captured after only this one brief skirmish. The Spanish sank all the ships in the harbour and then ransacked the town after which they set fire to the buildings starting at the eastern gate. The Spanish first put the torch to the Governor's residence, the hated Protestant churches, and then all the houses and businesses including the tavern and shipwright's shop. In all the Spanish made off with goods and silver to the value of £20,000 in cash - a prodigious sum in those days considering the small size of the community.

As they clambered towards the summit of the Blue Hills south of the town, the fleeing townsfolk could see the Charles Town burning in the distance. The townsfolk were fortunate indeed the Spanish did not pursue them into the woods. Instead the Spanish military returned to their ships and turned their attention to the settlements of Eleuthera. There they completely burned down the settlements of Spanish Wells, Harbour Island and Governors Bay. The latter settlement has not been re-built to this day. As at Charles Town, the inhabitants sought refuge in the bush hiding some of their vessels in small creeks in the mangrove thickets. After the Spanish left, many of the dispossessed settlers took to their ships and, ill-prepared for a long journey, headed north. In August that same year the people of Boston, Massachusetts generously took up collections to aid *'fifty persons, Men, Women and Children, which were, by the cruelty of the Spaniards, beaten off from Eleatheria'* and, who had arrived in New England so it was reported, *'naked and in great distress'*. The refugees were settled in the township of North Yarmouth on Casco Bay near Portland, Maine.

Almost no buildings were erected in New Providence for two years after the raid. The Eldings went to live in Exuma during this period and one of the Elding's ships carried Neptuna back to Bermuda. There, she received a formal pardon for her youthful indiscretion and, as a wealthy widow, made a good match by marrying a rich widower, Thomas Plummer. Neptuna died in her sixties, a colourful, yet much respected citizen of Bermuda. As a postscript to her death, the Bermudan records show that her ever-combative daughter Elizabeth 'Bahama' Elding tried, unsuccessfully, to sue the executors of the Plummer estate in Bermuda for alleged fraud.

Meanwhile from hideaways in the Bahamas, pirates continued to carry out attacks on Spanish ships and the residents of the islands soon resorted once again to wrecking. It is not difficult to understand the appeal of salvaging a wreck especially if she was Spanish. In 1687 a wrecked Spanish vessel in the southern Bahamas yielded treasure, mostly silver, weighing 26 tons! Lord Albemarle who financed the expedition received £90,000 and William Phipps, the captain of the expedition, was knighted and later made Governor of the Colony of Massachusetts. Little of the wealth however, filtered back to the scattered communities of the Bahamas.

Finally, the rebuilding of Charles Town recommenced. Many other former residents returned and the re-building of the community was further aided by other settlers who moved to Charles Town from Jamaica. The Eldings came back from their hideaway in Exuma and reconstructed the *Wheel of Fortune* tavern on the water-front next to an enlarged boat yard which was now run by Matthew and Read incorporating what was left of the shipwright's shop.

But Bahama soon got bored with her sedentary life even though she was now very well established as part owner of a busy shipping company besides being the proprietor of a profitable tavern. The call of the sea was in her blood and she felt she had a score to settle with the Spaniards. In the tavern she heard daily of the easy fortunes that were to be made in wrecking so she persuaded her husband Matthew to get directly involved 'in the trade'. With money from the tavern they purchased a new ship made in New England. She was a two-masted brigantine, with a square-rigged fore-mast and fore and aft mainsails and square main top sails. She was rigged and armed with cannon specifically for their new venture and was named - predictably perhaps - the *Wheel of Fortune.* Bahama and Matthew signed on a crew of competent sailors with a sprinkling of unemployed cut-throats and ne'er-do-wells that hung around the waterfront.

Sometimes Matthew and Bahama sailed together but more often than not they sailed in separate ships and on different missions. With the acquisition of the new vessel Bahama became a changed person. She pursued her new role with a determination that distressed her husband Matthew and embarrassed her son, Read. It might seem that a female master of a vessel would be repugnant to the *macho* rough-and-ready state of affairs aboard ship. But Bahama was but one of several females, Mary Read and Anne Bonny being others, who captained ships at this time and managed to keep the loyalty of their male crews.

The story goes that early in their piratical career Anne Bonny and Mary Read were on the same ship and nearly became sexually entangled until one of them bared her bosom to the amazement (and presumably amusement) of the other. It was the free spirit of these women that Bahama admired though unlike them, she was also able to preserve her chastity. This was due in part to the fact that all the hands who served with her were made to swear an oath of loyalty to their Captain whose 'private Person was to be inviolate' and doubtless the presence of her son Read Elding, a highly respected member of Council in the home port of Charles Town also had a moderating effect on their behaviour.

Bahama soon found that wrecking was too uncertain a trade. Months would go by without a wreck despite the dousing or posting of misleading navigation lights. So she again persuaded Matthew to become more directly involved in the 'wrecking' business. When the ruse of erecting misleading navigation lights failed to have the desired effect, they would board and search foreign vessels invoking the name of the Crown and charge a 'fee' for their service.

But when the business of wrecking did not bring the expected rewards, Bahama turned the *Wheel of Fortune* into an veritable pirate ship and, against the wishes of both husband and son, entered the 'old trade' to become for a time, the scourge of the Old Bahama Channel - the strait that divides Cuba from the southwestern Bahamas.

"Wi' a name like that," went the *braggadocio* of her crew, "...our capt'n owns the Old Channel!"

Using Long Cay (called in these days 'Fortune Island' with good reason) near Crooked Island as a base, 'Captain Bahama' boarded private merchantmen and even stragglers from Spanish convoys and, on one occasion, even brought a 'prize' to Charles Town. The 'prize' was a converted leaky old caravel that had been transporting some recent Spanish immigrants from Cuba to Puerto Rico. The passengers were relieved of their valuables but as a 'prize' it did not amount to much. Her husband expressed his displeasure at her action but inwardly could only admire her daring. Her son Read, on the other hand, who was charged with enforcing the orders of the Government Council of the Colony, was outraged. Read Elding arranged to have the 'prize' returned to its rightful owners in Havana by the colonial government with a devious diplomatic note to the effect that the ship had been "intercepted and saved from being wracked by ye boisterous sea and ye cruelle rocks(!)"

The presence of the *Wheel of Fortune* in the Old Bahama Channel was especially dangerous at this time since the strait had been declared as part of territorial waters by Spain. Nevertheless Bahama continued to patrol the Channel but almost all the sea borne traffic consisted of Spanish coastal vessels of little commercial value. Most of the important sea traffic between the Greater Antilles sensibly stayed close to the south shore of the larger Spanish islands or moved in great convoys attended by well armed men o' war. Occasionally the Spanish would send *Guarda Costas* gun ships to clear the Old Bahama Channel for the passage of small coastal convoys.

One day while on patrol near Diamond Point, the narrowest point of the Old Bahama Channel, the lookout from the *Wheel of Fortune* spied what looked like a straggler from a Spanish convoy. In fact it was a decrepit transport ship being used as a decoy. Shortly after the brigantine began to close in on the decoy, two Spanish coast guard vessels fore and aft of the *Wheel of Fortune* made a sudden appearance. The Spanish ships had been concealed among the cays lying off the Cuban mainland. Bahama realized at once she was about to be trapped in a vice and, faced with a decision as to whether to fight or run, true to her character, she chose to fight.

The brigantine with a following wind, headed for the downwind Spanish coastguard ship. Bahama chose this tactic because the Spanish ship would find it difficult to maneuver into the wind. With the assistance of a favourable wind the *Wheel of Fortune* under full sail sped towards the coast guard ship in the hope that she could ram her. But the Spanish ship held its position and turned head-on into the wind offering the smallest target.

As the *Wheel of Fortune* came within range, the coast guard ship quickly turned broadside to display its serried rows of cannon. The brigantine immediately matched the maneuver. But the Spaniard was able to fire off the first salvo. The spray shot raked the deck of the brigantine critically injuring two gunners. The *Wheel of Fortune* returned fire hitting the Spanish ship's rigging and then the cannons of both ships roared a continuous barrage at each other. At first the *Wheel of Fortune* got the better of the exchange but the Spanish ship boasted better armament and its broadsides started to inflict heavy damage to the upper deck of the *Wheel of Fortune.*

To make matters worse for Bahama and her crew, the other coast guard ship moved into position to engage the brigantine. With fire now coming from a different quarter, the sails of the *Wheel of Fortune* were shredded making Bahama's ship effectively immobile. After this several cannon balls hit the brigantine at the waterline causing water to flood into the vessel. Bahama stayed at the helm and shouted words of encouragement to the crew. But soon the *Wheel of Fortune* was listing so badly she was unable to fire. Then, she started to sink. Some of the crew escaped into the water and were picked up by the Spaniards to face almost certain execution. Slowly, silently the brigantine started to disappear below the surface of the water, for a moment a female figure was vaguely visible in the forecastle that was awash then, suddenly, the boat listed further dispatching the green-eyed terror of the Spanish Main to a watery grave.

It was inevitable perhaps, but in the high stakes game of piracy on the high seas, the *Wheel of Fortune* was sunk within only a year of flying the skull and crossbones. Bahama had outlived her mother Neptuna by only a few years. Elizabeth 'Bahama' Elding died in 1699, her 40th year.

AFTER JOHN WENTWORTH ineffectual governors came and went. Some wanted the Bahamas to be put under the protection of Jamaica. Others favoured Bermuda. But neither island really wanted the problem of administering so unruly a place and it is very doubtful they could have afforded the cost in any case.

In July 1688 a colourful Welsh governor by the name of 'Colonel' Cadwallader Jones arrived in the Colony. In no time at all he seems to have set himself up as a petty dictator, often imprisoning people without trial. It was said of him that he *'highly caressed those Pirates that came to Providence'*, indeed it was further reported that he, *'gave commissions to Pirates without and contrary to the advice of Council'*. Also, *'...he wilfully neglected to call a General Assembly till six months after the Time appointed by the Lords Proprietors' Instructions'*. One man that Jones brought to trial complained that the jury had been rigged with *'six pirates, three "strangers", two drunken sotts and a person arrained for buggary...'*

After many such incidents a minor 'rebellion' ensued and Jones was clapped into irons and put in prison but a month later an *'ignorant, seditious rabble...'* (who were clearly kindred spirits of Jones), *'...with force of arms rescued the governor and restored him again to the exercise of his despotic power...'*

Jones was finally relieved of his position by the Proprietors but such was the popularity of the rascally 'Colonel' that after the appointment of Nicholas Trott as the new governor, Trott found it 'expedient' to re-appoint Jones to a position of authority as a member of the Council.

Nassau (as Charles Town was now called) was taking on some of the characteristics of a thriving port city. One visitor described the community as having 160 houses, a church, governor's mansion and a fort at its centre forming a square. The visitor wrote, *'The Harbour of Nassau is formed by Hog Island'* (purchased by Governor Trott for £50) *'and runs parallel'* (to the town) *for five miles in length, lying east and west. At the entrance to the harbour is a bar over which no ship of 500 ton can pass; but within the bar, the Navy Royal of England might safely ride...'*

Towards the end of the seventeenth century the Bahamas was a veritable hornet's nest of piracy. The notorious corsair Henry Avery, after a successful engagement in the Indian Ocean that netted 100,000 pieces of eight and a similar number of Venetian chequeens, arrived at Royal Island north of Eleuthera. He requested of Governor Trott permission to take on provisions and water in Nassau. The governor was in no state to refuse, indeed there was a wild rumour that the French had just captured Exuma and were moving towards Nassau. It seemed prudent to the governor to have the additional force of arms to defend the country so Trott invited the pirates to dock at the capital city. The report of the French incursion - fortunately for the Bahamas - proved to be false.

Once in Nassau the pirates divided the spoils in a noisy brawl at the *Wheel of Fortune* and then slipped off to the mainland colonies. Avery bought a ship, the *Seaflower*, and sailed off to Boston with only £500 in cash but with all of the jewels. From there he went to Bristol and settled in Devon under a false name. When he died he was deeply in debt, still waiting to be paid for the jewels he had left with dishonest Bristol merchants. Trott supposedly did well, for he was reputed to have accepted twenty pieces of eight for each pirate who landed at Nassau! Needless to say when this news of this reached England, Governor Trott was also dismissed by the Lords Proprietors.

After Trott, the next governor to be appointed was Nicholas Webb who gave Read Elding, a member of Council, a commission and five ships to capture a 'rover' named Kelly, a notorious pirate. But Kelly evaded him and disappeared among the many islands of the Bahamas. Later Governor Webb made a hollow attempt to pass a law against piracy in the Assembly in 1699. But the new governor's credentials were questioned by many both in the Bahamas and abroad. The Governor of Boston suggested that Webb, '*...trod in the footsteps of his predecessor*' (Nicholas Trott), '*...who, if common fame lies not extremely, is the greatest pirate-broker that ever was in America*'. It was commonly believed that Trott's zeal in pursuing pirates was to line his own pockets and had nothing to do with ridding the islands of the scourge of piracy.

Webb resigned his position later this same year and departed for Delaware with all his worldly goods worth £8,000. But, the victim of incredible irony, in his aptly named ship *Sweepstakes,* he was captured by pirates on the high seas and lost all his worldly possessions and, at the shock of the encounter, his sanity too.

Before leaving, Webb had appointed Read Elding as his deputy with a commission to continue to apprehend pirates operating in the Bahamas. It is sad to recall that neither Neptuna nor Bahama were to see Read elevated to the position of acting-governor of the island country they loved so well. Matthew, now well on in years, could at least be proud of the elevation of his son to the supreme political post in the small colony. Matthew lived a secluded life as a widower but remained with the shipping company that by this time had turned its back on nefarious adventures on the high seas. Matthew outlived his wife by eighteen years.

Read Elding's second foray into the apprehension of pirates was confusing to say the least. On this mission he captured the *Bahama Merchant* that he asserted had been abandoned and so he claimed her as a 'prize'. For a short while Elding basked in the praise of his fellow citizens then, some time afterwards, the crew and owner of the *Bahama Merchant* unexpectedly arrived in Nassau. The owner claimed the master of the vessel had to '*quit his vessel to shift for his life*' when Elding appeared in command of three ships. But, whatever the truth of the matter, Read Elding was later to redeem himself by capturing some undoubted pirates.

Read Elding in fact proved himself to be the best law enforcer of all the governors and council members of the colony up until this time. In a short space of time he captured five pirates: Frederic Phillips, Ounca Guicas, John Floyd, John Valentin and Hendrik van Hoven (alias Hynde) the latter, one of the most notorious and vicious pirates of his day in the West Indies.

When the prisoners were brought before the Bench in Nassau the whole town turned out for what promised to be the greatest trial in the history of the Bahamas. From the sparse records that exist the trial must have been something of a melodramatic tragi-comedy.

On the appointed day the shackled pirates were dragged to the witness stand where Judge Taliaferro presided. Charges were read and the case, after many interruptions from all assembled, was heard.

"How d'ye plead?" the bewigged judge demanded.

Valentin held up his hand and said, "An't please your Worship 'not guilty' with an hexplanation your 'onour."

The crowd giggled.

Philips spat, Floyd and Guicas folded their arms and appeared disinterested in the proceedings while van Hoven fired: "This Court has no right to try me! I am a Hollander...a pox on this Court!"

A bailiff made to restrain van Hoven but the judge held up his hand.

'Stay your hand bailiff, we will hear him out!'

"...'tis true I have plundered many ships but I am mindful always to ensure they fly Spanish colours. My small country of Holland has suffered greatly at the hands of the Spanish cur..." The Dutch had long memories, fifty years previously, after a vicious uprising the Spanish had reluctantly recognised the independence of the United Provinces of the Netherlands.

'D'y hear how the pirate prates!' the Attorney General exclaimed, "what say ye then...have ye committed acts of piracy on the High Seas sailing under the colours of a bloody flag?"

"...and somewhile wi' no flag at all! And if ye mean, Sirraah, 'ave I slit the throat of many a Spanish dog?'- the answer is 'aye'!"

There was hearty laughter in Court at van Hoven's brazen declaration.

"Silence in Court!" the Bailiff intoned.

The trial dragged on for an hour or more, finally the Judge rose from his seat and for a moment, peered intently at each of the defendants, then sat down to offer his judgement. This action was a cue for the Clerk of the Court to place a black kerchief on the Judge's wig and then, with his gaze firmly fixed upon the face of van Hoven, the Judge announced his verdict:

"You have indulg'd in unlawful ways of living, and having no feare of God before your eyes, nor any regard for your oaths of allegiance to your Sovereign, nor to the performance of loyalty, truth and justice, but being instigated and deluded by the devil. Accordingly by the power invest'd in this Court and with the full Authoritie of the English Crown with jurisdiction concerning maritime Matters as they pertaine to this Colonie in and over ye Bahama Islands we now pass judgement. From your own Testimonie We find ye have sailed as a common Pyrate and robber on the High Seas...and accordingly...ye are found Guilty!...ye shall forthwith be taken to the Place of execution and hang'd by the neck until ye are dead! May God have mercy on your soul!"

The townspeople were unbelieving at the verdict. They had often seen trials of pirates and their like before but always the defendant had been set free on some finer point of law. They considered this judgment a preposterous turn of events and let the Judge know their feelings. A near riot ensued in the crowded Courtroom.

Read Elding, who had not been in Court during the proceedings, knew the townsfolk well. He had expected such an outburst and quickly dispatched ten constables to clear the building.

Three times more the Judge Tagliafero repeated the death sentence,

"...be hang'd by the neck until ye are dead! May God have mercy on your soul!"

The pirates took the news nonchalantly. Only Valentin was set free. His 'hexplanation' was based on his ignorance of the fact that England and Spain were at peace when he attacked a Spanish ship. He elucidated, "Your 'Onour, at the time I was not aware that no 'ostilities agin the Spanish was in heffect..." The judge hesitantly accepted his argument. Valentin looked sheepishly at the other pirates then rapidly left the Court never to be seen in the Bahamas again.

As he was being lead out of Court Philips shouted, "Pray, m'Lord, at least let us face a firing squad for we have served our nation as well as ourselves!"

"Now harkee! Be ye contente ye are not sentenced to be hanged, drawn and quartered for your wicked evil crimes!" Judge Tagliafero countered. "The Court will now adjourn!"

The Judge allowed the pirates six days to make their peace with God; then the four were publicly hanged on a gibbet in Nassau on October 30, 1699.

Some bystanders at the execution heard van Hoven utter the words, "...treasure ship can be found...at reef...south...Bahama..." as he was being strung up but the rope tightened around his neck smothering all further sound to a stiffled gurgle. It was some time before the unhappy pirates drew their last breath as they writhed and twitched in their last agonies.

Their bodies were allowed to sway in the breeze for three days as a deadly warning to Bahamians of similar propensities.

About an hour after this grisly diversion, the spectators drifted down to *The Wheel of Fortune* and discussed the hangings, piracy in general and the last words of van Hoven in particular.

"'Twere a sin for him to die and not tell where the treasure is to be found!" grumbled one.

"Why din't he mek a chart?" a one-eyed rogue asked of his tankard of rum.

There was a momentary silence as they considered the injustice of it all until someone added philosophically,

"...on'y he and 'is Maker know where it is and 'is Maker don' need it an' the Dutchman can't git it!"

A 'reef in the southern Bahamas' they declared could mean almost anywhere in an area of 50,000 or so square miles! It was a pity they were by this time drinking heavily and did not analyse the words more carefully. Two centuries later the words were to prove a surprisingly accurate geographical description as to where treasure would be found.

AFTER THE INTERIM STEWARDSHIP of Read Elding, Captain Elias Haskett was appointed governor of the Bahamas in 1701. He was little different from most of his predecessors. Commentators of this era did not mince words. His rule was described as 'arbitrary and tyrannical'. He was accused of taking bribes, levying illegal taxes and appropriating the property of the Crown. He even charged popular individuals like Elding with piracy - a backhanded form of hypocrisy to be sure - imprisoned them and then offered them their freedom for money.

A friend of Read Elding offered £50 for his release from prison but was told by the governor with astounding exactitude that the figure for his release was to be £67 and 10 shillings, *'as well as a rich ring and a piece of plate of value, a silver tankard, some drops of dry goods, a set of gold buttons and three gold drops'*. Read Elding forbade the debt to be paid and languished a full month in jail until an armed mob freed him. The mob was incited into a popular uprising against the governor and, together with Elding and some other prominent citizens, marched on the governor's residence and pointed pistols at the governor warning him to change his ways. Governor Haskett came out of his residence to confront the mob and brushed one pistol aside which then discharged wounding one of the demonstrators. At that a contemporary account reported that in the *mêlée* that followed the Speaker of the House stepped forward and *'broke His Excellency's head with the butt end of his pistol'* - a slight exaggeration perhaps but fatal at least to his reputation. Governor Haskett was arrested, put in chains and sent in a small ketch to New York to answer charges of unscrupulous behaviour and mismanagement. The governor counter-sued the leading Bahamians accusing them of treason and piracy. But Haskett's past as an undischarged bankrupt caught up with him and he disappeared from history without a trace.

A new governor of the Bahama Islands was appointed but before he arrived at the rebuilt settlement, a combined French and Spanish force attacked Nassau and once again it was razed to the ground. Guns were spiked and many men were put to the sword and about eighty persons, including the acting-governor, were carried off to Havana. The Spanish, realizing that the Bahama Islands were again becoming a haven for pirates, returned twice more in the next few years to complete the devastation. The Elding family once again escaped, this time finding refuge in Bermuda.

It was in Bermuda that Read Elding now 35 years old, married Esther, an Anglican clergyman's daughter ten years his junior. Read had remained unmarried mainly because of the dearth of marriageable females in Charles Town where he had spent most of his life. In this age his bride was also old in years to be embarking on marriage for the first time but Esther was a devout and practicing Christian and was happy to find Read, a respected gentleman, who was also a member of the established church. Esther was a handsome and resolute woman with a mission to save the world from pirates, pagans and Puritans. From her union with Read, a son William was born, the mother's religiosity patently apparent by naming her son after the religious reformer and first translator of the Bible into English. The birth, in elegant script, was the third entry in the family Bible:

William John Wycliffe Elding born to Esther and Read Elding Esq. in ye Parish of Paget and Christened in ye Churche of Sainte Peter in Ste George's,

Sommers Island (a former name of Bermuda) *on ye 7th day of April in ye Year of Our Lord 1708.*

William grew up to be a very different in character from his father. From an early age he expressed a great distaste for a life at sea. Even when very young he was acutely aware of his grandmother's illegal adventures at sea which ended in her early death and also the knowledge that his father had been responsible for committing several men to be hanged greatly concerned him. Then there was the incident of the capture of the *Bahama Merchant* that had not been sufficiently well explained to appear credible to the young man. And, as a constant reminder of the perils of the sea, the not uncommon sight of pirates hanging on gibbets horrified him.

When he became of age William announced: "Father I wish to make a break with the past. The Bible teaches that "'all who take the sword will perish by the sword'...and...and I have decided I want no part in war or fighting!"

His father tried to reason with him. "Sometimes force is necessary merely to survive and in any case who will defend us against the evildoers?"

William did not offer a reply but had already made up his mind to break with family tradition and not to go to sea. In this position he was quietly supported by his mother and more vociferously by his new wife Miriam, a zealous Puritan. Though there was some agreement on this particular matter, family differences over religion between Miriam and her Anglican mother-in-law were a constant threat to familial harmony that were largely evaded by their avoiding each other's company on the Sabbath Day. Despite having been christened in the established church William followed his fractious wife's lead and entered the Puritan persuasion.

The smallest incident could engender family discord. Shortly after their simple Puritan wedding the newly married couple were invited to dine with Read, Esther and old Captain Sayle, the former governor of Bermuda and initiator of the Eleutheran 'utopian' dream. Miriam arrived dressed in a severe grey smock, her hair rolled into a bun and hidden under a plain bonnet. Uncomfortable in a household where some were members of the despised established church, her demeanor suggested that of a frightened sparrow. William hovered around her and tried, without much success, to make her feel at home in his parent's home. But, despite William's efforts, Miriam was largely left out of the boisterous conversation that centered on the unruly politics of the new world colonies.

Immediately before the meal was served a set prayer of thanksgiving was recited and Esther made a sign of the cross. The gesture distressed Miriam and she made momentary eye contact with William.

When the meal was served Miriam only picked at her food and brusquely refused to take wine when it was offered. However, as the meal progressed the conversation became tolerably cordial.

In these times the movements of ships was always an important topic of conversation. The two captains discussed the ships that had recently called at Bermuda. On that very day two ships had arrived in the harbour, one from Virginia on its way to England, the other *en route* from the West Indies to New York. From the Dutch ship bound for New York, Read Elding was informed that she had called briefly in the Bahamas and had news about the state of the island colony.

The ship bound for Virginia elicited Captain Sayle to reminisce about the legendary John Smith who invariably called at Bermuda in the past, on his way to Virginia.

"'Aye, I wish I had time to visit your new colony at Eleutheria', the venerable John Smith told me, 'it is important we establish plantations, and of course fortified settlements, in ye Caribees. A small island like England must expand overseas if we are to keep the Spanish at bay and extend our commerce'...And I also recall the good Captain had many ideas of how to treat with the salvages. Did you know he visited Dominica and traded with the man-eating *salvages* of that isle? Aye, he stayed there three weeks and had many stories to tell. On his way from the Caribees to Virginia he told me he saw the Lucayos Isles, as he called them, but they did not tarry as they did not want to encounter any more *salvages*. I informed him that hitherto we have no news of any Indians now being in the Bahamas...I remember he said it was probably just as well..."

Captain Sayle lit a clay pipe while the assembled guests continued to converse about the legendary Captain Smith and that led onto a discussion about the former Indian inhabitants of the Bahamas and the rumours of their being sighted in the out islands from time to time. Sayle then offered a description of his first meeting with Smith.

"Aye, I first met that valiant soldier many years ago in a coffee house in London," he recalled, "a vigorous man...energetic, opinionated and tough, very tough. But not at all impressive to look at...he was very short I remember, and had a rounded, unkempt beard like a yeoman."

His audience was interested to hear first-hand about a famous man of the Elizabethan Age. Even to the younger generation, John Smith - for all his faults - was a heroic figure. As to his exploits or *'performances'* as they were called, one commentator admitted, *'laid at a distance they are cheaper credited than confuted'*. But for all that John Smith was generally acknowledged as *'bookman, penman, swordsman, diplomat, courtier, orator...'* to which list of attributes could certainly be added: *'imperialist'*.

Captain Sayle continued his narrative: "...Aye...John Smith lived an incredible life. He fought with the French against Spain. Then fought with the insurgents against the Spanish in the Netherlands. He had been a mercenary in the most brutal years of the German wars, a heroic defender of Hungary against the Muslim invasion, had been captured and endured torture in a Turkish dungeon, escaped to Morocco, visited Spain and even travelled to Moscovy. Great God...what a life!"

An interesting life indeed but, above all for the present company perhaps, he was the most famous of all the colonists of English America. Even Miriam was fascinated by Captain Sayle's narrative yet disturbed that a man who professed to be a non-conformist Christian would use the name of God in vain, but she let it pass. At the dinner table Captain Sayle further captivated his audience explaining how he had first met Smith when he was a young man in Bermuda and they discussed his idea for the colonisation of the Bahamas.

"And now *I* have a piece of news," Read Elding announced, "...I received some important information from the captain of the Dutch ship in the harbour today..." The visitors urged him to continue, "...I heard that a new English governor has been appointed and is already on his way to Nassau. I am sure you will agree with me that with a new governor in office the time is now opportune for the family to return to our Bahama homeland!" and, slapping his hand on the tabletop exclaimed: "Zounds! it is important that we lay claim to our property that was destroyed by those rascally bloody Spaniards!"

The derivation of the expletive 'bloody' is obscure and may derive from the impious expression: 'Blood of Our Lady' which was bad enough, but the word 'Zounds' was altogether too much for Miriam since the word was understood to be a sacrilegious contraction of 'God's wounds'. On hearing the words Miriam stiffened and, clearly distressed, cried,

"Father-in-law you have uttered evil curses! Even though one is a papist curse for repeating any such blasphemies you could go to hell!"

"God Damn it!" Read replied thoughtlessly, "don't heed the coarse language of an old seafarer!"

"...and you have once cursed again!" Miriam exclaimed and started to cry. "William I want to go home!"

William looking helplessly at his wife's outburst stammered, "She is right father, cursing is a sin and against the Law of God!" and he put his arm round Miriam and ushered her from the room.

Later the incident was explained away when it was discovered that Miriam was pregnant with their first child. But the altercation clouded relations between the generations in the Elding family even though Esther constantly made efforts to mend the rift. Read too tried to calm the situation but was privately exasperated at his son's sudden pacifism and empty piety. However, as life was continuing to be difficult for the Puritans in Bermuda some months later William made it known that he, his wife and their new-born daughter Chastity, would take up the offer to return to Nassau as proposed by Read.

The two generations of Eldings took ship and returned to Nassau to reclaim their property even though the town was in ruins and pirates still out-numbered the inhabitants. *'One small Pyrat with fifty Men that are acquainted with the inhabitants (which too many of them are) shall and will Run that Place'* wrote one contemporary commentator. On arrival Read found the eyewitness was exactly right. He also discovered that the shipwright's shop was a total ruin so he sold the waterfront land to a man who had clear ambitions to become a '*Pyrat*' and moved into a re-built house on East Street near the centre of the small town.

Once settled Read tried, unsuccessfully, to lend his services to the ineffective but legitimate government of the day. Robert Holden was the last of a long line of rogues to be proposed by the Lords Proprietors to be governor. Holden had argued to the noble Lords that he had great plans for the colony remarking that the goodly climate of the Bahamas might bring investment to fill the colony's coffers claiming the islands rivaled *"St. Helena and Bermoodas Islands, ye famed places of ye world for health'.* This may have been his only good idea but it was premature by two centuries. An astute wag at the time suggested that Holden, like many of the former governors, was more interested in wealth than health and noted archly: *'the Governors hitherto have work'd much at such ill Practices for filthy lucre'.*

After years of forced inactivity Read Elding was later able to aid the first 'royal' governor to be appointed to the colony but slowly succumbed to the quick sands of old age and died some time afterwards largely unrecognised for his outstanding services to the island nation. On his demise his wife Esther returned to the bosom of her Anglican family in Bermuda but not before she arranged for Read to be buried with full naval honours at sea. William, now the only surviving Elding heir, made a contract for the rental of the house on East Street - predictably to a '*Pyrat*' - and moved his family inland in New Providence to start a plantation far away from waterfront the nest of buccaneers.

Perhaps the most notorious pirate of them all, Edward Teach (alias Blackbeard) together with Hornigold, Jennings, Burgess, White and Vane all sailed from secret creeks and harbours in the Bahamas. Interestingly Vane was one of the few pirates who had the respect of his fellow pirate captains. He was even popular with his crew, something that certainly could not be said of Teach. By 1717 when Nassau had been rebuilt for the fourth or fifth time, all these pirates were openly using the town as a base again.

It was said of pirates that they were 'swaggerers, lovers of glory, sometimes cruel, often generous but cowards never'. This was certainly true of Edward Teach who was also tough, ruthless, and of frightening countenance. He is reputed to have shot his own first mate just to show how mean he could be. His hair was worn in dreadlocks (in engravings of the time he was shown with slow-matches in his dreadlocks smoldering like fuses!) and at his belt he wore a brace of six pistols and a sabre. He is reputed to have had fourteen wives. In 1713 he teamed up with Hornigold but did not obtain his own command until three years later.

Completely in character, Blackbeard captured a French merchant ship which he mockingly re-named the '*Queen Anne's Revenge*'. This ship he converted by installing cannons and a crew of the most bloodthirsty brigands he could find. He was more famous for his cruelties than the fortune he amassed. His victims counted themselves lucky if fate decreed that all they had to do was to walk the plank. Surprisingly he kept a log which would certainly have condemned him to a gruesome death if it had ever come to light. One extract from his log reads: '*Rum all out. Our company somewhat sober* (though later in the entry it is clear this condition will not last long) *damned confusion amongst us! Rogues a plotting, great talk of separation – so I look'd sharp for a prize...took one with a great deal of liquor aboard...*' After this encounter he met up with Vane and, after exchanging salutes, the two captains repaired to a remote Bahamian island, dropped anchor and proceeded to 'take a glorious debauch for several days'.

But perhaps the most memorable incident in his short career as a pirate captain was when he lit sulphur in the sealed hold of his ship and invited members of the crew to join him in 'hell' as he put it. 'Let us see who is closest kin to the devil by staying longest in it!' he challenged. Needless say Blackbeard was the last man to appear through a hatch.

About this time a report out of South Carolina to the Board of Trade in England stated:

'The unspeakable calamity this Poor Province suffers from Pirates Obliges me to inform Your Lordships of it, in Order that Your Majesty may know about it and be induced to afford us the Assistance of a Frigate or two to cruise hereabouts...This company is Commanded by One Teach Alias Blackbeard who has a ship of 40 of guns under him and 3 sloopes Tenders besides & are in all above 400 men...'

The British Governor of Virginia added to the chorus stating: *a nest of pirates are endeavouring to establish themselves at Providence,* and urged that, *'the place be made defencible'* even though the *'gang at Providence'* had said they would only seize French and Spanish ships, he stated that some trading vessels from the American colonies had already been plundered by Nassau pirates.

Since there were so many pirate ships operating out of the Bahamas, Edward Teach shipped up the North American coast to seek a new source of plunder and was finally cornered off Okracoke Island, North Carolina in 1718. Blackbeard avoided immediate capture by the British Navy and continued fighting for forty minutes after sustaining five musket ball wounds and three (some say twenty) sabre thrusts! When he finally died from loss of blood he was decapitated and his head was affixed to the end of the bowsprit of his ship.

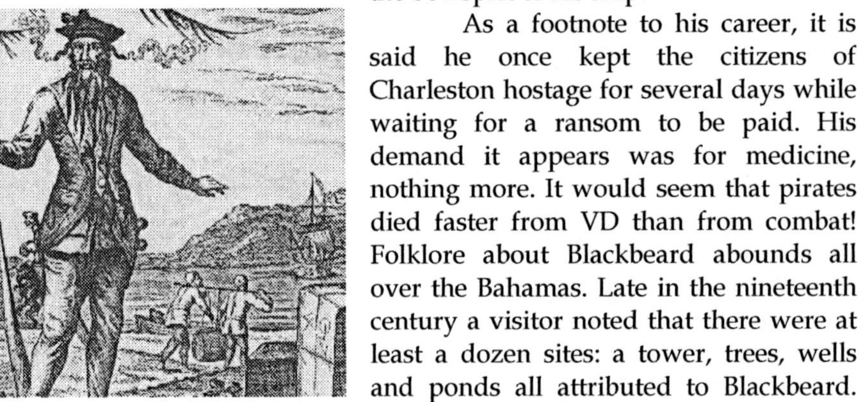

As a footnote to his career, it is said he once kept the citizens of Charleston hostage for several days while waiting for a ransom to be paid. His demand it appears was for medicine, nothing more. It would seem that pirates died faster from VD than from combat! Folklore about Blackbeard abounds all over the Bahamas. Late in the nineteenth century a visitor noted that there were at least a dozen sites: a tower, trees, wells and ponds all attributed to Blackbeard. The latter in particular, were thought to contain submerged chests full of treasure but if any pirate loot was discovered it was kept a wellguarded secret.

Around this time Thomas Walker (Judge of the Vice City Admiralty Court in the Bahamas) wrote to London that he had spent his time recently *'in takeing up pirates and routeing them from amongst these island'.* He had embarked on an almost impossible task. Beside the brigands in Nassau, many local men from Eleuthera had turned to piracy and formed a liaison with some blood thirsty 'strangers' that included Hornigold, Thomas Terrill, and Watlin. The Eleutherian pirates made two successful voyages to Cuba and captured a Spanish ship commandeering 11,050 pieces of eight that they took back to Eleuthera to the dismay (or possible envy) of the authorities in Nassau. A sailor named Captain Hearne, privy to what was happening in Havana, sent a note to Walker in 1715 advising him to subdue the pirates or at the very least return the vessel to the Spanish. He warned that an abortive Spanish attempt to attack the Bahamas had been made just a short while before and another was being planned:

Your takeing the piratts upp may save your life....The Spanish sent about two month, agoe to cutt you off, and all men, women and children. But it may be said as of the Invincible Armada against England, God did turne them home either by bad weather or elce by bad pilots. Sir, if you send the sloope you have seized to Havanna you will prevent their comeing and be rewarded as well...

Thomas Walker immediately set sail for Havana *'where he accommodated all matters with the Governor there for ye peace and safety of the inhabitants of the Bohama Islands'.* For the time being at least, Walker had prevented a Spanish attack on the Bahamas.

But matters were so bad in Nassau that the pirates robbed, raped and murdered at will. Their leader boasted he was the real *'governor'* and *'will make Providence into another Madagascar'.* When the seditious pirates mounted their own guns on the fort in 1716, Walker fled to South Carolina. He came back a year later, but prudently approached no nearer to Providence than Abaco (becoming the first recorded resident of Abaco and probably settling at the most northerly inhabited place in the Bahamas to which he gave his name: Walkers Cay).

One buccaneer was so closely identified with the Bahamas that he gave his name to a Bahamian island: John George Watlin. But even though the name 'Watlins Island' later reverted back to its original appellation of 'San Salvador', Watlin and his violent reputation have lived on.

Watlin became a 'buccaneer' when his plantation on the island failed and his wife took their children and left for the new colony of Virginia. Being destitute but at least possessing an Elding-made sloop and a few slaves, he decided to try his hand first at wrecking. But, like many others, he soon discovered that wrecking was a very uncertain line of work. So he equipped the sloop with two cannons and, after a few unsuccessful sorties, eventually captured a New England-made brig that was better suited his ambition to pursue a more violent occupation at sea.

He chose to make Pigeon Creek on the island his base as he knew that most shipping plying between North American ports and the southern islands of the Caribbean and South America would pass just a few miles east of the island arching round the eastern edge of the Bahamas. At this time most of the ships visible from the island were either involved in trading or slaving but he also understood he could expect few treasure ships in this vicinity. Nevertheless, Watlin was aware that there could be lucrative pickings from the steady flow of vessels carrying manufactured goods south and vessels carrying slaves, sugar, molasses and other produce travelling north. He decided that from now on, any ship, except the slavers, would be his quarry.

Soon after his wife left him he openly took his Creole mistress to his bed and sired several children, most of whom later sailed with him. Watlin's crew was mainly made up of former slaves who had been given a disagreeable choice: either to join his crew or be sold back into slavery. Most of the able-bodied male slaves chose to join his crew and, tutored by Watlin, developed into a savage bunch of cutthroats. In the years that Watlin and his crew sailed under the black flag they intercepted, boarded, plundered then sank nearly two dozen ships taking no prisoners. All their victims had their throats cut and were thrown to the sharks. The saleable booty obtained after they ransacked their quarry was bartered with other pirates in Nassau or re-sold at the port cities of Central America.

Only years later, at a rowdy meeting in the *Wheel of Fortune* in Nassau, when Watlin tried to cheat his fellow pirates he quit the Bahamas and hurriedly escaped to Jamaica. He even left his ship in Nassau harbour which was seized by the authorities and, because Watlin had not manumitted his crew, they were apprehended, flogged as run-aways and sold back into slavery.

In Port Royal in 1679, Watlin joined forces with Captain Sharp a notorious West Indian buccaneer. Their convoy of five ships sailed south with a view to attacking Cartagena. But, when they arrived off the bar, they discovered the city was too well fortified and so they decided to travel across the Isthmus of Panama to the Pacific coast with Kuna Indians as guides. After a grueling trek, recorded by William Dampier the inquisitive scholar-pirate, they finally arrived at the Pacific Ocean. Here the buccaneers used the Kuna canoes to seize two Spanish barks that enabled them to capture a large Spanish warship *La Santissima Trinidad* that they renamed the *Trinity* and which became their flagship.

But after eighteen of the crew had been killed and another twenty two wounded they decided that the city of Panama was too well defended to continue an assault. However, before they left, they were fortunate enough to capture a Spanish bark with 50, 000 pieces of eight and a large amount of powder and shot aboard that would replenish their dwindling ammunition supply. They now decided to plan attacks against the rich Spanish towns on the Pacific coast of South America and then 'go home round about America, through the Strait of Magellan'. But word quickly travelled along the coast that they were approaching and they were repulsed and lost two ships, half of their crew and many of the men were seriously injured. The pirates then withdrew from the South American mainland to re-group at the isle of Juan Fernandez.

On the island a bitter argument ensued about the failure of the assault. Since so many men had been killed or injured, several of the crew wanted to return home immediately. A small majority however, wanted one last engagement to obtain 'their fortune' before they returned home. Commodore Sharp was blamed for the defeat and was 'turned out of his commission' and Captain Watlin an 'old privateer' and 'stout seaman' was voted 'commodore' of the depleted fleet of pirate ships by a crew now numbering only 93 men. Since they needed all the hands they could get, Captain Sharp was retained but relegated to captain of one of the smaller ships. While on the island the crews were recompensed for their injuries. One sailor had lost a leg, two had lost arms, another had lost an eye, while yet another was completely blind from his injuries. According to normal practice among the fraternity of pirates for the loss of a right arm an injured sailor received 600 pieces of eight or 6 slaves, for a left leg 400 pieces of eight or 4 slaves and for the loss of an eye, 100 pieces of eight and one slave. Since slaves were useless to pirates who lived most of their lives at sea Watlin paid the men in plundered Spanish coin.

At the previous engagement on the South American coast Watlin had taken aboard an old Indian as prisoner and tried, by torture, to find out the weak points of the town of Arica that was to be their next target. The old man was either too frightened to talk or Watlin and his semi-literate crew could not understand his limited Spanish. In either case the old man did not know, or would not give Watlin any vital information about Arica, and so in frustration, Watlin brutally shot him in cold blood. Captain Sharp was enraged at this act of barbarity and announced that he 'washed his hands of it' and prophesied that the forthcoming fight at Arica would be 'a hot day for this piece of cruelty.' He was right, for as they commenced the attack on the town, three Spanish men-of-war with a full complement of 36 guns were laying in wait for them. The pirate assault failed completely and Watlin and half of the crew of his under-manned, under-gunned vessels were killed. To celebrate their victory the Spaniards carried Watlin's decapitated head around town on a pole. The remainder of the pirate crew, Dampier among them, limped back to the Isthmus of Panama.

Some believe that even today the cries of Watlins' victims can still be heard crying for vengeance at the ruined hill-top 'castle' on the island of San Salvador where, as a young man, he was reputed to have lived.

The two most notorious female pirates to operate from the Bahamas were Anne Bonny and Mary Read. Anne married a ne'er-do-well sailor-turned-pirate in the Carolinas named James Bonny. They both travelled to the Bahamas to join the 'rovers' but found the new governor had just offered pirates amnesty. James Bonny accepted the amnesty which of course him left out of work. Anne quickly grew to dislike her spineless husband and soon caught the eye of 'Calico Jack' Rackham, a pirate of some renown then biding his time in Nassau. Both Anne and Mary Read signed on to serve with Calico Jack and Anne became Calico's lover. The admiration between Anne and Calico was mutual. Calico Jack was a handsome man who knew how to spend money as well as steal it. Anne was a well-endowed lass with a fiery spirit and temper that matched any man (it was rumored that in her youth she killed a servant woman with a carving knife because the servant made her angry). Calico offered to 'buy' Anne from James Bonny but Bonny instead took the matter up with the Bahamian governor, who said that Anne should be stripped to the waist and publicly flogged and then returned to her legal husband. That night Calico Jack stole a sloop in Nassau and, with Anne Bonny and Mary Read aboard, recommenced a life of piracy.

Both Anne and Mary fought in men's clothing under Calico Jack's command and were experts with pistol and cutlass and considered as dangerous as any male pirate. In October 1720, however, the Governor of Jamaica, hearing of Calico Jack's presence, sent an armed sloop to intervene and captured his ship the *Revenge*. Jack was caught by surprise and much to the women's dismay, the pirates fought like cowards and were taken far too easily. Anne Bonny and Mary Read, were also taken prisoner but upon capture pleaded their 'belly' and asked to be tried separately after they gave birth.

Later they received trials separate from the men but were nevertheless still sentenced to hang. Upon being asked at her trial why a woman would turn to piracy, rather than giving an answer that might have brought her a pardon, Mary Read instead replied, 'that as to hanging, it is no great hardship, for were it not for that, every cowardly fellow would turn pirate and so unfit the Seas, that men (and women, she might have added) of courage must starve.' Mary Read escaped the hangman by dying from fever while in jail.

Anne Bonny received several stays of execution before mysteriously vanishing from official records. It is believed her father, who had influential contacts on the island, ransomed her back to the Carolinas where she assumed a new name and a new life. To illustrate how tough she was, while in prison she was granted a special favour to see Calico Jack on the day he was to hang. Anne's last words to him illustrate her incredible bravado, 'I'm sorry to see you here Jack, but if you'd have fought like a man you needn't hang like a dog...'

One other pirate of note, who was perhaps the most psychopathic brigand of them all, was the Frenchman Francis l'Ollonais. Though he generally operated out of the French islands of the Indies he occasionally paid a visit to Nassau for supplies or to careen his ships. In one engagement after leaving Nassau he boarded a Spanish ship but found it to be in ballast. So frustrated was he to find nothing of value on the ship, he is reputed to have drawn his cutlass, stabbed and cut open the breast of the Spanish captain, then while the poor man was still alive, pulled out his heart and began to bite and gnaw on it...The senseless and horrific brutality of the Caribbean pirates like l'Ollonais has probably never been matched in all the annals of history.

In England two ideas were debated as to how to rid the Bahamian colony of pirates. They could use force, but that would take time and money and, most important, tie up navy ships that were urgently needed elsewhere. The other idea was to grant the pirates a pardon and hope that overnight some of the most blood-thirsty brigands the world had ever seen would suddenly become law-abiding citizens. It was not a very plausible idea but it had the virtue of economy - all that was needed was a man who could enforce the will of the English government.

The man they found was Woodes Rogers.

CAPTAIN WOODES ROGERS came from a family of seafarers. He had made a privateering voyage round the world following the lead of Drake and Cavendish and had captured about 20 Spanish ships as prizes during his career. He was also a contender for the title of rescuer of Alexander Selkirk, better known as Robinson Crusoe, made famous in Defoe's novel of the same name.

Rogers made a **'Presentation'** to the British government outlining his proposals for the Colony. The Bahama Islands occupied a strategic location and should *'not be allowed to fall into enemy hands'*, he wrote, he also pointed out what everybody knew: it was infested with pirates and, if it was to remain in English hands, the pirates must be brought to heel. The Board of Trade were impressed by the **'Presentation'** to the Crown, the Lords Proprietors less so. But, reluctantly the noble Lords surrendered civil and military governance of the Bahamas to the Crown, the quit rents, royalties and they leased the company to Woodes Rogers for twenty one years.

After the business details had been settled to the grudging satisfaction of the Proprietors, Rogers was appointed Captain-General and Governor in Chief of the Bahama Islands. The monarch signed his name to a Royal Proclamation declaring Rogers to be the new royal governor. The proclamation began:

'Whereas we are privy to Information, that several Persons, Subjects of our sovereign Queen Anne, have since the 24th Day of June in the Year of Our Lord

1715, committed divers Pyracies and Robberies upon the High-Seas...' and goes on to state that if any of the aforesaid blood-thirsty villains will surrender themselves before the 5th September 1718 they *'...shall receive Our most gracious Pardon.'*

Rogers sailed to the Bahamas with a company of soldiers, the company ship *Delicia,* two navy frigates and two sloops.

He arrived off Eleuthera after fourteen weeks at sea.

The sparse inhabitants of that island told him that there were about a thousand pirates in Nassau and that the notorious pirate Vane, had publicly boasted he for one had no intention of surrendering to an English governor or anyone else. 'I am the governor here!' Vane boasted. Undeterred Rogers continued on to Nassau and, on the evening of 25th July 1718, lay just outside the main entrance to the harbour just west of Hog Island.

It was a momentous day in the history of the Bahamas.

The presence of Rogers blockading the main entrance to the harbour gave Vane pause and he directed a letter to Rogers (whom he deferentially referred to as the Governor of New Providence) as follows:

> *Your Excellency may please to understand that we are willing*
> *To accept his Majesty's most gracious Pardon on the following terms, viz.*
> *That you will suffer us to dispose of all our Goods now in our*
> *Possession. Likewise to act as see fit with every Thing belonging*
> *to us, as his Majesty's Act of Grace specifies. If your Excellency*
> *shall please comply with this we shall with all Readiness, accept*
> *of his Majesty's Act of Grace. If not, We are obliged to stand on*
> *our Defense. So conclude Your humble Servants Charles Vane*
> *and Company.*

And to underline the urgency of the matter Vane added a postscript:

> *P.S. We await a speedy answer.*

To such brazenness Woodes Rogers did not deign to reply. Vane notwithstanding, Rogers intended to enter the harbour at dawn. And before sunset Rogers sent *HMS Rose* to block the harbour mouth. Vane replied with volleys of grape shot and the *Rose* retreated out of range.

That night there were explosions in the town that confused Rogers and his officers. Were the pirates celebrating the fact that they would soon receive amnesty or were they preparing to defend the town? In fact it was neither.

Vane had just unloaded his ill-gotten gains from a French prize and then blown it up. Before the night was out, he sneaked out of the shallow eastern approach to the harbour with four score pirates and was never seen in the Bahamas again.

The following day, Rogers landed at the wharf and was greeted by two lines of people numbering about 300 who fired their muskets in the air and shouted the traditional - though probably not heartfelt - 'Hurrahs!' - for the new representative of the King. Outside the old fort the self-styled Chief Justice and the President of the Council bade him welcome.

The new governor read his Commission followed by the 'Proclamation of Pardon'. The inhabitants shouted more 'Hurrahs!'.

The following day, martial law was declared and the Chief Pilot was authorized to seize all cargoes in the harbour and make out an inventory pending the establishment of an Admiralty Court. After a week of re-organization Rogers nominated a civil government. Six members of the Council were drawn from those citizens of Nassau who were 'untarnished by piracy'. Thomas Walker was one, another was Read Elding who had recently returned from Bermuda with his family; the other six were appointed from those officials Woodes Rogers had brought with him from England. One of these was William Fairfax, part of whose family later moved to Virginia and became friend and benefactor to a man who would later become the *'great instrument to dismember the British Empire'*.

The first priority was defence and Rogers ordered that Fort Nassau be repaired, guns mounted and the militia housed. To add a degree of urgency to the situation there was news that the Spanish had raided Cat Island a little over 100 miles from Nassau. The report was fortuitous in that it helped spur activity along though it later proved to be false.

THEN, WITH THE AID OF COUNCIL, Rogers turned to improving the sorry condition of the town. He created a new plan of settlement giving lots of land 120 feet square and free lumber to anyone who would build a house within a year. Next he set about clearing the bush and clearing the roads of the accumulated filth. There was even a plan to send more salt to the cod industries of Newfoundland and to develop a whaling industry.

However, the sub-tropical climate and unsanitary conditions soon gave the well-meaning governor problems. An epidemic, probably typhoid, swept through the town and 86 people died. It is possible that even Rogers was infected, certainly it is known he became considerably weakened by disease about this time. The improvements which had been started with so much gusto, ceased. An eyewitness reported,

'...(in any case)...it did much not suit the inclinations of the pirates to work; and though they had provision sufficiently, and also a good allowance of wine and brandy to each man, yet they began to have such a hankering after their old trade that many of them took opportunities of seizing boats in the night, and made their escape, so that in a few months there were not many left.'

Woodes Rogers complained continually about the townsfolk to his officials,

'...(as) for work they mortally hate it, for when they have cleared a patch that will supply them with potatoes and yams and very little else, fish being so plentiful...they thus live, poorly and indolently with a seeming content, and pray for wrecks or pirates; and few of them have an opinion of a regular orderly life under any sort of government, and would rather spend all they have at a Punch House than pay me one-tenth to save their families and all that's dear to them...'

He found an occupation for those pardoned pirates who were useless on land and itching to go to sea. They were recruited as privateers to serve in the name of the King and were dispatched to search for Vane and any other piratical cut-throats they could find. Rogers was not to be disappointed. Vane evaded capture but two 'reformed' pirates, Hornigold and Cockram, captured thirteen pirates in the Exuma islands and cays though three died of wounds on their way back to Nassau.

Woodes Rogers had already sent three pirates to England for trial but decided that these brigands should be tried in Nassau, 'to make an example of the calamity the Pirates bring upon themselves.'

The pirates had an ingrained sense of the rightness of their calling. At their trial they defended their right to take others' property as being some kind of natural law which favoured the strongest. They even argued that the law could not be enforced when they stole from people who were of a different social group or nationality. And, when they saw that these arguments did not sit well with the Admiralty Court judges, they said that all blame should be attached to Phineas Bunch one of the pirates who had died from his wounds. The Court did not accept that argument either and sentenced them all to be hanged five days later.

At the appointed time the malefactors were given half an hour under the gallows to sing Psalms and listen to a lugubrious passage read to them from the Book of Deuteronomy:

...so you shall put away the evil from among you...and fear. If a man has committed a sin deserving of death, and he is put to death, and you hang him on a tree, his body shall not remain overnight on the tree, but you shall surely bury him

that day, so that you do not defile the land which the Lord your God is giving you as an inheritance; for he who is hanged is accursed of God…

And with these distressing words the executioner was told to go about his business but then, at the last moment, Rogers reprieved the youngest of them as being '…the son of loyal and good parents from Weymouth in Dorsetshire,' and he added, 'I hope this unhappy young man will deserve his life'. The remainder of the pirates were strung up and swayed on the gibbet for several days (the Biblical dictate about removing the body the same day would seem to have been overlooked). The grisly spectacle was to remind Nassauvians yet again that a similar fate awaited anyone else who reverted to 'ye olde trade'.

The lesson was slowly being learned. A few dozen pirates surrendered to Rogers in Nassau to seek clemency but it was estimated at the time that as many as two thousand pirates were still at large throughout the Bahamas. And, as if this were not enough, the Spanish were again threatening to invade the islands.

The following year a Spanish fleet arrived off Nassau but was thwarted in its attempt to make a frontal assault by Woodes Roger's ship *Delicia* which barred the main entrance to the harbour. So, with a superior force of 1300 men carried in four warships and eight sloops, the Spanish approached Nassau from the east and landing soldiers would have marched on the town late at night, *'but two valiant Negro sentries blazed hotly and happily away at the oncoming boats.'* The Bahamian sentries kept firing on the Spanish from the thick bush yet cleverly changed their positions so frequently that the Spanish thought there was a large contingent of men defending the town, thus the Spanish advance was stayed. The action has great significance since it was Bahamians of African heritage who first defended the country with valour from a hostile army on Bahamian soil.

The Spanish then tried to get ashore west of Nassau in daylight the following day but this time they were repulsed by 500 townsmen, most of whom were active or former pirates, who displayed a momentary if temporary loyalty to the Crown. It had been a close call. The Spanish left but the threat remained. Rogers appealed in vain to London for supplies and reinforcements.

'We have never been free from apprehension of danger from Pirates and Spaniards,' he wrote, *'though they expect an enemy that has surprised them these fifteen years thirty four times, yet these wretches can't be kept to watch at night, and when they do they come very seldom sober, and rarely awake all night, though our officers or soldiers very often surprise their guard and carry off their arms, and I punish, fine, or confine them almost every day…'*

It was not difficult to see from these lines why a disciplinarian like Woodes Rogers would be resented. Rogers was continually trying to improve the wayward Colony and used £11,000 of his own money on various projects but it was little appreciated by the populace. When he left Nassau in March 1721 for England he travelled by way of South Carolina and, ever mindful of the well-being of the Bahamas, arranged to have supplies sent to keep the soldiers victualed until Christmas.

He carried with him a **'Testimonial'** from some of the grateful citizens of Nassau hoping he would be well received at home for *'...it is owing to him, who has acted amongst us without the least regard for his private advantage or separate interest, in a scene of continual fatigues and hardships. These motives led us to offer the truth under hands of the most insurmountable difficulty, that he and this Colony has struggled with for the space of two years and eight months past.'*

But the **'Testimonial'** availed him little. On returning to England this remarkable man, certainly the best governor the Bahamas had ever had, spent some time in prison for debt.

But it was not the last time the Bahamas was to hear of Captain Woodes Rogers.

THE NEXT GOVERNOR was George Phenney who, thanks to Woodes Rogers, found the Bahamas a relatively tranquil place. He retained Read Elding and a few others from Rogers' administration as members of the government council. The islands were now engaged in relatively honest commerce. Fishing and lumbering being the principal occupations. Mastic, mahogany, lignum vitae and cedar were lumbered and used in building furniture, houses and ships. Indeed some of the lumber used in the British ships which fought at Trafalgar is thought to have come from the Bahamas. Other woods were used in the dyeing of cloth in the age before synthetic chemical dyes were in use. Of these green and yellow fustick and braziletto were lumbered commercially.

Salt-raking had long been an industry in the Bahamas which Phenney further encouraged. It was particularly suited to the more arid islands of the south. Salt pans were created by allowing the sea to flood a dyked area at high tide, then further access by the sea was closed off. If the evaporation was greater than the rainfall, salt crystals would form. Salt was most important as a food preservative in these days before refrigeration. Phenney, accepting the advice of Read Elding who had spent some time in Bermuda, even introduced Bermudans to come to teach Bahamians straw work.

Phenney was an able administrator with a keen eye on ways to improve commerce in the colony. But he was cursed with an overbearing wife who proved his undoing. It seems she was a rapacious businesswoman and used her husband's position to corner the market on everything from salt to straw. A contemporary observer wrote: *'Mrs Phenney sells Rum by the pint and biscuits by the half Ryal…'* She kept, *'the very Life of everybody there in her Mercy, who could not have any Provisions or Subsistence whatsoever without paying her exorbitant prices…'*, she has *'…frequently Brow beated Jurys and insulted even the Justice on the Bench.'* When the governor finally left the Bahamas to make way for the return of Woodes Rogers he was mildly criticized for *'conniving at or indulging his wife in so extravagant and oppressive a conduct…'*

WOODES ROGERS returned to the Bahamas in 1728, a colony in an uneasy peace with Spain but in a maelstrom of domestic political activity. The long-hoped-for Assembly of elected members had been established but the fledgling democracy was a hotbed of advocacy and intrigue. Rogers could not count on the Assembly to back any of his proposals for the betterment of the Colony, indeed the Speaker of the House became his arch political enemy and commanded a majority of the Members of the House. The governor fell out with many people including Read Elding who resigned his post as a Member of the Advisory Council but was later to occupy the position of Colonial Secretary. Revenues were down and the Colony's defence left much, to Woodes Roger's mind, to be desired. But Rogers never gave up trying to improve the lot of the Bahamians against their will.

This new term in the Bahamas found Woodes Rogers frail and in ill health. Less than a year after being re-appointed governor Rogers was exhausted and longed for a sea voyage. He left Nassau for Charleston for a stay of several months. When he returned, Rogers ordered the first census to be taken and encouraged foreigners and 'strangers' to settle the Bahamas. Newcomers came from the Palatine and St Kitts but most did not stay long. In the entire country only 1,388 people were enumerated.

Woodes Rogers was a hard taskmaster who thought the ship of state could in fact be run like a ship. He was estranged from his wife and had few friends. When he finally expired in 1733, the Colonial Secretary informed the English Secretary of State: 'Whereas it pleased Almighty God to take unto himself the soul of Woodes Rogers on the 15th day of the inst. We acquaint your Lordship therewith.' The epitaph signed by the President of the Council but penned by Read Elding in his capacity as Colonial Secretary unemotionally summed up in one sentence the common feeling for Rogers, he died respected but unloved. But the motto Woodes Rogers gave the country was a more fitting epitaph:

Expulsis Piratis Restituta Commercia
(Pirates expelled, commerce restored)

Chapter 9 - Reluctant Visitors (1748 - 1834)

For whom the Lord loveth he chasteneth, and scourgeth every son whom he receiveth.

Hebrews 12 v. 6

SLAVERY HAS EXISTED from time immemorial. But, nowhere and at no time, has the transplanting of people been so thorough or so demeaning as the transport of black Africans to the 'new world' of the Americas. And it had a further poignant consequence; slavery left a legacy which even today acts as a continuing irritant to social harmony in the Americas.

Slavery was already well established on the continent of Africa before the European nations arrived. Tribes enslaved other tribes and Arabs, among others, had long run a profitable business slave-running sub-Saharan Africans. Later they sometimes served as slave brokers for the Europeans involved in the so-called 'triangular' trade of shipping rum and sugar from the Caribbean to both old and 'new' England, then shipping trade goods to Africa and African slaves back to the new world.

As early as 1505 the conquistadores brought African bondsmen to the island of Hispaniola. Most slaves, however, were shipped to the Americas in the late eighteenth and early nineteenth centuries. In fact, for a time, prior to 1820, the number of Africans crossing the ocean outstripped the combined total of all European immigrants by a surprising ratio of five to one.

The slaves were captured mainly in coastal West Africa and transported on ships under circumstances of extreme barbarity to the new world. Once there, they would be auctioned as 'chattels' to be bought and sold like any other property. They were supposed to give of their labour for their natural lives yet the treatment they received from their 'owners' was demeaning at best, inhuman at worst.

Few slaves escaped from bondage in the Bahamas and those who did were generally soon caught and brutally punished. On rare occasions some managed to flee and by exceptional good fortune, remain undetected. This account follows the life of one slave who was brought from West Africa to Nassau. Though he died young, he became the patriarch of an African Bahamian dynasty. His family became embroiled in the problems of slavery but managed to escape the long arm of the law. One of the descendents of the family, two centuries later, gave the Bahamas one of its first Prime Ministers of African heritage.

Appendix B traces the genealogy of the male line of the original slave family whose surname, after the first generation, was purposely changed from Elding to Eldon.

Illustration of the interior of a slave ship bound for the Americas from West Africa

M'BUDA ROSE WITH THE SUN as he had done for most of his short life. Almost all of the tribe were already stirring and those who were still asleep would soon be awakened by the noise of drums and the chatter of the womenfolk in his little village of the Akan-speaking Fante tribe in the coastal jungle of West Africa. If that were not enough, the birds and animals in the forest reserved their most cacophonic sounds for the first hours of the day.

The little village consisted of only twenty houses built of mud bricks all laid out in a circle around a well-swept plaza. Their cultivated land was some distance from the village in clearings in the forest. As the village came to life several youths gathered in the centre of the plaza. This day M'buda and his friends were to go on their weekly trading mission to the Guinea seacoast. They would be transporting animal skins, okras and bananas to the coast that they would exchange for fish and salt. As the youths waited they discussed the festivities of the last few days. A small parade had been held in the village two days before with rival groups dressed in costumes and bizarre body paint. The original idea, mainly lost to history, was to honour their ancestors in a joyous carnival-like festival at which locally produced beer was consumed in great quantities. The concept of the festival would later be revived in a far corner of the world.

Less than an hour after sunrise when fifteen sturdy youths were assembled, the trading party started off down a well-trodden path carrying heavy baskets of produce on their heads led by a seasoned elder. Shafts of dusky sunlight randomly penetrated to the forest floor. Always, while the trading party trekked through the forest, they chanted a Fante song that established the pace of their march. The birds replied discordantly from the canopy of the forest.

After a few hours into their journey they made a customary stop to rest at the saddle of two hills where they would get a view of the distant sea for the first time. This day, when the trading party stopped at their usual resting place, they could see a square-rigged sailing ship at anchor in a distant bay. They mused it must be a trading vessel belonging to the white men who for many years had visited the local fort of Saõ Jorge da Mina along the south-facing coast that the white men called 'Guinea'. A Portuguese trading ship at the fort was not too an unusual sight. Though unknown to them, nearly three hundred years before a bright-eyed Italian youth had visited this same fort. A land far beyond the almost imperceptible arc of the horizon was to feature as part of their common destiny.

After a short stop the trading party recommenced their journey, now following a winding path down a steep hill. As they descended into a narrow valley the tropical vegetation became dense blocking out the sky above them. Though the path was well trodden every time they traveled this route they had to beat back luxuriant vegetation that seemed to grow overnight. They were only a few miles from the coast crossing a rare clearing when suddenly, from the cover of the jungle, they were surprised by fierce-looking tribesmen brandishing spears.

They were rapidly encircled in a carefully planned ambush. The warriors in frightening Asante war paint narrowed the circle.

Understanding only too well that they were in a perilous trap, one Fante youth dropped the load from his head and started to flee. But, as he did so, a hail of spears were hurled at him. One caused a great gash in his upper arm and yet another pierced his thigh emitting a torrent of blood. Another spear, which narrowly missed him, landed in the belly of the elder, grotesquely and fatally pinning him to the ground.

The terrified tribesmen were paralyzed with fear as the Asanti now completed the closing of the ring.

The warriors forced M'buda to the ground and shackled M'buda and his comrades together with metal manacles and chains. As soon as the Fante tribesmen saw the chains they grasped at once the reason for the ambush. The aim for the Asanti attack was not to steal their produce as they had at first assumed, but to take them captive. It was now quite clear that the powerful and aggressive Asanti with whom they shared a common language, were almost certainly in the pay of Arab slave traders and their European masters. They had heard what they thought were exaggerated stories of these new mercenaries operating further down the coast and how people from other villages had been dragged onto ships that they had seen lying so innocently at anchor. Now they understood the accounts were true. But, why they had been taken captive and where the ships went, they had no idea.

Fearful for their lives yet unable to offer resistance, the Fante tribesmen were dragged to the fort and thrown into a dungeon with eighty or so others. Every few hours more people would be thrown into their dank prison.

After some time they heard a foreign voice shouting words they did not understand:

"Mujeres! mas mujeres!"

It was not necessary to understand the words, for shortly thereafter women, young and old, were thrust in the hold with them. The captives spent a night of torment and anguish in their crowded prison.

The following day the prisoners were led out, manacled and chained together and then dragged to the ship that was berthed next to a temporary wharf. The tribesmen were forced on board the vessel by overseers armed with long sticks. The more recalcitrant prisoners were savagely beaten with whips. They were made to mount a narrow gangplank onto the ship and forced to jump, three at time, through an open hatch to the deck below. M'buda and the other captives were then dragged to a space on the middle underdeck which was just wide enough to lie on, and here their chains were secured to the framing of the vessel. There were three decks where originally there had been two. The height from floor to ceiling was less than five feet. And it was here that the frightened prisoners were left to the sweating darkness of the hold.

Amid the terror and dismay in the underdecks a young boy, barely thirteen, screamed the simple but unanswerable question:

"What is happening...where are we going?" followed by a plaintive scream: "help me!...help me!...someone please, please help me!" His cries reverberated through the underdecks of the ship.

Another youth less fearful, made the no less futile plea: "Escape!...let us find a way to escape!"

Amid the commotion an older man interjected: "Let us summon the voodoo spirits!...they can come to our aid!" and several men started nervously chanting a rite until a grave old man tried to silence the fear and panic of his fellow prisoners. In a frail but commanding voice he said,

"...there is nothing we can do...except to remember this day! Stay calm...breathe slowly...hold on to life!"

For short time an uneasy silence ensued but then the shouting, cursing and moaning resumed.

Within a few hours the ship began to move, the timbers creaked and the ship started to heave with the swell of the ocean. Orders were shouted on the deck above and, as the slaver left the coastal waters, the vessel started to pitch with the ocean swell. Some of the prisoners were seasick. The smell inside the hold became unspeakable.

Once a day for the next sixteen weeks they were given water mixed with stale wine and hard hunks of bread to eat. Then every few days a deck hand would throw buckets of seawater over them in some attempt at sanitation.

Some of the Africans went delirious and died. Others just quietly expired quietly in their sleep. The old man who had offered words of advice was chained opposite to M'buda. He was very frail, but in the same dialect as M'buda he kept urging;

"Hold on! Sleep boy if you can, but hold on to life!"

After three weeks out at sea, some of the Africans who had died were unshackled and thrown overboard. This grisly ritual continued from then on every few days. M'buda had lost count of time but the old man mumbled that they had been at sea nearly two moons.

At long last the constant pitching of the vessel changed to a gentle roll. Their nostrils detected a sweetness about the air.

A voice from the depths of the hold said: "I smell the forest!" and many of the prisoners sat upright straining their senses to try to discover what had caused the atmospheric change.

"We are arriving somewhere..." some of the shackled prisoners cried.

Fear and anticipation mounted in the hold but it took a further two days before the ship was secured to a dock. In the dim light of the underdeck M'buda saw that the old man who had given such reassuring advice during the voyage had not kept his own counsel. His sightless eyes were staring vacantly upwards.

The vessel bumped against something. Voices coming from the shore suggested a different language. They could not be sure. The words spoken were certainly meaningless.

"We want only a dozen men and three wenches...young, good breeding stock."

"Busquelos!" a crew member replied, *"tenemos prisa, debemos ir a La Habana."* A sailor from the slaver gave a halting translation. "Go down...look for them...and hurry...we have to set sail for Havana!"

Minutes later M'buda was dragged from below deck and brought out into the bright Bahamian sunlight. He was so stiff he could hardly walk, but a man on the dock, having the same skin colour as himself, supported him as they made their way to a small room where the fifteen of them were locked up for the night.

"You will feel better tomorrow," the local man said. The words were incomprehensible but M'buda discerned the tone of voice had a certain empathy.

The food they were given in their new prison was a great improvement. There was fresh fruit to eat and a bucket of fresh water to wash in. They could even see sunlight through the barred windows and M'buda could hear children playing nearby.

"I wish the old man was here...he would know what to do; just 'stay calm, hold on to life' I suppose is what he would say. Alright..." M'buda said to himself, "I will be strong and remain calm."

The next day the bewildered Africans were taken to a large stone building near the centre of the small town. There they were made to stand on a raised dais while white people stared at them earnestly and recited numbers in their general direction. One of the bystanders was Read Elding's eldest son, William who was now some forty years old, and an established farmer.

"Fifty!"

"Sixty!"

"Seventy!"

"Seventy pounds, ten shillings and sixpence,"

"Any other bids?..." and after a brief pause a mallet sharply hit the auctioneer's table top, "...lot 2, an African male is sold then to William Elding Esquire for seventy pounds, ten shillings and sixpence!"

A white man came from the assembled crowd to collect M'buda and placed a rope round his neck while the iron shackles were being released from his ankles. Like an animal he was led out of the Vendue House, Nassau and down the dirt road at the edge of the harbour that was grandly referred to as Bay Street. Fifty or so yards down the road he was made to wait while passers-by, both white and black, looked with curiosity at this new addition to their small community.

A short time later M'buda was joined by two other chattel slaves, for that was what they had just become, there was a man slightly older than himself of a different tribe and a young female, both naked except for a tattered tribal loin cloth.

An erect, portly olive-complexioned man now reappeared on horseback and signalled to his white overseer from a distance of about twenty paces to join the slaves together with ropes around their necks so that they would be able to walk in single file. A bridle rope was then handed up to William Elding, who led his strange human procession slowly in the direction of the Blue Hills. He hailed passers-by as they progressed up the dusty track. A coach drawn by a dappled stallion approached.

"Good day to ye Mister Elding!" Governor John Tinker exclaimed as he drove by in his open carriage.

"...and very good day to ye, Your Excellency!" replied William Elding tipping his hat.

"...two sturdy Africans and a fine wench you have there I see! - I trust your plantation fares well...?"

"Indeed it does sir!" William Elding replied beaming with pride.

No one could have imagined that the descendants of M'buda and the Eldings would meet under very different circumstances a century and a half later.

M'buda was taken to a plantation just four miles south of Nassau where he worked the fields from dawn to dusk. M'buda was re-christened 'Martin' which was about as near as his African name could be transliterated into English. And with the curious but customary irony of the new world he took the surname of his master. Martin made acquaintances with his fellow workers but remembered the advice of the old man on the slave ship to stay calm and hold on to life. He fought hard to survive. He

Vendue House a former Slave Market located on Bay Street, Nassau

was not severely abused except the work was hard and the soil rendered poor crops.

William Elding as resident owner of the estate took an active interest in the plantation which grew sea cotton, guinea corn, indigo and assorted fruits and vegetables. He and his wife Miriam kept very much to themselves in the Blue Hills area of New Providence. Mainly due to the influence of his frail devoutly religious wife, William had been good to his word and completely turned his back on the sea that the Puritans had often preached was the source of much wickedness and depravity. They even shunned the few upright members of Nassau society including his father's loyal friends. At best they had a nodding acquaintance with a few government officers and a Sabbath Day friendship with the Puritan congregation. At their plantation at Blue Hills besides Chastity, who had been born in Bermuda, William and Miriam had three other children; Felicity, Jonathan the eldest son, and the baby, Prudence. The family Bible duly recorded the births of their children besides untimely deaths of two young male infants. As the surviving family grew up they helped provide assistance on the plantation.

But to survive as a farmer in these times needed discipline and hard labour. William Elding provided the discipline, his unfortunate slaves the labour. At least at the Blue Hills Plantation the Sabbath was set aside as a day of rest for everybody. On this day the two generations of Eldings provided contrasting styles of worship. Read and Esther took their place in the front pew at the Anglican Church surrounded by the white elite of Nassau all bedecked in their Sunday best. William, Miriam and their family on the other hand, dressed in simple garments held services under a tree in fine weather and in a wattle and daub hut other times surrounded by their impoverished slaves who were often only half clad in hand-me-downs. Despite being exceptionally religious neither William nor Miriam saw anything wrong with slavery, using ambiguous texts of the Bible to justify acceptance of the 'peculiar' institution. Nor indeed did they see anything incongruous in providing pirates and their kin in the town with the produce of the plantation.

Everyone on the plantation was made to attend religious services at least twice on Sunday listening to long sermons preached by William or, on rare occasions, by a visiting preacher. The children, slave and free, attended three hours of religious instruction on Sunday afternoon conducted by Chastity who, true to her Puritan name remained a virgin all her life. Aided sometimes by Felicity the children were made to learn long texts from the Bible by rote and had to succumb to corporal punishment if their memories were not up to the task. Chastity wielded a cane that was often bought down sharply on the upturned palms of the recalcitrant youngsters. In later life Chastity became a schoolteacher where she continued with the didactic and disciplinary skills she had learned at the plantation.

One day a visitor arrived at the plantation to meet with William Elding with a letter of introduction from the governor. The newcomer carried a goose quill pen and some bound sheaves of paper and spoke impulsively to everyone including Martin, jotting notes everywhere he went.

The visitor entered in his notebook:

"William Elding the master of the ***Blue Hills Plantation*** *is typical of many West Indian planters. He is courteous to visitors, a fair master to the poor souls who provide their labour on his plantation and is a respected member of the small community of colonists on the island of New Providence. He and his wife are especially respected for their religious fervour but due to the isolation of the plantations few planters have considerable book learning and have few diversions lest it be the rum which is consumed at sundown after spending much time in the fields. The long days spent in the sun gives their skin the appearance of well burnished leather. From appearance, at least, it is not easy to imagine that two generations previously the same persons might have been country gentry in England..."*

The visitor was clearly unaware that William's link with the Mother Country was slender indeed and he was quite wrong to surmise that the proprietor of the Blue Hills Plantation imbibed rum or indeed any strong liquor at sundown. A page later in his notebook the visitor observed:

'...the negroes of the Bahama Islands discover, in general, more spirit and exertion than in the southern parts of the West Indies. Something perhaps may be attributed to a more invigorating climate as a physical cause; but I believe more is due to the circumstances in which they are placed. Their labour is allotted to them daily and individually, according to their strength; and if they are so diligent as to have finished it at an early hour, the rest of the day is allowed to them for amusement or their private concerns. The master also frequently superintends them himself; and therefore it rarely happens that they are so much subject to the discipline of the whip as where gangs are large, and directed by agents or overseers.'

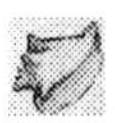  

IT WAS A DIFFERENT STORY at the southern end of the Bahamian archipelago at Grand Turk. Mary Prince, another slave from West Africa, wrote a book recounting the working conditions in the salt ponds which were worked for the Bermudans:

'When we were put to work in the salt ponds I was given a half barrel and a shovel, and had to stand up to my knees in water from four in the morning until nine, when we were given some Indian corn boiled in water...we were then called again to our tasks and worked through the heat of the day; the sun flaming upon our heads like a fire and raising salt blisters in those parts of our body which were not completely covered. Our feet and legs, from standing in the salt and water for so many hours, soon became full of dreadful boils which eat down in some cases to the very bone...when we returned to the house, our master gave us each our allowance of raw Indian corn, which we pounded into a mortar and boiled in water for our suppers.'

Medical attention for slaves was rudimentary. She testified that *'when we were ill...the only medicine given to us was a great bowl of hot salt water with* (more) *salt mixed in it, which made us* (even more) *sick.'* Mary Prince endured the Grand Turk salt ponds for ten years but was later able to educate herself. She sold her story to a publisher in England in 1831, three years before slavery was finally abolished in the Bahamas and the Turks and Caicos Islands. Part of her family later moved to Nassau.

On the island of Exuma in the central Bahamas matters were so bad there was even a slave uprising. Denys Rolle the father of Lord Rolle came to the Bahamas from Florida in 1784 after Florida reverted to Spanish rule. The Rolle family owned four estates on the island which were initially successful but after a few years ceased to prosper. By 1825, just nine years before the promised emancipation of the slaves, Lord Rolle was sustaining a net loss from his plantations of a hefty £500 per year. To try to resolve his financial difficulties he made a proposal to the governor to allow him to send most of his slaves to Trinidad where, he alleged, the slaves would be better cared for (and doubtless would have to work much harder). A skeptical Colonial Office turned down his request since the transportation of his slaves would have contravened the imperial law concerning 'trafficking' slaves.

When word of Rolle's proposal to send slaves to Trinidad reached Exuma there was great unrest and Governor Grant fearing a revolt, sent the militia to the island. As soon as the militia arrived it was reported the slaves put on a show of force themselves and paraded with firearms (eye witnesses may have exaggerated but claimed they had as many as ninety firearms!) Happily not a shot was fired. Isaac, an old slave who was the spokesman for the malcontents explained politely but forcibly that the slaves did not want to go to Trinidad or anywhere else. Despite assurances that there would be no transportation of the slaves out of the country they remained skeptical. And, to underline their distress and the poor conditions they had to tolerate on the Exuma plantations, Isaac further added they had been issued no new clothes for eighteen months.

Matters continued to fester. The Exuma plantations continued to fare badly, little work was performed and the slaves appeared to be getting the upper hand. It was thought if such a situation was permitted to continue it could be contagious. Lees, Lord Rolle's regular agent who was a member of the Council visited Exuma in 1829. Rapidly summing up the situation he planned to ship off 28 of the 'most troublesome' slaves and their families to Grand Bahama. When they refused to embark peaceably they were removed by force in Lord Rolle's sloop.

A short time later a slave named Pompey led an uprising when the agent said that some slaves were to be removed to Lord Rolle's plantation in Cat Island (there must have been duplicity or a misunderstanding somewhere because Rolle did not have a plantation in Cat Island). Then, when the slaves believed the militia were on the way to forcibly remove them, many ran into the bush and subsisted there for five weeks. Pompey their ringleader proposed they take their case directly to the governor and the runaways agreed. Late one night they commandeered one of Lord Rolle's boats and sailed to Nassau to plead with the new 'Gubna' Carmichael Smythe who was known to be sympathetic to the slaves. However, with the town of Nassau in sight, they were intercepted by a salt boat. The Exuma slaves were rapidly transported to Court and immediately convicted as runaways. All the adult males and five women were flogged (later it was discovered that two of the women had babes at the breast!)

Governor Carmichael Smythe (to the whites a misguided 'abolitionist') was not informed of the incident beforehand but when he discovered what had happened he immediately discharged the magistrate and two Justices of the Peace. Lees argued the case with the governor but was so 'insolent' that Smythe suspended him from the Council. The governor ordered Pompey and the other slaves to be immediately transported back to Exuma. On arrival there was general rejoicing but none of the slaves returned to work. When their defiance persisted the militia was dispatched once again to the island and Pompey, who had advised his people to flee again into the woods, was arrested and given the statutory 39 lashes in public.

Even after the Exuma incident Governor Smythe tried to persuade the House to rescind what he called the 'horrid business' of flogging female slaves. On this point, at least, William Elding agreed with the governor, possibly because he could find no Biblical text to support it, though there was evidence enough for flogging males. In Deuteronomy Chapter 25 verses 2 and 3 it is written: *And it shall be, if the wicked man is worthy to be beaten, that the judge shall cause him to lie down, and to be beaten before his face, according to his fault, by a certain number. Forty stripes he may give him, and not exceed: lest, if he should exceed, and beat him above these with many stripes, then thy brother should seem vile unto thee.* Thus, to keep within the Biblical mandate the stripes were limited to thirty-nine on any one day.

In 1831 a delicate female slave received an additional 39 lashes by order of a Member of the House when she said did not deserve the first 39. Because of this the governor dissolved the Assembly but the House remained adamant. The 'horrid business' was only resolved when the slaves were finally freed throughout the Bahamas in 1834. At that time Lord Rolle vacated his holding and was presumed to have donated the land to his former slaves quite simply because his Exuma plantations had little monetary value.

MARTIN ELDON WAS MANUMITTED on the death of William Elding and the plantation was put up for sale by his wife. Miriam had been frail all her life and by now had developed into a chronic invalid. The plantation quickly reverted to bush. The family moved to the house on East Street near the centre of town that had been owned by her father in law. William Elding's Last Will and Testament required for their only son Jonathan, aged seventeen, to be sent away to Harvard College in the New England Bay Colony to obtain an education befitting a Christian gentleman.

It was hoped he would become a Puritan Minister of the Gospel. But Jonathan was able to persuade his ailing mother to let him to stay near her in Nassau. He had in fact set his mind on joining the local militia. It was Felicity in fact who devoted her life to caring for her mother.

Jonathan took after his grandfather Read Elding and was a very different from his reclusive parents. He was tall and good-looking with hazel coloured eyes. Even though Jonathan was brought up as a strict Puritan, after his father died, to the chagrin of his sisters, he pursued a very different lifestyle. Out-going, he enjoyed a lively social life in Nassau especially after he married a teen-age daughter of the attorney general. His young wife Abigail was a pretty girl who, through her family connections, opened many doors for Jonathan. They built a house on Bay Street facing Hog Island where they had three children, two girls and one boy. George, the second child to be born, was named for the monarch of the day, King George II. Even though Jonathan was a strict disciplinarian in the militia, he was nevertheless well liked by his troops. For most of his military service in the islands he had little to do even though the Spanish and French remained a constant and serious threat. But all that was to change when the winds of change blew south from the North American continent.

Only two miles in distance from Jonathan Elding and his family but leagues apart in the social hierarchy Martin Elding, now a free man, was living in a shack in the community commonly known as 'over the hill'. As a former slave, Martin Elding was careful always to keep the signed, sealed and witnessed manumission in a safe place:

> *...and by these presents do manumit, make free and release from bondage, and all servitude, the said negro man slave named Martin Elding and his issue on my demise.*
>
> *signed* ***William Elding Esquire***
>
> ....

Martin was fortunate indeed to be freed. Most slaves and their issue remained the property of their owner for life and were bequeathed as chattels on the death of the 'Masta'. In the most illogical and iniquitous practice imaginable some slaves—as a privilege—were allowed to ***buy*** their freedom from their owner. After gaining his freedom Martin tried his hand at several jobs but found his employers treated him little differently from when had he had been a slave. He became a nominal Christian, married a free African girl born in the Bahamas, sired two children, John and Ezekiel, and even taught himself to read English a little. He had ambitions and dreams but they were not to be realized in his short lifetime. Before he reached the age of 40, M'buda (now commonly known to all in the small community as Martin Elding) died of smallpox. He was buried in a small churchyard marked by a simple wooden cross that for a few years carried the epitaph:

Martin Eldon—A Chriftian free African
Died 6th August 1775

Martin's eldest son John, was a good student and at the local missionary school he was selected by the Society for the Propagation of the Gospel to receive instruction into Holy Orders. The SPG sensibly reasoned that people of colour could more effectively carry the gospel of Christianity to their own race. On completion of his studies the Reverend John Martin Elding was appointed one of the first black Ministers of the Gospel in the Bahama Islands.

After serving as an itinerant preacher for a few years in the out islands the Reverend John joined the fast-growing Baptist sect that met fierce opposition from the established church and people like William Elding. The local newspaper opined that Baptist services would take on the look of a *'John Canoe'* parade and *'...their worshipping would be more in conformity with the noisy rites of Bacchus, than with the sober doctrines of the Christian faith...'* But despite the opposition 'Rev.' John became the popular minister of a small chapel for free blacks in the Delancey Town area of Nassau that served part of the 'over the hill' community. Interestingly the wooden chapel was named 'Bethel', the same name that Moravian missionaries gave their religious community in Alaska (Bethel is also a common Bahamian surname). At his chapel, the former Africans found much to learn from the Rev. John concerning Christianity and especially about the institution of slavery and how it applied to the Bahamian community.

The 'Rev.' John's parishioners were able to identify with the ancient Israelites being taken to Babylon in captivity and they could understand well the cruel Egyptian taskmasters the Children of Israel had to endure in Egypt. But in the New Testament teaching they were completely mystified by the seeming biblical acceptance of the practice of slavery. Their reading of the Bible seemed to sanction the institution of slavery as when St. Paul announced, without condemnation, the return of a slave to its master. In Colossians Chapter 4 verse 1 he wrote: *'Masters grant to your slaves justice and fairness, knowing that you too have a Master in heaven'*. The text was commonly accepted to condone a 'humane' form of slavery. The Epistle of St. Paul to Philemon was written down for St. Paul by Onesimus who was very probably himself a slave (his name means 'Useful'). St. Paul did however, suggest that 'in Christ' there was no distinction between slave and free. But by this expression St. Paul probably meant that freedom would be in the next life, not this. St. Peter also in his first Epistle Chapter 2 verses 18 and 19 would seem to both accept both slavery and the brutality it endorsed: *'Servants* (read 'slaves') *be subject to your masters with all fear not only the good and gentle but also the ill-tempered, For this is thankworthy if a man for conscience toward God endure grief suffering wrongfully'*. Yet, for all the ambiguity the new Bahamian acolytes were fervent in their devotion to the new Faith even though they were puzzled at some of its tenets.

One day the Reverend John was presented with a momentous problem that would completely change his life. Just as he was entering his chapel after nightfall a slave whom he immediately recognised named Magnus, appeared out of the bush. It was immediately apparent the unfortunate man had been brutally beaten by his master and had run away.

Magnus fearfully entered the small chapel and approached the Baptist clergyman. Everyone knew the law prescribed that a runaway slave when caught was to be given fifty lashes and any accomplices would also receive severe punishment.

In the misty darkness of the chapel Magnus pleaded:

"Rev. John you gotta protect me! God in heaven knows I been wronged...I showed the master he were planting cotton in the wrong field...he got very angry...I got angry...I told him that stony ground on'y good for yams...everyone know that...he shouted...I shouted back...I ain't going back...you gotta help me!"

The situation Magnus had outlined was not unusual. From years of working the land the field hands had a great knowledge of what would grow, where, and in what season. It was not in the interest of anyone to have a crop fail. But, right or wrong, the lash was the penalty prescribed by law for insubordination.

This was a brutal age and cruelty was not only reserved only for defenceless slaves. A seaman could expect to be flogged aboard ship for the smallest of offences and for something more serious he could be keel-hauled. There are records of women being stripped to the waist and publicly flogged by Puritans for being, in their estimation, heretics. For stealing a sheep the sentence was sometimes a death of slow strangulation by hanging. For heresy the offender was sometimes burned alive at the stake. While for the crime of treason, the malefactor would be tortured which was then followed by the grisly procedure of being hanged and, while still alive, he would have his entrails cut out. In short, to step out of line in these times was to invite cruel and terrible punishment.

The law against harbouring a slave was also very severe but a higher law still, permitted the Reverend Minister no option. Christianity it seemed to him, often seemed to favour the oppressors. 'Render unto

Caesar...' was the only advice that he could give. Magnus must surrender himself to his master.

But then could he in good conscience, Reverend John wondered, surrender this sorely abused man to more beatings for having run away?

The Baptist Minister pondered the matter for some time and decided that there must be another interpretation of Holy Writ. He quickly took the man to his small house attached to the chapel and gave him new clothes and bathed the broken flesh on his back. Then he contacted his younger brother Ezekiel, his faithful assistant. After a whispered conversation Ezekiel promised he would arrange for a small sailing boat to be made ready at the east point of the island. They had little time to consider that a conspiracy of this sort could bring the most brutal punishment down upon all of them.

"Magnus, you work your way through the woods to near the east point and wait. Make sure you are not seen! Around midnight come out of hiding when you hear a whistle. We will have a boat ready for you..."

Magnus was about to say that he hardly knew how to handle a boat but stayed silent. He would have to sail single handed northwards with the wind abeam Ezekiel explained to him, and he would have to try to reach the Berry Islands, some thirty or so miles away, by daybreak. They all held the unrealistic hope that people would not connect the missing boat with the runaway slave.

The rendezvous was made just after midnight and the two churchmen helped Magnus launch the boat. They pushed it beyond the waves and Magnus unfurled the sail and the boat moved slowly away from the shore. The Reverend John murmured a heart-felt prayer. Ezekiel added a too audible "Amen".

Magnus had almost no experience of sailing and there was hardly a breath of wind that night. He understood well it would be folly to be on the open water and less than twenty miles from New Providence at daybreak.

By 3 o'clock in the morning Magnus had travelled only two miles from Nassau. He could see a few of the oil lights still burning in the town. Then he heard distant thunder and within half an hour the wind picked up. During the squall that followed, he travelled a fair distance but as the sea got rougher, a gigantic gust capsized the boat. The small boat was heavy and he could not right it so he hung on to the boom until first light.

Magnus could not see land but in the early morning light he could make out the boat and its fittings better and was able to take down the sail. For many hours he remained in the water but the dark hulk of the boat attracted a shoal of silvery fish to seek cover. It was not long before the small fish attracted a large shark and Magnus decided quickly it would be safer if he lay on the surface of the upturned boat. The boat was now more visible but since the shark kept vigil for several hours he had no choice but to stay out of the water.

Only once that the day did Magnus see a another boat and she was a sloop far south of him probably *en route* to Nassau from the direction of Abaco. As the day wore on, with energy borne of desperation, he righted the boat. Then he bailed out as much of the water out of the hold as he could and waited. As nightfall approached Magnus hoisted the sail and got under way once more. The wind was shifty again in the night but by dawn he had reached a small island. He moored the boat among the mangroves in a small cove, making sure to take down the mast and covered the hull with branches and leaves.

Once ashore he searched for berries and grasses to eat. The island was a tangle of low shrubs and saw grass offering little in the way of nutrition. To quench his thirst, he drank from puddles of water left from the recent storms.

He lived like this for four days getting weaker and more desperate with time. He was painfully aware that he would not survive.

Magnus was half-asleep on the morning of the fifth day when, in the distance, he saw a small sailing dinghy heading for the island. His worst fears were realised. A search party was coming for him! On being returned to his master he knew he would receive incredibly cruel punishment but he would be alive at least. He made no effort to conceal himself but just waited on the beach as the small boat approached. He would submit without protest.

As the boat got nearer Magnus was able to make out two figures on the boat, he saw the man in the bow was black. That was not surprising, the man at the tiller would be the white overseer.

But, as the boat got even nearer, he found he was mistaken for the man in the stern was also an African and, as they got nearer still, he made out their faces - it was the Reverend John and Zeke his brother! They were waving furiously.

When they beached their boat, Magnus walked down to the shore to give himself up.

"It no good Rev, I die here…take me back…"

"No!" the Reverend John replied, "we are all in this together…you were seen at the chapel, they know a boat was taken…we are wanted for questioning as accomplices…a search is being organised for you…for all of us!"

"Then what shall we do?" Magnus cried.

"We will survive...I have heard tell of our people who escaped in other islands...they live free in the bush...they are called Maroons...we shall try to survive like them!"

And survive they did. The Rev. John had brought a little food and Zeke was handy with a fishing line. They cannibalized the boat that brought Magnus to the island. The ropes, tackle and the canvas sail would be used for several purposes including temporary shelter. The canvas would also come in useful later, Rev. John suggested, to make shoes and clothing. When all was ready they set sail just after dark.

They slowly worked their way up the shallow bank to the west of the virtually uninhabited Berry Islands. Zeke was at the tiller and they travelled only by darkest night to avoid being seen. Gradually Magnus's strength returned. Near daybreak they found refuge on small mangrove islets far from any of the larger islands that might have been inhabited. It took them nearly a week to reach Great Stirrup Cay near the northern end of the Berry Island chain where they were confronted by the deep water of the Northwest Providence Channel.

Assembling together in a cove the Reverend John dropped to his knees and led them in prayer then, just after nightfall, they started to sail due north.

With favourable winds, the crossing of the Northwest Providence Channel to the island of Grand Bahama took only two days. On their journey they saw only one large sailing ship on their passage but she did not alter course to hail them. To the merchantman *en route* to Europe the small boat in the distance was probably dismissed as a sloop belonging to some poor lost native fishermen.

The island the runaways finally arrived at was absolutely featureless. Indeed the only physical feature that caught their eye was a tiny rock poking out of the fringing reef of the southern shoreline as they approached the island. So Zeke headed for it and they landed on a nearby broad sandy beach. The Reverend John knelt to say another heartfelt prayer, then they lowered the mast, folded the sail and dragged the boat over the sand dunes and buried it.

That done, they started to explore the island and found it was virtually barren of fruit-bearing shrubs and trees but was covered with an extensive pine forest. The fugitives soon stumbled upon the creek that had been discovered centuries before by other visitors from another hemisphere of the 'old world'. In the shallows of the creek they captured some wading birds which gave them their first meal of flesh in over a month.

In their explorations they came upon the caverns that had once been inhabited by the Lucayan Indians. Magnus peering through the 'skylight' of one cave was terrified when he saw skeletons beneath the water of the bell-shaped cavern. He was fearful they were *jumbey* spirits and, emitting a loud scream, started to flee until the Reverend John stopped him. The Reverend Minister deduced correctly that they were the harmless bones of some former Indian inhabitants of the islands.

Near to the caves the fugitives found boat-shaped clay bowls, griddles, flint 'knives' and hammer stones all of which attested to the rapid departure of the former inhabitants. In fact, the hapless Lucayans had disappeared within just a few years of the first appearance of the white men on Grand Bahama. The fugitives were grateful indeed to have the use of the Indian implements and tools.

The visitors set up camp near the caves and Reverend John organized their days along the early Christian model. They prayed, they built a simple shelter, they fished the creek, they prayed, they cultivated wild cassava they found growing near the caves and then, after praying again, they slept. From here onwards each day became a replica of the last.

Throughout their sojourn they lived near the caves and were especially careful any time they went near to the beach.

For several years they were undisturbed living a life on the bare margin of survival at the caverns of the Lucayans. They were perhaps the only 'Maroons' in the Bahamas for the colony did not offer runaways either the cover or the sustenance of the larger islands of the Indies.

Meanwhile in Nassau a reward was being offered for information leading to the apprehension of Magnus and his accomplices. A notice was inserted in the **'Nassau Gazette'** of August, 1792:

> **RUNAWAY on the 25 of July last, a strong Negro Fellow named MAGNUS, about 25 years of age, field hand at Trident Plantation who is well known about town. He is probably associated with the Negro preacher John Elding, sometime known as 'Rev. John' and his brother Ezekiel Elding both of the Bethel Baptist Chapel who are absent and wanted for questioning. Whoever will deliver the said Negro to the subscriber and shall provide information leading to the apprehension of the said 'Reverend' and his brother shall receive *Twenty dollars* Reward.**
>
> *signed*
> *Gregory Carey*

The notice brought forward no information but it was common knowledge that a boat partly owned by Ezekiel Elding was missing from the eastern beach. There seemed little doubt that the wanted men had escaped on it. The most probable destination of the fugitives it was thought, was Andros, the largest island of the Bahamas, which at this time was virtually uninhabited and largely unexplored. A search party was sent to Andros and another to the Berry Islands but no trace of the fugitives was found. As time passed it was assumed the fugitives had been lost at sea.

The punishment for an absence of ten days and a flight of eight miles was decreed to be worthy of the maximum of 50 lashes. At a minimum Magnus could expect 61 lashes spread over two or three days if he was captured. The prospect for the Reverend John and Ezekiel hardly less severe,

'If any Free Negro or Indian shall be found guilty of...employing, hiding or assisting the escape of a runaway slave...he or she shall forfeit his or her freedom, and shall be transported off these islands by order of the Justices of the Peace.'

The punishment for white men aiding and abetting a runaway was a hefty fine of £60 or 60 stripes (interestingly 10 more stripes than the runaway!)

In Grand Bahama time dragged on, the occasional boat could be seen offshore but no one ever stopped. One summer's day a European visitor sailing near the south shore of Grand Bahama noted for posterity:

'...there was not the least appearance of cultivation on the island I could not but behold the beautiful and fragrant woods over the white sands, without recurring to the fate of that innocent race of people whose name it bears...'

The writer here correctly surmises that the island had been previously inhabited and suggested the original Indian name for the country was 'Bahama' but he could have had no idea he was being watched from the shore as he penned those words.

In 1792 some land was purchased at the western end of the island and a few years later a small plantation was established. For months the three fugitives furtively watched from the behind the cover of the bush as the plantation grew. Magnus was especially pensive as they watched.

Then one day the Reverend John said what they had all been thinking.

"Let us go and turn ourselves in. We will tell the plantation owner our story, he will detain us of course, but we will be fed before we are transported back to Nassau, we can ask for mercy, though doubtless we shall have to suffer punishment, but at least we shall save our lives...and..." he added, "...one day I would like to start a church again to thank the Good Lord for sparing our lives..."

So timidly they approached the owner of the plantation who was a Loyalist farmer whose first plantation had failed on Rum Cay. He had been directed to Grand Bahama by Doctor Benjamin Church, the eminent Loyalist and Member of the House of Assembly.

"Hey you men! What are you doing here?" the plantation owner shouted when he saw the three men approaching from the south beach and, without waiting for a reply, added, "...if you have come from Abaco seeking employment I can offer you work. Presently I could use a few good hands..."

The three men looked at each other realising that this man either did not know who they were or more probably was confusing them with somebody else. But at least he seemed most pleased to see them.

"Yes we need work, two of us know about farming...he can handle a boat too," the Reverend John said pointing at Zeke, "and I have worked in a house," he added stretching the truth a little.

"Good, then I'll show you your quarters...all are free men here...you will live over there," he indicated a small rectangular building without a roof. "Oh, yes it urgently needs a roof...if you could help old Kaleb..."

The three men fell in with the routine of life at the West End plantation and lived out the remainder of their days on the island of Grand Bahama. They completed the building of the servants' quarters just in time for Old Kaleb to have a roof over his head on his deathbed. The Reverend John became the chief servant of the household and confidant of the master who was a hopeless alcoholic. The loneliness of his existence and the problems of making ends meet in Grand Bahama had driven him to seek solace in homemade liquor. The Rev. John was indispensable in tending to the affairs of the plantation and helping the farmer lower his dependence on alcohol while Magnus and Zeke worked the plantation with a special energy. They had developed a deep faith from their association with the Baptist Minister and were content with what fate had decreed for them.

Seven years after they started to work, Ezekiel had a son, Theophilus Onesimus Elding by a pretty almond-eyed servant girl named Molly with whom he had a 'Christian marriage' that had been solemnized by the Reverend John in a ceremony in an old barn on the West End property. The union may have been a marriage in the eyes of God but it was certainly unknown to the State, for to publicize such a union would have been a sure way to invite discovery.

The continuing inter-marriage of people in the Bahamas may have been of little interest to any of the parties but Molly was distantly related to Mother Iya who, nearly two centuries before had produced offspring sired by the Indian *cacique* Caonoca. When the Spanish came to the Caicos seeking slaves part of her family escaped to Little Inagua. There, the small community survived for a century and a half inter-marrying with Taíno who escaped to the island from Cuba. Eventually the remnants of the community settled in Great Inagua and intermarried with Yoruba slaves brought there to work the saltpans. On that island Molly's great grandmother sired a son with a Bermudan overseer. The son, who was manumitted at birth, eventually made his way to Rum Cay where he worked on the plantation of Joseph Smith. When the Loyalist farmer's plantation failed on Rum Cay, Molly the daughter of the manumitted slave, was carried to West End.

The Loyalist farmer in his sober moments often pondered why providence should have sent him three men who never gave any trouble and always worked so diligently. Indeed, the soil of the island was very infertile and only by their considerable energy and resolve did they manage to get the land to yield anything. The plantation owner understood these men possessed some exceptional inner motivation.

Though in his sober moments he harboured suspicions he was content never to ask them exactly where they came from.

***THE BRITISH**, who had transported so many slaves to the new world, eventually relented of their involvement in the abhorrent trafficking of humans in bondage.*

In 1772 after the Somerset Case, slavery was abolished in England. This case involved a slave owned by an American colonist who was about to return him to America from England. The Court ruled that to permit the return of the slave would condone the practice of slavery in England. The event did not go unnoticed in the American colonies. By 1807 the transporting of slaves was abolished throughout the British Empire though it took another 27 long years for the slaves to be completely emancipated. The Emancipation Act came into force in the Bahamas on the 1st August 1834.

Emancipation in the Bahamas was achieved with 'utmost tranquillity' the governor recorded at the time, and the lieutenant governor issued guidelines setting out the 'chief points in the new system' reminding 'Masters' that for four years they still had to care for the people in their employ, and 'Slaves' that they still had to work in order to be fed and clothed.

In the United States it took another 31 years and a bloody civil war for the practice of slavery to cease. Brazil, in 1890, was the last country in the Americas to abolish slavery.

Chapter 10 - Red, White and True Blue (1770 - 1800)

A Loyalist is someone who has his heart in England and his body in America and whose neck should be stretched.

Contemporary Rebel witticism

TOWARDS THE END *of the eighteenth century the Bahamas was to get caught up in a web of events which had their beginnings in the British colonies of the middle Atlantic seaboard. These colonies decided at first to defy, then later to revolt, against the Mother Country. The event has been recorded with much extravagant and patriotic prose by the successful rebels but there was another poignant facet to the story which was played out in part in the small island colony of the Bahamas.*

At first there was little sympathy in North America for open revolt and, apart from royalist France, little encouragement from abroad either. But in the end the revolutionaries had their way and a radical but noble political experiment was begun. Many people in the American colonies who had been in government, the professions and agriculture (particularly the larger landowners) found themselves on the losing side after the Revolutionary War. They were branded by the victorious side as traitors and forced to leave the new republic for an uncertain future in Britain, Canada or the Caribbean.

This account follows the fortunes of Doctor Benjamin Church, a New England Loyalist, who risked his life for the Crown but whose patriotic actions were uncovered by Massachusetts 'rebels' who forced him into exile.

In this story he eventually makes his way to the Bahamas.

Fort Charlotte at the western entrance to Nassau harbour. The army barracks is left of the fort

THE ADAMS FAMILY of Braintree near Boston was the catalyst at the centre of a gathering storm. It was a storm that derived its early dynamism from John Adams senior, the patriarch of a clan of hardy settlers in colonial New England. The older Adams, according to one biographer, was a proud, pugnacious, independent-minded man with a hot temper and a very strong will. These character attributes resulted in his being constantly at odds with the British administration of the Colony. Though, if truth be told, he was probably of a mind to be opposed to all authority not of his own making.

The patriarch's restlessness festered for years in his household until it developed into open protest when his son John took up the gauntlet. Thereafter it found support outside the family hearth in the mysterious Long Room Club a directing force behind an even more sinister and secretive organization, the 'Sons of Liberty'.

The younger John Adams, his cousin Samuel and a few descendants of the original Pilgrim Fathers that included Dr. Benjamin Church, the Lothrops and the Warrens, were all members of the Long Room Club. To their enemies they were impolitely called, *'Sons of Licentiousness…obscure pettyfogging attorneys, bankrupt shopkeepers, outlawed smugglers, ignorant bricklayers…the foulest, subtlest, and most venomous Serpents ever to issue from the egg of Sedition.'* But despite the harsh epithets and official condemnation, the strength of their opposition to British governance in the colonies grew.

As long-standing members of the inner circle of the Long Room Club, Adams and Church were among the most vociferous in denouncing what they called British 'tyranny' and demanding bold and violent action. It later came to light however, that Doctor Church had been routinely supplying information about the rebellious cell to the British authorities. Benjamin Church was apprehended and summarily tried by the 'patriots' after they had found a message written in cypher to British General Gage.

In his defence Church cautioned the rebels, "...if you pursue this traitorous course you will create a schism that will divide forever the English-speaking world!"

Adams replied angrily, "...or it just might purge it of arrogance and expand its horizons!"

It took a long time for the rebels to decipher the coded message. But when the code was finally broken the fate of Dr Church hung in the balance. Besides information about rebel troop strengths and arms he ended his note, *'For the sake of the miserable convulsed empire, solicit peace, repeal the acts or Britain is undone. This advice is the result of warm affection to my king and to the realm. Remember, I never deceived you. Every article here sent you is sacredly true'.* Given the mood of the times and his daring deception, Dr Church was fortunate indeed that his life was spared especially since Washington wanted him hanged. It is quite possible that his fellow New Englanders, most of them former classmates at Harvard College, were responsible for the leniency of the judgement to their former friend and colleague. And there may of course, even have been a moment of self-appraisal as to who was in reality the traitor. After an agonising wait Church was finally released and with a brief sojourn in New York City made his way to the 'Indies'.

Many colonial settlers had genuine grievances with the government and administration that emanated from both the English and the colonial legislatures. There was also considerable disdain for many of the English landowners in the style of the Lords Proprietors who never visited the colonies or were absent for long periods. Indeed the discontent of the colonists might be accurately characterized as an early manifestation of the 'inevitability' of class conflict postulated by another, most unlikely revolutionary bedfellow named Karl Marx, half a century later.

Even people who had reached high office in the colonial administration yet were born in America were angered when they were not granted the titles and privileges that would have been their due had they been born in the British Isles. The predominant sentiment of the colonists was that they should be treated more like Englishmen that many considered themselves to be, or at the very least, as full participating members of the expanding British nation.

To further add to the colonist's discontent, England imposed a tax on her North American possessions that was embraced in the Stamp Act of 1765. The tax was intended to help defray the cost of defending the colonies from French incursions for, without this defence, the northern portion of the continent would, most assuredly, have fallen into French hands to the certain detriment of the interests of the English-speaking colonists. But the crux of the matter was that the British government, doing the bidding of the King, had simply imposed the tax as a *fait acompi* without reference to the colonists.

Lawyers, like John Adams, later to become the second president of the United States, were quick to declare that taxation imposed without representation was unjust and contrary 'to the inherent rights of mankind.' Though, in truth, the quixotic proposition he espoused was quite novel and certainly unpracticed anywhere in the political world of the eighteenth century. And Adams carried his fiery illogical reasoning to hyperbole when he further stated, *'opposition, nay, open avowed resistance by arms, against usurpation and lawless violence, is not rebellion by the law of God or the land!'* Angry, inflammatory words like that begged for trouble.

Matters soon deteriorated to the point when, in 1770, there was a 'massacre' (so-called by the rhetoric of the time) in Boston of seven belligerent townsfolk who provoked a riot and were killed by British soldiers.

The torch had been applied to an incendiary situation.

Adams and his rebellious cohorts were quick to exploit the situation and the first open conflict of the revolt, the Battle of Lexington, followed shortly thereafter.

There is no question that many colonists were disgruntled with British rule, but it was also true that very few wanted physical, open hostility. Indeed it has been estimated that out of the two and a half million people then in North America over half had no wish at all to support open revolt. A wag aptly summed up the feelings of the populace at the time:

'Which is better: to be ruled by one tyrant who is 3000 miles away, or by 3000 tyrants not a mile away?'

It is certain that the British did not do all they could have done to put down the uprising. There was a feeling, in the early years of the revolt at least, that the matter would somehow be resolved peaceably.

But it was not to be.

The man favoured by Adams into leading the insurrection was an ambivalent man at best who, before the Revolution had written to a correspondent in England, *'mankind when left to themselves are unfit for their own government'*. A slave-owning gentleman farmer, George Washington was chosen principally because he would bring the Southern Colonies into the conflict. Washington, a Virginian, had had an undistinguished career as a general in the British army in wars against the French and the Indians but in his new role he was able to mould a fighting force out of the feisty colonists.

Following Adams' lead, Washington relied on propaganda to sway the loyalties of the wavering colonists. Early in the conflict Adams enraged the colonists (and the English with relatives in the American colonies) by circulating the rumour that the British were sending bales of colonist's skulls to England as bounty. Washington, with more guile, urged his friends to fabricate tales of British atrocities, *'seemingly with indifference, drop it at the table before the servants'* (with this in mind it is strange to consider that Washington even today is considered a paragon of honesty). Yet it was only in the latter stages of the revolution that independence from Great Britain was being spoken about as being the principal object of the war.

Late in the conflict Washington still held the British to a stalemate on land while pinning his hopes on French naval intervention. And the curious fact is that perhaps the most decisive battle of the War of Independence was a sea battle in which not a single American colonist participated. Towards the end of the conflict French Admiral de Grasse was able to hold the British fleet at bay at Chesapeake and thus allow General Rochambeau to land thousands of French soldiers to tip the scales in the final battle of the war at Yorktown. So in the end, Washington triumphed in a land battle. In the final encounter at Yorktown over two hundred British soldiers were killed, and seeing further struggle was hopeless, the British army surrendered in 1776.

As is well known George Washington was elected first President of the United States of America. The year was 1789. Not so well known perhaps, is that when he died in 1799, he had been an unquestioning loyal British subject for over two thirds of his life.

IN 1775, WHILE THE WAR STILL RAGED, Lord Dunmore the governor of Virginia, who was later to re-appear in the Bahama Islands, ordered the seaport of Norfolk burned so it would be unavailable to the enemy. That same year he issued a proclamation offering freedom to all indentured servants and Africans willing to fight for the Crown. Dunmore formed the 'Ethiopian Regiment' for African Americans who wore a uniform boldly stamped with the words 'Liberty to Slaves'. Patrick Henry, the American patriot, known for his popular rallying cry: *'give me liberty or give me death'*, labeled Dunmore's action, *'fatal to public safety'*, forgetting for a moment perhaps, that it was 'revolution' that was fatal to public safety! It was estimated that some 100,000 slaves escaped behind the British lines, some of whom completed a full circle by eventually returning to Africa.

Contrary to popular belief, the rebellious colonists had few natural friends or allies. Many native Americans were quick to take sides in the conflict. The Crees and Chickasaws let it be known that, '*...they taught us to make war and discovered to us the blessings of peace...*(we shall)*...never desert our friends the English.*' But, to be precise, the Indians who joined in the conflict were fighting 'against' the expansionist colonists rather than for Crown and Empire. The Africans in America too could see that they would be better off under a British administration that was showing dim signs of conscience in the matter of slavery rather under a government of colonists who needed slave labour to thrive.

Even the French settlers stranded in Quebec after the defeat of the French in Canada elected to remain within the British domain rather than support what they saw as dour, abrasive, land-hungry Puritan rebels to the south. Whereas their compatriots in France, whose centrist absolute monarchy was diametrically opposed to anything to do with republicanism, provided important comfort and support to the American rebels out of hostility to their traditional enemy on the other side of the English Channel.

At the height of the turmoil on March 1st 1776, a naval squadron commanded by Commodore Esek Hopkins and under orders from the new continental government sailed from Philadelphia with eight ships bound for Chesapeake Bay to fight the British. Once there, Hopkins discovered that the British fleet was too strong to engage, so he conceived a daring, but less ambitious plan and sailed south to the British colonial outpost of the Bahama Islands.

On reaching Hole in the Wall, Abaco, he impressed two Bahamian 'conchs' to serve as pilots for his fleet. The Bahamians were astonished by the rebels' demands and tried to resist but were persuaded to cooperate upon threat of torture. At daybreak two days later the American ships appeared off the bar of the Nassau harbour to the great consternation of everyone in the town.

The harbour pilot reported to the Governor Montfort Browne that he had 'espied in the offing seven sails' (evidentally one of Hopkin's ships went undetected). The governor descended to the door of Government House in his nightshirt and grumbled agitatedly about being disturbed.

'What am I to do?' he inquired of the pilot.

The humble pilot was surprised to be asked for advice by the Royal Governor but mumbled that perhaps the governor should send the gunpowder away on a fast ship. The governor's actual words were recorded:

'I thank you for the hint; you are right...tell the captain of the sloop to prepare to sail...I will be down the hill directly.'

But for the governor this was a most inconvenient turn of events. To John Gambier, his aide, who was so lame with gout he could hardly walk, the Governor complained, "I fear I am as incapacitated as you!" adding, "and...it is yet so early in the morning!"

"But the rebels approach Your Excellency!" persisted Gambier.

"Zounds! The rebel fleet is now off? Then let us to the fort to sound the alarm!" Then, considering the worst possible consequences of the rebel intrusion he added, 'and now I must go home to make myself a little decent.'

The Council was summoned and three cannon shots were fired to alert the population to the danger. Hopkins, now sailing close to the bar of the harbour with his telescope trained on Nassau thought the cannon fire was aimed at his fleet so he sailed to the eastern side of Hog Island north of the city (the small cay would later to be re-named Paradise Island).

Preparations for the defence of Nassau were chaotic but finally about 150 militiamen were assembled and sent to Fort Montagu to engage the rebels.

Visual contact was made and the commander of the Bahamian militia, Jonathan the eldest son of William Elding, reported back to Government House that a defence had been organised but that there were between 250 and 300 fully armed marines about to advance on the town. In his *communiqué* he stressed the superior numbers and armaments of the hostile force. But while the homeland defence was being organised the rebel invaders distributed leaflets saying that if the community would surrender they would preserve life and property.

Admiral Esek Hopkins

This was all the Bahamian governor and colonists wanted to hear. Having no stomach for a fight they immediately surrendered. Government House was taken over by the rebels and a confusing new flag flew over the building. It was a British ensign with strange red and white horizontal stripes in the fly.

The Americans remained two weeks in Nassau and were entertained 'royally' by some of the republican-minded populace. A contemporary report suggests the officers were, *'countenanced by many of the principal inhabitants and elegantly entertained by some of the officers of the Government.'* George, the teenage son of Jonathan Elding was present at one of the receptions and declared boldly that, "he was for the new Republick if their deeds are half as good as their words!" Even Chastity, his prudish sister, found common ground with a few of the sailors from New England who shared her dour religious views. Prudence was even more impressed by the eager young militiamen. If she had been just a few years older she later admitted, she would happily have run away with any one of the fresh-faced young marines to the brave new American republic. However, fate decreed she was to remain in Nassau and, when only in her late teens, married a semi-literate white Bahamian sea captain by the name of Boaz Lowe and produced a brood of eight children.

While his children were fraternizing with the enemy in Nassau, Jonathan Elding had taken ship to Long Island in the central Bahamas to be out of harm's way. Under orders from the governor he sailed with a secret cargo across the Great Bahama Bank where, because of the uncharted shoals he was fairly certain the rebels would not follow him. With contrary winds he was forced to tack often but eventually he joined Exuma Sound then followed the string of cays to the safe haven of Long Island.

During the time the American sailors were occupying Nassau it was reported that many of them drank themselves to oblivion on sequestered wine and spirits. Even allowing for the high spirits over the success of their first naval engagement, with over one hundred men reporting sick, one has to wonder if their liquor might not have been laced by someone of royalist persuasions! Gossip had it that Jonathan Elding, whose rapid departure had been noted, was probably the culprit.

The invasion provided substantial ordnance to the rebels. Before leaving Nassau, Hopkins managed to find an extensive hoard of 88 cannons, 15 mortars, 5500 shells and 11,000 cannon balls but the commodity most urgently needed by the revolutionaries—gunpowder—had been expeditiously shipped out on the governor's orders. It fell under the custody of Jonathan Elding on Long Island.

Governor Montfort Browne (presumably in his best uniform) and the person occupying the hated position of Inspector-General of Customs in North America, who unhappily happened to be in Nassau at the time, were carried off by Hopkins. The bloodless victory lost some of its savour when the eight vessel American fleet was mauled on its return voyage by a solitary British man of war, *HMS Glasgow*. The *Boston Gazette* of the time reported that some of Hopkin's crew had come down with a 'tropical fever' (possibly typhoid) on their brief visit to Nassau which, together with throbbing hangovers, perhaps explains the poor performance of Hopkin's fleet in the ensuing unequal naval encounter. In June 1776 Hopkins was ordered by Congress in Philadelphia to answer charges of not 'annoying' the United States' enemies sufficiently. In 1777 Esek Hopkins was suspended from command and a year later, dismissed from the service.

The townspeople of Nassau would later charge Governor Montfort Browne with *'a neglect of, and an Inattention to, the Intelligence received of the designs of the Rebels; even when the Information was brought that they were not more than twenty Leagues distance from this fort.'* After the most turbulent years of the American Revolution were over, Browne was replaced by Governor John Maxwell in 1780.

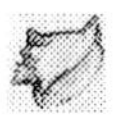 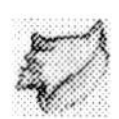 

HISTORY, IT IS SAID, is written by the victors. In the American Revolutionary War there can be no doubt that events have been glamourised for the sake of national pride. The Revolution was in fact a sorry conflict that need not have happened. It could perhaps, be more accurately called the 'first' American Civil War for it pitted countrymen against countrymen, friend against friend, family against family. For both sides were allied by blood, manners, language, laws, religion and commerce.

Indeed, to illustrate the point, it is interesting to note that many British troops who surrendered at Yorktown elected to stay in the newly independent country of their former enemy (possibly a circumstance unique in the history of human conflict). This fact alone compellingly suggests that there was a clearly understood commonality between either side. The ***Declaration of Independence,*** whining about perceived injustices and indignities of the King upon his American subjects makes reference to it thus:

'Nor have we been wanting in our attentions to our Brittish brethren…we have appealed to their native justice…they too have been deaf to the voice of justice and consanguinity…' (interestingly the word 'Brittish' was misspelled in the famous *Declaration*). Even a generation later during the period up to 1812, American seamen were impressed into service with the British navy on the contrived pretext that the American seamen could, when occasion required, serve as surrogates for British sailors.

In the near anarchy that followed the rebel's victory in the American colonies there was serious retribution against the considerable minority who, throughout the revolution, had remained either neutral or loyal to the Crown. The treatment afforded the unfortunate Tories remains one of the most sordid chapters in American history. For, after the ***Declaration of Independence*** was signed in 1776, each State of the Union enacted laws designating them as traitors. Thousands were deprived of their civil rights, debarred from earning a living, robbed of their possessions, imprisoned and, in many cases, banished from the land of their birth. In addition, all sorts of malicious indignities were inflicted upon them in the name of patriotism. Perhaps it was with this situation in mind that Dr Samuel Johnson, the famous lexicographer, noted around this time he considered '*...patriotism...the last refuge of a scoundrel*'.

The windfall rewards to the newly independent colonists were great. It was an unprecedented period of political and economic opportunism. Political appointments were there for the taking, buildings were pillaged, landowners were expelled from their houses - often at gun point - and unpopular Loyalists of rank were tarred and feathered. In an extreme case a mob '*...stripped an Anglican clergyman of his clothes, hung some women up by their heels after tarring and feathering them...(then they)...wretchedly abused others marking them with excrement in the sign of the cross.*'

The Loyalists, many of whom had been the very essence of the economic and political life of the nation, were conveyed out of the United States to an uncertain future in the Mother Country, Canada or the West Indies. The Loyalists, like the Moors and Jews who had been expelled from Spain exactly 300 years before had been an elite in their country but were summarily deported and, in many cases, within a generation were reduced to abject poverty.

AFTER HOSTILITIES CEASED, the port of Nassau regained for a time some of its former notoriety as a nest of pirates though now many of the pirate ships flew the colours of the new American republic. In 1782 Governor Maxwell notified London that 127 'rebel' (meaning American) ships had been apprehended and captured. Indeed there were so many American prisoners that the governor complained he could not *'keep or Victual them'* and so they were carried to the nearest American port where they were released, presumably to resume their former 'trade'.

As a consequence of the aftermath of the war the position of Great Britain in the Caribbean was seriously weakened. The ever-present threat of attack was realised later in the year when an allied force of 40 Spanish ships together with two large American frigates descended upon Nassau. Governor Maxwell immediately surrendered and Nassau was occupied by the Spanish for two long years. Many residents of the Bahamas escaped to Florida, then still in British hands. Among them were Jonathan Elding and his son George, together with his West Indian-born wife Anne.

Sometime later George Elding, who was then in his early twenties and rearing to rid the islands of Spaniards, heard of the plans of Colonel Andrew Deveaux, a British officer who had raised a regiment in South Carolina called the Royal Foresters to fight the rebels. Little came of the regiment except Deveaux gained the title of 'colonel' and gained command of a small group of Loyalist irregulars who captured two American generals in woodland ambushes. When the British evacuated South Carolina in 1782, Deveaux conceived a plan to seize Nassau (and thus the Bahamas) from Spanish control. George quickly volunteered to join Deveaux on a secret military mission. They were first sail to Harbour Island to obtain more men, and then wrest Nassau from the Spaniards. It was generally believed that under the terms of the Treaty of Versailles (which was not actually signed until September 1783) that the 'the islands of Providence and the Bahamas' would probably be restored to Great Britain. But Colonel Deveaux, did not wait for the Treaty to be formally signed. In April 1783 he transported his small brigade from Florida to Harbour Island where he and George Elding and hatched a plan to capture Nassau more by artifice than force.

Deveaux arrived in northern Eleuthera with 50 men. Enthusiastic volunteers from Harbour Island and Spanish Wells swelled the 'invasion force' to 225 that included almost the entire male population including free coloureds and black slaves. Deveaux set the scene: *'I have the honour to inform you that on the night of 14th inst. We arrived at Salt Cay with our fleet, four miles distant from the Eastern Fort* (Fort Montagu), *which consisted of thirteen pieces of cannon. I landed about a mile from it with my formidable body* (formidable? Just 225 men against 600 entrenched defenders!) *'...and proceeded against it...'* when the enemy saw him, they *'...in great confusion abandoned the fort and drew up in a field near the wood. As soon as I came up they fired upon us. My young troops charged them, made two prisoners and drove the main body in great irregularity into the town. We sustained no loss on our side'.*

The *'formidable body'* entered the fort but something did not seem right to Deveaux. So he locked the Spanish prisoners in the fort and withdrew some distance away. Soon loud shouts came from the fort. The prisoners screamed that the building had been booby-trapped and at that very moment a fuse was burning which could have blown the fort to pieces. George Elding was directed to enter the fort, disarm the mines and cut the fuse. The prisoners had saved themselves from being blown to pieces since there was less than thirty minutes of fuse left to burn. Once released the Spaniards happily surrendered information to 'Major' Elding about the location of other booby trap mines that had been planted. Once the clearing of the mines was accomplished Deveaux took over the fort and consolidated his position. Next he sent his two ships to proceed to Nassau harbour to board two Spanish galleys effectively giving himself command of the sea and leaving the Spanish no way to escape.

But Deveaux and Elding realised they would have to trick the Spanish governor into surrender as they could not defeat him with an open force of arms. So Deveaux suggested they perform theatrical tricks to confuse the enemy as to, *'...both to the number and description of the forces they had to deal with'*. Then *'a...show of boats was made continually rowing from the vessels, filled with men, who apparently landed but in fact concealed themselves by lying down as they returned to the vessels, and afterwards made their appearance as a fresh supply of troops.'* He dressed 'men of straw' on the high points to increase the apparent numbers of men he had under his command and after this elaborate pretense, he boldly demanded the Spanish governor to surrender.

Colonel Andrew Deveaux liberated the Bahamas from Spanish occupation

In a further inspired ruse Deveaux introduced two Cherokee and Choctaw chiefs in full regalia to the Spanish governor. The chiefs were there to inform the governor that their braves were hiding in the woods only waiting the order to take Spanish scalps. The governor was still hesitant until a cannon, well-aimed by a squad of artillery commanded by 'Major' George Elding, sent a shot through the Governor's residence. The Spanish governor capitulated immediately.

A little while afterwards the disarmed Spanish could hardly believe their eyes when they realized they had surrendered to a small, rag tag band of soldiers.

This engagement marked the end of hostilities for the Bahamas. A short time thereafter the British government paid the Lords Proprietors fourteen thousand pounds Sterling to relinquish all title to the islands that were soon to be settled by Loyalists escaping from the new republic.

HIS FIRST SIGHT of the Bahama Islands was the northern tip of the island of Abaco.

Dr Benjamin Church and his wife looked with apprehension at the flat and featureless island in the distance. As a prosperous doctor from one of the original Pilgrim families of New England, they pondered despondently what life would be like on these sub-tropical and 'desert' islands. Benjamin Church, a proud Bostonian, had left New England hurriedly and weathered the Revolutionary War in pro-British New York then a small city of around 30,000 inhabitants. Now he was in the vanguard of the United Empire Loyalists being transported to the Bahama Islands.

When the ship docked at Nassau, Loyalists were already filling the town. An almost undifferentiated mob of noblemen, tradesmen and slaves were constructing makeshift shelter for themselves. Army tents, lean-to's made of ship's sails, palmetto thatch huts and rough lumber sheds, indeed anything that would provide temporary shelter, was being erected. Among them were also a number of loyal Jews who also escaped the North American colonies in the exodus. They were to leave their surnames to posterity in the Bahamas.

On going ashore Dr. Church was astonished to be met by none other than William Bradford of the prominent family of Pilgrim Fathers. Bradford had been a graduate of the Harvard class of 1760 but left New England when it was clear the rebels were gaining the upper hand and accepted a post with the Crown in Nassau. The patriarch of the family, William Bradford senior had been with the original *'Separatists'* at Leyden in the Netherlands, sailed on the *Mayflower,* was the second governor of the colony, presiding officer of the United Colonies and is probably best known for his famous account of the trials of the early Pilgrims contained in a now famous manuscript entitled: ***'Of Plimouth Plantation'***. The two New Englanders spent many long hours discussing the strange turn of events in their lives.

"Do you remember old George Stafford who had a farm Duxbury near Millbrook Turning...class of 1756 I think?"

Church nodded his head eager to hear news of an old friend.

"...killed by the rebels I heard, his wife and family went north to Canada. All his land was requisitioned of course..."

Dr. Church was taken aback, "...then what happened to Archibald Weston his cousin?...you recall he was an attorney with chambers on King Street in Boston—he had great political ambitions through his connections in England I think".

"Oh! After he saw which way the tide was turning he became a devoted republican—accepted a lot of sequestrated property I was told, and incidentally King Street is now to be renamed 'State' Street", Bradford replied with an exasperated sigh.

And so the conversation continued. Many of their old friends had been either killed, imprisoned or had become turncoats.

In Nassau the trickle of migrants soon became a flood. Most Loyalists came from the American South though at least a thousand arrived from the port city of New York. The exact total of migrants may never be known but it has been estimated at between five and seven thousand in all. The slaves transported by the Loyalists brought the number of people of African descent to nearly three quarters of the total population of the Colony.

Most of the new arrivals were anxious to establish themselves in a semi-feudal plantation economy similar to that which they had just left. Their ideal was to create a plantation centred on the 'Great House' consisting of slaves' quarters, barns, mills and warehouses and, because of the maritime character of the country, with docks to move produce and materials in and out. Perhaps with good reason they favoured the more remote central and eastern islands of the Bahamas. Other Loyalists particularly those from the north remained in Nassau but soon found the town already had a surfeit of qualified administrators, doctors, lawyers and militia captains.

Unlike many Loyalists, Doctor Church did not attempt to settle in Nassau but opted to take a grant of land in Long Island near the geographic centre of the Bahamian chain of islands. There were many qualified professionals filling the squalid little town and he was influenced by the experience of a fellow Loyalist, Jas. Hepburn who bitterly complained to him, 'I have been refused permission to practice law in this petty town by the governor even though I have but recently been a Council member and King's Attorney General in St Augustine!'

Dr. Church explained to his friends: "...and I do not wish to practice medicine where it may cause resentment...I will take the offer of a grant of land from the Crown. It is important the British occupy these islands as a defense against our enemies. Then one day, after more sanguine heads rule in England, those of us that wish, may return to the mainland colonies all united once again under a beneficent and well-loved sovereign..."

Doctor Church, like so many of his compatriots, felt that the situation in North America was temporary and that matters would soon be resolved by diplomacy or force of arms and he would be able to return to his homeland. In the meantime he mused, "...as I become reconciled to this forced sojourn in the Bahama islands, to cultivate a plantation in the tropics might be an fascinating diversion." Since he had no practical experience of farming, he employed overseers exiled from the Southern Colonies to arrange for labourers to be acquired and for the distasteful but necessary of purchase of slaves. An 'iron law' of the age necessitated engaging slaves if a plantation was to be successful. Unlike Church, many Loyalists were from the South and brought slaves from their American plantations all of which swelled the black population of the Colony making them by far the dominant majority.

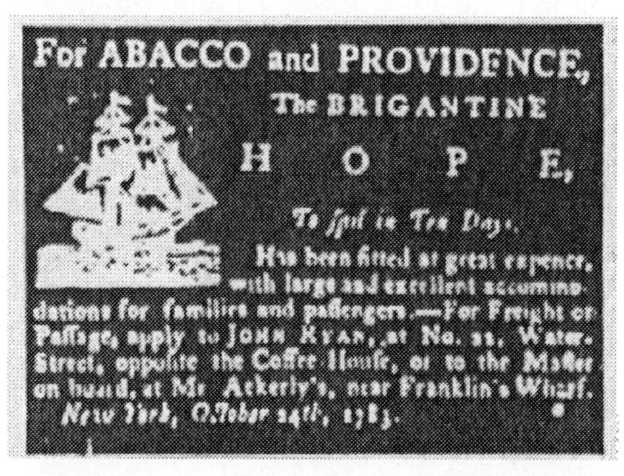

The overseers set the gangs of labourers to the task of preparing the land and building masonry walls round the fields with stone culled from the enclosed fields. In course of time they sowed sea island cotton. Coaxed by the warm sun it grew well and produced a profusion of bolls which split on maturity to reveal the white fluff which was the actual cotton stock. Land values soared. It was recorded that £20,000 was considered far too little a price for comparable property next to the Church's estate on Long Island.

Church and his genteel Bostonian wife set about designing a 'great house' for their hilltop property. It was to be built in the soft native limestone of Long Island with a roof of local split wooden shingles with wood for the joists and roof rafters from the pine forests of Abaco. It was hoped that some of the more important joinery, including some windows and doors, would be transported to the Bahamas from the Carolinas. He hoped too, to get some of his prized English and New England-made furniture that had not been 'requisitioned' by the rebels to be shipped to him from the port of Boston. In this hope he was to be disappointed.

The main facade of the Great House was to be in the then fashionable Georgian style of architecture with double height classical columns in the manner of the plantation houses of the Southern colonies. On the opposite side of an intended 'piazza' was a two-room kitchen building with a large open hearth constructed of imported bricks. To the left was a large barn with stalls for stabling horses and space for drying corn and peas. Another simpler structure to the right constructed of wood was intended as a cowshed. Nearby a cotton gin was planned to be housed in a circular structure but it was never built. Initially sanitation in the Great

House relied on portable commodes but later a stone built latrine was built some fifty yards from the Great House.

Careful attention was also given to the accommodation of his servants and slaves. The domestic servants were to have their quarters in the basement of the mansion. The slave quarters were planned downwind some distance from the Great House and were constructed of wattle and daub made of sand mixed with lime. Window openings were supplied with top-hung wooden shutters secured with leather hinges and the roofs were covered with palmetto thatch. The provision of furniture was the slaves' responsibility and consisted mainly of boxes for seats, handmade benches and, occasionally, a crafted rustic bed. For the slaves' quarters no provision was made for sanitation.

The daily life of the Africans, both slave and free, at this time in the Bahamas was ordered by the occupants of the Great House. Nevertheless the slaves were able to keep alive some African customs together with beliefs and practices they acquired in America. Almost all the servants and most of the slaves on the plantation were nominal Christians who, with Dr Church's consent, put on a small Junkanoo parade every Boxing Day. Many slaves lived in family units and farmed small plots around their living quarters. On most Saturday evenings there was music and dancing. Some evenings the older folks would tell stories of the 'old time' and, since none of them could read, it provided an oral record of their history that was passed down from generation to generation. It was well that the people from the Great House did not listen to the oral chronicles of the elders for they would have discovered that their slaves were reminded of the time they professed what was commonly considered to be the heretical faith of Mohammed once practiced in The Gambier in West Africa.

Dr Church engaged one of the old white settlers to assemble a team of black labourers both free and slave for the construction work on the Great House. The foreman had been recommended to him by 'Major' George Elding now a successful farmer on a plantation nearby who was considered to be something of a Bahamian patrician. It was a very long time since George had flirted briefly with republicanism in Nassau.

The Abaconian foreman was distantly related to the Elding's on the maternal side of the family. Like them he was a descendant of the original Eleutheran Adventurers whom some of the overbearing Loyalists derisively called 'conchs' after the lowly molluscs that formed an important element of their diet. The original white settlers of the Bahamas had known good times and bad and were little phased by the winds of change. They set a slow and steady pace in all they did that often found them at odds with the more energetic Loyalists. Josiah Pinder was a typical 'conch'. He was a boat builder by trade, blacksmith and sometime farmer. There was almost nothing he could not build or fix but was intractable in the extreme.

One day when Dr Church demanded of him why he was not at work the previous day Josiah calmly announced, "...from where I live it look like it gonna rain."

Dr Church started to get angry. "But heavens above man, you have to work when it rains, anyway it was only a shower! I have to tell you I cannot pay you for days you do not turn up to work".

"No Doc, I did not think that you would..." Josiah replied laconically.

"...and what about the workers...most especially the slaves, you are supposed to supervise the work, discipline and oversee them...set a good example..."

"Oh I thought they be off too, seein' as the sky was lowrin'."

Church was exasperated but kept his temper. He was slowly learning the ways of the islands.

The Church's reasoned that if they were to live in this outpost of Empire they ought to do so in a style to which they had been accustomed. When the house was finished it would be a pleasant enough place for them to raise a family. The first planting of sea cotton was proving successful and Dr Church realized he was in a happier position than many of the other Loyalists who had elected to stay in Nassau.

But the plantation was for him but a diversion, what really interested Benjamin Church was politics. He sat as a representative for Long Island in the House of Assembly and was a strong advocate of Loyalist rights. The House was dominated by Loyalists during the period 1783 to 1788 and their frustration and bitterness showed constantly in the debates in the Chamber. A newspaper was now published in Nassau that carried, almost exclusively, news about their former homeland. They learned that the new union of independent states experienced a serious financial depression immediately after the Revolution but the economy was gradually recovering. It rankled the Loyalists to find that the new and independent United States of America was learning to get along without them. By a cruel irony the Loyalists had no choice but to purchase most of their supplies from the former mainland Colonies. They particularly abhorred seeing the new 'stars and stripes' ensign being displayed on the ships that brought goods to Nassau. Many flags were ripped from the half-staff of the Yankee vessels. As a token measure to curb such excesses, Governor Maxwell ordered American sailors to stay on board their ships on the Sabbath, *'to prevent the Cause for Brawls and disorderly Conduct on the Day of the Lord'*. Dr. Church tried to force the Bahamian legislature to insist that all goods be brought to the Colony by British merchantmen but the idea, enshrined in the imperial Navigation Acts, proved impractical.

What most worried Governor Maxwell at this time was how he was to control the disillusioned Loyalists who, he feared, might take the government of the Colony into their own hands. He went so far as to write a confidential note to the British military commander of East Florida stating that a *coup d'etat* was imminent. What he did not know was that Benjamin Church had been able to assuage the thinking of most of the disaffected Loyalists and arrange for many of them to settle in the out islands or in other British islands of the West Indies thus dissipating their discontent. But one Loyalist, exiled in Abaco, poignantly summed up the predominant feeling of the Loyalists: '...the (Revolutionary) War never occasioned half the distress that this place has occasioned the Loyal subjects of the Crown!'

However as time went on, the Loyalists reluctantly adapted to Bahamian ways. At first the cotton crops were good, producing high quality fibre and the mills of Lancashire provided a ready market for their produce. In 1773 and 1774 exports of Bahamian cotton to England amounted to little more than £5,000. Twelve years later the figure had risen to £59,000.

Then the chenille bug appeared.

'Knowing how necessary your presence was on your Plantation after the very pernicious visitation you have had from that destructive insect the Worm, I delayed calling you together so long as the Public Business of the Country would permit...' wrote the governor to Dr Benjamin Church and the other members of government.

The output of cotton declined by more than 50 per cent from one year to the next. The reason for failure was readily understood by the planters. One of them attributed it to: 'the exhausted state of the soil, and clearing away more land than the Negroes could attend to, and not keeping down the bugs...manure would most certainly restore the lands to their original fertility, but where is it to be found?' And, as if the chenille bug and exhaustion of the land was not enough to contend with, the Bahamas was about to have another colourful character thrust upon it in the form of an irascible governor. His name was John Murray, Earl of Dunmore, formerly Governor of Virginia.

From the start Dunmore was unpopular. His record in the War of Independence had been anything but salutary; he had burned Norfolk when danger had threatened, withdrawing to a British warship anchored off Yorktown and claiming it as the seat of government of the unruly colony of Virginia. On his arrival in Nassau in 1787 he was immediately involved in nepotism when he arranged for his son to run for the House of Assembly from a constituency in Nassau. His son lost the Nassau seat but managed to get elected a month later from the Eleuthera constituency. Dunmore was accused of *'immorality in his private life and defects in his public character* 'for, besides conveying Crown Land illegally to his toadying friends, judging by the land records, he was quite prepared to speculate on land in his own name.

Dunmore fought with the Assembly constantly and the bitter exchanges found him sorely wanting in elementary political skills. With the example of the Thirteen Colonies still fresh in everyone's mind, he made the incredible blunder of trying to keep the House of Assembly from approving government spending. When it was clear the vote would be contrary to his inclinations, in desperation he tried to prorogue the Assembly. But he was too late and upon the issue of approval of monetary appropriations, the House won an important victory.

To his credit Dunmore constructed defences. A major fort named for Queen Charlotte, the wife of King George III, was constructed to command the main entrance to the harbour. Though it never fired a shot in anger, the fort was a serious deterrent to any potential invader and Britain at this time had no lack of enemies. The Spanish were, as ever, ready poised to attack from Havana. Then France at the end of the eighteenth century, energized with revolutionary fervor, sent a warship to patrol off Nassau for a time thus effectively blockading the city, while, at about the same time, the French Consul in the United States was urging a legion of American troops and privateers to invade the Bahamas.

But despite threats real and imagined, the inhabitants of Nassau were largely disinterested in defence; indeed some declared openly for the American republic and a former Chief Justice of the Bahamas actually left the Colony to settle in the fledgling United States. George Elding was 'conch' enough not to numbered among them. After the Revolution he had the opportunity to befriend many Loyalists and could identify with the injustice done to them in the name of opportunistic patriotism. Perhaps it was Lord Dunmore's fort, or more probably it was good fortune, but no attack on Nassau materialized even though the British Minister to the United States of the time, confirmed that an attack was imminent. Dr. Church continued to put pressure on the governor to bolster defences and to continue to solicit support from England.

A vocal opponent of the governor, he was approached by Lord Dunmore's cronies to "...toe the line and...support the Crown."

Church testily replied that he did indeed, "...support the Crown but could not find it in his reason to condone so poor a representative in the sublime office of governor..."

Other opponents of the governor expressed their feelings even more bluntly. Lord Dunmore was accused of being '...obstinate and violent by nature' with a '...capacity below mediocrity, little cultivated by education and ignorant of the law...'

It is certainly true that he was given to violent tempers and may possibly have been suffering from syphilis, gout or some other debilitating disease. Colonel Irving with the British militia in the Bahamas reported at the time: 'My Lord Dunmore has lately had several ugly attacks and is at this moment labouring under one of a very serious and alarming appearance...'

The noble lord's days were numbered.

After a relatively insignificant incident in Harbour Island where he broke a stick over a man's head, word reached his superiors in London and he was immediately recalled. He died in Scotland a few years later, as one critic put it, '...the lordly Despot of a petty Clan.'

THE PLANTATION that Benjamin Church had started in Long Island was, by this time, faring badly. He had been forced to change from cotton to subsistence crops and the ambitious plans for the Great House, had been considerably amended, yet even so the building work was far from complete. Old Josiah Pinder attended to the construction when he had the mind and did not complain if his wages were sometimes late. The principal overseer of the plantation on the other hand, had left for the Carolinas, setting a pattern of migration to the United States that Bahamians have followed in bad times ever since. Of Doctor Church's family, only the eldest daughter, a spinster, remained in the Bahamas living in the family house in Nassau. The other siblings left for England and were later to settle in colonial Africa.

Because of the decline in agricultural productivity many Loyalists moved away from the out islands. A visitor to Long Island reported, *'eight to ten plantations are entirely quitted and thirteen others are partially given up'*. One of the plantations that was *'only partly given up'* belonged to Dr Church. Two others that were *'entirely quitted'* belonged to George Elding and Burton Williams. The latter was a fellow Loyalist, Member of the House and Dr Church's good friend. Williams left Watlings Island for Trinidad with all his household and slaves. Like other Loyalists on the island he had been reduced to the level of subsistence producing only twenty bales of cotton for export in two years. But Williams had fallen in love with the beautiful Bahama Islands and returned to Watlings Island to die. After Emancipation he returned to Watlings bringing from Trinidad those of his workers and former slaves who wished to be re-united with their families. The governor of the time wrote to England that he hoped Burton Williams would take up a seat in the Assembly again because he is a 'sensible man ... (and) ... entertained the same views as myself'. He did not however, take up a position in the Assembly and, living on the very margin of survival, Williams outlived all his children to die at the age of 83 in 1852. A sympathetic writer penned the pathos of the event:

'Foreseeing that there would be no tools left with which to dig his grave when he died, he had it dug ahead of time, out of the limestone ridge. His foresight was wise, for when this once energetic and rich man died at an advanced age, a Negro...(one Joseph Ridley, who had been his erstwhile labourer) had only to shovel away the light leaf mould from the waiting grave, and to do this he used the only tool that was left,...a sharpened barrel stave.'

Dr Benjamin Church, also a proud man, was reduced to genteel poverty in his old age. In his fading years he felt bitter frustration at the continuing effort of the Imperial government he had served so faithfully to take away the one resource that continued to serve his needs—his slaves.

PART TWO

Chapter 11 - Emancipation & the Blockade (1801 - 1899)

Nassau is a quiet, hollow sort of place, with a bright sun always shining on its pure white streets.

J.H.Stark

AFTER QUEEN VICTORIA'S *accession to the throne a third of the way through the nineteenth century, the world enjoyed almost unprecedented peace. Two revolutions in France and America respectively had passed into history and the brief skirmish known as the War of 1812 was over. Britannia, it was said, ruled the waves. European imperialists were now in a race to accumulate new territory to add to empire. The main focus of the new acquisitions was now Africa and Asia and small island colonies like the Bahamas became backwaters in the imperial swell.*

After 1807, due mainly to the efforts of William Wilberforce, Parliament passed a law banning the slave trade, as a consequence of which, slaves in the British Empire could look forward to their eventual freedom. Twenty seven years later, on 1st August 1834, slaves living in the Bahamas were emancipated but their new-found liberty was immediately followed by crippling economic and social deprivation.

The Emancipation Act, needless to say, was unpopular in the extreme with the landowning class. The white population of the Bahamas considered the emancipation of slaves to be contrary to their financial interests inflicted upon them by an idealistic, but uncomprehending, imperial Parliament in faraway London.

The slaves, who now accounted for the majority of the Bahamian population, for good reason, were wary of change. Despite an apprenticeship system that was supposed to ease their transition to freedom, the result of emancipation they could clearly foresee, would mean that many of them would be put out of work and be homeless too. Indeed, when the Emancipation Act came into effect in 1834, the labour market predictably shrunk, yet more cargoes of African slaves kept being set free in the Bahamas which swelled the already under-utilized work force.

Not long afterwards however, the Bahamas became a staging post for supplies being dispatched to the Confederate Army in the American Civil War. In a century of stagnation the War brought a temporary economic boom to the Colony.

Cunard Line S.S. *Corsica* the first steamship in service between New York and Nassau 1859—67.

A RARE INCIDENT early in the nineteenth century serves to illustrate how some Africans, by now the largest segment of the population, arrived in the Bahama Islands.

Boaz Lowe II, a son of Prudence Elding, was a wrecker who operated his nefarious trade out of Hope Town, Abaco. One day 'Captain' Boaz was sailing *Shaving Mill,* his strangely named felucca, when his African Bahamian first mate espied a French 'prison' ship off the eastern Bahamas. They later discovered she was bound for New Orleans. Persuaded by the black members of his crew Boaz gave chase and boarded the unarmed French vessel with some well-aimed expletives but without a fight. In the sweating hold the ship's company discovered the usual horrific sight of Africans chained in rows, some of who were clearly near to death.

Outraged, the Bahamians tore the restraining chains from the framing of the vessel and carried several dozen manacled Africans to Cat Island and there, leaving them some meagre supplies they found on the French ship, they set them free. Despite their good intentions and help from the local residents of the island, only a few of the freed but emaciated Africans survived.

It was rare indeed for a privately owned ship like *Shaving Mill* to attempt to enforce the unpopular prohibition against trafficking in slaves. The apprehension of slavers was almost exclusively left to British warships that patrolled the Atlantic sea-lanes. The Admiralty records several interceptions of slavers around the Bahamas around this time. One of these occurred in 1829 when *HMS Monkey* captured the Spanish *Josepha* that she claimed as a 'prize' after she disembarked 202 slaves in Havana.

Later *HMS Monkey*, a small three-gun schooner built in Jamaica in 1826, challenged the Spanish slave brig *Midas* in the Northwest Providence Channel just off the island of Grand Bahama. The log of 26 June records that *Monkey 'enjoined and offered hospitality'* to an American brig that stayed during the action that followed. The next day *Monkey* made contact with the *Midas* just off the south shore of the island and prepared for action. At about noon they were within grapeshot range, *Midas* fired a broadside and the battle was joined. The tiny *Monkey* quickly rounded the *Midas* and fired her long guns that had a longer range than those of the *Midas*. After a sharp exchange of fire during which the Spanish had had its rigging torn to shreds, the *Midas* struck its colours and surrendered.

The *Midas* was a prize indeed. She was pierced for twenty guns but mounted only eight and she had a crew of fifty-three, of whom one had been killed and were three wounded. Slaves on the *Midas* were, typically, in a deplorable condition. On the same day as the naval encounter, three male and two female slaves died and before the two ships reached Havana in excess of forty additional slaves had died. The *Monkey's* log records that on 11 July the captain handed over the Spanish captain and the wounded to 'police officers' and 'boats came to remove the Negroes'. The log records that the captain received a receipt for the slaves but the number handed over, strangely, was left blank. It is perhaps surprising to note that of the *Midas'* crew five were English and two were American citizens.

A few years later in 1836, the *Vigilante* and *Creole* were apprehended and escorted by the Royal Navy into Nassau with 230 and 314 slaves respectively, many of who were desperately sick. Once landed, the slaves were usually given rudimentary medical attention then set free, generally on the nearest Bahamian island to their point of capture where they were left to themselves to survive as best they could. Sometimes however, freed slaves were settled in new communities like Adelaide in southwestern New

Providence, Bennett's Harbour in Cat Island and Williamstown in the Berry Islands. In an attempt to offer more assistance to the unfortunate freed slaves, in 1808 an Order in Council required the newly landed slaves to be bound as apprentices to *'prudent and humane masters or mistresses to learn such trade and Handicrafts or Employments as they seem from their bodily and other Qualities most likely to be fit for and to gain their livelihood most comfortably by, after the Terms of Apprenticeship or Servitude shall expire.'* Though well meaning, the Order often reduced the freed slaves to another form of servitude not so different from slavery.

The urgent need for slaves on the sugar plantations in territories where slavery was sanctioned caused slavers to resort to horrible stratagems to try to avoid the British blockade. If an attempt to outrun a naval vessel was unsuccessful the hatches were closed tight to conceal the slaves and 'in the putrid hold of the ship...the manacled wretches lay doubled up chin to knee, sweltering between decks scarcely three feet high' so that perhaps thirty of the 'gasping freight' died from suffocation. The Nassau *Royal Gazette* morbidly describes what happens next if it is clear the slaver is about to be boarded, '...the Negroes are confined to casks...laid with a sinking weight of irons...are swiftly lowered into the sea...one splash and one shriek and it is over...all evidence is gone...'

An unintended consequence of the British policy regarding slave trafficking was that once slaves were freed from slavers bound for the United States or Cuba they had to be settled in the increasingly destitute colony of the Bahamas. London glumly responded to the dilemma by noting that if the British government were to pay the captains of slaving vessels the value of the apprehended slaves, *'we shall have all the infirm Slaves of Charleston, St Augustine and the neighbouring coast of America sent to this colony'*. During these years many American slaves did in fact find themselves in the Bahamas by either accident or design. Some stayed but others returned to *'bear those ills we have'* rather than to *'fly to others we know not of'*.

But not all the non-white immigrants were Africans. In the period when Florida was under British control (1763 to 1784) Seminoles served as border guards in northern Florida and enjoyed a trade with the Bahamas. Governor Tonyn, governor of East Florida, reported *'they were well affected and I can confide in the headmen'* (he also noted that one Seminole had even been recruited in the Royal Navy!) Slave-owners in the fledgling United States (the states of Georgia and Tennessee in particular) were angered that runaway slaves were escaping to another jurisdiction across the border into British Florida. Once there many of them intermarried with the Seminoles (thus came to be known as 'black' Seminoles).

PART TWO

After the British ceded the territory of Florida to Spain, open wars broke out between the Americans and the Seminoles that caused the Indians to be pushed deep into the marshy prairie of the Everglades. Some even left Florida altogether. They had been told (presumably by Bahamian traders) that in the direction of the rising sun was a nation where Indians would find 'freedom' from American oppression. In 1819 it was reported that twenty-eight Seminoles arrived in Nassau who claimed they had been robbed and driven from their homes by the Americans. They were furnished with rations and temporary lodging by the Bahamian government, '*...to relieve their immediate distress.*' Other Seminoles used dugout canoes to migrate to the Bahamas and landed at Joulters Cays and Red Bay, Andros. From these migrations an 'Indian village' called Bowlegs Town was founded in northern Andros and existed well into the twentieth century.

The world at this time was in the throes of a major social and political upheaval which made the idea of conflict on the high seas likely. American independence brought rapid expansionism and the French Revolution had evolved from an enlightened egalitarian movement into expansive imperialism. Most of continental Europe had been defeated by Napoleon's armies and only northern Spain, where Wellington in concert with Spanish guerrillas were fighting the French, and the British Isles remained outside of Napoleon's clutches. It was thought that Bermuda and the British islands of the West Indies might soon fall to the might of France. But, mainly due to the British navy, the danger passed. Indeed by 1815 in the final land battle of the conflict, Napoleon was defeated at Waterloo.

THE NEW REPUBLIC on the North American mainland continued to pursue a self-proclaimed 'manifest destiny'. The Lewis and Clark expedition gave a grim warning to the native peoples west of the Mississippi that their world was about to change forever. In the wake of the expedition, land-hungry immigrants set about settling first the prairies and after that, the 'Far West'. Then followed the incursion into Spanish Texas and other southern territories by a vanguard of settlers of the new republic. Later they set their sights on Spanish Florida.

In the years immediately following the American Revolution the British in Florida, aided by native Americans, often had to repulse armed intruders from the new republic to the north who were seeking to capture runaway slaves. In 1784 Britain was forced to retrocede Florida to Spain and many of the English settlers left for the British colonies in the Caribbean region. Then, like Spanish Texas, Florida was infiltrated by aggressive

English-speaking people from the north. Most of the new arrivals were Indian traders or scouts seeking to retrieve runaway slaves though some of the newcomers came to settle.

The Revolutionary War and its aftermath introduced many fascinating people like Dr Church and Andrew Deveaux to the Bahamas. For indeed almost overnight a contingent of senior British army officers, politicians, plantation owners and lawyers arrived in the islands. Their presence was in stark contrast to the semi-literate 'old inhabitants' who survived mainly on fishing and wrecking—the latter profession only a slightly more peaceable version of piracy. As could be expected there was immediate friction between the old and new inhabitants exacerbated by imperious and insensitive governors sent out from England. And, as if the admixture of social classes and lifestyles was not enough, there was the further irritant of a growing abolitionist movement in the country.

One of the colourful characters who appeared in the Bahamas at this time was William Augustus Bowles. A dashing if eccentric Loyalist, Bowles had been dismissed from his regiment in Florida for disobeying orders. He moved to the Lower Creek Country of Georgia and, with a complete disdain for law, morality and prejudice, married two wives, one a Creek, the other a Cherokee. After the Americans declared independence he fled to Nassau where he was introduced by George Elding (by now a well known businessman with premises on Bay Street) to Lord Dunmore the colonial governor. Since Bowles spoke the native language of the Indians, the governor hatched a plan for him to return to northern Florida to oust a British trading company already doing business at St. Marks with the rebel Americans and to set up another trading post which presumably would do more to '...toe the line and...support the Crown.'

Bowles was accompanied by George Elding and, with fifty local men, most of them Seminoles, they made three attempts to capture the trading post but when most of his men deserted they finally gave up. Bowles and Elding then returned to Nassau. After the rough life of dodging bullets, wading through swamps and sharing his tent with red skinned savages, George Elding made it known he had had enough. For William Bowles, however, this was not the end of his quixotic career. He next visited London accompanied by some Creeks and Cherokees and obtained British support for the establishment of an independent state for the indigenous Americans near the Florida/Georgia border to be named 'Muskogee'.

He returned to northern Florida again in 1792 that at this time was under Spanish sovereignty and on this occa-sion managed with the help of some Indian friends to take over the trading post at St. Marks. While there

William Augustus Bowles adventurer extraordinaire

he was lured by promises from the Spanish and Americans that he thought would lead to greater business con-cessions. To pursue these concessions he was invited to visit New Orleans. His greed trumped his good sense. Once in New Orleans, the Spanish promptly arrested him and put him on a ship to the Philippines.

But the story did not end there.

Bowles jumped ship and made his way via Africa and Barbados back to Nassau. He again returned to northern Florida and with the help of some Indians managed to re-capture the trading post at St. Marks. He was then able to establish the 'free port of Muskogee' that had its own flag and operated for a time as a sovereign independent territory. However, in 1803 both the Spanish and the Americans moved against Bowles and his fiefdom. At a 'conference' he attended at Hickory Ground on American soil the Spanish, with the connivance of the Americans, seized Bowles and carried him to Cuba. Here he died a miserable, lonely death in Morro Castle Prison in 1805.

Back in Nassau George Elding was elected to the House of Assembly that was now dominated by the increasingly strident Loyalists. Governor Dunmore had become even more unpopular and was on especially bad terms with the Solicitor-General, a Loyalist, by the name of William Wylly. With the support of George Elding in the House, Wylly challenged the governor on almost every action he took—carrying his case to London more than once. Like Elding, Wylly was a slave owner but Wylly, influenced by an awakening of conscience after his visits to London, became a staunch 'theoretical' abolitionist. Sometimes they had conversations about the burning issue of slavery.

"This damnable business has to stop," Wylly opined.

"Slavery has existed since time immemorial and is accepted in the Scriptures," Elding pointed out, "besides, ***you*** own slaves."

"Yes that's the damnable part of it! If I did not have slaves my plantation would go to ruin. It's a dilemma that will only be resolved when all slaves are freed. When plantation owners pay a fair wage to their labourers the whole matter will be resolved. Those men practicing the dismal science they call 'economics' in England have said as much. In the future there will be a market for labour as there is for commodities."

"You jest! You cannot expect a black man to pick and choose whom he will work for!" Elding retorted.

"You must be aware that the recent government report, 'Enquiry into the Condition of Slaves' showed that our black seamen are perhaps equal to any in the world and many Negroes supply the town of Nassau with their produce. Often it happens that a slave is more intelligent, and perhaps a better man than his master!"

This was altogether too much for Elding.

"I know you reported as much in the House but it is very far from the truth. Anyway until this emancipation business is made law we would all do well to work our slaves to the utmost because soon other countries will have the advantage of us if we then have to pay our labourers..."

"That is where you are wrong," William Wylly exclaimed, "if we do not act with compassion and understanding this dreadful business will haunt us long into the future".

George Elding shrugged, "my father manumitted a slave called Martin some years ago due perhaps to misplaced compassion. What good did it do him? He died a pauper in a shack in the Negro shanty town," then, he added with conviction, "anyway, I believe the future can take of itself...I myself live in the present and I believe you should too!"

Over this conversation they parted company. In 1816 Wylly, citing the Somerset Case, caused a furor in Nassau when he refused to let an American slave be repatriated to the United States. George Elding and most of the other landowners ostracized him. But in the matter of slavery in the Bahamas, the end was now in sight.

John Lamotte, possibly Bahamian by birth, was another interesting man of the age. Lamotte, after many adventurers with the British navy, returned to the settlement of Carmichael in New Providence in his old age and appealed for his military pension to be reinstated. Lamotte had served in Nelson's flagship *HMS Victory* for seven years and had even seen action at the famous sea battle of Trafalgar in 1805. A true hero, he had been wounded three times and, after being demobilized from the Royal Navy, tried to return to the Bahamas from Britain. On the way his ship was wrecked and he was captured and carried by corsairs to North Africa where he was enslaved. A year later in 1816, he was fortunate enough to have been one of 1200 Christians freed by Lord Exmouth's expedition against the Ottoman Dey of Algiers.

John Lamotte finally arrived back in Nassau but due to his unhappy adventures understandably he had lost his Certificate of Pension. Lamotte was aided by George Elding, who by now was considered something of a hero in his own right, in his attempt to obtain a pension. But it is uncertain to this day if this incredible Bahamian ever received a veteran's pension for military service from His Most Britannic Majesty.

And yet another remarkable character to appear about this time was Robert Armbrister, son of James Armbrister, a Loyalist, who was born in Nassau in 1797. In his youth Robert had spent a short while in northern Florida and, like Bowles, had several connections among the Creek and Seminole Indians. Later he joined the Royal Navy, fought in the War of 1812, travelled to Europe and served with Wellington at Waterloo. Remarkably, he even spent time in Saint Helena guarding Napoleon Bonaparte in the former emperor's twilight years.

Returning to Nassau in 1817 and yearning for more adventure than the Bahamas offered, he asked permission of Bahamian governor Charles Cameron to return to northern Florida. News had arrived that the fort at St. Marks, which had previously been under Bowles control, had been blown up by an American raiding party killing nearly three hundred people composed mainly of black Seminoles and runaway slaves. (Interestingly one of the American raiders was the extravagantly lauded frontiersman Davie Crockett who later went on to invade another Spanish territory—Texas—where he lost his life defending the Alamo.)

The new Bahamian governor sensing that Armbrister could be helpful to the British cause, granted permission. He suggested Armbrister arrange to meet with an elderly Scot named Alexander Arbuthnot who lived in the Florida 'panhandle' and had official permission from the Spanish administration to engage in trading with the Indians. Arbuthnot was a sometime resident of Nassau and owned a schooner, the *Chance,* which he used to carry British merchandise from Nassau to the trading post near St. Marks.

Arbuthnot had a sympathetic if patronising attitude towards the Indians. He wrote in his journal:

'...these (people) are children of nature...leave them in their forests to till their fields and hunt the stag, and graze their cattle, their ideas will extend no further...they have been ill treated by the English and robbed by the Americans...'

Armbrister duly made contact with Arbuthnot at the trading post on St. Marks River and later met with some of his former Indian acquaintances in the Florida 'panhandle'. He was horrified at what he saw and wrote that he found them to be 'in a most pitiable condition' explaining it was not the Spanish but the republican invaders from the north who had brought them to this state after the invasion of St. Marks fort.

Robert Armbrister had chosen a very dangerous time to be in Florida especially since he was so near the Spanish-Georgia border. Under illegal orders from General Andrew Jackson, American troops pursued blacks, and especially runaway blacks, native Americans and anyone sympathetic to them, far into Florida territory. Jackson was particularly angry because blacks and Seminoles were often successful in ambushing the American troops in the ensuing skirmishes. His contempt for Indians was well known, he is reputed to have said of their ferocious tactics that, 'he would rather do battle with 500 white men than with 50 Seminoles'. Jackson's strict orders to his troops were to 'return the negros to their rightful owners' and, as he interpreted his orders, to eradicate anybody who got in his way. As Spain was unable to provide sufficient administration of the territory, this gave Jackson a pretext to make a full-scale military intervention in 1819.

History is a little unclear as to exactly what Armbrister was doing in the Florida panhandle at this time though it seems probable that with the tacit approval of the Bahamian governor he was helping the blacks, the Creeks and the Seminoles to secretly organise a defence against the American infiltrators. Had he been successful he might have stopped the expansion of the new American republic into Florida.

In 1818, having accomplished what he saw as his mission, Armbrister indicated that he intended to return on the schooner *Chance* to Nassau. However, before embarking he travelled to Bowlegs Indian Village on the Suwannee River well inside Spanish Florida to bid his Indian friends farewell and to take on provisions. It was a fatal mistake. On his journey inland he was taken captive by Jackson's troops.

Arbuthnot was also ill-fated. He was staying with a friendly Spanish commander at a fort in the Florida panhandle but decided to flee to his ship when he heard of the American incursion. He too was captured by American soldiers at St. Marks and both he and Armbrister were summarily tried and sentenced to death. The sentence was appealed but General Andrew Jackson, who had no love for runaway slaves, redskins or redcoats, declared Armbrister to be 'an outlaw and a pirate' and ordered the executions carried out. Armbrister was shot by a firing squad; Arbuthnot was hanged from the yardarm of his own schooner.

Jackson's 'atrocious conduct' was later criticised by the entire United States Cabinet, John Quincy Adams casting the only dissenting vote. After the deed became known in England the British considered demanding an official apology from the American republic but Lord Bathurst, speaking in the House of Lords, cautioned that if reparation was not immediately forthcoming '*...the demand...once made must be supported to the utmost extremity*', in other words with military action. It should be remembered this was less than a decade after the bloody and indecisive War of 1812. And so the matter was cynically dropped.

In 1821 Spain was forced to cede the Florida territory to the American republic that continued to harass the Seminoles and who, to this day, have yet to conclude a peace treaty with the United States. Indeed around the middle of the century some of the Seminoles, after continuing friction with the American newcomers, took to their canoes and, about a millennium after the Ciboney and Taíno, continued the trickle of emigration of Amerindians to the Bahama Islands.

THROUGHOUT THE EARLY YEARS of the nineteenth century the Bahamas endured crippling poverty as the colony settled into a kind of torpor. In Grand Bahama, if possible, the destitution was even more acute. Theophilus, the only child of Ezekiel Elding and his common law wife Molly, stayed on at a hut with his parents on the West End plantation until Ezekiel died then, when the plantation completely failed, he drifted into other temporary work in the West End settlement. Theophilus 'Eldon' (the spelling of his surname now matched more closely its Bahamian phonetic pronunciation and served to obfuscate the connection with a runaway slave) tried his hand first at slash and burn farming then fishing. His mother too worked at any small manual labouring job she could find but her main support was from the charity of the church.

However, after only two years of living in the small settlement, his mother Molly, from whom he had inherited his almond-shaped eyes, died of typhus fever. Because of the poor sanitation, typhus was a constant threat in the poorer settlements of the Bahamas. The epidemic also killed several other people in the tiny community at West End. Theophilus buried his mother in a cemetery just inland from the beach facing Indian Cay where it was recorded by Ponce de León that the last known Lucayan in the Bahamas was known to have lived.

Theophilus had hardly reached manhood when he found himself alone in the world and destitute. When the rare opportunity arose he worked for a shilling a day clearing the beach road of weeds in the settlement. The offer of work by the government for the indigent of the island gave special meaning to a popular saying of the day: *'a shillin' in Gran' Bahama wort' a poun' of money'*.

One day, John D. Smith, the financially spent son of the original plantation owner, asked Theophilus and three other under-employed men from the West End settlement if they would help him to 'settle a score' against his wife's lover since he entertained, as Smith put it, '...unfavourable suspicions of his wife's purity of character'. Theophilus needed money so he agreed readily enough. The situation, Smith explained to Eldon and his companions, was that his wife had deserted both husband and daughters and had taken Archibald W. G. Taylor, a well-known Bahamian landowner and sometime member of government, as her lover and they were presently at a house near Eight Mile Rock some ten or so miles east of the settlement of West End. Smith explained his plan of revenge and put it into effect a few days later when they all sailed under cover of darkness to a cove near the house where Taylor and Mrs. Smith were staying.

At about eleven o'clock that same night the four desperados approached the house and broke into the lovers' bedroom where they caught the pair in *flagrante delicto.* In the candlelight they could see Smith's wife completely naked porcelain white body spread-eagled on the bed and Archibald Taylor, her lover, likewise naked, *in coitus.*

The three black men pulled Taylor from the bed and seized him by the throat, whereupon Smith ran forward and pinned Taylor to the floor. Smith then pulled out a small knife and, according to a later newspaper report, crowed:

'I have caught the son of a bitch!'

'What are you going to do?' Theophilus cried.

'I am going to cut them both off!' Smith screamed, 'help me hold him down!'

And with that he cut off both Taylor's ears.

Punishments in these days were particularly severe. The testimony of Archibald Taylor, son of an extremely wealthy landowner who was once second-in-command to Andrew Deveaux in the re-capture of Nassau, was the sole witness. The impassioned testimony of Taylor, went unrefuted in Court in Nassau when Smith was found guilty as charged and sentenced to be hanged. At the same time the black men were convicted for 'felony as principals in the second degree' and were also sentenced to death.

They all had to wait in prison for a year with the threat of a visit to the gallows until May 1824 when they were granted a respite by the Court and then, in August of the same year, they all received a full pardon.

After this brush with death, Theophilus stayed on in Nassau living on the charity of the church in the African Bahamian community 'over the hill' known as Bain Town. Even though his criminal conviction had been rescinded, Theophilus understood well he had not the slightest prospect of regular salaried employment. But he had gained some useful experience in carpentry from his father, Old Zeke in Grand Bahama, so he put it to good effect. In his spare time, and he had plenty of it, he and his comrades built a small sloop. After it was launched they used the boat to go wrecking.

They first used Bimini as their base. The island was well located for people involved in the wrecking business. Bimini was settled only in 1847 and, as the most westerly of the Bahama Islands, is adjacent to the narrowest part of the Gulf Stream that at this point is only 45 miles wide. Wreckers soon outnumbered the 250 permanent inhabitants. Theophilus and his crew were often the first to locate many a wreck, but the government of the day permitted wrecks to be worked only by licensed wreckers. All the captains of the wreck boats were white men who were in possession of official government wrecking licenses so Theophilus and his comrades were invariably forced to move on from the wreck sites they found—or face harsh legal consequences and even physical force. Crime and violence was so common at this time that the circuit magistrate reported of Bimini:

'The occupation of the inhabitants is principally that of wrecking, and the harbour and roadstead are frequently the rendezvous of numerous wrecking vessels, at which time the licensciousness of the people is painfully manifested...the wrecking system every day develops its sad depravity, and indicates the urgent necessity of more prompt and effective measures, if not for prevention of enormous plunder, for at least the recovery of some of the portion of the articles stolen...' Indeed reports from all over the Bahamas at this time talked of civil disturbances that involved the contentious issue of sharing the spoils from wrecked vessels.

Reluctantly Theophilus and colleagues turned from wrecking to fishing and sold their catch near the Parade that would later become Woodes Rogers Wharf in Nassau.

In a short space of time after returning to the capital Theophilus fathered six children that bore his name though he did not marry. The mother of the children was a pretty girl of mixed race named Rachel Bethel. The family was fairly typical of the time as to both its size and character. There was strong family similarity about all the Eldon brood, indeed people declared when they saw Rachel's children playing in the dusty streets of Bain Town, "dem chil' wuz all look like pea in pod!" They all had ebony black skin, straightish black hair, almost Asiatic-shaped eyes and a bearing that could almost be termed regal. The children were all named for biblical characters: the boys Abel, Kaleb, Levi and Joel, the girls Miriam and Ruth.

Rachel brought up her children well, earning money as a kitchen helper at the house of the elderly widow of Dr Benjamin Church, the Loyalist, on well-to-do West Hill Street in Nassau. Theophilus helped Rachel with money when he could, though later he sired other children on his travels around the islands. In Abaco he fathered a male child with a comely but partly crazed daughter of an Abaconian 'conch'. From this ephemeral union, his male offspring brought a marked Caucasian strain to the Eldon bloodline. The progeny of the union, however, took his mother's name and, upon marriage, moved to Harbour Island where he became a respected member of the community. Ironically his descendents were rigidly opposed to permitting people of obvious 'colour' to reside in their small community.

Abel Eldon, the eldest son of Theophilus and Rachel, went to sea on an American clipper as a cabin boy when he was just fourteen. He was never heard from again.

Kaleb, the second son, scratched a living from growing Guinea corn which he sold at market and, for a time, he ran errands for a Bay Street haberdashery. The pay was poor but in these times he was happy if he earned enough to eat. He was father to several children but throughout his life he never formed a union with any woman for more than a few months. His offspring bore the mother's name. In his later life he became a victim to cheap rum and his brain, his neighbours declared, was 'confuddle up'.

Levi Eldon worked hard as an odd-job man and sometime carpenter. Sometimes he served as a crewmember on the fishing boat of his father Theophilus but the job paid almost nothing. He was one of many black Bahamians of his day who contributed to an *asue*, a kind of savings association that is thought to have its origins in Africa. Many people like Levi would pay a small sum every week into a fund that paid out its total proceeds to each of its contributors in turn. From the small capital Levi raised from the *asue,* he was able to purchase sufficient lumber and materials to complete the small house he had started to build on generation land in Fox Hill village east of Nassau. He was one of few black Bahamians who managed to obtain fee simple title to his land. Later part of the land was acquired by eminent domain by the government for construction of a new prison but he received monetary compensation. The money obtained allowed Levi to live fairly comfortably in his declining years. Levi Eldon sired two children from different mothers. In these times, because of custom and austerity, union in marriage was seldom a consideration. But Levi at least acknowledged his offspring and they lived with him for a time at Fox Hill and bore the Eldon name. Both sons died without leaving a male heir.

Miriam, the fifth child to be born to Rachel and Theophilus, produced a brood of children from at least three different fathers; one was a white sailor from a visiting sailing vessel, another was a Haitian fisherman, and the other a black Seminole Indian named Bowleg (the final 's' was now dropped from the original Seminole name as is customary in the Bahamian vernacular). The 'Indian' was from Andros, an offspring of a small band of Seminoles who escaped to the Bahamas in dugout canoes after the Second Seminole War of 1835. All Miriam's sons carried her surname. She lived her whole life on the charity of relatives and friends. When she died in 1906 at age 71 she was mourned by an extended family of over forty blood relations.

Ruth Eldon married a recently freed slave, Joseph Ridley, who had been granted 10 acres of land on Watlings Island (before and later known as San Salvador). In Watlins, Ruth and Joseph lived a desperately impoverished life but it was hardly different from the overwhelming majority of the black population. The smallholding provided just enough food for them to stay alive and, despite their poverty, they raised three live children and buried three others in infancy. They got through hard times by sharing with other subsistence farmers and Joseph was able to supplement his meagre income by doing odd jobs for the few impoverished white farmers who also found themselves trapped by economic circumstances in the out island. The most money he ever received on any one day in his life arrived from old Mrs. Church in Nassau. The envelope, which was carried to Watlins Island by the mail boat, contained two gold sovereigns to compensate Joseph for 'laying out' and burying the deceased Loyalist, Burton Williams. With the money there was a note addressed to his wife Ruth and signed by Rachel. The letter was almost certainly written by someone else, most probably Levi, it read:

> *To Ruth Ridley*
>
> *You mamma send her love. Here is our news. Abel never reach back. Miriam is four month with baby she now have four childs. Kaleb is sick agen with the trembles. Joel is well and he going to build boat to come wisit you one day. His son Absalom do well he got Govmen job.*
>
> *Try come Nassau to see me while God give life.*
>
> *Your loving mother*
> *Rachel Bethel*

But Joel never visited Watlings Island and the Ridleys' were never to return to the capital city after they sailed away on the mail boat in early 1844.

Joel Eldon, was the youngest son of Theophilus and Rachel and financially the most successful member of the family. He fell in love with Willamae, an attractive girl from a well-to-do black family who owned a funeral parlour in Delancey Town. The business was only a few yards removed behind the summit of the hill that divided the predominantly white society from the black community 'over the hill' in Nassau. Later after they married, Joel worked with his father-in-law, becoming in his later years, one of the wealthiest African Bahamians in the Colony and a member of the tiny 'coloured' middle class. Joel and Willamae Eldon had four children of whom Absalom was the eldest. Of their three girls, two died before they were twenty, the other who was mentally retarded died a spinster.

Absalom managed to obtain the best education of the 'extended' Eldon family and was in fact the only child to have a male offspring who carried on the Eldon name. Cognisant of the change in the family name from Elding to Eldon, as the most literate person of the family, he was always particular that the new spelling be adopted in official records of the family. Absalom graduated with high marks from a parochial church school in Nassau, studied for a semester in a 'Negro' college in Georgia and was considered something of a biblical scholar. Unlike the rest of the family who dressed in hand-me-downs, Absalom always managed to appear well-dressed sometimes wearing a black bowler hat and a cravat that was fashionable with the white set. Absalom was one of very few blacks of his time to serve in an official capacity with the government when, for three years, he was a member of the Bahamas Public Graveyards Board.

It might seem reasonable to consider that membership of the Graveyards Board would be a routine almost lackluster position but, just after mid-century, Absalom found himself in the middle of a small drama. Dissenting ministers of the Gospel tried to perform two burials in public burial grounds but were denied access under the law. A petition signed by 800 people was submitted to the governor but ignored. After which a near riot ensued and Absalom, as Board member, had to stay out of sight for fear of his life. Only when the Anglican Bishop of Jamaica intervened weeks later was the law changed to permit dissenting ministers to officiate at burials.

Absalom Eldon married Sheba a cousin, the daughter of his father's sister, Miriam. And, as is common in inter-family marriages, the distinct physical features of the Eldon clan became even more pronounced. Sheba had two children: a daughter who was born prematurely and lived only five years, and a son Romulus. Absalom continued to work with the family funeral business until he himself became one of its clients in 1918.

ON THE OTHER SIDE of town the lighter-skinned Eldings too, were caught up in the uncertainty of the age.

Gainful employment was in short supply even in the white enclave that stretched along Bay Street. Like many old Bahamians George Elding had turned to farming when cotton was king. For a time he had farmed a small plantation on Long Island near the estate owned by Benjamin Church. But, with Emancipation just years away, there was no market for slaves. Upon the death of the Loyalist doctor, his Great House and most of his plantation was sold for a pittance and his widow and eldest daughter moved to Nassau. Following the lead of Dr Church and Lord Rolle, once the wealthiest of the Exuma landowners, some plantation owners reluctantly gave the land to their workers, free and slave. Others stubbornly continued on farming though it now made little economic sense.

George also saw the inevitable end of the plantation era and tried to sell his modest plantation, but there were no buyers. So, assisted by his son Wycliffe, they closed up the house, dismissed the workers after the mandatory apprenticeship of four years was over in 1838 and returned to their property on Bay Street in Nassau where Wycliffe took over the reins of the family business. They were more fortunate than some. For shelter, they had an exquisitely constructed wooden-framed house that had been built by Wycliffe's grandfather, Jonathan Elding, in more prosperous times.

The residence was two storeys high with a steep pitched roof covered with pine wood shingles that had a few roofs of imported clay tile but most were of thatch. All water was collected from the roof by way of gutters that fed into an underground cistern. Water was drawn from the cistern by a bucket and later by a hand pump. The house was constructed of weatherboarding on a framework of rough lumber some of it re-used from old boats. The front of the house boasted a covered porch with fretwork brackets atop its wooden post supports. All the windows had top hung wooden shutters—an architectural invention that was later widely copied in the region. Inside the house was a parlour used only on special occasions, a dining room and a space that served as a family and work room. The kitchen and latrines were in separate shacks in the garden at the rear of the house that at one time also included another shack for the housing of domestic servants. Upstairs were three simple bedrooms and a box room. The furnishings of the house included a grandfather clock and many original pieces of English furniture as well as some ornaments and other *bric à brac* that had been recovered from wrecks. On a side table was a splendid, but unappreciated, collection of scrimshaw carved mainly from the bones of humpbacked whales. Artificial lighting was from paraffin oil lamps that afforded but a dim flickering light and caused the family to retire early to save on the cost of oil.

The house was separated from the cart rutted white coral street by a picket fence with two masonry posts either side of a gate that had long disappeared. The streetscape consisted of several houses of similar style though many were only one storey high, some having dormer windows to light an attic space that served as bedrooms. Sidewalks had appeared through usage rather than design. As one approached the centre of the town, residences gave way to a few commercial establishments hugging the waterfront like Elding's chandlery, all attempting to satisfy the needs of the townsfolk. The most important complex of buildings was the classical style parliament complex that was modeled on similar buildings in New Berne, North Carolina. The gridiron plan of the downtown area, dating from the governership of Woodes Rogers, featured the cathedral of the established church, a Presbyterian kirk, a Methodist chapel and some commodious residences of the few wealthy people in Nassau. Atop the hill commanding an imperious view of the town sat Government House, the seat of the governor.

To a visitor to Nassau at this time, the multi-racial character of the town would be immediately apparent. Though a second glance would suggest almost no inter-mixture of the two races. The whites were over-dressed for the climate, the women often hiding below parasols as if the sun were a shameful infection. Some of the white men sported waistcoats and even top hats. Many of the free blacks too were similarly over-dressed for the climate, the women wearing petticoats under dark but colourful print skirts specially sent to the Caribbean from the mills of Lancashire. Slaves and apprentices were immediately distinguishable by their ragged homemade clothing. Vehicular traffic consisted of carts pulled by skeletal horses and donkeys and there were a few carriages for hire pulled by the side of the road patiently waiting for a customer and also a few horse drawn carriages of the well-to-do.

A government report on the subject of the social and economic status of the Colony in 1838 sets the scene: *'...most of the people on the island(s) are in a state of great poverty owing to the gales last year and the drought this. The coloured population have suffered much from their having been suddenly and unexpectedly liberated at a time when but little could be gathered from the plantations, though they do not complain of that.'*

Though poverty was widespread in the Bahamas, a visitor to Nassau at mid-century noted that in the upper echelon of this largely expatriate Victorian society there was *'a graciousness, charm and beauty'* that would not be found later. The age, he reminded his readers, had not completely yet passed for which Johann Strauss wrote his waltzes. Quoting a local newspaper, he describes a garrison ball: *'The room was very tastefully decorated, flags overhanging each window in graceful festoons, while in two of the ample folds were placed...full length portraits of Her Majesty and Prince Albert. The nicely chalked floor exhibited appropriate devices, the Crown and Royal Initials, V.R. occupying a prominent position in the centre'*. The guests included Major

Clarke of the First West Indian regiment, Captain Barnett of the Royal Navy and his wife, Judge Sandilands whose name the writer notes *'is known to the visitor as it is applied to the Negro village, otherwise called Fox Hill'* (today his name is better known for its application to a psychiatric hospital). Governor John Gregory and Mrs. Gregory were there besides other 'notables' whose social significance has long since been forgotten. Needless to say, the Eldings' *cinderella* social status did not merit them an invitation to the ball.

Fort Montagu at the eastern approach to Nassau harbour

Wycliffe Elding was a poor businessman in hard times. The Eldings had property and may have had a certain prestige among the local white inhabitants in the Bahama Islands but even so Wycliffe found it difficult to make a decent living wage. The ship chandlers hardly put enough bread on the table for his large family. After much discussion with his wife Sophie, his family and friends, Wycliffe decided to look into the prospects for economic betterment in the southern United States of America. He booked passage on a ship to Savannah, Georgia where he hoped to seek work. If he found suitable employment Wycliffe asserted, he would briefly return to Nassau and then he and his family would emigrate to the United States.

His voyage to Savannah was the first sea voyage he had taken outside the Bahama Islands. After a painfully long but uneventful passage the sailing ship finally approached the Savannah River and took on a pilot. The ship then negotiated the few miles miles of river that led to the town. Wycliffe was immediately impressed at the beautiful late Georgian architecture on the walled bluff overlooking the river and was forced to admit to himself that it made Nassau seem very provincial. But as a British colonial its recent history seemed a favourable omen. In 1778 Savannah had been besieged by French and American forces who had been repulsed by British-officered American Loyalists. And, even though at the end of the Revolutionary War the town was turned over to the new American Republic, he understood Savannah was populated mainly by people from the British Isles who now enjoyed the relatively carefree and elegant lifestyle of the Old South. With the customary prejudice of his age he noted approvingly too that Southerners seemed to have a firmer grip on the black underclass than in his own country. Wycliffe was starting to become convinced that he and his family would quickly adjust to life in this Southern city.

Perhaps it was his colonial manner, or maybe he was just unlucky in the company he encountered, but on only his second day in Savannah, Elding got drawn into an argument in a saloon with an intoxicated patron that had undertones of Loyalist and Rebel.

"So you are from the Bahamas and you are looking for work in the Great State of Georgia?...Why do you not go to England or some far outpost of the great British Empire?" the Southerner sneered.

Wycliffe dismissed the question and said,"...if I can find suitable work, I would like to bring my family to Savannah...we British and Americans have a lot in common..."

"Like what?" the man demanded sharply.

"Oh, you know, a common language, system of justice, religion..."

"...and what religion would you be?"

"Why, I belong to the Church of England...' Elding replied unconsciously. The man took two steps towards him and only then did he realise the conversation was starting to take a bad turn. He became aware of an Irish brogue in the speaker's voice.

"...a church founded by a murderous and adulterous king that calls itself 'catholic'?" The Irishman was working himself up, "...a nation that impressed fine American sailors to serve in British ships!...a nation that attacked the United States and burned down Washington...a nation that denies the proud Irish a nation of their own..."

"Oh all that is in the past!...and I cannot imagine why the British parliament would consider Home Rule for a small portion of the British Isles...well sirrah, I really I think you may have been drinking too much!"

At this remark the Irishman grabbed the lapels of Elding's coat. "Oh, by the Holy Mother and all the saints ye do, do ye!"

Elding tried to resist by pushing the man away. At this, the man landed Wycliffe a knee in his groin followed by a blow to the face.

Wycliffe doubled up and fell to the ground his nose bleeding.

He staggered to his feet and put his fists together in a futile attempt to defend himself. People standing nearby sauntered over to break up the fight.

"Did you see what he did?" Elding gasped from a kneeling position.

"We saw you were in a fight with the mayor's brother...but let's see now...you are not from these parts are you?"

Wycliffe admitted he was not.

"Well, if you know what is good for you, you had better leave...and soon...you have made a bad enemy!"

The small crowd stepped away from them. Wycliffe got up, scowled at the Irish-American and left hurriedly. The brawl certainly helped Wycliffe Elding make up his mind.

He would return to Nassau on the first available ship…

Back in Nassau Wycliffe found things were as bad as ever. His wife Sophie was hoping to earn extra money as a seamstress to help support the family in their large house on East Bay Street. And it was hoped the children, when they were old enough, would help out by turning their hand to odd jobs but first they put their faith in the eldest son Triumph to contribute to their sustenance.

Triumph Elding, the firstborn, was typical of most of the male side of the Elding clan. In the family Bible his name had been entered as: 'Wycliffe Triumph Elding Jr.' but he preferred to be called by his unusual second name which at least distinguished him from his father (the reason for the curious name 'Triumph' was to commemorate the victory of Admiral Horatio Nelson over the French at Trafalgar in 1805 a few years before he was born). Triumph was a powerfully built, ruggedly handsome man and had inherited hazel-coloured eyes that had succeeded through almost every generation of the Elding dynasty. For a time he became a wrecker, but it was hardly steady work. The most important shipwreck he worked was a merchantman that sank off Cat Island. The trading ship was bound from the Mediterranean to Central America with a cargo of statuary and other ecclesiastical paraphernalia intended for several new churches in the Vice-Royalty of New Spain. Much of the unsaleable booty ended up in Nassau.

Triumph married young and his wife Jessica bore him just one son, Algernon Triumph Elding, before she died in childbirth. The family Bible was now contained in a crafted wooden case together with deeds and keepsakes, including a strange carved green stone. The sad event of Jessica's death was recorded in the Bible in the customary stilted language of the day:

'On the 1st day of February 1828 it Pleased the Lord to call His handmaiden Jessica to His side….'

Algernon's grandmother Sophie virtually adopted the child as her own since Triumph was away for a considerable amount of time on wrecking missions and sometimes served as a crew member on merchant ships sailing to the United States. He once even made a voyage to Europe. On his occasional visits to Nassau he sired several children by attractive young black women some of whom adopted the Elding name, but he never remarried.

THE GREATEST ECONOMIC EVENT of the century was the outbreak of the Civil War in the United States that started in 1861. The Bahamas was developing the ability to capitalize on the need or greed of other lands. Without missing a beat the Bahamas, ever ready for easy money, became overnight an *entrepot* for importing commodities from the South and in turn provisioning the Confederate States with anything they required, especially arms. The centre of this activity was Nassau. The value of both imports and exports in the capital city of the Bahamas shot up 500% in a 12 month period between 1861 and 1862.

So nicely has Nature dispersed the Bahamas that they afforded neutral water to within fifty miles of the American coast, and no sooner was the blockade declared than the advantages of Nassau as a basis of operations were recognised and embraced. The harbour was alive with shipping, the quays were piled with cotton, the streets were thronged with busy life.

In January 1862 when the Civil War became particularly savage the British government instructed the governor in Nassau to safeguard the neutrality of the Bahama islands by, '*...preventing as far as possible the use of Her Majesty's harbours, ports and coasts, and the waters within Her Majesty's territorial jurisdiction in aid of the warlike purposes of either belligerent*'. The loophole seemed to be the phrase *'as far as possible'* and also the interpretation of the instruction insofar as it applied to vessels in distress. In a manner of speaking, any vessel being pursued by an armed cutter was in distress! So little, in fact, was done to curb the naval traffic to and from the Confederate South. Indeed, an administrative order further helped the Confederates. If ships of opposing sides were in Bahamian harbours at the same time the first out was given a 24-hour start before the other could leave port.

In fact there was much sympathy for the South among the white population of the Bahamas. After all, some reasoned simplistically, "if it was legitimate for the original colonies to secede from the Mother Country, then it should be just as legitimate for the southern states to also secede from a union that is not to their liking." And indeed many of the second and third generation of Loyalists in the Bahamas still had ties of kinship with families in the Old South.

Besides the obvious need for arms, there were fortunes to be made in shipping cotton. In Charleston, cotton sold for eight cents a pound yet it could be sold in Nassau three days later for a dollar a pound. An observer described the contemporary scene in Nassau:

'Cotton, cotton, everywhere! Blockade runners discharging it into lighters, piled high upon the wharfs and merchant vessels, chiefly under the British flag, loading with it. Here and there in the crowded harbour might be seen a low, long, rakish-looking, lead-coloured steamer with short masts and a convex forecastle deck extending nearly as far aft as the waist, and placed there to enable her to be forced through and not over a heavy sea. These were genuine blockade runners, built for speed; and some of them survived all the hazards of war.'

Goods travelling the other way, worth say £6,000 in Nassau, could fetch £27,000 in gold at Richmond, Virginia. The captain of a ship out of Wilmington received £1,000 and the right to carry ten cotton bales on his own account, the pilot received £1,000 and the right to carry five bales, the purser and first officer £300 and two bales and so on throughout the crew.

Triumph Elding who by this time had gained the deserved reputation of being something of a rake, welcomed the chance of adventure and gainful employment. Encouraged by Boaz Lowe II, a distant relative by marriage, they both decided to join the blockade-runners and made two voyages to Charleston, South Carolina on the *Wild Rover.* After the first voyage the venture seemed like easy money but, homeward bound on the second trip, the *Wild Rover* came under fire from a United States Coastguard cutter north of the Little Bahama Bank. Boaz was killed and several others on board were seriously injured. Triumph received a wound in his leg that caused him to limp slightly for the rest of his life.

On this same trip when they were being chased by a Union cruiser to lighten the ship they had to throw overboard most of the cargo being carried on deck. As they were jettisoning some of the cotton bales they discovered a runaway hidden among the bales. The runaway was lauded for his audacity both on board and when they returned to Nassau. To the credit of the crew, some of whom were Southerners, the idea of returning the slave was not even mentioned. Had the runaway been returned to the Confederacy his captors could have received a handsome bounty of $14,000.

Certainly, there were enormous fortunes to be made but it was a hazardous gamble. After this brush with death, Triumph Elding retired from running the blockade and returned to the family chandlery business in Nassau that had picked up trade significantly during the Civil War. Money was spent with abandon when the ship's crews arrived safely in Nassau. The ships' owners were anxious to disgorge their cotton and re-load the ships with war *materiel* and other scarcities needed in the South as quickly as possible. The town was suddenly swarming with Southern refugees and seamen of all sorts. An American visitor captured the scene:

'Not since the days of the buccaneers and pirates had there been such times in the Bahamas; success paid larger premiums that were ever attained by any legitimate business in the world's commercial history, fully equal to the profits realized from the Spanish galleons by the buccaneers.'

The profits to be gained from the Civil War were great, but as Triumph Elding had discovered to his cost, there was considerable risk. After 1863, running the blockade with cargoes of arms and other essentials became an incredibly dangerous gamble indeed. To illustrate the point, of the steamships that left Nassau 42 were captured and 22 sunk - and the odds were much much worse for sailing ships.

But the ships that ran the blockade were the stuff of legend. The *Robert E. Lee*, built by 'iron mad' Wilkinson, ran the blockade 21 times and the *Banshee* of 217 tons, made especially for Thomas Taylor at Birkenhead, became one of the most celebrated of all the blockade runners. Taylor, who wrote a book about his exploits, records that the *Banshee* was captured on the ninth trip after a long chase off Cape Hatteras. But that did not stop him, the *Banshee* was followed by the *Banshee II* and others. One steamship, the *Will-o'-the-Wisp*, hurriedly built in England to run the blockade using Nassau as a port, travelled at an amazing speed of seventeen and a half knots over a measured mile.

It was calculated the blockade runners provided the Confederate forces with 60% of its modern arms, 30% of its lead for bullets, 75% of the armies' saltpeter and nearly all the paper for cartridges. Also most of the uniforms, leather for shoes also metals, chemicals and medicine. But the end of the old South was inevitable. In 1865 Robert E. Lee surrendered and a second fratricidal war on the North American continent was at an end. The South was crushed and the Bahamas, for whom the war had been a brief and profitable respite, sank into oblivion once again. A British army officer summed it up:

'What good came of it at last? There was...a good deal of drink...(and) many a Dinah owed her ruin to the extraordinary temptations offered by reckless sailors with more money than they knew what to do with, and with the very lowest notions of morality. A few undertakers may have profited, as disease became rather prevalent...and fatal; and the Government managed to pay off a small debt, but what became of all the money is a mystery...'

And the same writer recorded a physical picture of Nassau in those days,

'...the town faces the harbour, the commercial part straggling along the shore; while, sloping backwards and upwards to a ridge of rising ground which shuts in the town from the marshy interior, lie the villas of the wealthier inhabitants, buried in the foliage of palms and fruit trees. (The small colonial town)*...proclaims its maritime character unmistakably. Its stores are full of ropes*

and pulleys, tar, red herrings, and preserved provisions, and the very rafters of the houses tell of the dangers of the sea. Ecclesiastical windows, intended for some church, have been secured by wreckers for the windows of a grocer, and monumental urns may be found ornamenting the gate pillars of a comfortable villa (identifying the house and ornaments owned by the Eldings' on Bay Street). *Nassau is a quiet, hollow sort of place, with a bright sun always shining on its pure white streets, and the blue sea forever sparkling and dancing, and generally alive with pretty little schooners just back from one wreck and starting for another.'*

The Elding families' finances improved but they certainly did not get rich from the Civil War. Triumph continued to work with the family business renting a small house near Fort Montagu on East Bay Street. When his father, Wycliffe died in 1881, Triumph Elding returned to the ancestral family home.

Shortly afterwards Triumph's son Algernon (predictably called 'Algie' by his close friends) left home on his marriage to Chloe, a vivacious freckle-faced girl, the daughter of a wealthy Jamaican planter of Anglo/Irish heritage, whose maternal grandmother had been black. Algie and his wife lived for a time on the plantation in Jamaica. With Algernon out of the house Triumph Elding shared his bed with a Southern lady of dubious reputation who found herself stranded in Nassau after the Civil War ended.

After nearly a year Algie returned to Nassau where he pursued a career with the family business working as store manager under his father's direction. In this capacity he was able to persuade his father to expand into the hardware business. And it was around this time Algernon was able to purchase several plots of vacant land fronting Bay Street in his own name. It was a shrewd investment and became the foundation of the Elding family's future wealth.

THE REST OF THE CENTURY involved not very Christian religious squabbles, which resulted in the disestablishment of the Church of England in the Bahamas. Successions of new crops were tried; pineapples, sisal, citrus, tobacco all were successful for time then failed. Conch shells for cameo broaches had a moment of glory and then fizzled out, finally sponging took hold on the world market. The Greeks were prominent in the business that, though few fortunes were made, lasted well into the twentieth century.

The Bahamas continued to be a racial melting pot; the fine lines between the descendents of the white Adventurers and Loyalists on the one hand and the Mandingo, Fulani, Fante and Yoruba of Africa on the other became blurred toward the end of the nineteenth century. A wag put the happy dilemma into verse:

God bless the white folks one and all, though hark ye,
I see no harm in blessing too the darkey!
But which is the darkey and which the white;
God bless us all! That is beyond me quite!

Tourism was seen to be a possible saviour for the economy. Many foresighted men had already noted the ideal climate, the beautiful beaches and the relaxed atmosphere of the islands. But tourism got off to an inauspicious start. The first steamship to bring visitors from New York to

Loading bales of cotton for re-shipment to Lancashire, England

the Bahamas was the *S. S. Jewess* but she burned to the waterline in Nassau harbour in 1851 so the service was promptly suspended.

Samuel Cunard eight years later started a monthly service from New York to Havana by way of Nassau. His first ship, the paddle steamer *Corsica,* first docked at Nassau in November 1859 two years before the Civil War began. An unfortunate consequence of the new steamship service was that disease was spread from country to country. Shortly after a ship from Havana docked in Nassau there was an outbreak of cholera. Many people in Nassau died. The outbreak was blamed on the steam ship.

The Royal Victoria Hotel, fortuitously completed in the first year of the Civil War, soon reaped a handsome financial reward for its owner and became the virtual offshore headquarters for the blockade-runners. At the end of the century Henry Flagler, the indefatigable tycoon who pushed a railway to Key West, Florida, bought the hotel. The tremendous growth that Flagler brought to southern Florida was a safety net for the unemployed in the Bahamas.

BECAUSE OF THE SCANDAL brought upon the household by the 'un-Christian' liaison of Triumph Elding, now in his middle age, and the woman townsfolk referred to under their breath as the 'Southern harlot', Algernon and his father had a bitter argument. As a result of the altercation Algie and his family moved to Florida for a time. It was in Florida that their first child Walter was born, thus becoming an American citizen. A genealogical sleuth would have to infer that the family Bible at this time must have remained in Nassau since the birth of Walter was inscribed in the Bible in the same hand as the announcement in 1885 of the marriage of Walter and Eunice and also the entry announcing of the birth of their first child Randolph in 1899. The family Bible, contained in an old wooden box was crammed to capacity with sundry deeds, bills of sale, jewellry and a strange egg-shaped carved green stone of unknown provenance.

By now most of the white community of Nassau ostracized Triumph even though his uncharitably-named lady friend, the 'Southern harlot', departed shortly after the rift in the family. Triumph ceased to attend the Anglican Church and was often seen in the company of 'coloured' friends. He soon gained the unflattering reputation of being a free-thinking radical.

In 1886 a kindred spirit arrived in Nassau.

In this year a new Stipendiary and Circuit Magistrate was sent out from England who, in a very short space of time, stirred up a hornet's nest of controversy in the small Colony. Louis Diston Powles was a Roman Catholic with progressive views on many things, especially race relations. He had the opportunity to show his true colours in one of the first cases to come before his Bench. The case involved a white Methodist named Lightbourn who had savagely beaten his 'coloured' maid. Despite considerable pre-trial pressure from the white community, Powles found Lightbourn guilty and promptly sentenced him to prison. In the clamour that followed, Powles was overheard saying to Triumph Elding that 'he would not trust a Methodist (like Lightbourn) on his oath.' Triumph, who knew the defendant well, heartily agreed with him.

The unpopular sentence and Powles' indiscreet remark when it became known, caused an uproar in the Colony. The Methodists sent letters and petitions to Governor Blake. And, when the governor did not act, the House, which was largely controlled by Methodists, refused to reimburse Powles the money for his passage from England to the Bahamas. The governor at first supported the magistrate but after Powles further aggravated race relations by encouraging a black Bahamian to publish a community newspaper entitled ***'The Freeman'***, even Governor Blake wavered in his support. An article by the editor of the ***'The Freeman'*** serves to illustrate why the white establishment wished to curb the newspaper:

Ever since 1837, this country has been dominated by a small gang of whites and so-called whites, whose main object has been, since they could no longer keep the coloured people in slavery, to prevent their ever rising to be anything more than hewers of wood and drawers of water. They look upon them as dogs, and as dogs they treat them, not unkindly as a rule, but with the kindness shown to dogs, neither more nor less.

As a circuit judge Powles made extended visits to the out islands that he recorded later in a delightful book. However, when he arrived back in Nassau after his last 'circuit' of the out islands, matters came to a head. The governor informed him that the Methodists had brought charges against him and there would be an investigation before the Executive Council. Since most of the members of the Council were Methodists, Powles knew his cause would not prevail and so, encouraged by the governor, he resigned.

Powles left the Colony under a cloud. Many blacks and even some whites who had opposed his judgement in the Lightbourn case, were honourable enough to decry the treatment he received. Triumph Elding was foremost in drafting a petition on his behalf to the Secretary of State for the Colonies (recorded in full as Appendix F). But it availed Powles little and he was effectively barred from making an appeal or ever again working in any capacity in Her Majesty's dominions.

While this drama was being played out in the Bahamas, Walter Elding attended the University of Virginia and, on returning to Florida, used his dual nationality and knowledge of American business to good effect by becoming an agent for many American-made products. These he consigned to the family business run by his grandfather, Triumph, in Nassau. The ownership of an 'agency' in these days was a passport to wealth in the Colony. Many of the early agents later became the core of an oligarchy of 'Bay Street Boys', so-named because they often had premises on Bay Street, the main thoroughfare of the capital city. Algernon, despite being estranged from his father Triumph, encouraged young Walter, to pay frequent visits to his ailing grandfather in Nassau that, up to this time, was a larger and more prosperous community than any in south Florida.

Algernon Elding and his wife Chloe returned permanently to the family home in Nassau on the death of Triumph in 1901. Walter returned a year later with his American-born wife Eunice and became floor manager of the family business. With their Florida connections, the Eldings' hardware and chandlery business slowly started to improve. Not so the general economy. It was estimated that at this time one in five Bahamians left to find work in Florida, most of them never to return. The new immigrants settled all over south Florida but were concentrated mainly in the communities of Coconut Grove near Miami and in Key West. The vast migration became commonly known as the 'Miami Craze'. Many surnames of Bahamian origin can still be found today in the three southeastern counties of the State.

One man who decided that he would seek his fortune in Florida at this time was Vincent Williams who lived in one of the Abaco cays. Unlike most Bahamians the Abaconians favoured Key West and some actually transported some of their houses there by sea. Williams decided to sail to Key West with all of his personal belongings on a twelve foot long open dinghy. After arrival he stayed only a short time deciding that the small Floridian community was not to his liking. On his return he ran into a terrible storm and was rescued by a passing Norwegian ship. But he refused to stay with the ship to be dropped off in some distant port, so he set sail for Abaco again. Shortly afterwards another storm almost sank his boat and he was again rescued, this time by a Spanish ship that dropped him off in Tobago. Once there he appealed to the British authorities but had difficulty convincing them who he was and where he was from. The authorities thought he was trying to enter the country illegally and returned him to the Spanish ship that carried him to Corunna in Spain. From there he was put on a ship for England which docked in the River Thames. Again, he had problems identifying himself and he was confined to a workhouse for a year. Finally a protestant minister was able to understand his strange accent and his even stranger story. He was then placed on a ship bound for Nassau and returned to Abaco with an unbelievable tale about where he had been for the past two years!

Getting to the Bahamas in these days before airplanes, was a major problem. Quite extraordinary disasters dogged the efforts of the steamship companies. The *S.S. Missouri* burnt at sea in 1872 on its way to Nassau with the loss of 84 lives and another five cruise ships serving the Bahamas were

Sunday morning after attending the 'Shouters' chapel—'Over the Hill', Nassau c. 1880

all wrecked or destroyed by fire before 1895. But, despite the misfortunes at sea, as the nineteenth century slipped away the Bahamas was well on its way to becoming an important tourist destination.

In the nineteenth century the lifestyle of Africans in the Bahamas had developed to the point where they had become a distinct social entity. Then as now, the great majority of the Bahamian people looked to Africa for their roots. Yet, by the late nineteenth century there were almost no direct cultural links with Africa. Tribal African distinctions had been obscured by several generations of inter-marriage so that Bahamians began to think of themselves as a distinct people. Many families had become a creolized racial mixture of many West African peoples often with some Caucasian and even native Indian blood in their veins.

Though the religions of Africa had been lost along the way, the fervent spirituality of Africa was re-born in the many Christian faiths practiced in the Bahamas. The most popular was the Baptist Church that stressed devotion to God but also personal freedom. The Christian religious experience for African Bahamians was supplemented with emotional sermons, rousing music, lively singing and hand clapping. Sometimes heartfelt and exceptionally demonstrative spirituality gave rise to popular congregations known as 'shouters', 'jumpers' or 'holy rollers'.

Obeah was perhaps the only religious cult to survive from Africa. This practice was a combination of ritual, superstition, alchemy, religion and some might suggest, extortion. The priests of *Obeah* created a spell (called a 'hex') that could only be negated by an even greater and more potent spell. There was a belief that errant *jumbey* or *duppie* spirits could be made to cause mischief especially between enemies and star-crossed lovers. *Obeah* is akin to Voodoo but in the Bahamas at least has, throughout time, had many fewer followers.

Bush medicine practiced in the Bahamas relied on knowledge brought from Africa though many new world potents were substituted for the original African bush medicines. Love vine, aloe, sage bush, milk wood and many others have been used with differing results. The most common bush medicines used in the Bahamas throughout time are probably cerasse for the cure of colds and fever, shepherd's needle to cure wounds and aloe for skin disorders and used as a purge. Older women in rural areas tend to be the most knowledgeable practitioners. An aphorism the Africans brought to the West Indies suggested, *'tout hazié sé remèd'* (every bush has a remedy).

The premier Bahamian cultural phenomenon that had its origins in the African experience was Junkanoo. Similar customs also survived in Georgia, Jamaica and Bermuda but it was in the Bahamas that it became the pre-eminent cultural event. As early as 1801, Junkanoo, a lexical corruption of 'John Canoe' (possibly the name of an African chief from Ghana), was firmly established in the Bahama Islands. Performed every Boxing Day and New Year's Day from about 3 o'clock in the morning to about 9 am, the 'rushers' parade in crepe paper costumes to the accompaniment of cowbells, goatskin drums and whistles through the principal communities of the island country. Illuminated first by artificial light, then through the ethereal colours of dawn to morning light, the parade is a never-to-be-forgotten visual spectacle enhanced by a haunting repetitive rhythm. For the few brief hours of the parade, Junkanoo opens a window to the African soul of Bahamians.

In short, cultural and social life for Bahamians of African heritage, throughout the nineteenth century revolved around church and community. They were closely tied to the sea though for subsistence most families invariably kept a plot of land on which to grow fruit and vegetables. They enjoyed a cooperative form of existence in which 'community' often took precedence over family, though in many settlements most of the community were in any case bonded by being related, however distantly, to one another. In adverse times their strong community spirit pulled them through.

Chapter 12 - Ebb and Flow: The Twentieth Century (1900 - 1949)

Can it be possible that the Bahamas will not turn up in the centre of things, adventurous and glamourous?

H.M.Bell

ALTHOUGH QUEEN VICTORIA *died in 1901, the first fourteen years of the new century could be said to belong to the old. Nevertheless, little by little some of the wonders of the new age appeared and changes were slowly introduced into the island colony. Shortly after the turn of the century the motorcar made a debut on the dirt roads of the capital city. A submarine telegraph link between Nassau and Florida was instituted and finally in 1907, a telephone system for Nassau was established by the government that was a full two years before there was a reliable supply of electricity.*

In the first half of the twentieth century two major wars enveloped the world and the Bahamas rallied to the cause of Empire. The period between the wars was marked by Prohibition which, as in the American Civil War, turned the Bahamas into an entrepôt for boats running the United States blockade. But this time, instead of arms, the cargo was liquor. The end of the Second World War surprisingly did not bring the expected depression, instead tourism started to flourish. At the same time there was an emergence in the Bahamas of political awareness.

Demographic statistics tell an interesting tale of incipient metropolitan dominance in the Bahamas. The population of the Colony at the turn of the nineteenth century was around 50,000 people, 11,000 of whom lived in Nassau

(New Providence) and only fractionally less on Eleuthera (including Harbour Island and Spanish Wells). One hundred years later the population of New Providence had increased 500% while the population of Eleuthera and adjacent islands remained about the same. The population in the rest of the Bahamas for the next hundred years also remained fairly constant except for Grand Bahama which, because of the development of Freeport, enjoyed rapid growth in the second half of the century.

Bay Street, Nassau around 1905

ROMULUS, THE SON OF ABSALOM ELDON, had personal entrepreneurial ambitions and chose not to work for the family funeral parlour but instead took his small share of the inheritance and looked for other employment. Understanding well the material needs of the common people he opened a general store near Bay Street intending to cater principally to black Bahamians. His enterprise was unusual insofar as he rented space from a white Bahamian in an enclave of poor whites east of the centre of Nassau. A handpainted sign over the door advertised the shop as:

GROCERY AND DRY GOODS STORE
Union Street, Nassau
Romulus Eldon, Proprietor
Dry & Stable Goods
Groceries & Provisions

The interior of the shop was typical of such establishments. It had the pervasive but not unpleasant musky odour of disinfectant and over-ripe fruit. On the floor were open sacks of rice, chili peppers and grits, a few baskets of mangos, avocados, okra, black-eyed peas and squash. A bunch of sugar cane stalks and a few Eleuthera pineapples were stacked in the corner. The lower shelves were well stocked with a miscellany of items like ginger beer, lemon barley water, lye, carbolic soap, face creams and patent remedies, while on the upper shelves were dusty cans of soups with names sounding strange to Bahamian ears: tinned sardines and salmon, tomato ketchup and yellowy halved peaches. One wall was devoted to a display of dried conch and salted cod that flies seemed to find more appealing than the sticky fly paper suspended from the ceiling. On the counter were jars of boiled sweets, chocolate bars and baskets of freshly baked bread.

The business enterprise certainly found a ready market and soon it was the small white community who were among Romulus's best customers. But the Bay Street merchants objected to competition so close to their historic 'sphere' of commercial influence and, as agents for many of the products Romulus stocked in his store, they refused to grant him credit and often withheld supplies from him.

Within a year he was forced out of business.

Embittered, financially crippled and unable to find other employment in the Colony he took ship to work as a labourer on the construction of the Panama Canal. Romulus was one of hundreds of Bahamians to work on what was at that time, the biggest civil engineering project in the world. While in Panama, unlike many of his compatriots, he was able to avoid the scourge of malaria, yellow fever and industrial accidents that affected so many of the workers in the Canal Zone. Three years later he returned to Nassau, by Bahamian standards, a relatively wealthy man.

He purchased a wooden house 'over the hill' in a corner of Bain Town that he converted to accommodate another general store. Later Romulus incorporated two other small wooden framed buildings nearby to serve as living and sleeping quarters. With additional capital and being now more worldly-wise he was able to stock the new store without antagonizing the Bay Street agents. The business did relatively well in the new 'over the hill' location given the economic circumstances of the time.

Not long after his return, he met Verna a serious-minded Turks Island girl and distant relative of Mary Prince. After years of co-habitation with Verna, who worked as a room maid at the Royal Victoria Hotel, they were married in a quiet ceremony by a justice of the peace. They reared five children in Bain Town all of whom bore the Eldon surname. Their sons were Joshua and Constantine, the girls bore the unlikely names of Proudencia, Savelita and Clotilda. All three of the girls had large families though Clotilda was not legally married so her offspring continued to carry the Eldon surname.

EVENTS IN EUROPE slowly started to affect the torpor of the Colony. As a portent of a gathering storm the German battleship *Karlsruhe* found itself in Bahamian waters at the outbreak of the First World War but managed to escape to the neutral port of San Juan, Puerto Rico. War fever started to mount.

About 1800 Bahamians signed on to fight the foreign foe. But, as almost all of the Bahamian contingent were of African descent, they found it was difficult to see, in physical terms at least, the German 'Huns' as being so very different from pink-complexioned Englishmen. Joshua and Constantine Eldon, signed on to fight with the British North Caribbean Regiment (later re-named the Bahamas Battalion) while most white Bahamians joined the better-paid Canadian armed forces.

Three years after the outbreak of the Great War, the United States entered the conflict in 1917 by which time the local economy of the Bahamas was near collapse. Revenue from tourism dried up and obtaining supplies from the United States became exceptionally difficult. At the same time the Bahamas experienced severe inflation and, to make matters worse, a local bank failed.

Randolph Elding, the eldest son of Walter Elding a property owner and Bay Street merchant, was one of the first white Bahamians to enlist in the armed services. Together with a handful of others of both races he was publicly acclaimed by Governor Sir George Haddon-Smith in a public ceremony just after war had been declared. The pomp and circumstance of the event encouraged many unemployed men of both races to join the forces. The flag waving, martial music and patriotic speeches hardly prepared them for the carnage of Flanders. The enlisted men were to understand little about the killing fields of the European theatre of war until they came face to face with a fusillade of German machine gun fire. The carnage of the 'Great War', as it came to be called, was a living hell. In the words of a nostalgic popular song of the time, 'Its long way to Tipparary' the Bahamian soldiers would soon find out soon enough it was a long, *long* way back to their tranquil and idyllic isles of perpetual June.

Following in the steps of his wife's father, Randolph joined the British West Indian Regiment. After training in Jamaica in the early years of the war, the regiment was transported to Europe and saw action in Picardy in northern France and in Belgium. Some of the regiment even got to serve in southern Palestine and Egypt. In Picardy, Elding obtained a commission, rose to the rank of major and had the debatable distinction of being 'mentioned in dispatches' from the front line. On his record he was classified by the army as 'white' but his men recognized him as being a man of 'colour' which helped him forge a special relationship with his men. His physique and a knowing look into Randolph Elding's hazel eyes revealed the African lineage, albeit distant, in his heritage. As most of the men under Elding's command were from the West Indies or the Bahamas he was able to create a bond with them that a 'white' European officer might have found impossible.

When a section of the 'front' next to them was so severely battered that it almost ceased to exist, the uninjured remnant were transferred to Randolph Elding's platoon. Lance-corporal Joshua Eldon was one of the soldiers who increased the number of black Bahamians in Randolph's platoon to nineteen. It was almost an axiom that in the deadly trench warfare of Flanders that units with high morale managed to survive, while the opiate of despair meant almost certain death. Randolph and Joshua were to survive.

When the Armistice was finally signed in November 1918, the economic situation in the Bahamas, with the troops returning home was, if anything, worse than before the Great War. Of the 670 Bahamians of both races who actually saw action in the war, 50 were killed in the cause of Empire. The bullet-riddled body of Constantine Eldon was buried in Belgium and marked by a simple cross. In all, a million men of the British Empire had been sacrificed in this horrendous 'war to end all wars'. A cenotaph memorialising the sacrifice of Bahamians was later erected in a public garden behind the parliament building in Nassau.

Shortly after arriving back in Nassau, Joshua Eldon married Naomi, a bright worldly-wise Long Island girl and, like Joshua's parents, they had five children. For a time Joshua worked at his father's general store but he had great difficulty settling down and was often away from home. His war experiences had made him unsettled and moody. Naomi was philosophical about Joshua's protestations that everything was well with him. She explained it in a Bahamian proverb, "when a man say him no mind, den he mind". The way she reasoned it was, that even though Joshua did not act responsibly, he really wanted to.

So with Joshua away, despite having five children to rear, Naomi had to find time to help her father-in-law Romulus mind the store. The children were brought up in time-honoured fashion by their mother though their aunts sometimes acted as foster parents. The oldest son Charlten was a model student at school with a passing grade in the top quartile at a government high school. Good-looking, polite and intelligent, judged by his character and academic achievements every one said he would go far. However, after leaving school things started to go terribly wrong. He could not find a job suited to his talents and was often found in the company of a street gang. He was briefly incarcerated for being part of a gang that had been involved in petty theft even though he had not been present at the time of the crime. Charlten never forgot the injustice and the biting supercilious remarks made by a white bewigged magistrate at the time he was sentenced. It became a turning point in his life. When he left confinement he was seldom seen at home. Naomi, ever loyal to her family, quoted a proverb to try to stem the gossip: "when eye no see, mout' no talk..."

After many years Joshua came back to live with his family permanently and took over the management of the general store from his ailing father. After World War II started, business picked up just a little and he made sufficient money for the family to survive. In 1943 in the middle of World War II a policeman mounted on a motorcycle came to seek Joshua at his place of business. The black policeman called from outside the shack that he had an official notice to deliver to 'Mr. Joshua Eldon'. Joshua crept outside with some trepidation hoping the visit had nothing to do with his son Charlten whom he knew had been shooting his mouth off again at political rallies.

The policeman explained the reason for his visit: "Mister Joshua because you is male, a businessman, ex-serviceman and property owner you name bin selected to a pool of purtential jurors for an up-comin' trial".

Joshua stammered some questions but was given no answers.

"Make sure you appear at the Court in Rawson Square at the appointed time..." He was given a piece of official paper to sign and then the motorcycle carrying the policeman roared off.

Joshua had no idea of the drama that he would soon witness. Relieved at least that the summons was merely procedural he felt sure that as a black man he would be overlooked for jury duty and promptly dismissed the matter from his mind. Charlten's problems with the law and his being out of work continued to give the family increasing unease. Naomi, as always, was ready with a rationalization for the families' adversities and explained away Charlten's misfortunes to her neighbours and friends: 'Erry day fishing day, but not erry day catchy fish".

Fortune was kinder to Joshua's superior officer. After demobilization, Major Randolph Elding had a lightning romance with Sarah Newcombe, a daughter of the Colonel in Chief of the West Indian Regiment whom he met in Britain. Fearing lest parental approval might be withheld, the couple eloped to Nassau, married and started a family. Colonel Sir Richard and Lady Newcombe visited them in 1920 after their first child, Leonard, was born. If the proud grandparents had any misgivings about the union, they never expressed it publicly.

THE END OF THE WAR brought the expected slump but hopeful signs of economic betterment for the Bahamas once again came from North America. The Volstead Prohibition Act was signed into law in the United States in 1919 disallowing the public sale of beverages containing more than half of one percent of alcohol. Unpopular from the beginning, it was soon clear that Prohibition was contrary to the wishes of the great majority of Americans and many entrepreneurs energetically set out to redress the deficiency of liquor in the United States.

The Bahamas, because of its geographical position, soon became an important centre for the traffic of alcoholic beverages to the United States. It was a situation not so very different from 1861. Perhaps the major difference had to do with the exalted ideals which were expressed and fought for in the Civil War, while during Prohibition it was simply a law enforced upon the nation by a minority of idealistic teetotalers meeting dogged resistance from the 'outlaw' tipplers.

The Bahama Islands were soon the homeport for as many as 400 boats that ran the cordon of US Coastguard vessels trying to interdict the traffickers. The three major ports for transshipping liquor were Nassau, West End, Grand Bahama and Alice Town in Bimini. Besides fast boats, the bootleggers sometimes even used airplanes to take liquor to remote airstrips in the Everglades in Florida. As in the Civil War, vast fortunes were to be made,

'...bootleggers played poker for $100 notes on the piles of empties, competed at pitch and toss with gold pieces on the wharfs, roared loud choruses as they trekked to their boats for outward runs...timid folk stayed home o' nights, preachers threatened all and sundry with the wrath of God...money ruled...'

The 'big' money to be made in bootlegging encouraged Al Capone and other notorious members of the American gangster scene to become frequent visitors to the Bahamas, especially to West End, Grand Bahama. When competition got too brisk, inter-gang rivalries spilled over into fights for 'turf'. In the early 1920's the notorious Ashley Gang from Florida raided West End and held up the entire village with machine guns and small arms and then made off with 'loot' stolen from their competitors. At least four warehouses were raided and about $8,000 was taken in cash. The raid was ill-starred though. On the morning before the raid at least $250,000 in cash had been sent on the rickety old mail boat to Nassau!

But for the Ashley Gang worse was to come. On October 19, 1921, Ed and Frank, two of the Ashley brothers left the bar of the St. Lucie Inlet on the east coast of Florida under cover of darkness. They passed under the very eyes of a federal cutter but with lights extinguished and motor muffled they were not stopped for questioning. The boat scurried out of Stuart Harbour and was soon bucking the cross current of the Gulf Stream just offshore. So strong is the northward urge of the Stream at this point that the small craft changed course and headed toward the southeast, battling for an additional twenty miles so that when it was out of the influence of the Stream they were in a direct line with Settlement Point at the western end of Grand Bahama.

Barrels and crates of liquor in Nassau awaiting transshipment to the United States

Once safely in West End, box after box of liquor was packed into the small boat until there was scarcely room for its crew and but a scant few inches of freeboard showed above the water line. The West Enders warned the brothers that they were over-loading the boat but they laughingly passed off the danger. The Ashley brothers' departure for Florida, under ordinary circumstances, should have taken place the same night but a threatening sky and the counsel of the islanders was finally heeded and the Ashley boys decided to wait until the following day. The whole of the next day the sky was still overcast and the sea choppy, and effort was again made to prevail upon the youths to wait yet another day. But, the Ashley brothers' devil-may-care attitude prompted them to cast off. Impatient to realize their profit, they started out even though in West End's protected harbour the white caps could be seen to be licking menacingly toward the gunwhale of their boat. A few West Enders gathered at the dock to watch the pair disappear over the horizon in their small boat.

The Ashley brothers were never ever seen again.

During the Prohibition years the small West End community was a den of iniquity, bars and poolrooms sprouted up, tarts touted their charms and drunken orgies and gunfights were commonplace. Yet, to keep the peace in this volatile situation the Bahamian government entrusted the maintenance of law and order to a commissioner and two unarmed policemen!

Liquor brought into the Colony was subject to a small duty and even though a drawback was allowed on liquor re-exported from the Colony, the government and populace prospered. Roads were paved, the harbour in Nassau was deepened and the wharfs lengthened. In the private sector churches were refurbished, charities refinanced and new houses and hotels built. But the good times did not last. In 1933 the Prohibition Act was reversed by the Twenty First Amendment and Alice Town and West End reverted back to sleepy out island fishing villages. Nassau fared little better.

IN THE EARLY YEARS of the Great Depression, Major Randolph Elding now considered something of a war hero, was appointed to the Legislative Council and became a *confidante* of the governor during the remainder of the inter-war years. The amity between the two men cooled somewhat when Harry (later Sir Harry) Oakes, appeared on the Bahamian scene.

Oakes was a larger-than-life character who, though born in the United States, became a Canadian citizen. He was an incredibly ambitious man with a burning desire to succeed. With great perseverance and not a little luck he became fabulously wealthy from mining in Canada but he greatly resented the crippling Canadian taxes he had to pay. In Palm Beach, Florida he met Harold Christie, then a member of the House of Assembly, who persuaded him to bring his fortune to the tax-free haven of the Bahamas. Cynics of the time suggested that it was quite apt that he should move to the Bahamas for, like the pirates before him, much of his fortune was derived from plundered gold.

Oakes took Christies' advice and bought 7000 acres of prime land on New Providence where he built many houses, constructed an airport, gave to the right charities, became the largest employer of labour in the private sector and, by so doing, after changing his nationality, acquired a knighthood. In 1938, a year before the outbreak of the Second World War, Sir Harry Oakes was elected a member of the House of Assembly. His meteoric ascent from foreigner, to investor, to elected politician, to Knight of the British Empire, to Member of the Legislative Council was surely without precedent in all His Majesties' dominions. The local oligarchy, Randolph Elding among them, held their breath.

"I wonder what will be next?" Randolph asked.

"Oh at this rate and with his money and influence how about Premier, Governor, King...or how about God Almighty!" was his son Leonard's cynical reply.

In 1939 Britain, to again honour its Treaty obligations, was forced into another war with Germany. The worldwide Empire, upon which the sun was about to set, once again was dragged into the conflict including of course, the Colony of the Bahamas where the loyalty displayed towards the Mother Country was nothing short of remarkable.

As the distant thunder of World War II shattered the tranquil islands of the shallow sea, a son Peter was born to Leonard and Lorna Elding. The family Bible faithfully recorded the birth of Peter Leonard Wycliffe Elding christened in the Anglican Cathedral in Nassau in August 1939. Two years later his wife presented him with a daughter. Several names were discussed for their green-eyed daughter born two years after Peter but they finally decided upon the first name inscribed in the yellowed pages of the old family Bible: Elizabeth Neptuna. Her childhood name for herself was 'Bamie' and her family and close friends adopted the name for the precocious little girl with chlorine and sun-bleached blonde hair though later, on Elizabeth's pre-pubescent but explicit instructions, she demanded to be called 'Bahama'. All of her friends and most of the family concurred.

On the political scene in the colony most of the members of the Legislative Council, including Randolph Elding by now had great resentment for a *nouveau riche* outsider like Oakes dabbling in Bahamian affairs but they kept the matter to themselves. With a war now waging in Europe and a sputtering economy in the Bahamas, they well understood this was no time for divisive behaviour. But it was not easy. Oakes had an over-bearing nature and he hardly disguised his contempt for the 'callow' colonials, black and white. In the second year of the war he started acting coyly and wearing a Cheshire cat smile on his face that suggested that he was a party to some important news.

Randolph Elding hoped it might be good news to do with the conduct of the war since, despite all inducements, the Americans were still sitting on the fence and the Axis powers were advancing in all directions. In northern France, Dunkirk had been a military defeat made to look like some heroic tactical retreat, the North African campaign was going nowhere and the news from the Far East theatre of war was appalling. "Yes" thought Elding, "I hope this news is something very special."

The smile on Sir Harry's face turned to a broad grin when the news was finally announced to the public:

"Yes my dear chap, the Duke of Windsor—former King Edward VIII no less—is to become the new governor of the Bahamas!" he crowed.

The governor of the time, Sir Charles Dundas, was packed off to Africa and Government House was spruced up to receive the Duke of Windsor and his wife, the former Mrs. Wallis Simpson. As if to set a pattern for her future conduct, the Duchess immediately upon arrival, declared the interiors of Government House uncomfortable and outmoded and called in the best decorators from New York that money could buy. She was probably right about the state of the building but with a desperate war waging around the world, the timing was indeed unfortunate. The Duchess missed the high society of Europe and soon let be known that she considered Nassau society 'moronic'. And that was not all. 'The heat is awful', she wrote to her aunt, 'I long for some air that isn't caused by electric fans...I hate this place more each day...where did you stay when you came to this dump?' A gratuitous question certainly, her aunt would not have access to the most luxurious residence the colony afforded...

Bahamians of course were not consulted about the choice of governor but a local songwriter summed up their feelings in a local catchy melodic form of calypso called 'Goombay'.

I din't know Ms. Simpson was a woman like det
She wear tight dresses to make King Edward fret
Now she got some money and she got a talk
And a fancy walk – just to suit New York
Let de organ play, let de church bell ring
Let de nation sing, 'God Save the King'.
It was love, love, love alone
dat caused King Edward to leave de trone

Around this time some hard questions were being voiced about the Duke of Windsor's political sympathies. In August 1939 he had cabled Hitler: 'I address to you my entirely personal simple, though very earnest appeal, for you to use your influence towards the peaceful solution of the present problem.'

Hitler cabled back: 'Assure you my attitude towards England remains the same. My wish is to avoid another war between our two countries. It depends however...on England...'

At this same time in the critical history of the world many well-to-do people sought refuge from the war in the Bahamas. One such was an enigmatic foreign millionaire from Sweden. In September 1939 Axel Wenner-Gren sailed from Gotenburg to Nassau to escape the war. *En route* to the Bahamas his colossal yacht passed close to the north coast of Scotland where the first marine casualty of World War II was recorded. Well within view of Wenner-Gren's yacht the British liner *Athena* was torpedoed by a German U-boat. He was able to save 376 survivors. But questions remained about the number of aerials on his boat and his being at that particular place, at that particular time. Wenner-Gren spoke fluent German and it was well known he had links to the Nazi hierarchy.

Hitler with the Duke and Duchess of Windsor

Nevertheless when Wenner-Gren arrived in the Bahamas he was immediately be-friended by the Duke who was a frequent guest on his yacht the *Southern Cross*. During his stay in Nassau, Wenner-Gren was suspected by the Secret Services of Britain and the United States as being a Nazi go-between. The allied Secret Services were unsure about the Duke's loyalties in the early war years and surmised that if Britain lost the war Hitler might try to place the Duke as a puppet king on the throne of England.

After being installed as governor of the Bahamas, the Duke was defensive at being sent to an outpost of empire and wanted his voice to be heard. He wrote to his lawyer in England on 30 May 1941: 'the average American is interested in what the Duke of Windsor has to say'. And one gratuitous thing he had to say was, '...this doleful succession of (British) defeats does cause one to doubt the ability of the strategists...'

Sir Winston Churchill, the British wartime prime minister was infuriated and wrote:

'I hear from various quarters of very unhelpful opinions being expressed by both the Duke and Duchess (in Nassau). What is wanted is an important American publicist who will try to instill sound ideas into that that circle' (here Churchill anticipates the need for 'spin doctors' to influence the 'media'). And he added quizzically: '...it does not matter if there is a row.'

Some time after arriving in Nassau, Wenner-Gren visited Mexico where he established a bank. He invited Avilo Camacho, brother of the Mexican president and a known fascist sympathiser, to come to Nassau even though Britain had closed relations with Mexico. The Duke, and possibly Harry Oakes and other Nassau notables, were believed to have transferred money to the safety of a Mexican bank in violation of wartime currency regulations. Such actions were considered to be 'trading with the enemy'—a most serious violation of wartime regulations. Later the Duke was even invited by Wenner-Gren to visit him in Mexico. But after the full machinations of Wenner-Gren were known, he was denied permission to return to the Bahamas even though he made many requests. He also, unsuccessfully, kept up a barrage of correspondence from Mexico with the Roosevelt administration to get himself off the United States 'blacklist' of undesirables.

Before the United States entered the World War II, an Accord was signed between the British and American governments permitting the United States to create bases in many British territories in the Caribbean in exchange for fifty old, some preferred the word decrepit, destroyers. Several of the bases were built in the Bahamas. The airfield that Oakes had constructed near the city of Nassau was considered unsuitable for war planes and so plans were drawn up for a new airfield (later named Windsor Field in honour of the royal governor) which was to be built at the western end of the island.

The Bahamians were very happy to find employment on the airfield project but when it was discovered that American labourers were being paid $1.50 an hour while they were only being paid four shillings (about 60 cents) for the same work, there was loudly voiced anger.

After a few days, the discontent started to turn violent and a mob from 'over the hill' descended on Bay Street and broke windows and looted the shops. The anger of the mob was directed at the Bay Street merchants (most of whom were members of the House of Assembly) since it was believed that they were the perpetrators of what was termed the 'dirty deal'. The riotous behaviour was so serious that the troops were called out and two men were killed and twenty-five injured. It was, in its way, the Bahamian version of the Boston Massacre.

Charlten Eldon the only surviving son of Joshua and Naomi, and now a young union activist, helped to stir up the protest. Charlten had political ambitions he never seemed able to attain. He changed jobs frequently, failed at the enterprises he started and expressed his radical opinions too forcibly. For a time he worked at the docks like his father where he tried, unsuccessfully, to organize the stevedores into a union. Marcus Garvey the Jamaican-born activist and leader of the Pan-African Movement who wanted to carry all the 'transported' black people back to Africa was his sometime idol. To many people of African descent in the 'new world' Garvey was considered a kind of black prophet. Garvey even acquired three ships with a view to carrying out his mission but, in a related case, was sent to prison in the United States for alleged fraud. Over 35,000 mainly African-Americans invested in his project which eventually failed, loosing $750,000 of the subscriber's money. Garvey visited the Bahamas and made a lasting impression on several people who passed on his message of hope (and some would say hate) to the young Charlten Eldon.

In the middle of a crowd of rioters in Bay Street, Charlten Eldon led the chant, "what do we want?" and the thundering reply from the mob blocking the airport road was, 'we want more money!' Two of Charlten's henchmen were arrested but not before they burned a photograph of the Royal Family in public. Questioned about their disloyal behaviour, one of them made the reply, 'Man, I willin' to fight under the flag, but I aint't gwine starve under it!' In true Bahamian fashion the incident called for music and the rioters started by singing patriotic songs but quickly turned to a new strangely enigmatic anthem of dissent: 'Burma Road declare war on Conchie Joe, don't lick nobody, don't lick nobody...'

Charlten Eldon understood the need for political and social change but was far ahead of his time. His moment in the spotlight of Bahamian history was passing. He had a stormy marriage with a schoolteacher, Ranetta Lightbourne, and they had two children together, though he also fathered two or three 'out' children in the town.

The Duke of Windsor, in his capacity as governor, was spared direct criticism for the Bay Street incident but thereafter his popularity waned. Even before the anger over the so-called 'dirty deal' had broken into the open, Leonard Elding, a recent but dynamic member of the Executive Council, had tried to persuade the governor to let him talk to the ringleaders to work out a compromise.

"I am acquainted with one of the ringleaders Your Excellency, let me talk to him, I know I can bring him round. He is a man named Charlten Eldon..."

"Elding? Not a relation I trust!" the governor joked.

"Err, no, Your Excellency, Charlten E...l...d...o...n," (he spelled out the name), "...a coloured fellow who considers himself something of a disciple of Marcus Garvey. Of course we shall have to offer more money...about six or seven shillings an hour would be acceptable I am sure..."

The governor was sympathetic but Harry Oakes and others later convinced the governor that such an action would be tantamount to capitulation, "...and who knows how much more they will demand?" they declared. The Royal Governor, by not speaking his mind, concurred. Indeed at this moment the Duke had some other important business to ponder. Harold Christie had brought him a proposal from some 'businessmen' in Havana to introduce gambling into the Bahamas. Though gambling had a bad reputation in Cuba it would doubtless bring in much needed hard currency to the hard-pressed Colony. Harold Christie convinced the Duke that any bad elements could be curbed with help from the British police. Sir Harry Oakes was at first enthusiastic but on consideration he tried to turn the governor against the idea. He did not want the idyllic Bahamas overrun by hordes of middle class visitors and anyway it was possible the gambling bosses might gain political influence at his expense as had happened to the political elite in Cuba.

"No," he told the Duke, "on further consideration I believe gambling will destroy the character of the Bahamas and drive well-to-do people away from Nassau." The Duke concurred about the unsuitability of mass tourism but the prospect of revenue to the colony—liberally spread around—could not be overlooked. He indicated he would like to consider the matter further.

Sir Harry Oakes, in his meteoric rise to fame and fortune, destroyed many people. One day, when he was in the British Colonial Hotel in Nassau with some important friends, a waiter was rude to him. That was too much for Sir Harry. A few days later he purchased the hotel and had the man dismissed on the spot. Oakes also had an acute dislike for the husband of his teenage daughter, a Mauritian, with a mouthful of a name: Count Marie Albert Fouquereaux de Marigny.

Just after her eighteenth birthday Nancy Oakes ran away to marry the twice divorced de Marigny in New York. Oakes, a crabby old miner, had reluctantly to accept the playboy de Marigny as his son-in-law. To make matters worse Nancy soon became pregnant which threw Harry Oakes into a rage. Nancy lost the baby but it was the crowning of a mutual hatred. And de Marigny did not only upset Oakes. He snubbed the Duke of Windsor and other notables and then befriended a bunch of French ex-convicts who washed up in Nassau after having escaped from the notorious penal colony of Devil's Island.

On a stormy night on the 7th July 1943, a ghastly crime was committed in Nassau. The event was so shocking that, even though it occurred in the middle of World War II with news blackouts and emergencies, it still managed to capture the headlines making news of the raging world war secondary. The crime remains to this day an intriguing mystery.

Sir Harry Oakes, whose wife was away at Bar Harbour, Maine for the humid summer months, had spent the evening quietly at his palatial house *Westbourne* with two others and Harold Christie. The two guests left the house at about 11:30 for home while Christie, a bachelor, stayed on to discuss a business deal and was given a spare bedroom next but one to Oakes's. There were no servants in the house. Though two watchmen were thought to be in the grounds, they mysteriously disappeared and did not appear when a trial was later convened. Then, there were two alleged 'hit men' who were reported to arrive (and depart) by fast boat at Lyford Cay on the fateful night. The two men were seen by caretakers at Lyford Cay but both caretakers died, under mysterious circumstances, before a trial was held.

When Harold Christie awoke at about 7 a.m. the following day he discovered Sir Harry Oakes had been brutally murdered. His head battered, he had been thrown on the bed, sprayed with an inflammable spirit and set alight. Some chicken feathers were strewn about the place. Oakes's head had been smashed, and he been thrown on a bed which had then been doused with kerosene and set on fire (astoundingly Christie later declared he had heard nothing in the night and had slept soundly all night).

The Duke of Windsor's first reaction to the news as governor of the Bahamas, was to apply his powers of censorship. But he was too late. The local editor of a newspaper, with whom Oakes and Christie had an early appointment, had been the first to hear of the murder and telegraphed the story to the far corners of the world. It took the Duke of Windsor several hours to decide what to do. As an irreverent writer for a sensationalist American magazine put it, '...he was somewhat rusty at making decisions ever since he decided to forego the Crown six years before...' By now very concerned, the Duke, ignored the local Bahamian C.I.D., the American F.B.I. and the competent criminologists attached to the forces in Nassau and telephoned Miami to request the services of two police officers with whom he was vaguely acquainted.

Shouldering aside the local police, the Miami police went resolutely to work. On the evening of 9th July, Alfred de Marigny, the husband of Nancy Oakes, was arrested and charged with the murder of his father-in-law. The case against de Marigny seemed clear. Notoriously estranged from Sir Harry and Lady Oakes, whose daughter he had married without their consent, he was without an unimpeachable alibi for the night of July 7. In fact, he was known to have been in the vicinity of *Westbourne* after midnight and, when his house was searched, he was unable to trace the shirt he wore on the night of the murder. The Miami police examined de Marigny's arms and beard and declared that his hairs were singed. Then, six days later, they announced that they had discovered de Marigny's fingerprints on the screen in Sir Harry Oakes' bedroom. The unfortunate Mauritian seemed to be headed straight for the gallows.

The same sensationalist American magazine writer continued: 'the fact that Harry Oakes had attained his sixty-eighth birthday without being knocked off was as much a mystery as the murder itself. He had, all his life, been asking for it. The Miami dicks...learned that Sir Harry Oakes was an autocratic old buzzard who had enough enemies to populate a fair-sized island. A sporting instinct caused him to look down upon coloured folks...as a form of life best used as punching bags and footballs'. Then, the reporter continued, there were the five escapees from Devil's Island the notorious penal colony off French Guiana who were good friends of de Marigny which sounded 'fishy'. So in the foreground of the police inquiries was de Marigny who had recently said of his father-in-law, 'its about time that somebody killed that old bastard and...from that moment...the Count's goose was in the oven and the...imported flatfeet began to turn up the gas...'

Joshua Eldon was called to appear at the Court for jury selection. When he arrived in his best suit he was not surprised to find most of the other people selected were white. He assumed he would be dismissed but to his complete surprise he was the first person selected to serve on the jury and was informed he should be prepared to be held *in camera* once the murder trial began. He tried to object but was made to understand it was his civic duty and, after he was informed he would receive payment for his services, he quietly acquiesced. He returned home with the news. Miriam quietly pleased at the turn of events, helped him pack a bag and assured him she would mind the store in his absence. "Dat Mr. Mariney him never do what dey say he do", she declared. But Joshua was not listening. He was pondering on the strange episode that was about to overtake him.

PART TWO

The sensational trial opened before a bewigged Lord Chief Justice and an all-male multi-racial jury on 16th October 1943 and lasted almost three weeks. Counsel for the prosecution was the Attorney General of the time, assisted by a highly respected black Bahamian attorney. Counsel for the defense were two were two young local white attorneys.

There was a tense moment in Court when a handcuffed de Marigny was sworn in and sat as defendant in the dock. The jury were seated on benches situated along the sidewall of the Court where they could see the nervous defendant, the impatient judge and the eager counsels for both prosecution and defence. Joshua fidgeted nervously in his seat. After the preliminaries, the detectives gave evidence that claimed that they had found the fingerprints of de Marigny on a screen in Oakes' bedroom. It was evidence all the jurors realised could have sent the defendant straight to the gallows. Glances were exchanged along the jury benches and murmurs arose from the spectators in Court.

Nancy Oakes took the stand and strongly defended her husband. Her mother however, Lady Eunice Oakes, told of the bitterness the marriage had caused in the family thus adding weight to the case of the prosecution against de Marigny.

A nervous Christie explained to the Court, somewhat implausibly, how he had slept soundly on the night of the murder and how de Marigny was angered because Sir Harry would not let him take title to some property in Nassau.

Meanwhile the Bahamian Commissioner of Police who knew a great deal about the crime was mysteriously transferred to Trinidad and so was unavailable when the trial began. The local newspaper editor commented on his absence: 'one would have thought that he would have been called as a witness by the Crown, but later I had the impression that he might have held views that did not fit comfortably with the Crown's case'. The Duke of Windsor who might have been called as a witness also arranged to be away from Nassau during the trial.

Nancy, de Marigny's wife, who was away in the States at the time of her father's death, had commissioned a well-known American detective by the name of Schindler to travel to Nassau to assist with the investigation. It was Schindler who probably noted the sloppy work of the Miami detectives in the gathering of de Marigny's fingerprints. The antenna that all good detectives have told Schindler he was about as welcome in Nassau as an outbreak of the bubonic plague. He soon summed up the character of de Marigny and confided to the defence attorneys, '...the French fancy pants may have been a slayer of the ladies but he was not a slayer of men.' And the sensationalist magazine agreed: '...the case against the French Count

Alfred de Marigny turned out to be as full of holes as a screen door. If he didn't do it, then apparently nobody did…'

The crux of the trial was the three-day cross-examination of one of the Miami police, in which the defence practically reduced the Miami detective to an admission that he had forged the incriminating finger-prints which were not produced on the screen on which they had been found but had been lifted onto a piece of rubber.

At this point the defense counsel objected to the presentation of a lifted 'latent' (fingerprint) as evidence.

'My lord, I reluctantly ask leave to interrupt my learned friend; but I must in all candor point out that this is the first time the defence has heard anything about 'lifted' prints. When the evidence was submitted in the Magistrates Court, I assumed that the fingerprints referred to were photographs of prints on the screen. I only learn today officially of something on rubber.'

The Lord Chief Justice shared the defence attorney's concern and almost imperceptibly nodded to the jury to take notice.

'When was the photograph of latent number-five print taken?' the Chief justice asked.

'The photograph was taken on July 9.'

'My lord,' the attorney for the defence continued, 'that is exactly what I object to. This piece of rubber is not the best evidence; and I know of no case in which it has been produced in Court before. The proper evidence would be to produce the print on the article on which it is found, and I submit that there is no print now on that screen!'

The defence attorney's robed arm swept toward the screen at the corner of the bench in a motion of defiant challenge. Joshua and the other jurors followed the theatrics with rapt attention.

'We have only this witness's word to suggest that the print in question came from that screen,' he pressed. 'We for the defence are in a position to prove that a photograph of a lifted print cannot be produced as the original latent raised print of number-five digit of the accused, and that the best evidence is the screen itself on which the print should be produced, and on which there is now no sign of a fingerprint.'

The Chief Justice raised a question: 'You would not object to a photograph of a raised print on that screen?'

'I would not, my lord, and that is precisely my point. By a 'raised' print, I mean a print that has been dusted with powder and is visible. It can then be photographed *in situ.* The original fingerprint can be preserved by covering it with Scotch tape. The original fingerprint in this way is not destroyed. It is there for all to see.'

The Chief Justice: 'Your point is that they should have powdered the print, left it there, and taken a photograph?'

'That is it precisely, my lord.'

The Chief Justice: 'What you say then is that since they did not powder the print and leave it on the screen, it might be a forgery?' There was a gasp from gallery. The Jury squirmed on their bench realizing the case was taking an interesting turn.

'That is exactly my fear and my contention. Whether this print came from that point on the screen which the witness describes now depends upon the uncorroborated evidence of the witness himself.'

The Chief Justice: 'It seems strange to me that no case on this exact point has come before the Courts, either in England or America?'

'I have searched the authorities, my lord, and assure the Court that I can find no case in point.'

The Lord Chief Justice was having difficulty controlling his Irish impatience. He addressed his question to the Miami Police Captain:

'Why was the print not powdered, photographed, and left on the screen?'

'I did not have my fingerprint camera with me so I had to lift the print from the screen,' the detective replied.

The Chief Justice queried: 'And why did you not have your fingerprint camera with you?'

'As I was proceeding originally on the theory that the case was a suicide and did not involve any criminal act, I saw no need to bring the latent-fingerprint camera with me from Miami.'

'Would it not have been easy to powder the print and leave it there?'

'There is always a chance that it will be accidentally smudged or destroyed.'

'Could you not have had a latent finger-print camera flown over from Miami in a relatively short period of time?'

'Yes, I suppose that I could have.'

'So by your process of lifting this print on the rubber matting, you deliberately destroyed the best evidence which was the print itself?' The Chief Justice asked.

'This manner of lifting the print does destroy it. Yes.'

'And a photograph of this print *in situ* taken with a latent-fingerprint camera would also have shown the background so that there would be no doubt where the print came from now?'

'Well, the background doesn't always positively tell you exactly where the print came from.'

The Chief Justice confessed some doubt. Some of the jurors hurriedly scribbled notes.

'I have no hesitancy in admitting that I am taken by surprise. It seems highly unlikely that no Court has ever been called to pass upon this exact question in the past, but if counsel assure me that they find no cases for precedent, I accept their representations. It occurs to me that I may well admit this print into evidence and let the jury decide whether it is legitimate and what weight to give it. If they have reason to doubt its genuineness, they can discard the print, and for that matter, the testimony of this witness altogether. We approach the hour of adjournment. The Court needs time to reflect upon this critical matter. You will have my decision when we sit again on the morrow.' The Chief Justice stood up and the Court was adjourned.

The jurors, before being led out of Court, were sworn again not to discuss the case with any one. They passed through a cordon of inquisitive bystanders who called out questions as they passed. Under police guard they were accommodated in a tourist hotel on Bay Street where, if Joshua had appeared requesting a room under different circumstances, the management would probably have found some reason to deny him access.

The American magazine took up the story of the trial again: '…the print of his little finger…might have been faked. Yes ***faked…*** There's not one chance in ten million that this fingerprint came from that screen' (said a fingerprint expert at the trial). 'The detective began to bite his nails and sprinkle a little more profanity into his speech…one thing is certain…officials in Nassau don't want…anybody to prove guilty the real killer…'

'I can prove that it is improper to raise a print,' counsel for the defence exclaimed after the trial resumed and the jurors had examined the screen. 'Now we have only have the police's uncorroborated word that it came from the screen, I cannot find a case in which a lifted print ever was submitted in evidence. This is the first time the prosecution has testified about something on a piece of rubber.'

A controversy then arose over the inability of the Miami policeman to specify exactly at what spot on the screen he had lifted the evidence exhibited. The defense counsel hammered at the fact that he could not fix the precise place from which the print in evidence was taken. This admission was enough to give the defense another loophole. De Marigny's attorney asked the Captain if he was sure the print in evidence was that of the defendant.

Barker replied, 'My conclusion is that they were made by the same person.'

Here the Chief Justice spoke up. 'Is the defense contesting that these are the accused's finger prints?'

'No sir,' was the astonishing reply of the defense lawyer.

'Do you mean to imply that the lifted print might be a forgery?' asked the judge.

'We do,' responded the lawyer. Then he intimated the witness had swept aside the truth in his desire for gain and notoriety. He did not contest that the print in evidence was that of the defendant's finger but charged that it had been taken from some other object touched by the defendant since the discovery of the murder. He presented that the incident of de Marigny's having been taken to the Oakes home for further questioning by the Miami officers while the screen was being examined could have offered the opportunity to get his imprint.

'I doubt whether the print actually has been lifted from the surface of the screen,' the defense attorney said raising his voice. 'There is no evidence on the screen now. We have only the police captain's word for it, and he himself is unable to point to the exact spot from which he says he took it.'

He turned to the witness and declared, 'I suggest you—the police—planned to get the accused alone to get his finger prints.'

'I did not,' responded the witness.

'I suggest this exhibit never came from that screen!'

'It came from the screen,' retorted the police detective.

In a dramatic scene, at 7:30 p.m. on 8th November 1943 after being out for only an hour, the jury returned a verdict of 'Not Guilty' nine to three. Joshua had had little doubt from the start of the trial of de Marigny's innocence but had listened carefully to all the evidence which confirmed his belief. Joshua, however, was swayed by the arguments of the white jurors, three of whom wanted the death penalty, that Marigny should be declared an 'undesirable'. Joshua reasoned that if de Marigny was to be acquitted with the hatred some white people held for him, it might be better for him to be out of the country. It was not until the next day that the public heard of the further recommendation by the jury.

Even though he was set free, invoking the exigencies of wartime, the spokesperson for the jury recommended de Marigny be deported from the Colony as an undesirable. In a terse sentence it read: 'The jury recommends that de Marigny be deported from the Colony immediately.'

When the Judge heard this he said, 'that's something I cannot contend with, but no doubt the proper authorities will take proper cognizance of your recommendation.' The 'proper authorities' doubtless included the Duke of Windsor and de Marigny was shortly thereafter declared an 'undesirable' and made to leave the colony.

The matter of Oakes death would not go away. The mystery surrounding Sir Harry's death was too bizarre and too intriguing to be forgotten. Stranger than fiction, it was a murder drama with a real twist—Agatha Christie (no relation to Sir Harold!) could not have come up with a better plot. The suspects included de Marigny of course, but also Sir Harold Christie (some would even add—with the knowledge and possible collusion of the royal governor), two 'hit men' who were reported to have arrived (and departed) by fast boat at Lyford Cay on the fateful night, the mafia (master-minded by Meyer Lansky from Havana), the cut-throat criminals who arrived from Devils Island whom de Marigny had befriended, or any one of a number anonymous people acting singly or severally, black and white, whom Sir Harry had treated atrociously. A further intriguing, though remote possibility that might explain the presence of the chicken feathers, was that it might have been somehow connected with *obeah,* the obscure Bahamian form of witchcraft and revenge. But intriguing though the unsolved murder was, the world Press again turned their attention to the war raging on the Russian front and in the Pacific theatre leaving the Bahamas to sink into oblivion once more.

The Bahamas House of Assembly had, for most of its long existence, been a parliament representing minority interests. The country had been gerrymandered to allow tiny out islands to have a seat in the Assembly while large, mainly African-Bahamian constituencies in Nassau had inadequate representation in the House of Assembly. Since there were far more out islands than there were constituencies on New Providence, the minority interests inevitably won control of the government. Free liquor and glowing, but empty promises, also had a persuasive effect on a gullible electorate. In addition, the disenfranchisement of women and the exclusion of persons from the voting lists who were not landowners virtually guaranteed the elitist white interests would continue to be confirmed as rulers of the country.

The turning point was the labour riot during the construction of the new airstrip in Nassau during the war. The riot was a clear demonstration to the majority of the people that, for good or ill, if they acted in concert they could effect change. Even so, it took a very long time for a grass roots political organization to become established. Disenfranchisement was but one element of the social malaise. The Duke of Windsor sent a telling note to

Westminster on racial relations in the Bahamas shortly after arriving when he reported to Lord Moyne at the Colonial Office:

The Bahamas...maintain a very staunch and American attitude towards the coloured problem...white Bahamians will not allow their wives to sit down to dinner with coloured people. One of the main arguments against the inclusion of the coloured element into the social life of the Colony is that it would hurt the susceptibilities of the American winter visitors...

The end of World War II did not bring the expected slump. The Duke of Windsor left the Bahamas to return to France and another governor was sent out from England. A local Bay Street merchant, Tristram Cornforth, accepted the position of Chairman of the Development Board and was able to increase tourism to the Colony in dramatic fashion and was later knighted for his extraordinary promotional abilities. He became Deputy Premier of the newly formed Bahamian National Party (BNP) which particularly favoured the interests of the wealthy white people in the Colony and continued to pursue the social policy outlined by the Duke of Windsor.

Investment from overseas was accepted without question and land was rapidly being subdivided and sold mainly to overseas buyers. Randolph Elding with bitter memories of impoverishment and the dark legacy of the 'Great Depression', accepted the *laissez faire* policies of the Bay Street government but his son Leonard was concerned at what he saw as the 'selling out' of the Bahamas to foreigners. It seemed to him that if you were of any nationality with a white skin you could get business concessions providing you had a Bay Street 'partner' but, if you were Bahamian-born and of darker complexion it was another story. Leonard Elding did not need to be reminded that to some of the 'purists' in the Bay Street oligarchy that even though the Eldings had 'old money' and a prestigious name they should be considered 'coloured'. Leonard and his father were prudent enough never to apply for membership of *The Sayle Club* of Nassau which blatantly banned persons of colour from membership.

When he could stand the glaring inequity no more Leonard Elding went to Sir Tristram direct to raise the issue of the foreign landowners,

"...you know sir, I really wonder about the wisdom of selling enormous acreages of land in the out islands to foreigners", he said, "they don't develop the land, they make a tremendous profit which is sent abroad and they effectively deny our own communities the space to expand."

Shuffling papers on his desk Cornforth did not look up. He really did not want to be lectured by a young liberal but had seen Leonard Elding in deference to his father. After a pause he said, "but they pay stamp taxes to the government, they use the services of our legal profession and in so doing they put some money into circulation you know!"

Leonard was angered because he knew Cornforth was talking down to him.

"That may be so sir, but do we really know who these people are? I heard, for instance that Trinity Consolidated Enterprises is an unholy front for organized crime—the Mob!...and did you hear that three families were evicted from generation land in Exuma without compensation...without an explanation even!"

Cornforth looked up unfazed and grinned, "...well I haven't heard anybody complain yet about the colour of the investor's money!"

Leonard Elding could hardly hide his irritation and left the room as Cornforth was fortuitously called to the telephone.

The time is ripe for change, Elding thought.

PART TWO

Chapter 13 - Pride, Prejudice, Progress (1950 -)

If I may so express it, he has a right to be proud.

Jane Austen

THE BAHAMA ISLANDS *were one of several countries of the former British Empire which underwent a major, but quiet political revolution in the second half of the twentieth century.*

Though largely unnoticed by the world, in 1973 the island nation was rapidly catapulted from the status of colony to that of a sovereign and independent nation. The old British ensign with the Bahamas coat of arms in the fly was replaced by a new tricolour flag which fluttered in the trade winds. Its colours intended to represent, black for a strong people, turquoise for the sea and gold for the sun. Since the new flag has been unfurled, the Commonwealth of the Bahamas demonstrated, in contradiction to naysayers, that it has a vigorous democracy and is well able to stand on its own feet.

Within a lifetime that spanned this event, a typical Bahamian family of African heritage, witnessed an enormous change in its economic, social and political standing. This chapter follows the life of Darrell Eldon a young Bahamian who could trace his forebears to an African slave who arrived in Nassau in 1748. In the early 1960's this young man was fortunate enough to be educated abroad and, on his return to the Bahamas, moved rapidly from poverty to affluence and into the fast track of the new society. This, in turn, was to lead ultimately, to significant political power.

Bahamians, like all human beings, are the product of both their genes and their environment. There is little genetic reason why Bahamians of African heritage should be very different from, say, Haitians or the black race of Cuba and yet a cultural chasm exists and it is not only because of language. Indeed, what has most shaped Bahamians is their environment. First, the archipelagic character of the Bahama Islands resulted in an inward-looking lifestyle fashioned by the encircling sea. Then, there was an invisible but pervasive cross-culturisation resulting from the two races living in close proximity to each other for over three hundred years which had the effect of influencing the other more than either appreciated. All this coupled with a powerful belief in God. More recently, there has been additional cultural influence from the Western World, especially from the United States of America. With some obvious exceptions, lifestyle, economic motivation, political philosophy, religion and morality in the Bahamas today, all derive from this pervasive background.

Other important cultural factors are the institutions of the country. Though strong social and cultural influence emanated earlier from Africa and then more recently from the United States, a lingering but diminishing influence of the former Mother Country continues in many of the institutions of the Bahamas, particularly in its form of government, education and system of law. And, though a minor case in point, there are numerous labour unions that were adapted to Bahamian conditions, in part, from the British model. These latter were to play an important part in the quest for fair labour practices and also led to the political arena from whence the African Bahamian majority ultimately attained its political independence.

The historic setting of the second oldest parliament in the Western Hemisphere From left to right: Public Records Office, the Senate, the House of Assembly.

LEONARD ELDING decided to talk to the outspoken labour leader Charlten Eldon whom he had first met at a Labour tribunal in Nassau a few years earlier. Leonard had serious qualms over the recent industrial disputes by workers some of which he felt were justified but more importantly he was concerned about the lack of political representation for the mass of the Bahamian people. Wise and foresighted, Elding realized that great and immediate political change was necessary in the Bahamas. He knew that on most points Charlten would share his views.

After his secretary tracked Charlten down at his sweetheart's small house, they arranged to meet at a bar located in a small wooden shack 'over the hill' in Nassau on Sunday morning after church.

Charlten Eldon had matured considerably and was now a powerfully built man with a physique fashioned from having been a stevedore. Street smart and outspoken he had participated in the riots of '42 when he gave a policeman a black eye and was lucky indeed not to have been 'arraigned for questioning'. Charlten had built up a loyal following in the Stevedores, Harbour and General Workers Union that he had been able to form and for this, he was anathema to the Bay Street oligarchy.

Charlten Eldon had already drunk three bottles of Guinness stout by the time Leonard Elding arrived. Elding sat down at the painted periwinkle blue table and they exchanged some banter about the 'out' children Charlten had sired. Charlten, now slightly inebriated, declared that it was the stout, that gave him his sexual drive ('put lead in his pencil' was the way he expressed it). During a racy, and sometimes humourous exchange, Charlten expounded his theory that the size of a woman's hips ('boongy' was the Bahamian term he used) was directly related to her performance in bed. The conversation after several circuitous diversions eventually led to the more substantive discussion about the increase in cruise ship traffic to Nassau and its generally positive economic effects. At this point Elding sensed the mood was right and turned the thrust of the conversation towards his real reason for being 'over the hill'.

"Charlten, we have known each other a long time. I have come here today to discuss some very important matters with you; first like you, I am concerned about the worsening labour situation in our country, then I would really appreciate your opinion and your help on some other matters too...this country is on the wrong track and we need help."

"You tellin' me the country on the wrong track, man!...it damn'd hard for a fella to get work, more hard for him to keep it, and the pay and conditions, they is the worst!"

"Yes Charlten I know all that, and there is the added problem of bad elements coming here to settle..."

Charlten laughed.

"I don't know about them comin', they is already here and your cronies be some of them!"

Elding shrugged. "Well be that as it may Charlten, let us agree it is a time for change, it is time people got organized—politically I mean..."

"Oh yea man...and you wanna help?"

Elding did not like the sarcastic tone of the remark but replied, "...to build up political support it will take help from many sources."

"Maybe, Mister Leonard, but it like 'chalk and cheese' as they say..." Charlten Eldon pondered for a minute, then finished, "you are one of they!...we's we, ain't nothing's going to change that, you have my respec' Mister Leonard but we don' need no help!"

Charlten Eldon realized that what he had said was a little strong since Leonard Elding commanded the respect of almost everybody. Even so, he knew he was speaking the minds of his colleagues when he said that the new worker's unions and the new political movement they were spawning would have nothing to do with anybody who, at some time, had not felt the stigma of being poor, black and downtrodden. Too many times in the past white politicians had made great promises, provided free booze, handed out small sums of money even, then forgotten their constituents immediately they were elected to the House.

Elding re-stated his position but found Charlten immoveable. Indeed Charlten recited at length all the wrongs suffered by people of colour in the Bahamas. Elding did not interrupt him but nodded understandingly. When Charlten had finished he paid for the drinks and left the bar disheartened. So that was it! The radical elements wanted confrontation, it seemed that time was already running late for reasoning or even rational discussion.

And confrontation was not long in coming.

In January 1958 the airport, which had been built at the western end of New Providence, was again the touchstone. The new passenger terminal was about to be opened when angry members of the Taxi Union blockaded the approaches to the airport. They were objecting to visitors to the island being carried by buses and tour company cars effectively denying taxi drivers income. Traffic was paralyzed, flights were cancelled and the tourist trade came to a sudden halt.

For two days guests volunteered to serve meals in the hotels and wash dishes. Then the hotels closed completely. The governor, Sir Raynor Arthur, hastily telegraphed Jamaica for a detachment of the Royal Worcestershire Regiment to be flown in. *HMS Ulster* arrived with technicians to maintain essential services and public utilities and tough pink-faced soldiers who, if ordered, would not hesitate to establish law and order in the Colony.

Labour negotiations began in an atmosphere of mutual distrust. Charlten Eldon, fidgeting and with very blood-shot eyes, sat opposite to Elding.

"Well you can't say I didn't warn you!" Charlten snarled from across the table.

"...and if you had listened to me this whole unnecessary confrontation could have been avoided!"

"You still don't understand do you Mister Leonard! 'Confrontation', if that's what you wanna call it, is what it's all about!" Charlten hissed back.

The negotiations dragged on for over a week. Many privately-employed and some government workers stopped work in sympathy. A general strike had begun. Finally the Taxi Union, backed by the Bahamas National Labour Federation, got what it wanted. Contrary to conventional wisdom, buses and tour company cars were banned from servicing the airport.

Nineteen days after the first confrontation, the strike ended. On the economic front a great deal of damage had been done but, out of the conflict a political organization was born: the Bahamas Peoples Alliance, popularly known by its initials BPA.

The grass roots movement aimed at starting a political party with an appeal to the low-income workers in the Bahamas and was already well established before Darrell Eldon returned from Middle Temple and the London School of Economics fired with idealism and something akin to revolutionary zeal. As the recipient of a foreign scholarship Eldon had had the almost unprecedented chance for a Bahamian of his race to study overseas.

Darrell, the eldest son of Ranetta and Charlten Eldon was the product of a one parent home. Charlten had deserted his wife after a stormy relationship lasting about seven years. Darrell's mother Ranetta had imbued him with a thirst for knowledge and he gained his political instincts from his absent, radical and disillusioned father. Darrell was an exceptionally good looking young man with what Bahamians refer to as a 'bright' complexion. While away, Eldon had been exposed to other ideas and cultures in the stimulating cosmopolitan atmosphere of London that allowed him to unmask his previously concealed pride in his race and nationality. It also developed in him a righteous anger at those who would deny his people their rightful place in the world. He could not accept that he belonged to a 'coloured' race of people. A people who were somehow graded by the colour and shade of their skin. He saw only too well that if this system continued, there would be constant division between dark skinned and the not-so-dark skinned people of African origin.

When he returned to Nassau he immediately sought out the new political movement. Darrell Eldon sat in on the early meetings of the new Bahamas Peoples Alliance saying little as his estranged father and the other labour leaders expounded their unrealistic and naive dreams for a new society. Darrell was quick to realize that they had neither the skills, nor the eloquence, to lead a political movement that would break the hold of the Bay Street merchants.

Little by little, Darrell Eldon made himself useful by providing legal expertise to the Party, soon he was to become indispensable. When voting took place for Party offices, Darrell, aided somewhat by his family connections, was elected to the BPA Steering Committee. It was only a short time before he was popularly elected as spokesman for the Party. His father Charlten was unhappy to see power slipping from his grasp but happy that his son seemed to carrying forward the mantle. Charlten too, perhaps foresaw his usefulness to the Bahamas Peoples Alliance was coming to an end.

Darrell Eldon had another advantage not shared by the other members of the Party. As one of the few black Bahamian attorneys, he had a thriving law practice that gave him the financial resources and the opportunity to visit the out islands to make new contacts. These new friends were made for the Bahamas Peoples Alliance but they would never forget that it was Darrell Eldon who first fired them with his zeal, enrolled them, and then gave them status in the Party.

The fealty of the out islands was critical if anyone was to hope to change the political destiny of the Bahamas.

The major problem confronting the BPA was a paradox. For the first time since Prohibition, things were going well with the Colony. Tourism was booming. It was common knowledge that Sir Tristram Cornforth was involved with graft but, for all his bombast and petty dishonesty he was doing an excellent job in encouraging investment to the islands. Grand Bahama in particular, was now being considered as a suitable site for a major new development. Bahamians of colour were better off than they had ever been. True they lacked political power but, if the pundits were correct, a change to black rule would kill the goose that was laying a giant golden egg.

The Bahamas National Party (BNP), true to their promise, encouraged many foreign investors to the Bahamas. In Grand Bahama over 200 square miles were sold to an American financier on condition he build a harbour and encourage industry to locate on the island. The venture started slowly but eventually became a spectacular success by creating the new city of Freeport.

As a favourable omen, just after the first major hotel in Freeport opened, a richly laden treasure wreck was found only a mile offshore from the new hotel. The remains of a sunken 'prize' was discovered exactly where the Dutchman, van Hoven, in his last words, had tried to explain two centuries before. The wreck was the remains of a ship captured by Piet Heyn, another Dutchman, in his astounding feat of capturing the entire Spanish treasure fleet in 1628 worth 15 million guilders. Van Hoven's abbreviated description of the location of the treasure on the scaffold was, '...treasure...can be found...reef...south...Bahama'. What was found near Freeport was indeed 'treasure', at a clearly identifiable fringing 'reef', at the 'south' (no more than a mile from the southernmost point of the island) of 'Bahama' (the former name of Grand Bahama Island). The wreck was to yield about $10 million in gold, silver and precious stones!

DARRELL ELDON used his time well in Nassau. He was correctly friendly with everybody. He was invited to many functions and parties as well as official government receptions. He was sympathetically regarded by the Bay Street-controlled Bahamian news media since he projected a voice of reason on the left of the political spectrum. But in the early 1960's it was unlikely he would ever be invited to sit at the dinner table of a Bay Street merchant.

At one of the many Nassau gatherings he attended, his eye caught sight of Bahama, the only daughter of Leonard Elding. She had blossomed as an exotically beautiful young woman with a sylphlike figure, flawless olive complexion, tantalising green eyes and sun bleached hair but, besides her physical charms, she came from a well-to-do and highly respected Bahamian family. Bahama was known to be charming, extremely intelligent but she was strong-willed, fickle and refreshingly open-minded. Without doubt she was one of the most attractive, and some might say eligible, women in the Bahamas.

She was talking to her brother Peter as Darrell Eldon approached.

"Well hello Darrell! How was your stay in England?" Peter asked. Darrell and he had been at the Government High School together.

Eldon grinned, "Informative, cold, and correct—'fratefully' correct'," he replied.

They laughed.

Darrell turned to Bahama and asked her how she had liked her schooling abroad.

"Positively awful," was the blunt reply.

The men laughed again and Peter moved away as Bahama and Darrell got onto the subject of the dashing new president of the United States and that led them to the subject of politics in the Bahamas.

"This situation can't go on," Bahama huffed throwing her head back, "there is no way that ten percent of the people should govern the remaining ninety percent. It doesn't matter how good they are at administration, or juggling the ballot, or what ever it is they do to stay in power, it just isn't right!"

Eldon agreed but carefully avoided sounding over-zealous.

He proffered, "...of course, but the government has got the economy rolling..."

Bahama smiled wistfully, then retorted, "...that's what they would like you to believe but with the United States booming, our growth in tourism was inevitable."

"The *Journal* ran an editorial yesterday about the need for us to stay under the British umbrella like Bermuda. What do you think about the importance of the so-called 'British connection'?" Eldon probed.

"Yes I read it. Oh, I doubt that counts for much, it was useful once I suppose, but certainly not now...Oh, there's Phyllis Cornforth, you must excuse me, but I must go and talk to her." And in a moment she was in the middle of a circle conversing with half of the Bay Street oligarchy.

The next time Darrell met Bahama they were at the luxurious cottage home of Percy Ritters, an American magnate, who had settled in the well-to-do residential neighbourhood known as Cable Beach west of the City of Nassau. Ritters was one of those people who like to know what was going on. The Bay Street merchants had invited him to relocate himself and his fortune in the Bahamas but that did not mean they were going to invite him into their counsels. So Percy Ritters made a practice of inviting people to his house of any race and nationality who, he felt, were going places. This time he used the excuse of a party to christen his new swimming pool.

Ritters particularly liked Bahama who, besides being young and beautiful with a rebel streak, also came from an influential family. Besides being decorative she could be relied upon to liven up any party by sometimes saying the most outrageous but hitherto unspoken truths. Darrell Eldon was Ritters' lawyer, whom Ritters found to be always formally correct and good at his work. He discerned a burning ambition in the handsome young man. The rest of the guests were his neighbours: an expatriate Bahamas Airways pilot and his socially mobile wife, the second secretary from the American Consulate whom everyone declared was with the CIA, the senior black Bahamian from the Customs Department and his girl friend, an Italian-American businessman, a Nassau Greek and a young Southerner Percy Ritters casually introduced as 'Lu-Anne'.

As Darrell arrived he immediately noticed Bahama across the swimming pool. She was clad in a scant bikini with a pink-coloured lacy cover-up, she was sipping rum and ginger and talking heatedly to the CIA man. Through the corner of his eye he saw her laugh, throw up her hands and then move on to talk to Theo about his family, some of whom still lived in the Greek island of Kalymnos. She had visited the island the year before and knew it was from Kalymnos that most of the Greek community in the Bahamas originated.

Darrell moved towards them. Theo knowing of Eldon's political ambitions, said,"...well I see that labour matter was resolved Darrell!"

"Yes the BPA won a moral victory of sorts but of course we could not afford the bad publicity or to lose the tourists," he replied tactfully.

"Nonsense," Bahama interjected, "buses or some other means of mass transit serve every airport in the world—so why not here?"

Eldon disguised a wince.

"Yes, but have you considered the hardship there would be to the taxi drivers' families if they had competition from buses?" he asked.

"They could always learn to drive buses you know!" Bahama shot back. "That is what is wrong with so many people, they have to know how to adapt, become engaged..."

It was impossible to argue with her today, her eyes were blazing and even if Bahama had not comprehended all the nuances of the case, she was eloquent, impassioned, defiant...and absolutely irresistible. Darrell felt a sudden surge of desire.

His reverie was broken as Lu-Anne spoke for the first time and announced in a Southern accent, "Buffet is ready, y'all!" and everyone filed to the ritual of serving themselves from tables displaying a ridiculously lavish assortment of food.

"Oh how frightfully *gauche!*...I just can't understand why they mix peaches with turkey!" the English pilot's wife exclaimed loudly.

"Oh super! I love caviar!", her husband remarked to deflect his inebriated wife's gratuitous observation.

"'Champers over here!" Ritters announced proudly. "...Bahama, my dear," he hailed her from a distant corner of the terrace, "...do come and chat."

Bahama by now was getting bored with the party but dutifully went to sit on a *chaise longue* next to her host. Ritters held his finger up, "I heard you denouncing the taxi driver settlement, Bahama - that won't do you know!"

"Mr Ritters, I have a right to my opinion, this is," she said archly, "my country after all." Anyone but Percy Ritters might have recognized the sarcasm in her voice.

"I heard say that your father had a meeting with that big coloured guy from the Union, what's his name?..." Bahama did not reply. "Eldon, yes that's it, Charlton Eldon."

"You seem well informed Mr. Ritters,...oh no, no champagne thank you Courtnel," she purred to a uniformed servant who came over to fill her glass. Percy Ritters then delivered a short lecture to Bahama about how he thought the matter should have been handled. Bahama said little.

After an extravagant baked Alaska and coffee were served, Bahama announced, "well I really think I must be leaving soon...I promised to play tennis with the Johnsons." She stood up and cast a glance in the direction of Darrell Eldon and smiled for the briefest moment, she then briefly thanked Percy Ritters for the invitation and left hurriedly.

There is something about Darrell Eldon that really intrigues me, Bahama thought.

Darrell's eyes followed her departure from the house.

LATER THAT EVENING Darrell Eldon was sitting in his new red MG thirty yards or so away from the Blue Hills Tennis Club. Just as it started to get dusk he heard Bahama's unmistakable voice as she came down the driveway of the tennis club. He quickly pondered what indecipherable urge had placed him in this location and at this particular time.

Bahama, in the latest London fashion mini-skirt, was surrounded by several young men, scions of Bay Street with a sprinkling of young English attorneys. Darrell regretted the impulse that brought him there but knew it was too late to leave. He waited until most of the young men had sped off and Bahama was left talking with a young English attorney. Darrell realized he could not escape notice when they left, so he opened the door, got out, and walked to the front of his car. For good measure he pretended to adjust the outside driving mirror. Elizabeth noticed him.

"Darrell! What are you doing here?" she shouted.

"Oh...well, at this moment I am...checking something on the car," Darrell lied pathetically.

Bahama and her friend spoke a few moments and then the Englishman walked to his car and drove away. Bahama immediately came over to him.

"Well this is a surprise!" Bahama sounded effervescent. "By the way I love your new car!"

"Yes…well, the car seems to be alright." Then, after an awkward pause, he added even more clumsily, "I say, you wouldn't like to join me at the *Travellers* to have a drink would you?"

Bahama, acting on impulse, enthusiastically replied, "Oh wow, yes…I'd love to!"

They drove in tandem at high speed to the *Traveller's Rest,* a rustic bar on the coast not far from Bahama's home at Old Fort Beach and not too far from luxurious expatriate estate then being constructed (clearly only for white people of considerable wealth) at Lyford Cay.

The conversation avoided politics and any serious subjects were deflected by Bahama as 'tiresome'. After several rum and gingers the conversation turned to gossip, then to sex.

"Oh Jonathan," Bahama said referring to the Englishman at the tennis club, "he has brains, a beautiful body but no sex drive, plays tennis well though."

"So, you are not serious about him?" Darrell questioned.

"Heavens no! I tried to seduce him once. It was embarrassing…" Bahama changed the subject. "Now, what about your love life? No…" she held up her hand, "let me guess…you have a 'brown skin gal' whom you visit late at night but then you disappear before dawn…"

"Wrong, quite wrong!"

"Oh?" Bahama feigned surprise.

"I don't always disappear!"

They both laughed.

"Another drink?"

"Thanks. It's a beautiful evening…let's walk on the beach," Bahama purred.

By now the sun was setting and the western sky was flaunting an astoundingly brilliant sunset. Screaming sea birds formed a bridge across the sky and the velvet black of the coppice was silhouetted against a fluorescent setting sun. Soon the stars were twinkling and the palmettos gently rustled their fronds. The night was mild and scented with jasmine while the sibilant hum of the crickets added a special ambiance to the scene. The waves gently lapped the white sand beach known to another headstrong girl known by the same name over two centuries before.

They walked to a small cove.

A demasted sloop that would never sail again had been washed high up the beach. Bahama seductively ran away from Darrell to the boat and clambered onto its deck of bleached wooden planks. Play-acting from the storied past of her namesake ancestor, she announced that she was now a pirate captain and would repel all boarders. Darrell, amused at her co-quettish behavior joined in the charade and solemnly announced that if she would spare his life he would show her where treasure was hidden.

Continuing to act out the charade, she mockingly acquiesced to his request and followed him to the foot of the dunes. Darrell marked a cross in the sand. Bahama tip-toed to the spot and sat down.

She held out her hand, Darrell took it, and knelt at her feet.

Soon they were in each other's arms. Bahama looked into Darrell's pale brown eyes.

"Sometimes words just get in the way," she murmured.

Darrell kissed Bahama passionately for many minutes as they both gently touched each other's bodies with their hands.

"I need to get comfortable," Bahama whispered and she unhooked her bra.

They left the beach just as dawn was breaking.

DARRELL ELDON could not understand himself. He was madly in love!

Other things that two days before mattered so much to him seemed now to be of small consequence. He had arranged to meet Bahama after work the day following a night of ecstasy.

He found himself in his office but his mind was distracted.

As he was walking to his office later than usual he fielded questions from the typing pool:

"Oh tell Mr. Ritters I will call him later!

"No I can't meet Oscar Pyfrom tonight…tell him I am sorry. I know he came in from Exuma but it can't be helped."

"A call for you from Miss Bahama Elding, on your private line," another secretary announced.

"I'll take it in my office. Please make sure I am not disturbed…"

The three secretaries exchanged glances without a word being spoken.

Darrell Eldon went into his office and grabbed the phone.

"Hello…"

Bahama sounded subdued.

"Darrell, I have to talk to you. Last night was very special but…" Eldon's heart sank, "…but, well things are getting complicated and I think we should talk about it."

"OK, but can't you tell me what this is about? I thought we were going to see each other tonight…remember we made some promises last night…"

"Yes, yes I know, I feel terrible about it but Jonathan came round this morning. We…we had a serious discussion…"

"Go on…"

"Well…I think I am going to marry him…" Bahama blurted out.

Darrell was dumbfounded.

"But I thought…well anyway at least lets talk about it…we arranged yesterday to meet at *Traveller's Rest* at six tonight…let's still meet there!"

"Alright I'll see you there then…but Darrell, it won't make any difference…I'm sorry…"

The meeting at *Traveller's Rest* was brief. The western sky managed to display another spectacular sunset but it went unnoticed.

Darrell Eldon went home crushed and angry.

LEONARD ELDING WAS BITTER about his meeting with Charlten Eldon and the outcome of the Labour Tribunal.

Before he met Charlten he had already decided to disassociate himself politically from the Bay Street establishment and lend his support a broad-based movement that truly represented the aspirations of the Bahamian people. He discussed his feelings with his Canadian-born wife Lorna and with Peter and Bahama who all were, as ever, sympathetic and supportive of his feelings. Bahama was saddened because she was particularly close to her father but realized, better than he, that the political ground swell was turning against people like him. There was little chance of a third political force emerging at this time in the Bahamas. Only the formerly dispossessed blacks would inherit the new political order of the Bahamas.

"I say Bamie, did you see the *'Journal'* this morning?" Peter asked suddenly. He started reading the headlines, "'DARRELL ELDON TO RUN FOR CAT ISLAND ON BPA TICKET'," and continued, "there's a bye-election you know—then the paper quotes him as saying he wants 'full Bahamianization of the country in three years'. He has some very unkind words for that development in Freeeport, Grand Bahama, says the Agreement with the Developer should be abrogated. He calls the present owners 'untimely Lords Proprietors'...My God! I wonder what Cornforth and the Premier will make of this!"

"Yes", Bahama replied, "I heard too, he was particularly angry about the young English attorneys whom, he claims, are stealing work from Bahamians like him. Jonathan wonders if he will get his Work Permit renewed. Do you realize that when I marry Jonathan we may have to leave the country!"

Just over three weeks later Darrell Eldon was elected from the Cat Island constituency by a landslide. He was now one of seven Opposition members of the House of Assembly. Omar Newcombe, the firebrand BPA leader, gave Darrell the job of 'shadow' Minister of Out Island Affairs. It was Eldon's job to follow the workings of the government's Ministry of Out Island Affairs so that he could, when necessary, oppose their policies in the House. It was a critical time in the political life of the Colony, an election under Parliamentary rules, had to be called within the next eighteen months.

The Bahamian National Party, headed by Sir Elvin Dowdeswell but in fact run by Sir Tristram Cornforth, was fighting for its political life. Constituency boundaries on New Providence had been manipulated as far as was legally possible to help the BNP cause but the critical deciding vote would be held by the scattered and under-populated out-islands. The ruling Party controlled the only radio station of the Bahamas and they had money for public relations experts, printing, travel and everything necessary to mount a *blitzkrieg* of a campaign. The BPA had some funds from the Unions and that was about all.

There were, however, white expatriates associated with the Bahamas who had nothing to gain by another Bay Street victory. Ritters was one of them.

The BNP had ensured that the Bahamian economy was strong but their autocratic rule was increasingly seen as flawed and their support was faltering, so they decided to call a quick election before the Opposition could get organized.

Darrell Eldon met Ritters at 8 o'clock in the evening on the day the 'Notice of a General Election' was published.

"Nothing to worry about!" Ritters beamed, "I got friends who can help with the political organization and they have the money too!"

They moved into the sitting room, "...you remember Rico?"

Darrell remembered meeting the American businessman at the party Ritters held a year or so before. How could he forget? That was the day he had fallen in love with Bahama.

"Oh yes, nice to see you again..."

Sometimes fact is stranger than fiction. At the general election that was held in 1968 the two main political parties were tied with an equal number of elected candidates when the votes were counted. Two other non-party candidates were chosen by the electorate, one representing the Unions and the other, a white man standing as an Independent, was the other. Sir Elvin, the Premier and Omar Newcombe, the leader of the BPA, had hurried meetings with the two men who held the destiny of the nation in their hands.

The following day the momentous result was announced: the Union candidate would be awarded the prestigious post of Minister of Labour and the Independent would become the Speaker of the House. The Bahamas Peoples Alliance was now the official government of the country!

Darrell Eldon was appointed Deputy Premier and Minister of Out Island Affairs. The first order of business for the new government was to improve education in the country though the golden egg of tourism was not forgotten. His father Charlten, was appointed to the Senate, a British parliamentary ruse copied in the Bahamas for elevating someone away from the real corridors of power. Charlten Eldon served in the Senate for a year and then disappeared from the political scene. Leonard Elding's name was sympathetically considered as a possible candidate for a Senate position but his previous attachment to the Bay Street establishment went against him.

The election victory had not come without cost. Rico the American businessman had been given a firm verbal promise that he would get a casino license in Nassau if the BPA won.

"You know how much we are indebted to Ritters' friend," Darrell Eldon reminded the new Prime Minister Omar Newcombe, "we did not say in writing we would grant him a casino license but we sure as hell had better have a good excuse to turn him down!"

"I know, I know! But the Baptists won't let us open another casino, they and the evangelicals are our greatest supporters, a casino license is out of the question, a casino license simply cannot be granted. Difficult business, I say we let them down gently...please, you handle it."

Not an easy assignment Eldon thought.

He went first to Ritters and tactfully explained the problem.

Ritters was angrily disappointed and evasive. "I think you had better talk to Rico yourself about this, I can tell you this, he is not going to like it!"

Eldon then had an idea. Instead of using the sole excuse that the Bahamian domestic situation would not support the proposed new casino, what about using the pretense that forces outside the country were opposed to the idea? He phoned Chip Simpson at the United States Consulate.

Two days later Eldon was shown a confidential telex copy of Rico's extensive biography. "Wow, incredible! That man is into everything!"

"You are going to have to be very careful, he has got a powerful organization around him—and even more influential lawyers—so far there is nothing major anyone can pin directly on him...anyway, let us know if we can help. I'll tell State we had this conversation." Eldon motioned to take the telex, "oh no, sorry!...I can't let you take that!"

This was going better than I expected Eldon thought.

Eldon spoke to the Premier and then arranged to see the British governor, Sir Walter Woodcock-Walters. The British were still responsible for internal security and foreign affairs in the Colony and Eldon realized this blemish on complete Bahamian political independence could be turned to advantage. An appointment was arranged for him at Government House.

Passing over Gregory's Arch in a chauffer-driven government car he was admitted by a uniformed guard into ante-room of the imposing building that dominated the Nassau skyline. Wearing his best suit with finely pressed creases and a neatly folded handkerchief in his top pocket he refused to be seated explaining to the obsequious servant that he preferred to stand.

"Very well sir..." the aging servant intoned.

Fifteen minutes later an *aide-de-camp* ushered him into an impressively large room proportioned as a double cube with impressive Italianate moulded cornices but with wooden floors that creaked. The furniture dated from the golden age of European joinery, the walls hung with portraits of former governors looking out with imperial majesty from their gilded frames. Darrell just had time to notice that the faded drapes needed either cleaning or replacing when the governor appeared and welcomed him warmly and asked him to sit down.

The discussion was brief and to the point. "The meeting is going well but why do I always feel inferior when people talk to me in the measured tones of the Queen's English?" Darrell had time to reflect. Suddenly the governor announced:

"H'mm, I quite see the problem, Minister. These American gangsters really! But you can count on my support now you have decided to decline the casino license application." The governor stood up. The meeting was over.

"Thank you, Your Excellency."

Eldon was about to leave the governor's office in Government House when the governor surprised him.

"You know Minister, by choosing to involve the American State Department and the Commonwealth Office you may have saved yourself and the Premier from a tough spot...I have already spoken to London and Washington about it...you have been dealing with some very mean-spirited people who would not hesitate at the idea of...hmm...assassination you know...be very careful! I shall be taking this matter up with the Premier and the Chief of Police..."

Eldon was trying to think of something to say as the *aide-de-camp* ushered him from the room.

Two weeks later Darrell Eldon and Rico had a meeting in Bimini. The Chief of Police, with the full authority of the governor, had drafted a long tersely written letter explaining the security arrangements for the future ownership and management of casinos in the Bahamas. Eldon showed it to Rico. He read it carefully but his face showed that it was immediately clear to him that, however devious and inventive he and his lawyers were, there was no way he could comply with a set of regulations like that. Prominent among the clauses were the screening requirements for casino personnel, the procedures for checking the gaming winnings and a further clause that permitted only British subjects to have management and ownership of gambling operations in the country. It was crystal clear Rico would have to look somewhere else to set up an off-shore casino.

Ritters became the sacrificial lamb. Three weeks later a brief article in the local newspaper stated:

CABLE BEACH RESIDENT DROWNED AT SEA

The body of Percy Ritters 65, of New York City a long time resident of Cable Beach was washed ashore on Rose Island last night. He had been alone on a fishing expedition. The police reported that it seems he accidentally fell overboard as he was reeling in a fish. He is survived by a wife from whom he was legally separated five years ago.

The circumstantial evidence was such that no one, not even Darrell Eldon, suspected the death might involve foul play.

Bahama and Jonathan were married in Nassau the following year. Darrell Eldon was invited to the wedding but sent a polite hand-written note explaining that he would be in London for a constitutional conference on the day of the wedding. The talks in London culminated in the Bahamas gaining independence from Britain some 325 years after Captain Sayle first arrived in Eleuthera. A Grand Bahamian poet put the momentous event to verse:

Sumpum big done happen,
De bigges' change ta date,
'Cause de Gubman wa did alwis rule,
Bin defeated here o' late.
Bahamian's heads start lif'in,
Deyself dey proud ta be
'Cause de voice dey had in Gubman
Did just make history

National independence has an inexorable way of changing people's lives.

The Bahamas Airways pilot and his outspoken wife ended up in Singapore. The privately-owned airline collapsed when the government ostensibly refused to support the airline, but the real reason, which leaked out later, was that some members of the government were secretly in process of forming a separate privately-owned airline to take over the more lucrative routes of the flag carrier.

Jonathan predictably lost his Work Permit. Bahama and he went to live in England for a time but the lure of the Bahamas was too great and they returned. Jonathan was later granted 'resident status' and permitted to open a plant nursery in Nassau. Bahama was elected President of the Bahamas National Trust, the organization charged with preserving the natural environment of the Bahama Islands. It was a happy choice.

Bahama's brother Peter, was effectively denied a chance ever to serve in politics. He continued to work as a highly paid attorney from his Bay Street chambers mainly offering legal services to offshore banks domiciled in Nassau. He confessed to being staunchly apolitical. He and his wife had three children, two of whom were boys, fairly assuring the continuance of the Elding dynasty.

The work force of the country was Bahamianized and several thousand foreigners were forced to pack their bags and leave. Foreign speculation in land was halted. Major foreign investments in the country dried up.

The development of Freeport on Grand Bahama was effectively halted.

The Unions gained in strength (the number of Unions actually grew to over 40) and the Taxi and Transport Union successfully continued to evade all attempts to have buses service the airports, and many of the hotels in the country.

The Bahamas National Party disappeared as a political force.

Several splinter parties to the right and the left of the Bahama National Front were formed but none were able to successfully challenge the xenophobic appeal of the BPA.

Joel Pinder, the senior customs officer, went to New York to become the representative of The Bahamas to the United Nations.

Charlten Eldon was awarded an OBE on the advice of the Prime Minister after he contracted a terminal disease. He enjoyed the imperial honour only a few weeks before he died.

Leonard Elding was appointed to the Senate as an independent Senator on the advice of the Governor. He too was awarded an OBE on leaving the Upper House.

While all this was going on, the Bahamas became a major staging point for drug trafficking to the United States. There was a persistent rumour that many members of the BPA were indirectly involved in the trafficking, including Theo the Nassau businessman who was elected to Parliament by constituents in the Ragged Islands on the BPA ticket.

No indictments were ever handed down.

Eldon became engaged to a dazzling Brazilian lawyer who had once been a beauty queen. In his public life it was an open secret that a rift was developing between Eldon and the Prime Minister. Darrell Eldon let it be known that he felt that the BPA reforms did not go far enough and he warned privately about the excesses of the Party.

But throughout it all, the tourists continued to flow to the Bahamas. Nassau and Freeport together became the major cruise ship destinations of the world. As in times past, the Bahamas survived, when times were bad elsewhere it actually flourished. Perhaps, the expensive public relations people were right, maybe it really was:

'Better in the Bahamas'

And that would have been the end of the story but for the capricious intervention of fate.

JONATHAN CARLISLE was not very content in his new profession.

That is not say that there was not money to be made, but the job of a nurseryman did not have the glamour of law. He worked long hours and his home life with Bahama started to become fractious. At the end of the day he was tired but for Bahama the day was just beginning. There were parties, meetings, functions. Jonathan dutifully attended but to get through the excessive socialization he started to drink a little too much. Soon the habit followed him to work. He was caught up in a pattern of behaviour that affects so many people, both residents and visitors alike, in the Bahamas.

It took its toll on the marriage. After a time Bahama went to the meetings alone, later she went unaccompanied to parties. At one of them she saw Darrell Eldon, who was also alone, it was the first time they had seen each other socially for several years.

"Well Mr. Minister, it's nice to see you again!"

"You too Bahama, it has been a long time!...how is Jonathan?"

Bahama shrugged, "Oh, he couldn't come this evening—too much work."

Darrell had heard about the drinking problem.

"Would you like a drink?"

"No, I'd rather not, I feel little warm in here Darrell, let's go onto the terrace...I want to hear about your glamourous fiancée...I hear she's a lawyer..."

Darrell forced a smile.

"Yes, she visits our law chambers sometimes...international law you know."

"Sounds interesting, have you set a date for the marriage?"

Eldon looked a little uncomfortable as he fielded the inevitable question. "No, nothing is decided yet, Mirabelle is in Brazil at the moment." He pronounced 'Mirabelle' with a Brazilian accent.

They had both done some verbal prying and, as if by mutual consent, Bahama changed the subject. "I see the American press is still unhappy with the drug situation over here..."

"Yes. And why wouldn't they be!" Darrell replied happy the subject had changed, "nearly one third of all drugs entering the United States pass through the Bahamas. Crack was introduced to the States from here and untold amounts of other drugs get there via the Bahamas too".

"So I understand," Bahama said, "so what's the solution?"

"Frankly there isn't one simple answer, but something is certain, the Americans should put more resources into eradicating drugs at the source and in the marketplace, interdiction in the conduit isn't going to have a great effect, if trafficking dries up here...and hope it does...it will most certainly start up somewhere else."

"I'm sure you are right," Bahama agreed.

"What I care most about are the Bahamian kids who get hooked because it is so available, that is perhaps why we Bahamians should do more. I wish I could convince the Prime Minister!"

Darrell gave a hint of the difference of opinion that was emerging in Cabinet. Darrell and Bahama continued talking for about twenty minutes and both were aware that something was beginning to happen again.

"Well Darrell, it has been so good to see you again, I am still very ashamed at what happened before...do let's be friends..."

"I should love that," Darrell replied but because other people were also seeking the solace of the terrace they reluctantly moved away from each other.

It was two weeks before they met again. This time it was at the Annual General Meeting of the Bahamas National Trust at their picturesque headquarters in Village Road, Nassau.

Bahama, in her opening remarks as President of the Trust, looked in his direction and announced, "...and the Chair is delighted to acknowledge the presence this evening of the Honourable Darrell Eldon Minister for..." and, as she was making the announcement she realized she *really* did feel delighted. Something told her that his presence at the AGM was somehow a portent of something she did not exactly understand.

When the long meeting finally dragged to an end and all the members and visitors who attended the AGM of Bahamas National Trust had slipped away, Darrell was still in his seat.

"Thirsty work, Bamie. How about a drink?"

"Gosh I'd love one," Bahama answered noting he used her childhood nickname that he had learned on the fateful night on the western beach. And Bahama remembered too, when she had uttered similar words before.

After some discussion they decided to go an elegant club on West Hill Street. They were both too well known to escape attention but at least at this time of night most of their social set would be at home, or so they thought. After all, they were only going for a social drink.

When they arrived in their separate cars at the club there were half a dozen or so Bay Street merchants and a few politicians and their wives near the doorway. Darrell stopped his BMW in the street and walked to Bahama's car.

"Would you mind very much if we went somewhere else?"

"No, not at all," Bahama said. She understood how gossip began.

"Follow me..."

They arrived at the palatial house of Darrell Eldon on Prospect Ridge, a geological extension of the 'Blue Hills', in the centre of the island. The electronically operated gates slid open and the two cars parked in the driveway side by side.

"Hope you didn't mind...but I did not think the West Hill Club would be appropriate," Darrell explained.

Bahama nodded her understanding.

"Do come inside."

The interior of the house belied the exterior. *Bric a brac,* giant stuffed fish, ugly vases, framed certificates and other proclamations adorned the walls. The marble floor was covered by a giant imitation Tabriz carpet. The expensive furniture was horribly mis-matched. Indeed the house was in desperate need of a woman's' touch if not Mrs. Wallace Simpson's decorator.

Darrell led her to a small poolside bar which was pleasantly unostentatious.

A servant appeared.

"No, I will take care of the bar, Ranier. You can take the night off." The servant nodded and was heard to leave the house by the side door.

"I thought the AGM went well," Darrell offered as an opening to the conversation, "I never cease to wonder at the interest and generosity of foreigners towards the Bahamas and its environment."

"You are so right," Bahama replied," and I am not so churlish as to suggest that the money they give is just a tax write-off. There are plenty of tax loop-holes without giving away hard-earned money for the upkeep of flamingos in Inagua or the caves of the Lucayan National Park..."

Darrell looked admiringly into her eyes as she enthusiastically warmed to the defence of the Bahamas National Trust. He added, "have you ever considered that almost everybody who came to the Bahamas came reluctantly; the Indians suffered population pressure, the Eleutherian Adventurers came because they were being persecuted, the slaves were brought here in bondage, the Loyalists were exiled here..."

"...and today the paradox is that people who genuinely want to come here are welcomed for two weeks or so and then the welcome mat is taken away...oh! You remembered..." Bahama murmured.

Darrell placed a small glass of white wine in front of her.

She looked at it pensively for a moment, "I remember in our careless youth we once drank rum and ginger!"

The conversation harmlessly drifted from one subject to another until Bahama bluntly offered, "why don't you ask me about Jonathan?"

Darrell, a little taken aback, smiled. "I was getting to it."

"Well Darrell, I think I should tell you I still love Jonathan, actually I love him more than ever now we have the prognosis..."

"Oh no! what's that?"

"Liver problem...two years max. the doctors said, he has to go to the States for treatment...it's awful!" Darrell moved his hand and put it on top of Bahama's. Bahama stifled a tear. Several minutes passed.

Slowly she turned to Darrell and forced a smile.

"I had better go," she announced.

Darrell saw her to the car and put both his hands on her shoulders. They looked for a moment into each other's eyes then Bahama slowly freed herself and drove away.

A year later at a Bahamas Peoples Alliance Conference in Nassau it was clear that more fifty five percent of the delegates favoured Darrell Eldon's leadership. He was able to attract honest men, and not a few women, who were interested in restoring respect and integrity to Bahamian public life—besides introducing meaningful social programmes and aiding in the diversification of its economy. He even had a change of heart and stated publicly that foreigners would be welcomed back to invest and live, and in some cases work, in the Bahamas.

That same year Jonathan Carlisle died and his body was taken England for cremation. A respectable eighteen months afterwards Bahama and Darrell Eldon were married. When they left Nassau for their honeymoon in Asia, Bahama wore a carved jade talisman in a necklace that had been a family keepsake for years. The jade talisman, it had long been thought, was of Central American provenance but, while in China, it was positively, and most surprisingly, identified as having come originally from Central Asia. Bahama promised herself she would research her families' history to see if she could discover more about the origin of the enigmatic pendant that exhibited pre-Taíno carving yet now, she was told, was made of Asian jade.

However, when they returned to the Bahamas, the couple found the country in a political crisis and her small family research project had to be delayed. Most of their time was now spent in political caucus's and promoting a new vision for the Bahamas. A hotly contested election ensued and, after electioneering in the scattered constituencies of the Islands, the Honourable Darrell Charlten Eldon MP was resoundingly elected the new Prime Minister of the Commonwealth of the Bahama Islands.

Epilogue

The story of the Bahama Islands related herein has taken some liberties with historical facts, most especially in recent times.

Evidence of a migration of a Stone Age people from central Asia to the Americas is now incontrovertible. But exactly when and where the canoe was developed may never be known, though historians have suggested it was probably first introduced, as is suggested here, in eastern Siberia. Without the timely invention of the canoe, the colonisation of the Americas would have been greatly delayed and it is possible the Bahama Islands would not have been discovered before the coming of the Europeans. The manner and date of the first human crossing of the Bering Strait are also still open to speculation but the resulting colonisation of the Americas by people originating from Asia is, of course, a self-evident reality.

The circumstances of the actual human discovery of the Bahamas will never be known, though we can approximate the date when the Casimiroid settlers first arrived in their dug-out canoes from the Greater Antilles to sometime in the first century before the Christian era. Though Tsgot is purely fictional, there were doubtless many brave men like him who undertook grave perils to discover a 'new world' of islands in the north of the Caribbean Basin long before Europeans ventured much beyond the world of their clan.

There are several theories as to route taken to the Bahamas by the first Lucayans. In this account the Ciboney from Cuba are credited with being slightly ahead of the Island Arawaks who arrived later from Hispaniola. The story of the Lucayans is told as far as possible in the words of the first European eye-witnesses to visit the 'new world'. The heroics and the pathos of the first encounter are real. It should be understood that Columbus was by no means the first person to arrive in the Americas and it is now very clear that, with the limited technology available to them, the 'Indians' performed a far greater feat than the Europeans in arriving at, and settling, this astounding 'new world'.

The excerpts from the log of Columbus are from a recent English translation but the words put into the mouths of Columbus and his crew are generally fictional. The break away voyage of Martin Pinzon in the *Pinta* to Inagua is recorded fact and we know he had Indian captives aboard his vessel who directed him there in his quest to find gold. Though it is easy to imagine the frustration he felt at not finding gold which would have absolved from being accused of mutinous behaviour, there is no recorded evidence that he seriously abused the captive Indians.

The hypothesis that the fabled ***'Fountain of Youth'*** was to be found in Grand Bahama is simply that: an unproved and fanciful theory. People familiar with the island of Grand Bahama will recognise the supposed site of the first Lucayan settlement as being set in the present Lucayan National Park. Though the account of the voyage of Ponce de León and the incident involving the wreck of the Spanish treasure ship *Santa Maria de la Maravilla* on the Little Bahama Bank are generally factual, the Marques de Montealegre existed, though the beautiful Condesa did not.

The effect of the collision of the European and native cultures was real enough and was so devastating that by the time the English arrived in the Bahamas from Bermuda in the mid-seventeenth century, they started with virtually a clean slate in an uninhabited country. Captain William Sayle, a remarkable man, was responsible for organizing the ***Company of Eleutherian Adventurers*** and establishing the first English colony in the Bahamas. William's son Thomas captained the ship that brought many immigrants to the Bahamas from Bermuda. The two family dynasties introduced into the narrative, the Eldings and the Eldons, are pure invention, but the incidents of their lives are told against some of the actual recorded history of their time.

Neptuna Downham and Read Elding were indeed real people though most aspects of their life recorded herein are fictional. Neptuna was deported from Bermuda (and, as we know from the records, eventually returned there) and Read Elding, who may have been of mixed race, was Acting-Governor of the Bahamas for a time but certainly did not marry Neptuna's daughter to create an Elding dynasty. A man called Richardson found a treasure wreck in Eleuthera but neither Neptuna nor Elding aided in retrieving it. The Quaker elder did not exist though it is possible that after the treatment they suffered in Massachusetts some members of the Society of Friends may have made their way to the Indies. There was also about this time, a tavern called the *'Wheel of Fortune'* in Charles Town (modern Nassau) that the governor of the time, Robert Lilburne, is known to have often frequented. And it quite possible that Robert Clark was put to death in the hideous manner described in the text.

The stories of the pirates are based on much-quoted secondary sources. Unfortunately little is known about the actual career of John Watlin who lent his name for a time to the island of San Salvador. The content of his crew and his sphere of activity in the Bahamas are supposition. However, we know from records that a pirate named Watlin attacked several Spanish cities in the new world and was killed in one of the engagements.

M'buda, is totally fictional though the early experiences attributed to him were repeated with sickening regularity. The Slave Market, now called the Vendue House, is still standing in Bay Street in downtown Nassau and looks much as it did in the eighteenth century. In the twentieth century the building was used for a time to house generators of the government-owned power company. Today the building has been converted into a museum. A Bahamian of African heritage opened a church in the western district of Nassau at about the time suggested in the text but the rest of his story is also pure fiction. There was a slave revolt on the island of Exuma in the first half of the nineteenth century led by a slave named Pompey the events of which are similar to those recorded in the book.

The events surrounding the Loyalists are largely true. They suffered incredible indignities at the hands of so-called 'patriots'. But what makes their story more tragic was that they were persecuted by an idealistic political movement that was ostensibly acting in the name of democracy and human rights. It is a chapter in American history that has often been overlooked. To illustrate this episode in human events, Dr Benjamin Church a descendant of one of the more prominent Pilgrim families was selected for the story. As the text suggests, when it was discovered he was lawfully informing the then legitimate government of the American Colonies of sedition, he was expelled by 'rebels' from his native land. The rest of the story about his life is fictional. In fact it is most unlikely he ever visited the Bahamas. Interestingly though, records suggest that William Bradford whose forebears arrived in North America on the *Mayflower*, was already established in Nassau at the time the Loyalists arrived.

Towards the end of the eighteenth century a remarkable imperialist named William Augustus Bowles operating from Nassau married two Indian wives and tried to carve out an independent Indian 'state' in the Florida panhandle. Alexander Arbuthnot a Scot and a resident of Nassau and Robert Armbrister, a Bahamian, were also later involved with the native Americans of northern Florida and were captured in Spanish Florida and brutally executed there on the orders of General (later President) Jackson.

The principal events of the 19th century, the emancipation of the slaves and the Civil War, were real enough. The capture of several slave ships including the interception of the 'prison' ship is recorded fact. And, the unfortunate Archibald W. G. Taylor did lose both his ears in circumstances similar to those recorded in the text. Towards the end of the nineteenth century a very remarkable man, Louis D. Powles became a

Circuit and Stipendiary magistrate in the Bahamas and fearlessly pursued his profession in face of prejudice and insult.

In the 20th century, the appointment of the Duke of Windsor as wartime Governor of the Bahamas and the murder of Sir Harry Oakes are factual. After Count de Marigny was acquitted of murder no suspect was ever brought to trial again. Scotland Yard was invited to re-open the case twenty years later but with many of the parties dead or unavailable for questioning the case was closed for lack of evidence.

The riot in Nassau during World War II concerning the wages paid to Bahamian labourers at Windsor Field and the subsequent troubles over the carriage of passengers to and from the new Nassau airport were also actual historical events. An election held in 1967 had similar results to that suggested in the text, but there all similarities end. And, it may be fair to surmise, the enigma of the origin of the Asian jade talisman, was never solved.

Other personalities portrayed in the book, particularly in recent times, are not based upon or represent any person living or dead, and are completely fictional.

APPENDIX

Appendix A

1. WHICH WAS THE FIRST ISLAND DISCOVERED BY COLUMBUS? AN ANALYSIS DERIVED FROM THE LOG OF COLUMBUS AND EARLY WRITINGS

Significant Features of Guanahani (San Salvador/Watlins Island) as Described by Columbus

	Watlins	Cat Island	Samana	Mayaguana	Caicos
Island should be around latitude 24 N	yes	yes	yes	no	no
Island should be shape of lima bean	yes	no	yes	no	no
Island should be generally flat	yes	no	yes	yes	yes
Island should be surrounded by a reef	yes	no	yes	yes	yes
North should have space for many ships	yes	no	no	no	yes
In southeast there should be a peninsula	yes	no	no	no	no
Island should have large lake in centre	yes	no	yes	no	no
Rum Cay should be 21 NM southwest	yes	no	no	no	no
Requirements					
Present	8	1	5	2	3
Missing	0	7	3	6	5

Adapted from the study by Dr. Pedro Grau Triana in his book,
SAN SALVADOR—THE FORGOTTEN ISLAND.

In his zeal to promote Watlins Island as San Salvador, Dr Grau has not been completely fair in his allocation of his 'yes's' and 'no's'. For somebody coming from the rugged terrain of western Spain, Cat Island could be said to be 'generally flat' (though if Columbus had actually visited Cat Island it would be surprising if he did not mention the small rise of just over 200 feet near the centre of the island). But then it is doubtful that the Pigeon Creek entrance could be defined with any certainty as a 'peninsula' in the southeast of Watlins Island. Also some would argue that a definable reef does not extend around the entire circumference of Watlins. In addition, a whole line of 'no's' can be deleted if Rum Cay was not the second island Columbus discovered as many contend. But, having noted these exceptions, it is still clear that, given Dr Grau's listing of significant 'features', Watlins Island still gains the most 'yes's'.

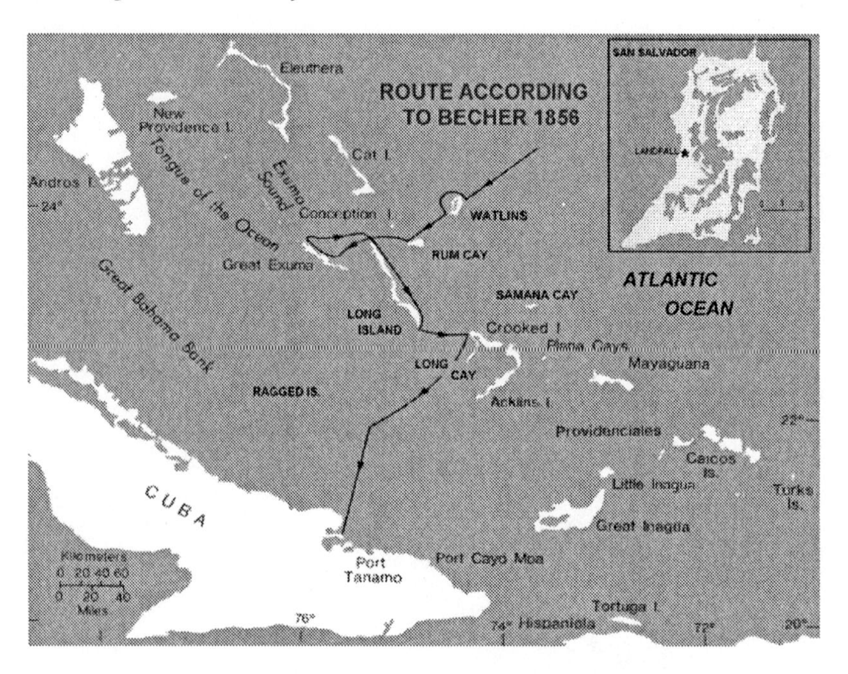

Route taken by Columbus through the Bahamas as suggested by Captain A. B. Becher RN

2. ARCHAEOLOGICAL EVIDENCE

And, if further evidence were necessary, Dr Charles Hoffman excavated 19 two metre squares between 1983 and 1985 at Long Bay on San Salvador and discovered many items of fifteenth century Spanish provenance lying side by side with Lucayan artifacts. Among the Spanish objects were some green and yellow glass beads which Columbus recorded in his log as gifts given to the Lucayans in 1492, there were also two bronze buckles of Spanish or Italian manufacture and a coin of Spanish origin minted in Spain between 1454 and 1474.

3. EVIDENCE FROM THE LOG OF COLUMBUS

Bearings and distances in the Log of Columbus indicate with only slight inexactitude the present-day island known as San Salvador as the landfall of Columbus. Other theorists base their claims for other island landfalls on the shaky supposition that Columbus was off course and did not know it. More recent proponents have based their arguments on state-of-the-art computerized naval navigation and also which measurement Columbus used to measure distance (which is subject worth an entire book on its own!) Many experts quibble about the number of Spanish and nautical miles in a league but Robert Fuson cuts through the confusion to suggest that three nautical miles, or a trifle less, equals one league. But certainly let us agree there was much room for error. We know that Columbus had few navigational instruments. He certainly knew about celestial navigation to measure latitude by using the North Star. To find the ship's position from the stars he used a crude quadrant which was inaccurate on the rolling platform of his vessel. His compass would have had the inherent inaccuracies of deviation by pointing to magnetic, not true, north. Most inaccurate of all would have been his method of calculating his speed. For this he relied on a half-hour glass and, to make things more complex, there can be little doubt he underestimated the distance he travelled so as not to alarm his crew.

For scientific convenience the islands visited by Columbus in the Bahamas have been designated by Roman numerals as follows:

Island I = San Salvador
Island II = Santa Maria de la Conception
Island III = Fernandina
Island IV = Isabela

Depending on which island is taken as a starting point all the other islands change to meet the criteria of the various proponents. Nowadays one is on dangerous ground to suggest any sequence but a semi-official consensus accepts **Island I** as Watlins (presently re-named San Salvador), **Island II** as Rum Cay, **Island III** as Long Island and **Island VI** as Crooked Island/Aklins/Long Cay. There seems less controversy about Columbus' sailing close to the Ragged Islands that he called *Islas de Arena* before making a landfall in Cuba.

Eris Moncur, a Bahamian from Cat Island, makes a well reasoned argument for Cat Island as being the island first discovered by Columbus, and a long historical tradition in the Bahamas would seem to support his claim - including endorsement by Governor Woodes Rogers. It should be remembered it was only on the 6th May 1926 that Watlins Island was officially declared by the Bahamas government to be the landfall site and not Cat Island. Little San Salvador, an island northwest of Cat Island (and nowhere near Watlins), and Conception Island (named for Santa Maria de la Conception, the second island Columbus visited) further reinforce the toponymic claim for the proponents of Cat Island.

However, we know the Spaniards stayed in *Guanahani* only two days and Columbus' log suggests they did not start to circumnavigate the island on the first day of their arrival. This being so, it is highly unlikely that they could have circumnavigated Cat Island, a distance of about 100 miles, in a single day in a small sailing dinghy on the 13th October. Further if, as seems likely, Columbus landed on the west side of *Guanahani* and had wanted to circumnavigate Cat Island, he would have had to sail northwest not nor-northeast as described in the log. Also as mentioned above, if Columbus had landed at Cat Island it is very surprising he did not note that the island possessed the highest point of land for many miles around. The translation from the log (reproduced below) makes it quite clear they sailed nor-northeast. This inclusion in the log also creates a major problem for the proponents of Samana Cay which is a narrow island lying east/west.

Extract from the original Spanish in the Log of Columbus dated 14th October 1492.

English translation of part of the entry in Columbus' Log of 13th October 1492:

'…this island is fairly large and very flat…in the centre of it there is a great lagoon…' So Columbus had obviously explored the island on foot possibly the first day he arrived on the island and noted the strangely-shaped large body of water. He called the water a 'lagoon' and not a 'lake' presumably because it contained salt water. Few contending islands have a 'great' lake or lagoon actually centred in the island besides possessing 'several other bodies of water' (lakes or ponds) as described in the log.

Translation of part of the entry in Columbus' Log of 14th October 1492:

[In the ship's boat]*…I went along the island toward the nor-northeasterly direction, to see the other part, which lay to the east…a great reef of rocks…encircled the whole island, while within there is deep water and a harbour enough for all the ships of Christendom, the entrance of which is very narrow. It is true that inside the reef there are some shoals* (this fits Watlins Island and is patently not true of several other contending islands), *but the sea is no more disturbed than the water in a well…I examined the whole of that harbour, and afterward returned to the ship and set sail…*

And now for the most telling evidence. The argument to date would bring the contenders for the title of San Salvador down to two: Watlins Island or Samana Cay. No one, except Becher perhaps, has really addressed the statement in the log: '*that I saw so many islands that I could not decide where to go first.*' Columbus could be wrong about many things but he could see the '*many islands*' with his own eyes. Then to confirm his testimony the Indians who were with him, '*...made signs indicating there were so many islands that they could not be counted, and they named, in their language, more than a hundred*'. An exaggeration perhaps but where in the Bahamas are there a plethora of inhabitable small islands that somebody would bother to name? The answer would seem to point to the Exuma Cays. Incidentally in some of the semi-official literature about the Bahamas it is claimed there are 365 Exuma Cays. The claim for one cay for each day of the year sounds a bit contrived but the assertion of '*more than a hundred*' islands starts to sound very reasonable. Then very importantly the log notes: *All the islands I saw were very level without mountains, and very fertile, and most of them were inhabited.* Columbus (or his captains) obviously saw the '*many islands*'. If he could see actual people and that the land was flat and fertile these were clearly islands not headlands over the horizon or shadows of clouds. But, though he doesn't say it, the small islands did not strike him as places where he would find gold and anyway he had set his mind on finding the mainland so, after sighting, and possibly landing on the Exuma Cays, the ships turned round. Only with a landfall at Watlins—and nowhere else - would have enabled Columbus to see, '*...so many islands that they could not be counted, and they named, in their language, more than a hundred*'.

4. EVIDENCE FROM THE TURIN MAP DATED 1523

Of particular significance on the map published in Turin, Italy in 1523 (shown below) is the sequence of the islands shown by their Indian names (north is to the right of the map). Note that *Guanahani* (Watlins Island) is placed between Mayaguana and *Guanima* (Cat Island) thus obviating both Mayaguana and Cat Island from contention. Also it should be remembered that Ponce de León on his voyage of 1513 also cited the names of the islands in this same order. So if the map and the evidence of de León is correct then the factors favouring Watlins Island as the landfall site are fairly convincing. (Note Florida is denoted as an 'island' on this map!)

But perhaps Fitzpatrick Sale in his book, **Conquest of Paradise,** is on the safest ground when he states that twelve islands have seriously been put forth as the 'landfall' island. He claims to have studied and been swayed by each claim and then concludes the landfall question can never bedecided with any certainty noting that after the expenditure of over one million dollars by the ***National Geographic Society*** to promote Samana Cay, the question of the landfall site, in his opinion at least, is as open as ever.

Turin Map of 1523

Appendix B

SOME CONSEQUENCES OF THE EUROPEAN CONQUEST OF THE AMERICAS

A largely positive aspect of the Spanish discovery of the Americas and its aftermath was the exchange it allowed between the two worlds. Take for instance, foods:

From Europe came traditional condiments such as clove, ginger, cardamom and almonds. The new world, which was deficient in meats and dairy products, obtained pork, lamb, goat and beef which yielded milk and cheeses; it also obtained the vegetable seeds, (wheat, oats, rye and barley) as well as chickpeas, onion, watermelon, citrus fruit and sugar cane (the latter of which was brought by Columbus from the Canary Islands but actually originated in New Guinea).

From Africa came the banana and okra. In exchange Africa, which had previously been confined to a narrow range of foodstuffs, obtained maize, sweet potatoes, manioc and green beans from the new world.

From the new world came such important staple vegetables as potatoes, tomatoes and corn. It has been suggested of the latter, that kernels of new world corn became, for a time, a yellow currency, more valuable to the well being of the world than nuggets of gold. Columbus sampled *maiz* (corn) in Cuba and declared it to be, 'most tasty boiled, roasted or ground into flour.' It was to transform eating habits and trigger population explosions from Africa to China. When it was introduced to Africa it immediately became a staple. Indeed, some Africans relied on corn so much for sustenance that even to today they are afflicted by pellagra or 'mealie disease', a sickness related to malnutrition from over-reliance on corn. By the mid-16th century corn was a familiar food in southern Europe and formed the basis of such national dishes as Italian *polenta* and the Romanian staple *mamaliga* (a sort of cornmeal mush).

It would be difficult to imagine what northern European cuisine would be like today without potatoes and the cuisine of Italy and Provence without tomatoes. But one can add to these staples, green beans, pumpkin, avocado, peanuts, chocolate, vanilla and pineapple which were also introduced from the new world to enrich European palates.

Few meats travelled east except for the now ubiquitous turkey. The guinea pig and hairless dog, delicacies in America, were not much favoured in Europe. Venison and bison were of course, available in both the new and old worlds.

The daffodil, tulip, daisy and dandelion were introduced to America from Europe. While flowers like the petunia, sunflower, black-eyed susan, dahlia, marigold, and wild rice, travelled in the opposite direction. A less welcome plant introduced from Europe to the new world was crab grass. But perhaps the most pernicious plants of all were to come from the Americas: tobacco and the narcotic, coca. When introduced to Britain, King James 1st of England (James 6th of Scotland) dismissively remarked of tobacco: *'Smoking is a custom loathsome to the eye, hateful to the nose, harmful to the brain, dangerous to the lungs, and in the black, stinking fume thereof nearest resembling the horrible Stygian smoke of the pit that is bottomless'.*

European food before the discovery of the new world was fairly bland so the Europeans went literally half way round the world to the East and West Indies to find spices. The West Indies supplied nutmeg and allspice and the Bahamas is a major source of cascarilla used in the Italian cordial *Campari*. The Lucayans used a concoction of the tree *lignum vitae* as a treatment for syphilis and, after the Spanish conquest, it was much in demand in Europe. The spicy peppers of the new world were a great culinary success all over the world. They flourished in southern climes and took hold in Italian dishes like *'arrabiata'* (angry) sauce. Eventually the capsicum pepper of the new world made its way into the cuisine of India and the Sichuan and Hunan provinces of China. By obscure channels they arrived in Hungary as paprika.

Food consumed in the Bahamas owed much to the sea. Besides the conch that could be diced and eaten raw, it could also be fried in batter and made into a chowder. Nassau grouper would be common fare as were the smaller fish like grunts, snappers and yellow tail. Occasionally deep-sea fish like tuna, marlin and sailfish would find their way to the table of the white settlers, especially those engaged in fishing as an occupation. Lobster was occasionally eaten by the poorer classes but was more highly regarded by the whites.

Though cattle were bred on stock-raising islands, meat would probably have been eaten only once or twice a week even by the well-to-do white inhabitants. Before refrigeration the problem of keeping food fresh was a major consideration. Chickens were commonly reared and were perhaps the only flesh, apart from an occasional goat, that the black population tasted with any regularity. Vegetables included many native root vegetables though strains of peas, beans and tomatoes were plentiful. Melons and bananas too were common. Coconut and other introduced fruits like mango and citrus were also readily available.

Among beverages beer was commonplace though almost all was imported from Europe and North America. But the most common alcoholic drink until the early twentieth century was rum brought mainly from the sugar-producing islands of the Caribbean. Coffee was more easily available than tea until the late nineteenth century, though people with close English connections found a way to import sufficient tea for their own use and often kept it under lock and key. And it was about this time too that food imported from Europe and North America made its appearance in jars and tin cans on the shelves of the more upscale grocery stores.

For a time the Bahamas exported citrus, pineapples, sisal and sugar cane. While from the sea the exportation of conch and sponge were once major industries, the latter especially found a ready market in Europe. During the Second World War there was even a seafood packing plant at West End in Grand Bahama.

The interchange was not confined only to plants and foods. After the ship, the horse was the most important (and fastest) means of transport of the age that was carried from Europe to the new world. The European colonists set them to familiar tasks: pulling wagons, ploughing, carrying soldiers. It would be difficult to imagine how the great land masses of north and south America could have been conquered without equestrian aid. Some of the horses escaped or otherwise fell into the hands of the indigenous peoples who adopted the horse primarily for personal transport and warfare. In the Bahamas, until the advent of the motorcar in the early twentieth century, horses were extensively used as beasts of burden and for transport. The Nassau horse-drawn Surrey is a relic of this era.

Some other exchanges were less happy. European diseases like mumps, smallpox, measles, whooping cough and gonorrhea found the natives of the new world immunologically defenseless. In Mexico, for example, it is thought that the population fell from thirty million before Cortes, to a mere three million after his arrival. A similar devastation shook the Caribbean islands and the entire northern and southern continents. The great germ migration was largely a one-way affair though it is thought that possibly syphilis travelled from the old world to the new. It claimed Vincent Pinzon as one of its victims and it soon spread throughout Europe. In England it was sometimes known as the 'Spanish' disease.

America afforded cures for many ailments. Quinine, derived from Peruvian bark, eased malaria, Ipecac from Amazonian roots, cured amoebic dysentery and a tonic from Canadian pine needles was found to be a remedy for scurvy. Mark Catesby the famous naturalist writing in 1731 noted that Ilathera (Eleuthera) bark, a member of the croton family, gave a fine 'perfume' on being burnt and that, infused with wine, and yielded a fine aromatic bitter. Today American herbs enhance over 500 prescription drugs.

Timber was a major resource and from early times tropical hardwoods were sent to Europe to create fine furniture and for use in the shipbuilding industry before ships were made of iron and steel. The main pine islands of the Bahamas; Abaco, Grand Bahama and Andros exported yellow pine to North America and Europe. In America the pine was used in the manufacture of cardboard and in Europe it found its way down the coalmines of Wales and the Ruhr in Germany for use as pit props.

The other great exchange was the great precious metal wealth which was drained from the new world to the old, while at the same time, technology and masses of people, important resources of a different kind, were moving in the opposite direction.

□ This Appendix on the subject of cultural and other exchanges between the two 'worlds' has borrowed liberally from the **Newsweek Special Issue**, 'The Great Food Migration, Fall/Winter 1991

Appendix C – GENEALOGY OF THE ELDING AND ELDON FAMILIES

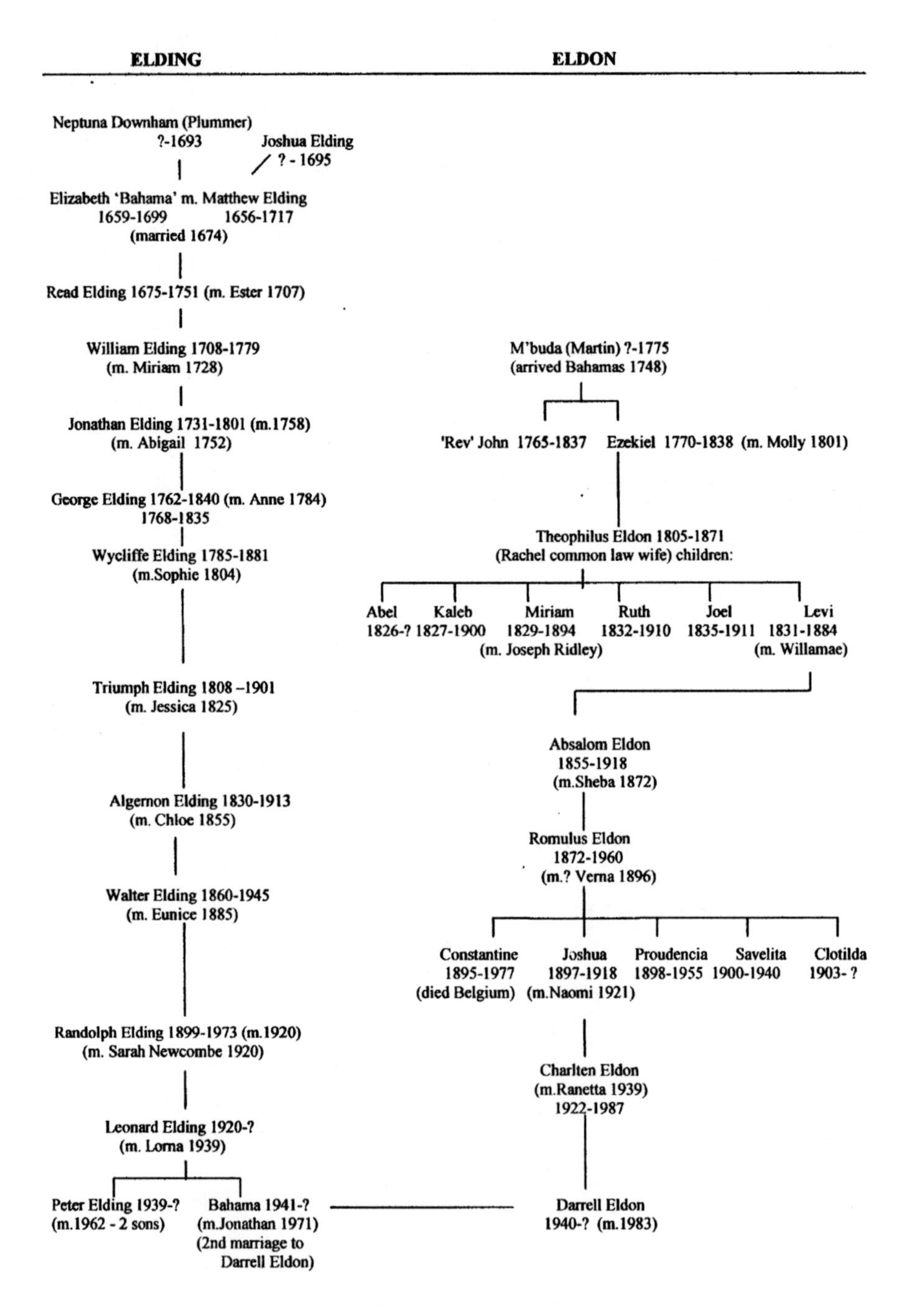

Appendix D

GOVERNORS OF THE BAHAMAS REFERRED TO IN THE TEXT

Eleutherian Adventurers

1648 William Sayle
1661 Nathanial Sayle (not ratified)

Lords Proprietors

1670 Hugh Wentworth (died before being installed)
1671 John Wentworth
1680 Robert Clark
1682 Robert Lilburne
1690 Cadwallader Jones
1693 Nicholas Trott
1696 Nicholas Webb
1699 Read Elding (acting governor)
1700 Elias Haskett

Crown Colony

1718 Woodes Rogers
1721 George Phenney
1729 Woodes Rogers
1738 John Tinker
1774 Montfort Browne
1780 John Maxwell
1787 Earl of Dunmore
1820 Lewis Grant
1829 Sir J. Carmichael Smythe
1849 John Gregory
1864 Sir R.W. Rawson
1884 Henry Blake
1887 Sir Ambrose Shea
1912 Sir George Haddon-Smith
1936 The Hon. Sir Charles Dundas
1940 H.R.H. The Duke of Windsor
1945 Sir William Murphy
1957 Sir Raynor Arthur
1970 Sir Walter Woodcock-Walters *

Independent Nation

1972 Sir Augustus Simmons *

* indicates fictitious

Appendix E

PETITION TO THE TO THE RIGHT HONOURABLE HER MAJESTY'S SECRETARY OF STATE FOR THE COLONIES 1888

The petition of the undersigned British inhabitants of the Island of New Providence, humbly showeth:

(1) *That your petitioners are informed and verily believe that his Worship, Louis Diston Powles, Esq., one of the Stipendiary and Circuit Magistrates, now absent on sick leave, does not intend to return to the Colony.*

(2) *That his Worship has, during his tenure of office, so fearlessly and impartially discharged his magisterial duties that his memory is affectionately cherished by a large majority of the inhabitants not only of New Providence, but also of the outlying islands of the Bahamian Group.*

(3) *That your petitioners believe that his Worship has left this Colony chiefly in consequence of a persecution organized against him by persons who do not wish to see justice equally administered towards all classes of the community, irrespective of race or social position.*

(4) *That the vast majority of the inhabitants of the Bahama Islands are coloured people, and neither of the two judges, nor of the two Stipendiary and Circuit Magistrates, are coloured men.*

Wherefore your petitioners humbly pray:

(a) *That Her Majesty's Principal Secretary of State for the Colonies will use his exalted station to induce his Worship, Louis Diston Powles, Esq., to return to this Colony, either to take up his present or some higher post should a vacancy occur.*

(b) *That in the event of a vacancy occurring in the office of Stipendiary and Circuit Magistrate, her Majesty's Principal Secretary of State for the Colonies will cause that vacancy to be filled (i) by a member of the English, Scottish, or Irish Bar, or (ii) by a properly qualified coloured magistrate.*

POST SCRIPT

It is interesting to note in the 'Petition' signed by 519 British subjects living in the Bahamas in 1888 that reference is made in clause (4) (a) to Powles being offered 'some other post should a vacancy occur'. This was probably a guarded reference to their preference for the appointment of Powles as a future governor. But as Powles noted at the time, '...I have applied to the Colonial Office for re-employment on various occasions. Whether I shall be ultimately successful or not is a question time alone can answer.'

No reply was ever forthcoming from the Colonial Office in London. In fact, when Governor Blake was recalled, the Colonial Office in a display of astute diplomacy, appointed Sir Ambrose Shea, a Roman Catholic from Canada, as the new governor of the Bahamas. Louis Diston Powles however, was never to hold another position in the British Colonial Civil Service.

Extract of Reviews

BAHAMA SAGA: The Epic Story of the Bahama Islands

A saga that fully deserves the label 'epic'. In retelling the two thousand year story of The Bahamas and its people, Grand Bahamian maven Peter Barratt imaginatively fills in the gaps where the historical record is silent or unclear. For the modern period he heightens the narrative by presenting real-life characters in thinly veiled disguise. If this astute mixture of fact and fiction is what the public wants, *Bahama Saga* could well become a best seller of the stature of Robert Wilder's *Wind from the Carolinas.*

Peter Barratt's ***Bahama Saga:*** *The Epic Story of the Bahama Islands* lives up to its title. "Saga" is a sensuous sweep of Bahamian history, a vivid result of his love affair with the Island. From the first chapter, when humans set foot in the Americas, to the last chapter, when the flag of Independence lifts into the Bahamian sky, Barratt's epic is richly textured with historical detail and human motivation.
For those who like their history fictionalised and their fiction historicalised this is the book to choose. Any nervous Bahamas historians are herein advised to read the Epilogue first, for Barratt's sincere and straightforward disclaimers. All other readers please open to page one and enjoy Peter Barratt's epic story: ***Bahama Saga.***

Sandra Riley – historian, novelist and playwright. Riley wrote a definitive history of the Bahamas: ***Homeward Bound*** *and, with illustrations by Alton Lowe,* **The Lucayans.**

About the Author

Peter Barratt claims to have fallen in love with the Bahamas after he first visited the islands in 1960. This is the second book written by Barratt about the Bahamas. His first was **Grand Bahama,** published by Macmillan, which was about the island where he first settled in 1964. He has also written many articles on a variety of subjects about the Bahamas. This new work **'Bahama Saga'** is an ambitious fictional work based closely on historical fact that follows the history of the islands from the orignal aboriginal tribes who first discovered the island around the time of Christ, right up to the present day. Barratt was formerly the town planner formerly in charge of the development of the new city of Freeport. He is an avid amateur archaeologist and founder of the Lucayan National Park. A tennis player and licensed pilot, Barratt also sails and dives the amazing waters of the Bahamas as he continues to explore the waves of tide and time that have captivated so many people with its beauty from around the world.

Printed in the United States
33103LVS00004B/43-279

9 781410 798299